39965339
V2

Encyclopedia of Family Life

Encyclopedia of Family Life

Volume 2

Compadrazgo – Fertility and infertility

Editor

Carl L. Bankston III

University of Southwestern Louisiana

Project Editor

R. Kent Rasmussen

SALEM PRESS, INC.
Pasadena, California   Hackensack, New Jersey

Managing Editor: Christina J. Moose
Project Editor: R. Kent Rasmussen
Manuscript Editor: Robert Michaels
Development Editor: Wendy Sacket
Research Supervisor: Jeffry Jensen
Acquisitions Editor: Mark Rehn
Photograph Editor: Karrie Hyatt
Production Editor: Joyce I. Buchea
Design and Layout: James Hutson
Indexer: Robert Michaels

Frontispiece: James L. Shaffer

Library of Congress Cataloging-in-Publication Data

Encyclopedia of Family Life / editor, Carl L. Bankston III; project editor, R. Kent Rasmussen.
    p. ; cm.
Includes bibliographical references (p.   ) and index.
ISBN 0-89356-940-2 (set)
ISBN 0-89356-942-9 (vol. 2)
    1. Family—North America—Encyclopedias. 2. Domestic relations—North America—Encyclopedias. 3. Family services—North America—Encyclopedias. I. Bankston, Carl L. (Carl Leon), 1952-   . II. Rasmussen, R. Kent.
HQ534.E53 1999
306.85'097'03—dc21

98-42491
CIP

First Printing

Contents

Encyclopedia of Family Life

Compadrazgo

RELEVANT ISSUES: Children and child development; Kinship and genealogy; Religious beliefs and practices

SIGNIFICANCE: *Compadrazgo*, or godparentage, occurs when a close family friend sponsors children during religious sacraments and serves as a social device for acknowledging mutual obligations

The personal intimacies that Latinos require in their social dealings with other individuals is bolstered by persistent patterns of kinship. Latinos feel that members of their families as well as a larger kin group understand their unique qualities and provide the sort of intimate contact that allows them to relax. Kin relationships include strong ties to *compadrazgo* kin. Latino families tend to include a much wider circle of relatives than has been common in U.S. families in the late twentieth century. The small immediate family, consisting only of a husband, wife, and minor children, is still an anomaly among Latinos, even in urban areas. Latinos have always maintained a strong allegiance to extended family groups and regard outsiders with suspicion.

Compadrazgo became a vital element in Spanish life beginning in the Middle Ages. Later, Spaniards introduced it into the New World. The practice has both formal and informal connotations. The formal ritual ties are usually established at baptism, confirmation, or marriage ceremonies among parents (*padrinos* and *madrinas*), godchildren (*ahijados*), and godparents (*compadres* and *comadres*). The terms *"compadre"* and *"comadre"* also indicate an informal reference to adults in a relationship of mutual friendship and respect, which differs from the established, ritual forms of godparentage.

Compadrazgo also implies dependencies as well as mutual advantages. Young persons can benefit from their godparents' financial resources, experience, and wisdom as well as business skills and contacts. Godparents are expected to attend birthday parties and all major social events of *ahijados* from childhood to adult life. Frequently, *padrinos* arrange initial employment and financial credit for their godchildren. Most important, godparent ties provide protection from the fear of parental death, because godparents are expected to provide for godchildren in such situations.

Historically, *compadrazgo* has cut across racial lines in Latin America, beginning in the colonial period. This was particularly true in the seventeenth century, when the labor system of debt peonage created personal relationships previously lacking in forced labor systems. Spaniards established godparental relations with indigenous peoples that pervaded colonial society and continued into the nineteenth and twentieth centuries.

In all its manifestations *compadrazgo* also serves as a social metaphor to acknowledge obligations to godparents, particularly to *padrinos*. In all their dealings with outsiders, *padrinos* can expect the loyalty and unswerving support of *ahijados*. In rural Latin America and the southwestern United States such commitments could involve political support to godfathers' political ambitions or service in the armed forces to overthrow opposing leaders.

Once the Southwest came under U.S. control after 1848, *compadrazgo* became a vital element of community survival in Mexican American culture, when resources were scant and loss of land as well as declining standards of living made personal contacts essential for everyday needs. The hegemony of an often hostile white culture frequently drew families closer together, with *compadrazgo* serving as a necessary foundation.

—*Douglas W. Richmond*

See also Baptismal rites; Child support; Death; Extended families; Fatherhood; Filipino Americans; Godparents; Latinos.

Competition during childhood

RELEVANT ISSUES: Children and child development; Parenting and family relationships

SIGNIFICANCE: Although competition in childhood can contribute to children's developing into competent adults, it can also create emotional problems for them and put emotional and financial strains on families

Competition in childhood can take many forms. Athletic contests, beauty pageants, club activities, academic quiz bowls, science fairs, and spelling bees all represent venues in which children might compete during childhood. Children can begin to

Organized sports, such as baseball, allow children to mimic adult competitiveness. (James L. Shaffer)

engage in competitive activities from infancy and continue to do so all the way through early adulthood. The activities in which children engage and the extent of their engagement vary from child to child. Some children become involved in competitions during early childhood, spending many hours each week on their competitive activities. Others may begin competing at a later age or may never engage in competitive activities.

Forms of Competition. How much time children spend on competitive activities and when they begin depend on many factors. One such factor is the amount of parental encouragement and involvement. Some parents, for various reasons, encourage their children to become involved. Such parents often believe that competition, such as athletic events and beauty pageants, will help their children to become self-confident, poised, and adept at social skills. It is also true that parents who encourage their children to compete on athletic teams often feel that this form of competition increases children's leadership skills, their ability to contribute to a team, and their general health. Parents of very young children may feel that participation in athletics will help them to develop motor skills and eye-hand coordi-

nation. Parents who encourage their children to compete academically may feel that this form of competition helps their children to do well in school, to get college scholarships, or to achieve career goals.

Economic factors may affect whether children engage in competitive activities, particularly in beauty pageants or athletic events. To participate in beauty pageants, children must be able to afford the costumes, lessons, and coaching that contribute to their competitiveness. To participate in athletic events, children must be able to afford insurance, special shoes, uniforms, and equipment, such as racquets and balls. Children in-

Organized competitions among children are most likely to make positive contributions to their development when emphasis is placed on participation and effort instead of winning. (James L. Shaffer)

volved in sports may also need to pay for special coaching in order for them to be competitive.

Factors of location may also affect whether children are able to engage in competitive activities. Some communities and school systems encourage certain types of competition over others. Football, basketball, and baseball teams as well as cheerleading and musical activities are fairly ubiquitous in communities and school systems throughout the United States and Canada. Children who want to compete in ice hockey events, however, will be more able to do so if they live in the northeastern part of the United States or in such Canadian provinces as Ontario or Quebec. While beauty pageants occur throughout the United States, young children are more likely to be able to participate in them if they live in the South, where beauty pageants for young children are most common. Children who have serious athletic or musical career goals may have to move to areas where they can receive first-class training and use state-of-the-art facilities.

Another factor which may motivate children and affect their interest in engaging in competitive activities is their own innate characteristics and abilities. Children, like all humans, enjoy doing those things which make them feel successful. Children will feel most successful in performing those activities for which they possess special characteristics or abilities. Thus, children who are physically attractive, talented in dance and music, or who possess personal charisma may be drawn to the competition of beauty pageants. Children who are well coordinated or who have unusual physical prowess may feel drawn to the types of sports activities at which they can succeed. Those who possess special intelligence may devote their energies to competing at the academic level.

Advantages of Competition. There are many advantages to competition in childhood. Competition in sports contributes to children's physical conditioning, overall good health, poise, and self-confidence. Children who compete in athletic events develop motor control and eye-hand coordination. Participation on sports teams helps children to develop leadership skills and to know how to contribute to group success. Because they must be present at games and practice at certain times and must learn to compete while being responsible for keeping up with their schoolwork, partici-

pation in sports activities also helps children to develop time-management skills.

Success in athletic competitions can lead student athletes to receive college scholarships and, although such cases are rare, to careers as professional athletes. Yet, whether or not children who play sports go on to become professional athletes, their participation in sports activities often leads to a lifetime of involvement in sports hobbies and activities which contribute to their happiness and well-being.

Competition in beauty pageants can certainly contribute to children's feelings of self-confidence and self-esteem. Children who possess high self-confidence and self-esteem are more likely to be happy than those who lack these qualities. Participation in beauty pageants may also encourage children to develop certain interests such as dancing or drama that will enrich their entire lives. Children who participate in beauty pageants may develop poise and grooming skills, thus enhancing their ability to achieve career goals in later life.

Participating in academic competitions, such as academic quiz bowls, science bowls, and spelling bees, or striving to make the honor roll, to be merit scholars, or class valedictorians can help students to learn facts and skills that will improve their overall academic performance, grades, and test scores. Strong grades and test scores may enable students to win scholarships or attend the colleges and universities of their choice. Participation in academic competitions also helps students to develop good study skills, which can contribute to further success in their academic careers.

Club competitions offer many worthwhile advantages to participants. Children who win blue ribbons in 4-H competitions know the value of hard work; they have learned much worthwhile information along the way and have increased their sense of self-worth by winning. Children who strive to win badges in Girl Scouts and Boy Scouts competitions gain much valuable information as they work toward their badges. Boys who work for an Eagle Scout rating not only gain valuable information, but they also develop self-confidence and character. As children participate in all sorts of club competitions, such as model aviation contests, equestrian events, twirling competitions, band battles, and writing contests, they develop hobbies and interests that will make their lives

Children—especially boys—often need little encouragement to find ways to compete among themselves. (R. Kent Rasmussen)

more meaningful. Children who participate in music and dance competitions not only develop their talents, but they also develop interests that enrich their lives. In all such competitions, students may develop skills, interests, and knowledge that they can put to use in their future careers.

Disadvantages of Competition. While there are certainly many advantages to competition during childhood, there are also disadvantages. Competition in sports can result in both physical and emotional injuries. Children are most at risk of being physically injured when they engage in contact sports; however, any athletic activity can lead to physical injury. Children who lack athletic ability and coordination or who cannot physically keep up with their peers may find that athletic competitions injure their spirits. If children do not perform well, their self-esteem can be damaged. This sort of competition can also be injurious to children who are pushed to compete in athletic events in which they have no real interest. Children very much want to live up to the expectations of parents and teachers. When parents and teachers push children to participate in athletic competitions in which they have no real interest, the children may feel upset or lose self-confidence.

Participation in beauty pageants can also cause problems for children. This type of competition can be detrimental to children's value systems. Competition of this type may encourage children to value the superficial over the complex, appearance over substance. Children who lose beauty contests may develop feelings of low self-esteem. In order to make themselves more attractive to judges, both winners and losers may engage in activities that are detrimental to their health, such as excess dieting, overexercising, plastic surgery, and taking laxatives. Paying for costumes, coaching, and transportation to contests may take money away from family budgets that might possibly be spent for other purposes.

Academic competitions are often most detrimental to the most academically talented children, but they can also harm less talented children who wish to achieve academically. Academically talented children may place themselves under enormous pressure to achieve or they may feel pressure from their parents to do so. Children who are less academically talented may feel the same pressures, but they may also feel greater dis-

appointments because they are less likely to meet the demands placed on them. In some countries, such as Japan and South Korea, the pressure to achieve academically is at times so great that teenagers who cannot live up to the pressure to go to certain universities or to get high grades commit suicide.

Academic competitions are not only detrimental because they create stress and pressure in the lives of children, but also because an overemphasis on academic pursuits may cause children to fail to develop necessary social skills. Children who feel pressured to perform academically may not engage in social events such as football games and homecoming dances, preferring to spend their time attempting to get good grades. Such children may not develop friendships because they do not have time for them or because they feel competitive toward those who would be most likely to be their friends. Lack of social skills and lack of friendships often cause children to feel unhappy and alone in the world.

While striving to win club competitions, science fairs, and musical competitions, children may also place enormous pressure on themselves or experience pressure from parents and teachers. At times this may make them feel so under stress that they become physically ill. Such competitions may cause children to spend so much time practicing, preparing, and participating in competitions that they cannot devote needed time to schoolwork, friends, social activities, and family events.

Effects on Family Life. When children choose to participate in any sort of competitive activity, all members of the family may be affected. Members of the family may not be able to eat together because children must rush off to participate in practice, recitals, and games. Parents may have to curtail their own pursuit of hobbies, entertainment, or sports activities so that they can drive their children to practice, contests, recitals, or games. A family's financial situation may be affected by children's needs for equipment and services to make them more competitive, such as lessons, uniforms, costumes, and coaching.

Competition in childhood may affect relations between siblings. Sibling rivalry may result if one child in the family outstrips the others in talent or ability. One child may strive to be as good as a brother or sister who is exceptionally talented.

Sometimes children may feel humiliated because they cannot compete as well as their siblings. Competition can also bring out the worst in parental egos. Sometimes parents may view their children's successes—or failures—as their own. This intense involvement of parental egos in children's competitive efforts will often create emotional difficulties for children. Children may strive to please their parents to the extent that they no longer view a competitive activity as their own, but rather as something which they perform to satisfy their parents. Children may refuse to compete whatsoever if they believe that they cannot live up to their parents' expectations.

Competition Throughout the World. In the United States, Canada, and Europe children's competitive activities are highly organized. In these parts of the world it is generally believed that children who participate in various types of competition are better prepared for adult life than those who do not, for adult life is highly competitive. In highly developed Asian countries such as Japan, there are also organized children's competitions. In these countries, however, there is a general feeling that all children should compete and that the reason for children's competition is so that children can learn to function as members of a team.

—Annita Marie Ward

BIBLIOGRAPHY

Cross, Gary. *Books/Kids/Stuff.* Cambridge, Mass.: Harvard University Press, 1997. Discusses how childhood has changed in the last century and how toys and games reflect that change and the changes in society.

Joravsky, Ben. *Hoop Dreams: A True Story of Hardship and Triumph.* Kansas City, Mo.: Turner Publishing, 1995. Five-year study of two adolescent basketball players and how their participation in competitions affected their entire lives.

Matthews, Gareth B. *The Philosophy of Childhood.* Cambridge, Mass.: Harvard University Press, 1996. Outlines the development of a philosophy of childhood and how the development of such a philosophy could contribute to better childhoods.

Postman, Neil. *The Disappearing Child.* New York: Delacorte Press, 1982. Discusses childhood and how it has been changed by modern events.

Torbert, Marianne. *Secrets to Success in Sport and Play.* Englewood Cliffs, N.J.: Prentice-Hall, 1982. Explores attitudes and techniques that contribute to successful competition.

See also Community programs for children; Educating children; Entertainment; Favoritism; Schools; Youth sports.

Computer recreation

RELEVANT ISSUES: Children and child development; Economics and work; Parenting and family relationships; Sociology

SIGNIFICANCE: With the advent of personal computers and the home video market, families have gained access to recreational activities in addition to television

When the American company Atari created a computer game called Pong in 1972 and installed it in a California bar, it laid the foundation for a significant change in family home entertainment. Atari moved into the home video-game market by selling its product through Sears. Over the next eight years, sales of home video games (by then joined by the toymaker Mattel) reached $1 billion annually, with more than 1,500 different games available. Although many Americans thought it worthwhile to purchase a game system for their homes, they found that the games were similar to each other and that Atari and Mattel did not offer any upgrades or new technology to keep the products interesting.

Computers for Family Entertainment. Although Atari quickly dominated the relatively small video-game market in the 1970's, it failed to maintain its edge. Its games were simple and indeed crude by later standards, featuring flat, two-dimensional action and controllability that involved little more than ninety-degree turns. Atari's research and development teams, however, continued to produce an expanding number of titles, saturating the market and planting the seeds of the company's destruction. Within a few years after reaching its peak sales Atari was out of business and Mattel was nearly bankrupt.

Meanwhile, Nintendo of Japan had transformed itself into one of the world's most powerful companies, beginning with arcade games. Mario Brothers and Donkey Kong became instant arcade classics, leading Nintendo's management to conclude

To keep young customers coming in, computer arcades have had to offer increasingly sophisticated action games. (AP/Wide World Photos)

The growing power of home computers has enabled them to offer both entertainment and education in forms that hold the attention of children. (Long Hare Photographs)

that homes on both sides of the Pacific were ready for real home video-game computer systems. In 1985 Nintendo premiered its eight-bit Nintendo Entertainment System—an eight-inch, compact computer game player that utilized cartridge-type computer games such as Mario Brothers in a home format. Suddenly, parents who had become concerned about the potentially negative impact of computer arcade games saw an opportunity to bring the games into the home and play them as families. Many of the games featured separate play features and dual controllers in which persons could play against the computer or other players.

The usefulness of computers as family entertainment underwent an abrupt change in the early 1990's. The introduction of increasingly powerful sixteen-bit machines meant that more realism was possible than previously. Furthermore, competi-

tion with Nintendo by another Japanese company, SEGA, led to an effort to capture the largest market of home and arcade video-game players: teenage males. SEGA introduced digitally reproduced human actors in a bloody and violent game called Mortal Kombat, which became an instant hit and propelled SEGA into the lead in home system sales. Nintendo, aiming for more wholesome market elements, targeted younger children and females with Mario Brothers follow-ups and cartoon games. However, the popularity of Mortal Kombat and other sports games created a highly specialized type of game industry, marking the end of the "family fireside game," just as television in the 1950's had ended the family radio hour.

By 1995 SEGA and a new, powerful computer-game manufacturer, Sony, had introduced thirty-two-bit systems that provided even greater realism.

Should Children Be Supervised on the Internet?

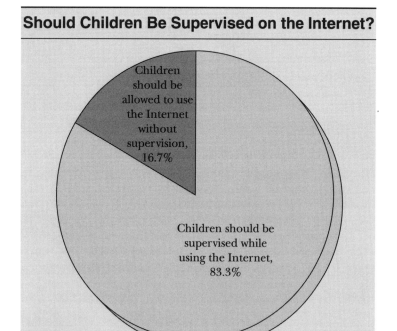

Children should be allowed to use the Internet without supervision, 16.7%

Children should be supervised while using the Internet, 83.3%

Source: Parentsroom website (1998)

Note: Parentsroom conducted an informal poll among visitors to its website. Visitors—mostly persons with an interest in parenting—were asked if children should be allowed to use the Internet. This chart summarizes the responses.

growing number of Americans had home PCs for work-related activities. Early PCs lacked sophisticated software and hard disc drives, limiting them to accounting and word processing functions or primitive computer games such as Pac Man. Like the game-only systems, however, the capabilities of computers rapidly expanded and costs fell, so that a system that might have cost more than $10,000 in the mid-1970's cost less than $3,000 in the late 1980's. Game manufacturers had already begun to develop programs specifically for PCs, but soon educational software developers offered encyclopedias, science packages, and history games.

Family use of PCs increased further in the mid-1980's, when America Online (AOL) and other online Internet services began targeting noncommercial users. By 1990, when Prodigy entered the competition for online Internet services, such services already had nearly ten million subscribers, and the number began to grow exponentially. Online providers offered teenagers and young adults in the home a crucial service: a way to talk to friends (or total strangers) without leaving the house. Chat rooms appeared, allowing participants total anonymity and, ultimately, creating a somewhat natural offshoot of online dating services.

Regulation of the Internet. The great strength of the Internet, namely its ability to provide access to any online server or information source, has also proved a great liability. Children browsing the web (Internet information sources) on their parents' computers accessed (deliberately or inadvertently) pornography and hate-group web sites. Worse, some children were lured by Internet contact to meet with pedophiles. Many of the same forces that protested against video-game violence demanded that government control the Internet in some manner.

In 1995 Congress passed the Communications Decency Act, which made it a federal crime to use telecommunications devices to transmit or solicit

Long before that, however, the hue and cry from family and children's advocates had pressured Congress to regulate the sale of exceedingly gory or violent games. The gaming industry recognized the public mood and began to provide warning labels similar to those found on musical recordings and television ratings, cautioning parents that certain games contained violence and bloodshed. Ironically, the threats to regulate video games attracted a new market for the most bloody and gruesome products, and the industry boomed again. By 1995 the United States alone had become a $6 billion market split between Nintendo, with about 50 percent of market share; SEGA, with about 35 percent; and Sony, with 15 percent and rapidly growing.

Personal Computers and Family Recreation. Although growing at a slower initial pace than the strictly game-based computer systems, computer entertainment on personal computers (PCs) started to take off in the 1980's, at which time a lewd, lascivious, filthy, or indecent requests or comments that could be construed as harassment and prohibited using telecommunications devices to transmit indecent images or communications to minors, even if the minors themselves have placed the calls. Pornographic web sites began to install "certification sites," at which viewers or users have to certify that they are adults. This protected maintainers of web sites legally, but it did not entirely solve the problem of children gaining access to restricted sites by lying about their age.

In response, several Internet child-filter, parental control systems appeared, such as NetNanny, CYBERsitter, Cyber Patrol, Cyber Snoop, and Surf-Watch. Created in the early 1990's, these services provided adult "lock" mechanisms by establishing a series of words or phrases that the screening software would identify and exclude from transmission to computers. Based on estimates by Net-Nanny, which controlled 25 percent of the market in 1997, approximately 600,000 families employed screening software. Such screening services also provided lists of web sites, newsgroups, or other online uses that parents could choose to eliminate and allowed parents the option of requesting which sites should be excluded without the use of identification codes. Attempting improperly to gain access to a site could cause a computer to shut down.

WebTV. Television, which, like radio, had gained acceptance almost immediately as the center of family entertainment, continued its evolution in the 1990's with the introduction of WebTV. By adding sleek set-top boxes to existing television sets, companies such as Philips-Magnavox transformed ordinary televisions into Internet cable boxes at a fraction of the cost of a PC. WebTV adaptor boxes used traditional hand-held, remote-control television controllers to point and click at desired web items. Viewed by some as a way to introduce new consumers into the computer culture, WebTV generated hopes for a way to orient families around the computer the way families had once gathered around the radio or television. However, there are fundamental differences between television and the web, the most important of which is the fact that television programming can appeal to several people at once, while browsing the web is highly individualized.

—Larry Schweikart

BIBLIOGRAPHY

Biggar, Bill, and Joe Myers. *Danger Zones: What Parents Should Know About the Internet.* Kansas City, Mo.: Andrews and McMeel, 1996.

Gilder, George. *Life After Television.* Knoxville, Tenn.: Whittle Direct Books, 1990.

PC NOVICE: Guide to Going Online 5 (April 1, 1997).

Sheff, David. *Game Over: How Nintendo Conquered the World.* New York: Vintage Books, 1994.

See also Couples; Entertainment; Family albums and records; Family economics; Matchmaking; Recreation; Television depictions of families.

Conjugal families

RELEVANT ISSUES: Kinship and genealogy; Parenting and family relationships

SIGNIFICANCE: The concept of the "conjugal family" refers to a family composed of a husband and wife who may or may not have children

The term "conjugal" refers to a relationship established through marriage. A conjugal family is a form of nuclear family that necessarily includes a husband and wife. A conjugal family system emphasizes marital ties over blood ties, which are central to a consanguinal family system. A conjugal family system is also characterized by a mate-selection process controlled by the participants on the basis of romantic love and sexual attraction as well as by strong ties between the husband and wife, who live independently from the kin group.

The focus on the married couple in the conjugal family highlights two dimensions: marriage and parenthood. The adjectives "conjugal" and "nuclear" are often used interchangeably to refer to a married couple and their children. Both terms, however, stress different aspects of a family system. A single-parent family is a nuclear family, but it is not a conjugal family, because one spouse is missing as a result of abandonment, divorce, widowhood, or the birth of a child to an unmarried female. The growing incidence and acceptance of various forms of families and living arrangements—singlehood, cohabiting couples, never-married mothers, divorced parents, childless couples, and extended families—contribute to enhancing the symbolic value of marriage and the relevance of the concept of the conjugal family.

A conjugal family may or may not include children. According to data gathered in the 1990 U.S. Census, the childless married couple is the most common type of family, representing 29.4 percent of all U.S. households. An increasing number of married couples in the United States and Canada remain childless temporarily or permanently. In 1991 only 25.9 percent of U.S. households consisted of married parents living with at least one child over the age of eighteen, compared to 43 percent of such households in 1970. At the same time, American women have chosen to wait longer before having children. In 1990 more than 40 percent of women between the ages of twenty-five and twenty-nine were childless. Lifelong childlessness may be involuntary or the result of a conscious decision. According to 1990 U.S. Census figures, 5 percent of wives and 15.8 percent of never-married women between the ages of eighteen and thirty-five did not expect to become mothers during their lifetimes. Overall, 10.8 percent of never-married women between the ages of forty and forty-four had not given birth and were

The keystone of a conjugal family is the marriage tie. (James L. Shaffer)

The essence of consanguinal families is blood ties, such as are shared by brothers. (R. Kent Rasmussen)

unlikely to give birth at a later age.

A conjugal family system contributes to minimizing the importance of having children as well as limiting their number. Children are vital to the continued existence of the extended family by ensuring the transmission of heritage and the care of elderly parents. At the same time, children represent a pressing burden for nuclear families. Many young married couples have decided to postpone or forgo childbearing, because they know that a child costs money. In the 1990's it was estimated that middle-income families would spend $120,000 over seventeen years to raise a child. Young married couples also know that parenting is a demanding occupation and that their earning abilities, especially women's, are likely to be affected if they have children.   —*Jacques M. Henry*

See also Childlessness; Communities; Consanguinal families; Equalitarian families; Extended families; Nuclear family.

Consanguinal families

RELEVANT ISSUES: Kinship and genealogy; Parenting and family relationships

SIGNIFICANCE: Consanguinal families are those composed of people related by blood through a chain of parent-child ties

"Consanguinal" refers to connections through descent or "blood" between family members. Coined from Latin (*con* "with," *sanguis* "blood"), the term was originally used by scholars and later by anthropologists to distinguish blood ties from marriage ties. A consanguinal family is composed of people who can trace their descent to a common ancestor. Relatives through marriage, or in-laws, are not part of the consanguinal family.

Despite its relationship to "blood," descent is not a natural phenomenon; rather, it is a product of human organization. Descent can be patrilineal, matrilineal, or bilateral. In a patrilineal system, individuals are related to their consanguinal relatives along the male line, through their fathers. In a matrilineal system, individuals are linked to their consanguinal relatives along the female line, through their mothers. In a bilateral system, such as that in the United States and Canada, individuals are affiliated to the consanguinal kin group through both parents. Members of one's consanguinal family are known as consanguines, which literally means "those of the same blood."

Knowledge of consanguinity is important for individuals because consanguinal ties regulate marriage and structure daily life. In all known societies, the incest taboo prohibits sexual intercourse and marriage between close relatives so that sex and blood do not mix. This taboo is universal for relations between fathers and daughters and between mothers and sons. In the bilateral systems found in most Western societies, the strength of this prohibition decreases as distance between relatives increases. For example, U.S. law prohibits marriage involving parents and children, grandparents and grandchildren, siblings, aunts and nephews, and uncles and nieces. Although most states also ban marriages involving first cousins, few forbid marriages involving second cousins. In matrilineal and patrilineal systems, individuals are usually forbidden to marry within their own descent group. For example, among the Navajo and Hopi—matrilineal peoples living in Arizona and New Mexico—individuals cannot marry within their mothers' clan and their fathers' mothers' clan. Yet, in some societies, such as among North African Muslims or Western European aristocracies, marriage within the consanguinal family is preferred in order to protect "blood" purity and group cohesiveness.

In consanguinal systems, in which blood ties are emphasized more than marriage ties, consanguinity organizes residence, economic endeavors, religious functions, and political activities. Members typically live close to one another, are expected to cooperate economically with their consanguines, provide them with assistance when requested, and worship together. In modern societies, the relevance of consanguinal ties in everyday life is limited because of the importance of the nuclear family. Knowledge of descent is important for people who wish to reconstruct their genealogies, such as members of ethnic and racial groups searching for their European or African roots. It is also important for people who believe they have a legitimate claim to an estate or who seek consanguinal relatives for medical reasons.

—Jacques M. Henry

See also Affinity; Bilateral descent; Extended families; Kinship systems; Matrilineal descent; Nuclear family; Patrilineal descent.

Cooney, Joan Ganz

BORN: November 30, 1929, Phoenix, Ariz.
AREAS OF ACHIEVEMENT: Art and the media; Education
SIGNIFICANCE: Joan Ganz Cooney founded the Children's Television Workshop, the production company responsible for the creation of *Sesame Street*

After working as a reporter in her native Arizona, Joan Ganz moved to New York City in 1954. She wrote publicity copy and worked in network drama until 1962, when she became a documentary producer at WNDT, a New York educational television station. She married Timothy J. Cooney in February, 1964. In 1966 she did a study on behalf of the Carnegie Corporation on the potential of television for preschool education. Two years later she formed the Children's Television Workshop and began seeking funding to research children's tastes in television.

The product of that research, *Sesame Street*, debuted on the National Educational Television network in November, 1969. The new show invited children to "come and play" on a fictional urban street populated by live actors and lively Muppets, puppet characters created by Jim Henson. Using music, animation, and humor, the show's episodes taught children around the world about numbers, letters, and about generally getting along.

The Children's Television Workshop also produced *The Electric Company*, a reading-based show aimed at older children. Cooney served as president of the Children's Television Workshop from 1970 to 1988 and as chief executive officer from 1988 to 1990. In 1989 she was inducted into the Academy of Television Arts and Sciences Hall of Fame.

—P. S. Ramsey

See also Cultural influences; Educating children; Television depictions of families.

Corporal punishment

RELEVANT ISSUES: Children and child development; Parenting and family relationships; Violence

SIGNIFICANCE: Stemming from English common law and practiced in the United States through much of the twentieth century, corporal punishment can lead to the abuse and injury of children

Family life and changes are best viewed within the sociohistorical context in which they occur. For the majority of Americans, corporal punishment has been practiced as part of an Anglo-European tradition that has been supported through religious teachings. English common law allowed men to use corporal punishment to control their wives and children, as though they were chattel or men's property. These laws helped form the basis of the legal system in the United States. In the North American colonies in the 1700's, corporal punishment was prevalent in parents' attempts to control and teach their children. Corporal punishment meant any kind of physical discipline, including a range of behaviors from spanking and hitting to injuring children.

Corporal punishment within families remained prevalent in the nineteenth and through much of the twentieth century. However, with the advent of two great social movements in the United States, the Civil Rights movement in the 1960's and the feminist movement in the 1970's, more attention was paid to the family and oppression of any type. Children's rights were examined in ways heretofore neglected. Corporal punishment came under close scrutiny by the state, and legislation was enacted to protect children from their caregivers, whether parents, grandparents, or unrelated individuals.

Incidence of Corporal Punishment. In an often referenced study published by Murray A. Straus, Richard J. Gelles, and Susan K. Steinmetz in 1980, 71 percent of the parents surveyed reported that they hit their children, while 20 percent said they did so with objects. One-fourth of the mothers in the study reported that they hit their children before they were six months of age, and this figure rose to nearly one-half by the time the children had reached the age of one.

In the late twentieth century corporal punishment in the home accounted for 60 percent of the incidences of child abuse in the United States. Corporal punishment can lead to abuse and injury of children. Legally, persons are required to report suspected cases of child abuse. Parents who use corporal punishment may be approached by law-enforcement and legal officials to answer questions about their parenting, and they may have charges brought against them by the state. If cases of child abuse are substantiated, a range of out-

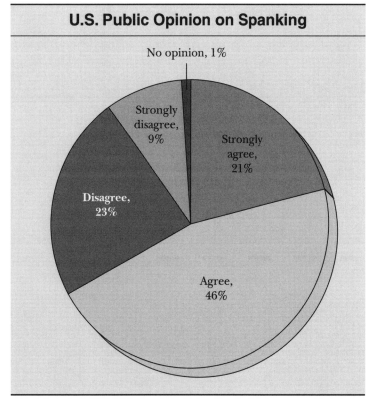

U.S. Public Opinion on Spanking

No opinion, 1%
Strongly disagree, 9%
Strongly agree, 21%
Disagree, 23%
Agree, 46%

Source: CNN/ *USA Today*/Gallup Poll

Note: In 1994 a cross-section of Americans were asked if they agreed that it is sometimes necessary to "discipline a child with a good, hard spanking."

In Tom Sawyer's time the right of adults to use corporal punishment was rarely challenged. (Arkent Archive)

comes are possible. Caseworkers may decide to work with affected families to increase parents' skill level, or children may be removed from the home if future injury appears to be likely.

These changing social attitudes toward corporal punishment have meant that parents, who may once have thought that their disciplinary rights included the right to injure their children, have had to shift to other forms of discipline for teaching and punishing their children. Because corporal punishment has a long legacy in Western history, it may be difficult for parents to employ other methods of teaching, which may have important consequences for children's behavior.

Corporal Punishment and Aggression. A generation of family members who have often used corporal punishment may encourage such tactics and even attempt to undermine other forms of discipline attempted by new parents. While the social values of modern culture may reject injury to children and assert that child abuse is abhorrent, many persons uphold their rights as parents to use corporal punishment.

Furthermore, aggression is a behavior in North American culture that is celebrated in different forms. Words such as "competitive" and "hostile takeover" are applied to businesses in congratulatory ways. Physical aggression is applauded in sports events. Violent acts in the media, fictionalized and real, are ingested daily. If one combines these factors with corporal punishment in the home, it is logical to see how children might resort to physical aggression as an alternative in social interactions. For these reasons, it is important for new parents and those couples who are considering marriage and children to examine their own childhood histories and discuss forms of discipline that do not employ corporal punishment.

Not all groups, which differ by virtue of religion, class, or ethnic origin, view corporal punishment as a negative factor. Some religious sects approve and encourage corporal punishment of children by adults in the home and use their interpretations of religious texts to support their claims, as do some Muslim and conservative Christian groups. Scandinavian countries have viewed corporal punishment of children as illegal for decades. Their reasoning is that since physical aggression toward one's neighbor is abhorrent, adults' conduct toward their own children should be held to the same level of accountability. While diverse voices may be heard on the subject of corporal punishment, there exists abundant research suggesting that corporal punishment may have a negative impact on children.

Developmental Outcomes. Negative sanctions by the state are the least of the arguments for rejecting disciplinary techniques that include physical punishment. Developmental data suggest that children are adversely affected by corporal punishment. One factor of parenting that is a blessing and a curse concerns the extent to which children mimic their caregivers. Developmental researchers have shown that modeling aggressive behaviors serves to show children several logical links with outcomes. Modeling corporal punishment conveys to children the messages that when they are angry, they may hit others; that when they are bigger, they may hit others and get away with it; and that physical aggression is a form of behavior to be repeated. More often, those children from homes in which corporal punishment is practiced are the most physically aggressive toward their peers in day care, at school, and on the playground. Modeling is one of the most powerful teaching tools employed by adults. Modeling corporal punishment is almost guaranteed to promote the same behavior in children.

Researchers have found that corporal punishment is an important factor in adverse early rearing. Adverse early rearing promotes antisocial behavior. Negative social interactions in families means that children's worldviews will be affected. For example, such children may come to think that "might makes right." Children from such homes may develop negative attitudes at school and may develop fewer cooperative techniques for their interactions in other social settings. Subsequent rejection by peers and teachers may put children at risk of developing larger problems. Thus, children who have been physically punished will be vulnerable to antisocial disorders, including delinquency, dropping out of school, and, later, adult criminality.

Suggestions for the Future. There are organizations and institutions in the United States and Canada that provide parenting support and education for people who do not wish to use corporal punishment. The American Humane Association, Children's Division is one such source. Counseling centers at universities can provide this service or refer parents to these resources. Local mental health care providers are also an excellent information resource. These professionals have access to local counseling and education groups, and they can help adults find needed resources. Parenting children is truly a beautiful experience. Releasing the shackles of corporal punishment from modern culture will provide a better future for everyone. A legacy of cooperation and caring can be the task for the next century.

—*Sharon K. Hall*

BIBLIOGRAPHY

Cicchetti, D., ed. "Advances and Challenges in the Study of the Sequelae of Child Maltreatment." *Development and Psychopathology* 6 (1994).

Dinkmeyer, Don, Sr., and Gary D. McKay. *The Parents Handbook: Systematic Training for Effective Parenting (STEP)*. New York: Random House, 1989.

Eisenberg, N., and P. Mussen. *The Roots of Prosocial Behavior in Children*. New York: Cambridge University Press, 1989.

Miller, W. H. *Systematic Parent Training*. New York: Research Press, 1979.

Straus, Murray A., Richard J. Gelles, and Susan K. Steinmetz. *Behind Closed Doors: Violence in the American Family*. New York: Doubleday, 1980.

Walker, H. M., G. Colvin, and E. Ramsey. *Antisocial Behavior in School: Strategies and Best Practices*. New York: Brooks-Cole, 1995.

See also Battered child syndrome; Child abuse; Child rearing; Childhood history; Disciplining children; Parenting; Straus, Murray; Time-out.

Corporate families

RELEVANT ISSUES: Economics and work; Sociology
SIGNIFICANCE: Family-owned businesses have long played a major role in the American economy

Before 1900 most American families engaged in farming or ran small businesses. Even as small business firms grew, sometimes to employ several hundred workers, their management tended to remain in family hands. Both ownership and management were passed on generationally, mostly to sons, but occasionally to widows or daughters. Structural change only occurred with the appearance of the railroads, whose special demands for capital and subsequent securities sales caused a separation of ownership from management. At that point, most corporate families lost control of their companies as their shares of ownership diminished and as professional managers assumed responsibility for daily operations of the increasingly large-scale businesses.

That change—the separation of ownership from management—has been used by historians to differentiate between "small business" (no matter how large) and "big business" (no matter how small in terms of workforce size or capital worth). By definition, virtually all family-owned firms are thus considered "small business." Exceptions have included such companies as Wal-Mart and, until the 1960's, Ford, whose family owners managed their companies and possessed most of the stock.

By the twentieth century most of the well-known corporate and company families—including the Vanderbilts, Rockefellers, and Gettys—had passed from owners to inheritors and administrators of wealth. Although still associated with huge companies or entire industries, the "inheritor" families had little daily contact with business in any way. Neither Walt Disney's daughter nor J. Paul Getty's sons showed any ability to perpetuate their family businesses or demonstrate the entrepreneurial vision and vitality of their famous fathers. Nevertheless, most Americans associated family names such as Vanderbilt, Rockefeller, and Getty with "corporate families" and the wealth derived from active businesses.

In contrast, the Waltons, owners of Wal-Mart, remained an integral part of their firm well into the 1990's and were annually listed among the Forbes 400 richest Americans. Despite remaining a family-owned and family-run firm, Wal-Mart expanded from 200 to 1,600 stores during the 1980's and created 212,000 new jobs. In the same period, family-owned firms hired the vast majority of minority and female workers.

Small Business Firms and Company Families. American families' most common form of economic activity in the business sector in the twentieth century was running small businesses. Although even the federal government's Small Business Administration used a variety of definitions to determine which firms constituted "small businesses," most companies with fewer than 250 employees fell within that definition. Economists,

The murderous Corleones of the Godfather *films represented a type of corporate family.* (Museum of Modern Art, Film Stills Archive)

especially in the first half of the twentieth century, tended to emphasize large corporations as the centerpieces of American business activity. By the 1960's, however, the growth of large corporations was slowing. During the 1980's, while the assets and sales of many big companies continued to grow, their workforces and market shares had shrunk.

By 1997 small, family-owned businesses employed the majority of workers and comprised the bulk of the "new rich." Between 1974 and 1984 the workforces of the Fortune 500's largest companies fell by 1.5 million, while net employment in small businesses rose. By some estimates small business employment accounted for three-fifths of the 20 million new jobs. Start-ups of new businesses reached new highs, as a record 9.5 percent of the workforce became owners of businesses.

Once family-owned firms achieved a measure of success, they became targets of established companies. During the 1970's some 95 percent of the nearly five thousand corporate mergers involved small companies. Small family firms took advantage of incorporation laws to expand, while families retained control of their companies. After the mid-1980's more than 650,000 new incorporations occurred. Many of these newly incorporated, small family businesses failed, often reflecting the fact that, after their principal owners retired, their families did not want to continue running the businesses. The apparent high failure rates of family-owned businesses therefore often reflect the absence of heirs who want to continue the family enterprises.

Immigrant Family Firms. As a nation of immigrants the United States has been a haven for

Immigrant families, such as the Jamaican Americans who own this shoe-repair shop, often become corporate families. (Hazel Hankin)

entrepreneurs from other parts of the world. Immigrants who have started businesses have often employed their own children, allowing these businesses to maintain longer business hours. One study of Lebanese-owned businesses in Atlanta, Georgia, found that they were open sixteen to eighteen hours a day. A similar study of Koreans found that family members worked an average of sixty hours a week in their family-owned stores. The 200,000 Cuban refugees who arrived in Florida during the early 1960's founded most of the 25,000 Cuban-owned businesses operating by 1987 in Dade County, Florida. One Cuban entrepreneur, José Pinero, peddled second-hand records until he could open his own record store that featured Latin imports. His Ultra stores soon expanded into shopping malls across the nation.

Numerous studies of Haitian, Jamaican, and Vietnamese families in the United States have shown that they capitalize on family labor to achieve business success. As a result, they have higher per-capita incomes than many white families. Proportionally, far more black Jamaicans, Haitians, and Dominicans in the United States run businesses than do American-born whites.

Child-labor laws and compulsory education have limited the extent to which immigrants have been able to utilize family labor to expand family wealth. Moreover, not all immigrants have the same cultural perspectives. Adult Chinese immigrants, for example, sometimes work extra hours so that their children can concentrate on their education. Immigrant couples often run businesses as a team. More often, however, immigrant wives manage their households while their husbands concentrate on their family businesses.

Wealth, Families, and Capitalization of Business. The fame of exceptionally wealthy American business families, such as the Vanderbilts, has propagated the myth that most successful entrepreneurs and family businesses inherit wealth. In fact, studies have shown that inherited wealth is a detriment to business success. One study of thousands of American millionaires found that 80 percent were first-generation rich. Other studies of male multimillionaires revealed that 33 percent had inherited no assets at all. Of those worth two million dollars or more, more than 70 percent had no inherited assets. More than half of the names in the Forbes 400 in 1996 had not appeared on the list in 1990, and more than half of all millionaires had received no inheritance. Marriage and the maintenance of a family structure appeared to be critical to the business success of the millionaires, even if their spouses did not work outside the home.

Nearly all major American corporations were started with accumulated personal savings from work or from small sums contributed by families; only a small fraction were founded with money from inherited wealth. An example of a family participating in the start-up of a successful corporation is the Gordy family of Detroit, Michigan. When Berry Gordy was a line worker at General Motors, he received a $500 loan from his mother to help start Motown Records.

Corporate Downsizing and Family Relationships. In the 1990's media attention to large-scale layoffs by a few major corporations bred the myth that American corporations were "downsizing" at substantially higher rates than previously, generating anxiety and stress at unprecedented levels, especially within families. In fact, since 1979, while 43 million jobs were lost, 70 million new jobs were created; and the number of working Americans rose by 32 percent after 1982. Massive layoffs at AT&T made headlines, but equally massive new hires at MCI, Sprint, and cable companies did not.

It was often asserted that families were under more stress than ever because the new jobs did not pay as well as the old jobs and because housewives were driven into the workforce to help maintain the standard of living. However, studies of labor-force participation showed that involuntary part-time work did not increase in the 1980's and 1990's and that so-called service jobs paid, on average, as much as blue-collar jobs (mainly because those in service jobs included accountants, professors, attorneys, salespersons, and other relatively high-payed white-collar employees). Finally, inflation-adjusted incomes of the baby boomers were shown to be higher than those of their parents. A 1996 survey of Americans showed that nearly half rated themselves better off than the year before, and the overall rating of "how people feel" was the highest since 1976. Other studies showed that the number of poor families remained almost constant between 1972 and 1990, while the number of middle-class families shrunk and the number of upper-income families rose.

One study concluded that "the rich have become richer, and the poor richer faster."

Another variant of the corporate-family relationship is the continuing tension in American business and labor relations as to the appropriate role of firms in the lives of employees. Well into the 1920's, many businesses employed "welfare capitalism" to offer employees family-type services, including medical care, cafeterias, playgrounds, child care, company stores, and other benefits. Welfare capitalism was abandoned in the Great Depression, as companies could scarcely afford to pay salaries. Although it revived in some forms in the 1980's and 1990's, it has remained a tool that only a few companies can afford to use. Moreover, with the exception of medical insurance, most American employees have expressed the desire to be compensated directly in cash rather than in kind, further diminishing the effectiveness of companies that want to be "a family" to their employees. —*Larry Schweikart*

BIBLIOGRAPHY

Becker, Benjamin M., and Fred Tillman. *The Family Owned Business.* 2d ed. Chicago: Commerce Clearing House, 1978. Textbook approach to family businesses examining at length the structure, problems, management, and operations of small family firms.

Gilder, George. *Recapturing the Spirit of Enterprise.* San Francisco, Calif.: Institute for Contemporary Studies, 1992. A classic, enhanced reprint of Gilder's *The Spirit of Enterprise,* this book explores the political and economic factors that encourage small business formation, while at the same time devoting space to case studies of Cubans, Lebanese, and other minority success stories.

Marsh, Ann. "Meet the Class of 1996," *Forbes 400* (October 14, 1996). Provides a snapshot of dozens of entrepreneurs, including several families who have made their fortunes through enterprise.

Solomon, Steven. *Small Business USA: The Role of Small Companies in Sparking America's Economic Transformation.* New York: Crown, 1986. Useful for statistics on small- and family-owned businesses.

Sowell, Thomas. *Race and Culture: A World View.* New York: Basic Books, 1994. Argues that cul-

tural characteristics that emphasize entrepreneurship, hard work, and savings explain more about family economic development than does race. A crucial book for comparisons of intra-race income and wealth gaps.

See also African Americans; Baby boomers; Family businesses; Institutional families; Japanese Americans; Jews; Public education; Vietnamese Americans.

Couples

RELEVANT ISSUES: Marriage and dating; Parenting and family relationships

SIGNIFICANCE: As definitions of families and intimate relationships have been challenged and modified because of changes in society, an understanding of this diversity and its impact on families is necessary

In the 1990's changes in society resulted in a variety of intimate relationships that were previously not recognized, accepted, or even possible, relationships which were seen by many as a threat to "the institution of the family." For example, numerous articles and letters appeared in magazines and advice columns highlighting the dangers of relationships initiated over computer networks. Stories in the print and broadcast media have questioned the parenting abilities of lesbians and gay men. At the same time, family members and friends have questioned the commitment of individuals in commuter marriages, because they live far apart from each other.

Despite increases in divorce rates and alternative arrangements to "traditional" marriage, the desire for permanence and commitment in relationships is still as strong as ever. In *Families in Canada: Social Context, Continuities, and Changes* (1994), Lyle Larson, J. Walter Goltz, and Charles Hobart note that by the age of sixty-five, only about 8 percent of men and women have never been married. What appears to be changing is not the importance of family relationships and marriage, but rather the nature or structure of individuals' commitment to each other.

Old Assumptions About Relationships. In the mid- to late twentieth century, the "family life cycle" assumed there was one type of family and one way for families to develop. A (heterosexual) man

Coupling often becomes serious among teenagers. (James L. Shaffer)

The late twentieth century saw a growing public acceptance of openly gay and lesbian couples.
(James L. Shaffer)

and woman met, fell in love, got married, and then moved in together. Following marriage and the birth of children, the wife typically stayed at home to care for them. As their children grew up, predictable events and challenges were experienced. Children eventually left home as young adults, and later the husband (or both parents) retired from the paid labor force. This was assumed to be the natural and most effective form of family development. All other types of families, if they were even recognized, were assumed to be "deviant."

A closer look reveals that not all individuals followed this pathway, while increasing numbers of people rejected it. Furthermore, despite contrary claims, "alternative" relationships were just as effective as "traditional" relationships in meeting families' needs.

Societal Changes. Technological advances have resulted in more technologically advanced homes. In the 1990's the majority of homes had televisions and videocassette recorders. Furthermore, personal computers provided homes with access to the world of the Internet. This technology has given people the opportunity to initiate and experience relationships that exist solely "within" computer networks, whereby individuals never physically meet or speak to each other. Access to the Internet has also changed how individuals communicate with their partners when they are geographically separated from each other, making communication faster, more efficient, and quite different from phone conversations or letters.

The number of women working in the paid labor force increased dramatically in the late twentieth century. As a result of the feminist movement, women began to question the satisfaction they were expected to derive from caring solely for their families. The traditional roles of women and men within families and society have been challenged. With the slight decline in men's incomes during the 1980's, women needed to work in the paid labor force to maintain an adequate standard of living for their families. Many women work not only because they want to work, but also because they have to. Additional "downsizing" in the workforce has resulted in unemployment and increased competition for jobs. Individuals must often move to obtain paid work. The economic and psychological importance of jobs for women

and men has resulted in partner separations, giving rise to long-distance dating and commuter marriages.

During the 1980's increasingly liberal attitudes toward cohabitation resulted in higher numbers of individuals living together, with or without the intention of eventually marrying. For example, the percentage of Canadians in cohabiting relationships increased from 6 percent to 12 percent from 1981 to 1990. This increase was the result of several factors, including an increased wariness toward marriage because of high divorce rates and a view of cohabitation as a step leading to marriage.

Homosexuality was viewed in the United States as an illness until 1974, when the American Psychological Association withdrew homosexuality from its list of "mental disorders." Since then, individuals have become increasingly tolerant and accepting of lesbian and gay relationships, although many still view such intimate relationships as controversial and questionable. Nevertheless, increasingly liberal attitudes toward individuals' different ways of meeting their intimate needs have resulted in greater numbers of open and accepted lesbian and gay relationships.

As technology and attitudes and beliefs have changed, so too has the definition of relationships. This has resulted in different dating and marital experiences. In the 1990's five types of relationships existed—the result of societal changes.

Internet Relationships. The advancement of technology has changed the nature of relationships forever. Individuals can initiate and maintain romantic relationships over computer networks with people they have never met. They can exchange messages in real time with others in a shared computer space or leave messages for others to read later. In some cases, the anonymity of computers and the lack of physical presence (or physical appearance) can quickly lead to intense levels of intimacy. Anecdotal information has revealed that individuals have valued these relationships highly, declaring that they know the people they have met on the Internet much better than those with whom they interact face-to-face.

Such relationships have given rise to a variety of concerns. For example, high levels of intimacy can lead to unrealistic expectations about both computer and noncomputer relationships. Cases have also been documented of computer users misrepresenting their identities; for example, partners have lied to each other about their sex, names, or occupations. Some have questioned whether computer-mediated relationships are "real" or suitable substitutes for face-to-face interactions with others and whether computer relationships affect the face-to-face relationships that computer-users maintain.

On the other hand, the use of electronic mail has changed the nature of long-distance relationships, allowing for inexpensive instantaneous communication between partners. Long-distance relationships have often benefited from partners' ability to communicate by e-mail.

Long-Distance Relationships. Many adults find themselves in long-distance dating relationships when they move to pursue educational or work opportunities. Furthermore, commuter marriages have become increasingly common among couples who are highly committed to their careers as well as their partners. As persons move to obtain new jobs and set up separate households they highlight the strong relationship between work and home life. Those who are unhappy with their work situations (or lack thereof) can be negatively affected in their personal lives.

Living apart from one's partner does not imply lack of love or commitment. Rather, this arrangement often illustrates that couples are highly committed to each other, successfully maintaining their relationships in the face of constraints such as loneliness and increased financial burdens. On the other hand, persons have benefited from separation by developing their personal interests and goals, enhancing communication with their partners, and coming to a greater awareness and understanding of what they really want in a relationship.

Cohabiting Relationships. The term "marriage" has become a complex term. Approximately one full page in Canada's 1996 income-tax guide was dedicated to defining "spouses." Thus, common-law spouses were persons of the opposite sex living with each other for at least twelve continuous months, including separations of less than ninety days. The legal identification of such relationships for income-tax purposes pointed to their staying power.

Research initially indicated that individuals in cohabiting relationships had more liberal views regarding marriage and relationships than those who were married and that the stability of cohabiting relationships was lower than that of marital relationships. Since cohabitation has become more common, the rates of marital and cohabitation breakups as well as the attitudes, beliefs, and behaviors of cohabiting and married persons have narrowed. It has been suggested that as nonmarital (heterosexual) cohabitation has become more and more common, it could almost be considered a societal institution. Yet, much is still not known about these relationships, including how partners develop a sense of commitment to each other.

Gay and Lesbian Relationships. In a 1995 journal article, Michelle Huston and Pepper Schwartz noted that, like heterosexuals, many lesbians and gay men have maintained long-term committed relationships, despite the difficulties they faced in meeting partners and maintaining relationships because of societal disapproval or lack of support. However, tolerance or acceptance of these relationships seems to be increasing. Homosexual couples deal with the usual issues of communication, support, power, sexuality, and connection versus autonomy.

Implications for Families. Because of the diversity of dating, cohabiting, and marital relationships, it is no longer considered acceptable to think of family relationships as following only one pathway or course toward commitment and happiness. This indicates that individuals have found creative and innovative ways to connect with and relate to their partners in a changing society.

Additional research is required to learn more about the experiences of individuals in such relationships. For example, how do individuals negotiate closeness with their partners when they are separated? How are children affected by these relationships? In her 1992 review of research on the children of lesbian and gay parents, sociologist Charlotte Patterson found that children raised by lesbian or gay parents were not significantly different from children raised by heterosexual parents in terms of their gender identity, gender-role behavior, sexual orientation, personal development, or their interpersonal relationships. Furthermore, existing research has contradicted the common opinion that gay and lesbian individuals make

During the 1990's, films such as True Romance *offered startling new—and often violent—views of modern love and couples.* (Museum of Modern Art, Film Stills Archive)

"bad parents." Researchers still need to examine how children experience growing up with parents involved in commuter marriages and cohabiting relationships.

A review of the gamut of relationships reveals that they provide benefits and opportunities for individual and interpersonal growth which, in turn, lay the foundation for effective family relationships. For example, communicating effectively with dating partners by e-mail requires being able to communicate thoughts and feelings accurately and creatively. Commuter marriages require that couples manage their finances effectively in order to deal with the extra expenses of geographical separation. Couples must be able to negotiate the challenges of living together or separately, deal with the possible negative attitudes of others, and communicate well if they want their current and future relationships to be successful.

As more becomes known about families, it can be argued that family processes, rather than family structure, seem to be important for individuals' well-being. Love, support, affection, companionship, and socialization can occur in any relationship and are not necessarily dependent on whether couples are heterosexual, whether they live in the same geographical location, or whether they are legally married. A happy, secure, committed relationship between two individuals, regardless of sexual orientation or marital status, may be more relevant for the secure development of children than obligatory heterosexual marriages, which may, after all, be conflict-ridden.

—*Áine M. Humble*

BIBLIOGRAPHY

Baker, Maureen, ed. *Families: Changing Trends in Canada.* 3d ed. Toronto: McGraw-Hill Ryerson, 1996. Discusses various changes in Canada's culture which affect families, including definitions of families, impact of technology on families, and trends in sexuality, cohabitation, and marriage.

Cunningham, John D., and John K. Antill. "Current Trends in Nonmarital Cohabitation: In Search of the POSSLQ." In *Under-Studied Relationships: Off the Beaten Track*, edited by Julia T. Wood and Steve Duck. Thousand Oaks, Calif.: Sage Publications, 1995. Provides an overview of attitudes toward cohabitation, descriptions of who cohabits, and discussions on issues such as relationship quality, childbearing, and their links with marital stability.

Gerstel, Naomi, and Harriet Gross. *Commuter Marriage: A Study of Work and Family.* New York: Guilford Press, 1984. Covers factors contributing to long-distance marriages, challenges and benefits of being separated, impact on parents and children, and the relationship between marriage satisfaction and paid work.

Huston, Michelle, and Pepper Schwartz. "The Relationships of Lesbians and Gay Men." In *Under-Studied Relationships: Off the Beaten Track*, edited by Julia T. Wood and Steve Duck. Thousand Oaks, Calif.: Sage Publications, 1995. Describes the initiation, maintenance, and ending of these relationships, effects of gender socialization on partner preferences, and the impact of society at large on these relationships.

Larson, Lyle E., J. Walter Goltz, and Charles W. Hobart. *Families in Canada: Social Context, Continuities, and Changes.* Scarborough, Ontario: Prentice Hall Canada, 1994. Discusses the development and maintenance of dating and marital relationships, while looking at relationships in transition and the future of Canadian families.

Patterson, Charlotte J. "Children of Lesbian and Gay Parents." *Child Development* 63 (1992). Discusses various lesbian and gay families and summarizes research which, overall, indicates that children with homosexual parents do not differ significantly from children of heterosexual parents in their sexual identity or levels of well-being.

Rohlfing, Mary E. " 'Doesn't Anyone Stay in One Place Anymore?' An Exploration of the Under-Studied Phenomenon of Long-Distance Relationships." In *Under-Studied Relationships: Off the Beaten Track*, edited by Julia T. Wood and Steve Duck. Thousand Oaks, Calif.: Sage Publications, 1995. Explores the challenges and benefits of long-distance romantic and friendship relationships.

See also Cohabitation; Computer recreation; Dating; Domestic partners; Family life cycle; Gay and lesbian families; Marriage; Monogamy; Persons of opposite sex sharing living quarters (POSSLQ); Serial monogamy; Women's roles.

Courting rituals

RELEVANT ISSUES: Marriage and dating; Parenting and family relationships

SIGNIFICANCE: Although courting rituals have changed dramatically throughout the twentieth century, society still maintains certain forms of conduct that guide young men and women toward the common goal of matrimony

Prior to 1900 distances between towns and homesteads dictated a practical approach to finding spouses. Social activities were limited to church and agricultural functions, and it was not uncommon for men to pay overnight visits to the homes of the young women they were courting, even chastely sharing their beds. Called "bundling," this practice allowed couples limited privacy while maintaining young women's virtue by a variety of means, including placing a low board between the man and woman or even tying the woman's legs together.

As the distances closed, it became accepted practice for men to pay "courting calls" on their prospective brides. Such courting calls took place in women's homes in the presence of their parents

The time when a young man would not think of proposing marriage to a woman without first asking her father for permission has long since passed. (James L. Shaffer)

or other suitable chaperones. Women held the upper hand; mothers and daughters controlled how long the call lasted, whether or not refreshments were served, and even suitable topics of conversation. Social rules were strict, dictating everything from the time between the invitation and the actual visit to what role the chaperones played. After a suitable period, a prospective groom asked the young woman's father for her hand in marriage.

As society changed to a city-based culture in the early twentieth century, courting rituals changed as well. Restaurants, theaters, and parks offered alternatives to the parlor and provided relief from the watchful eyes of chaperones. Despite initial resistance by the upper classes (who considered it

Once regulated by strict traditions, North American courting rituals have steadily become less formal. (James L. Shaffer)

"compromising"), dating became commonplace, eventually replacing the courting call altogether. Consequently, women no longer controlled the early stages of the relationship. Men planned and paid for meals and entertainment and determined how long the evening would last. By way of recompense, more and more proposals were made directly to prospective brides rather than to their fathers.

Relationships changed dramatically in the mid-1960's. Understood as everything from a response to decades of repression to the utter collapse of morals, the free-love movement cast aside ritual for "anything goes." Women were free to ask men out on dates and even propose marriage to them, while many young couples chose to forego marriage altogether and simply cohabit. These open attitudes lasted through the discos and the singles' bars of the 1970's, until a sharp rise in sexually transmitted diseases dampened promiscuous lifestyles.

This increased wariness, coupled with an office-based lifestyle, forced many professional singles to turn to dating services. Late twentieth century matchmakers use computers, voice mail, and video cameras to aid others in their courting rituals.

—*P. S. Ramsey*

See also Arranged marriages; Bride-price; Bundling; Couples; Dating; Engagement; Love; Marriage; Matchmaking; Weddings.

Cousins

RELEVANT ISSUES: Kinship and genealogy; Marriage and dating; Parenting and family relationships; Religious beliefs and practices

SIGNIFICANCE: Cousins are an integral part of extended family and kinship networks

For many people, family is the basic social unit composed of married parents and their children. Extended families include grandparents, aunts, uncles, cousins, and other relatives. The nuclear or traditional family was far less prevalent in the late 1990's than it had been in earlier decades. This notion of the nuclear family became popular early in the twentieth century and is very much a Western or European-American ideal.

Family Systems, Structures, and Boundaries. The family can be viewed as a system. The members in the family form their own system within the extended family or kinship network. Within the family system are subsystems. Spouses create a spousal subsystem. Children create a sibling subsystem. Beyond the nuclear family is the extended family system, which includes subsystems among adult siblings, parents and grandparents, grandchildren and grandparents, and among cousins.

The concept of boundaries is important in family structure. Boundaries can be thought of as abstract lines between parts of the system, determining how members interact with each other.

Teresa Marciano and Marvin B. Sussman developed a concept of the wider family that has become more visible and more accepted. This wider family is similar to kinship network. Kinship networks are most often discussed in terms of African American and other ethnically diverse families as extended family networks. The extended kinship network can be viewed as a family strength found in the African American family and may include grandparents, aunts, uncles, siblings, and cousins, all of whom may participate in shared child rearing. Siblings are defined as brothers and sisters, or persons who share parents. Half siblings share one parent. Stepsisters and stepbrothers occur in cases in which parents divorce and remarry.

Defining Cousins. In order to define cousins, it is necessary to understand that an aunt is the sister of one's mother or father and that an uncle is the brother of one's mother or father. First cousins are the children of one's aunt or uncle. A person's cousins are also that person's mother's or father's nieces or nephews. Cousins can be divided into cross-cousins and parallel cousins. Cross-cousins are one's mother's brother's children or one's father's sister's children. Cross-cousins have parents who are siblings of the opposite sex.

Parallel cousins are either one's mother's sister's children or one's father's brother's children. Parallel cousins have parents who are siblings of the same sex.

Second cousins are the grandchildren of one's great aunts or great uncles. If two people are first cousins, their children will be second cousins to each other. Third cousins are the great-grandchildren of one's great-great aunts or great-great uncles. If two people are second cousins, their children will be third cousins to each other.

To make matters more complicated, there are also "cousins once removed." Cousins once re-

The fact that the fathers of this boy and girl are brothers makes the children parallel cousins. (R. Kent Rasmussen)

moved are the children of first cousins. The children of a person's first cousin are that person's first cousins once removed. One's children will be one's first cousin's first cousin once removed.

Half cousins occur when only one of two parents is a blood parent. This follows because half siblings share only one parent. The children of two half siblings would be half cousins, because they share only one grandparent. Double cousins occur when two brothers marry two sisters from another family. The children are cousins to each other not only because their mothers are sisters, but also because their fathers are brothers. Double cousins can also occur when brothers and sisters from one family marry sisters and brothers from another family.

Marriage between first cousins has been restricted in North America; about half of the states in the United States do not allow legal marriage between first cousins.

Cousins in the United States. There are many variables that can determine the nature of relationships between cousins. These variables in-

clude the proximity of the family households, the relational closeness of the cousins' parents as adult siblings, the influence of mutual grandparents, and cousins' ages and interests. Some cousins are as close, and perhaps closer, than siblings. Some cousins never even meet one another.

Not all cultures and groups view families in traditional ways. Kinship networks are common among nonwhite ethnic groups in the United States. A brief history of the notion of cousins in African American families is given by Niara Sudarkasa. Two ideas are important in looking at cousins in African American families: conjugality and consanguinity. Conjugality means relationships between spouses and consanguinity means relationships between blood relatives. European and American families tend to emphasize the conjugal relationships in nuclear and extended families. African and African American families have traditionally been organized around consanguinal relationships. These kinship networks are often formed by adult siblings of the same sex. The kinship network often includes spouses and children and siblings and their children. The extended family in Africa often differs from the family in America in that among the former the extended family exists as an umbrella group. The extended family often lives together in a family compound. It is not unusual for all the children of the same generation within the compound to regard themselves as brothers and sisters rather than as cousins. Adults in the extended family often take on responsibilities for all the children without distinguishing whether the children are their own biological children or nieces and nephews. African families do not draw the rigid boundaries that the European-American families often erect around their nuclear families.

Native American, Asian American, and Hispanic American Families. There are many differences between the tribes of Native Americans. One common thread found among Native American groups is that the basic family structure for most tribes is the extended family, often extending to second cousins. Derald Wing Sue and David Sue explain that Native American children are often raised by relatives such as aunts, uncles, and grandparents. Cousins raised together often relate very much like siblings in nuclear families.

Asian American and Hispanic American families are also diverse groups that include ethnic heritages from many different countries. Yet, both of these broad groups share the extended family or kinship network orientation. The extended family as the basic unit creates a greater sense of closeness with cousins than does that of a basic unit with boundaries drawn more tightly around parents and biological children.

Siblings Versus Cousins. In the majority of European American families siblings are much more likely to be closer to siblings than to cousins. Siblings are more likely to grow up in the same household than are cousins. Some variables that can affect the relationship between cousins are how close the families live to one another, how close

Integral parts of extended family networks, cousins often develop intimate relationships with one another when they are close in age. (Long Hare Photographs)

cousins' parents are, cousins' involvement with mutual grandparents, and cousins' ages and interests. In families based on extended kinship networks these same variables may exist, but the boundaries between each set of parents and children may be much more relaxed. It is more likely that cousins who spend some time in their childhood residing together will have a relationship more like the traditional sibling relationship than that between cousins who have never shared the same residence. —*Cynthia Semlear Avery*

BIBLIOGRAPHY

Goldenberg, H., and I. Goldenberg. *Counseling Today's Families.* 2d ed. Pacific Grove, Calif.: Brooks Cole Publishing, 1994.

Marciano, Teresa, and Marvin. B. Sussman. "The Definition of Family Is Expanding." In Salvador Minuchen, ed., *Families and Family Therapy.* Cambridge, Mass.: Harvard University Press, 1974.

Sudarkasa, Niara. "Interpreting the African Heritage in Afro-American Family Organization." In Mark Hutter, ed. *The Family Experience: A Reader in Cultural Diversity.* 2d ed. Boston: Allyn & Bacon, 1997.

Sue, Derald Wing, and David Sue. *Counseling the Culturally Different.* 2d ed. New York: John Wiley & Sons, 1990.

Swisher, Karin, and Viqi Wagner, eds. *The Family in America: Opposing Viewpoints.* San Diego, Calif.: Greenhaven Press, 1992.

Walsh, F., ed. *Normal Family Processes.* 2d ed. New York: Guilford Press, 1993.

See also Cross-cousins; Extended families; Parallel cousins.

Cross-cousins

RELEVANT ISSUES: Kinship and genealogy; Marriage and dating; Parenting and family relationships

SIGNIFICANCE: Cross-cousin marriage is a prescribed form of marriage found in either patrilineal or matrilineal kin systems that tends to reinforce socioeconomic relationships of the offspring of parental siblings of the opposite sex

Early anthropologists explained sister exchange as a basis for cross-cousin marriage, but modern explanations are that sister exchange is intrinsically related to cross-cousin marriage. Societies that subscribe to cross-cousin kinship terminology also have parallel cousin terminology, based on what anthropologists usually call bifurcate merging, whereby one calls one's father's brothers "father." Conversely, one calls one's mother's sisters "mother." The obvious extension of these kinship ties makes the offspring of "father" and "mother" parallel cousins, whom one calls "brother" or "sister." Persons' cross-cousins are normally determined as the offspring of one's father's sister or mother's brother, and it is not considered incestuous if one marries a cross-cousin. Cross-cousin marriage is often considered to be a preferred or even a prescribed form of marriage, as it tends to reinforce the alliances of the sibling parents of the married pair. A further function of cross-cousin marriage is that it maintains wealth inheritance and economic holdings within kin groups, particularly between moieties (the complementary halves of a society).

Matrilineal cross-cousin marriage tends to promote greater social integration and solidarity than patrilineal cross-cousin marriage, because wife providers and wife takers regularly stand in the same relationship. —*John Alan Ross*

See also Clans; Cousins; Kinship systems; Lineage; Marriage; Matrilineal descent; Parallel cousins; Patrilineal descent; Tribes.

Cruelty as grounds for divorce

RELEVANT ISSUES: Divorce; Law; Marriage and dating

SIGNIFICANCE: Concepts of cruelty as grounds for divorce have paralleled changing attitudes about women's rights and various important aspects of marriage

The attitudes of Western societies toward marriage have changed dramatically over the last three hundred years. The Protestant Reformation in Europe initiated the concept of divorce as a remedy for marriage dissatisfaction and established the doctrine that marriage is a civil contract between two people.

As early as 1639, the Plymouth Colony identified grounds for divorce as adultery or desertion lasting seven years or more. It was not until the middle of the nineteenth century that the southern states accepted the view of the New England and

Before the advent of no-fault divorce laws, many women seeking to escape unhappy marriages found the legal requirement of proving that their spouses had been cruel to them an insuperable burden. (Skjold Photographs)

334 • Cult of True Womanhood

middle states that jurisdiction over divorce rested with the state courts. From the middle to the late nineteenth century, societal attitudes toward marriage changed. There was a growing belief that marriage was a partnership of equality and affection, not just a civil contract. Women gained more legal control of property and the wages they earned. All of these factors contributed to the establishment of physical cruelty as grounds for divorce nearly two hundred years after the legal system had defined what constituted cruelty of one person toward another. By 1887 thirty-three states and the District of Columbia had enacted laws that not only gave women the right to manage their own property and wages but also identified physical cruelty as grounds for divorce. In addition, by the end of the nineteenth century the emotional and intimate aspects of marriage were viewed as increasingly important.

By the beginning of the twentieth century, the definition of cruelty as grounds for divorce expanded to include mental and emotional, as well as physical behavior. The widely accepted definition of cruelty between marriage partners encompasses a pattern of physical violence or threats to a spouse's safety that may include expressing ridicule, showing contempt, or performing acts of physical mistreatment. Some states have also recognized personal indignities, rudeness, disdain, or vulgarity.

Establishment of cruelty as legal grounds for divorce has given men and women recourse when mistreated by their spouses. It has also helped define a societal norm for acceptable behavior within a marriage. Children are protected from the disorganization and pain that result from cruelty in a family. In the first half of the twentieth century, however, many women were unable to benefit from divorce because of the financial and emotional costs involved. Lengthy court proceedings and public testimony to prove alleged cruelty place additional burdens on persons already subjected to physical, emotional, or mental cruelty. Establishment of no-fault divorce laws reduced the need for proving cruelty, thereby sparing already victimized families additional emotional and economic stress.

—*Janet C. Benavente*

See also Child custody; Divorce; Domestic violence; Marital rape; Marriage counseling; Marriage laws; No-fault divorce; Violence Against Women Act.

Cult of True Womanhood

RELEVANT ISSUES: Children and child development; Marriage and dating; Parenting and family relationships

SIGNIFICANCE: The Cult of True Womanhood, prevalent throughout the nineteenth century, maintained that women's sphere should be limited to the family home

Throughout the nineteenth century, American women were expected to adhere to the Cult of True Womanhood. This ideology, which was prevalent in women's literature and other forms of popular culture, held that a woman's role should be confined to the home. As men entered the industrial workforce and market economy, certain books, including Catharine Beecher's *Treatise on Domestic Economy* (1841), underscored the importance of household work and established a code of conduct that restricted women's economic opportunities.

The Cult of True Womanhood encouraged women to cultivate four basic traits: piety, purity, submission, and domesticity. By serving as the spiritual head of the family in providing a pious example, women were expected to serve as role models for their daughters and curb and reform the immoral tendencies of their husbands and sons. Intellectual pursuits for women were discouraged, since education would conflict with the time women were supposed to devote to evangelical commitments. Purity was considered to be the greatest gift a woman could bestow upon her husband. Novels and literary magazines emphasized the value of virginity, and published stories encouraged the notion that women who participated in premarital sex often succumbed to insanity or death. Acceptance of submission symbolized that women were weak, fragile, and in need of the protection offered by men. As a result, women were expected to remain passive and never offer advice unless asked. Most important, women were expected to display enthusiasm for domestic tasks. Since their work was confined to the household, women were expected to provide a cheerful, loving, and spiritual home environment.

The ideals of the Cult of True Womanhood excluded women from the public sphere of politics and business. As a result, many social reformers, including Susan B. Anthony and Elizabeth Cady Stanton, refused to accept this doctrine. They eventually organized America's first significant feminist movement.   —*Robert D. Ubriaco, Jr.*

See also Family: concept and history; Gender inequality; Marriage; Menopause; Motherhood; Women's roles.

Cultural influences

RELEVANT ISSUES: Children and child development; Education; Parenting and family relationships; Race and ethnicity; Religious beliefs and practices

SIGNIFICANCE: As a powerful vehicle for transmitting cultural norms, the family may be a culture's most influential socializing group and have the most lasting impact on a child's ability to function in society

Babies are not born into a social vacuum, but rather into colorful environments of people who form complex social groups. Cultures define solutions for group members' handling of basic human problems, as well as for how people should relate to one another, the significance of time, valued personality types, the relationship of humankind to nature, and the innate predispositions of human beings. A culture determines what should be eaten and worn and how children should be raised. Cultures also define beliefs and provide frames of reference for making sense out of the surrounding world.

Within each culture the process of socialization teaches individuals not only what to do, but also how things are and why they are as they are. Young children begin to absorb and construct for themselves a description of the world as it is. The foundations of this ordering of the physical world of objects and all the events which impinge on an individual's consciousness are laid by parents. Later, siblings, friends, teachers, and the media complement parents' influence.

Socialization occurs through a number of processes in addition to direct teaching. Through the process of identification, children more than two years of age tend to behave as their parents and adopt the latter's mannerisms, roles, values, restrictions, and ideals. Therefore, identification is viewed as an important vehicle through which parents transmit not merely ways of being but also worldviews.

Modeling is another important process in the child's socialization. Again, parents transmit explicit and implicit values, attitudes, and behaviors as a result of their words and actions. Closely related to imitation is the process of role-learning, which integrates children into the different facets of the social matrix as they acquire behavior appropriate to each facet. Role behavior is reciprocal, as parents influence behavior by shaping it to conform to their conceptions of appropriateness. The process of role-learning leads children to acquire their identities through their perspectives on the social world viewed from their particular roles.

Families mediate the cultural experiences available in their children's society by designing opportunities for participation in religious instruction, music lessons, and sports activities; by providing certain toys; and by situating themselves in certain neighborhoods and school districts. Families also provide models of children's interactions by interacting within and beyond the home. Thus children develop patterns for establishing relationships and preferences for those with whom they choose to relate.

Each cultural belief and practice that becomes well established within an individual through experience is internalized and learned at various levels. Children learn many things as simple habits. They later come to defend them. Eventually the concepts or patterns take on added levels of meaning, at which time young persons can provide intellectual arguments, experience emotional attachments, and attach values to concepts or practices.

Process of Ethnic Identity Development. Ethnic identity takes root in families, the foremost agency of ethnic socialization. Unless children learn and experience their basic ethnic identities within their families or other early primary groups, it is unlikely they will ever feel them strongly. Child-rearing practices reflect broad diversity in techniques used to socialize children according to belief systems, values, and ethnic norms. Scientific writings on African Americans, for example, suggest that the cultural and social values most important to the acquisition of ethnic attitudes are bicultural adaptation, religious orientation, and strong family ties.

Families that are not part of a society's dominant culture must socialize their children not only in their own ethnicity but also in that of the dominant culture. Their children must also be socialized in how to survive in a hostile environment. Families, by providing a positive sense of ethnic identity, serve to buffer children from society's negative impacts.

Children initially acquire their ethnic identities as perceptive differences. These differences are later perceived in relation to belief systems, values, and feelings of pride and attachment. To know and recognize one's ethnicity is cognitive; to feel its sentiments and emotions is affective. After this recognition occurs, an individual might begin to focus on rituals, group singing or dancing, and ceremonies or traditions.

Development of Values, Opinions, and Prejudices. At an early age, children develop ideas and feelings that may grow into real prejudices through reinforcement by family members and society. These early feelings and ideas may be based on children's limited experience and developmental level or may be imitations of adult behavior. According to social learning theory, identification is a major factor in prejudice acquisition. Children learn social behavior through imitation and reinforcement. Conformity to a collective image, modeled by parents, helps individuals know what to expect. Labeling others as different serves to maintain community boundaries. Therefore, the children most likely to be prejudiced are those who have prejudiced models; those who have been given explicit reasons to be prejudiced; those who

Although music is a central component in most cultures, music instruction is typically an early casualty in educational budget cuts. (Hazel Hankin)

These Milwaukee, Wisconsin, schoolchildren are participating in a festival designed to emphasize individual cultural heritages. (James L. Shaffer)

have expressed, rehearsed, and practiced prejudice; and those who have been rewarded for their prejudicial behavior. Social learning theory also attributes the acquisition of gender-role attitudes to children's imitation of, and reinforcement by, people similar to themselves—in particular, their same-sex parents. Although personality and gender roles are not rigidly fixed in childhood, individuals are strongly conditioned by their early social learning experiences.

Psychodynamic theory attributes negative intergroup attitudes to an authoritarian personality structure. According to this theory, children raised by harsh and rigid parents direct their frustration and hostility toward outgroup persons. Research has shown that highly prejudiced children have mothers who have stressed obedience, preferred quiet children, and used physical punish-

ment. It has also been hypothesized that prejudice tends to accompany ethnocentrism, political conservatism, chauvinism, and patriotism. Also included in this profile of the prejudiced individual is an unresolved history of parent-child conflict.

Prejudice acquisition may also be viewed from an interpersonal vantage point, which assumes that it stems from learning through interaction with the sociocultural environment. According to this model, children acquire prejudice through kinship as they conform to their parents' beliefs, values, and attitudes. Children can adopt prejudices by taking over attitudes from their family environments. They develop prejudices as a result of childhood and rearing experiences that breed suspicions, fears, and hatreds. The transmittal of ethnic attitudes from parents to their children provides little evidence that direct verbal instruc-

Helping to select a pumpkin for a Halloween jack-o-lantern is part of the culture training that children receive from their parents. (McCrea Adams)

tion is a dominant form. Often parents are unable to answer their children's questions about group differences and either change the subject, portraying race as an anxiety-arousing issue, or utilize derogatory stereotypes. Rather than verbalize their prejudices, some parents are known to shape children's prejudices indirectly through rules that prohibit or punish their children for playing with outgroup peers.

Impact of Cultural Traditions and Norms. Culture is based on customs and traditions. Individuals within specific cultures are expected to behave according to those norms. Family systems theory can be an important vehicle for viewing families' cultural impact on their children. Children cannot be understood outside their place in the family and environment. This framework places influences of history and tradition, as well as of modern experiences, in perspective.

At birth children are welcomed in various ways into their family religion. Religious beliefs assist families in deciding what elements from the environment should be transmitted to their children. Belief systems have strict ideas about such questions as birth control, divorce, obedience, and good and evil. Studies have identified the characteristics of strong families. Among them is a religious or spiritual orientation that provides members with common beliefs and promotes family values.

—*Robin C. Hasslen*

BIBLIOGRAPHY

Allport, Gordon W. *The Nature of Prejudice.* Reading, Mass.: Addison-Wesley, 1958.

Bandura, Albert, and Richard H. Walters. *Social Learning and Personality Development.* New York: Holt, Rinehart & Winston, 1963.

Belsky, Jay, Richard Lerner, and Graham Spanier. *The Child in the Family.* Reading, Mass.: Addison-Wesley, 1984.

Goodman, Mary E. *Race Awareness in Young Children.* 2d ed. New York: Macmillan, 1964.

Hoppe, Ronald A., G. Alexander Milton, and Edward C. Simmel, eds. *Early Experiences and the Processes of Socialization.* New York: Academic Press, 1970.

Katz, Phyllis A., ed. *Towards the Elimination of Racism.* New York: Pergamon Press, 1976.

Leichter, H. J., ed. *The Family as Educator.* New York: Teachers College Press, 1974.

National Commission on Children. *Beyond Rhetoric: A New American Agenda for Children and Families.* Washington, D.C.: Government Printing Office, 1991.

Radke-Yarrow, Marian, Helen Trager, and J. Miller. "The Role of Parents in the Development of Children's Ethnic Attitudes." *Child Development* 23 (1952).

See also Child rearing; Communities; Enculturation; Family: concept and history; Family values; Literature and families; Parenting.

Culture of poverty theory

RELEVANT ISSUES: Sociology; Economics and work

SIGNIFICANCE: This sociological theory provides an explanation of the mechanism through which poor families transmit poverty to the next generation

The theory of a culture of poverty was first articulated by anthropologist Oscar Lewis, who drew on his research among rural communities in Mexico during the late 1950's. The core idea of his theory is that the culture of people living in poverty is distinct from the mainstream culture, which emphasizes achievement and success. The culture of poverty, by contrast, is a culture of "getting by." Lewis later applied the concept to his studies of Puerto Ricans in San Juan, Puerto Rico, and New York City, indicating that the phenomenon is not confined to less developed countries. Rather, Lewis found that a culture of poverty is present among the lower class in the wealthiest society in the world, the United States.

The theory has both positive and negative implications. On the positive side, it holds that living in poverty is a creative act requiring great ingenuity. The ability to survive on starkly insufficient resources demonstrates that the impoverished are highly adaptable. This runs counter to the traditional view of the poor as lazy, unintelligent, and backward. On the negative side, the culture of poverty tends to be intergenerational, perpetuating itself through the process of socialization. The skills, norms, and values learned by the poor, which enable them to survive under difficult circumstances, are not very well-suited to success or upward mobility. Principal among these cultural aspects of poverty are an inability to recognize opportunities for advancement as such, owing to a view of the world in which advancement is impossible, and a lack of future orientation, a psychological predisposition toward the present that forecloses all potential for planning, saving money, and working toward a career.

Beginning in the 1960's social scientists sought to answer the question: How can poverty continue to exist in the midst of an affluent society? The findings of scholars such as Michael Harrington and Edward Banfield were soon translated into public policy. This resulted in such initiatives as the Office of Economic Opportunity (OEO) and the Head Start program. The OEO was an agency created under the administration of President Lyndon B. Johnson, which represented an institutional attempt to break the cycle of poverty by providing jobs and a stake in society through community action programs. The Head Start program

The culture of poverty theory attempts to explain how poverty is transmitted from one generation to the next within families. (James L. Shaffer)

aimed to remedy the academic and material disadvantages of poor children at an early stage of their education.

Ultimately, these programs failed in their mission to eliminate poverty in the United States, although the Head Start program has been successful in making educational opportunities more accessible to the children of poor families. Ironically, the culture of poverty model has been validated to some degree by the failure of the programs it inspired, since it implies that poverty cannot be erased by government fiat or tangible efforts but only by a change in the culture of the poor.   —*Aristide Sechandice*

See also Aid to Families with Dependent Children (AFDC); Cultural influences; Feminization of poverty; Head Start; Poverty; Welfare.

Curfews

RELEVANT ISSUES: Law; Parenting and family relationships; Violence

SIGNIFICANCE: Curfews are government-mandated restrictions on the hours during which unaccompanied minors are permitted in public

Many cities and towns have enacted ordinances prohibiting unaccompanied minors from being in public during certain hours. Typically, people under eighteen are not allowed to be in public places during late-night and early-morning hours unless they are with an adult, traveling from one place to another, or working.

Although curfews have existed since the nineteenth century, they became especially common in the 1980's and 1990's. The primary justification for enacting these laws has been to reduce the incidence of juvenile crime. Some proponents of these laws also argued that they help to protect children from harm and from the temptation to get into trouble. By the late 1990's some places had also created curfews that applied during school hours. These curfews were meant to reduce truancy and to assist law-enforcement officers in enforcing truancy laws.

Although curfew laws have been popular among legislators, they have also been criticized by many people. Critics have claimed that the laws usurp parents' rights to control their children's activities. It should be the parents' choice, not the government's, as to whether children are allowed out at night. Supporters of curfews respond that the laws actually support parents' efforts to control their children by threatening with legal sanctions those who defy parental authority. Furthermore, some argue that too many parents do not appropriately regulate their children's behavior. Undisciplined youth not only victimize others but they also endanger their own safety and futures. When parents are unwilling or unable to control their children themselves, it is argued, it is appropriate for the community to do so through curfew laws. In fact, in some jurisdictions parents may be punished if their children violate curfews.

Another common criticism of curfew laws is that they unlawfully restrict the liberty of youths. As these laws would almost certainly be unconstitutional if they applied to adults, it is argued, they should be unconstitutional when applied to children. Most courts, however, have held that curfew laws are constitutional. Courts have generally allowed greater restrictions on children than on adults, because children are considered particularly vulnerable. As long as curfews have legitimate purposes, such as protecting children and reducing crime, courts have permitted them.

Research has not generally shown that curfews significantly reduce juvenile crime. One explanation for this is that in many communities curfews have not been enforced very strictly, in part because of limited law-enforcement resources. Another explanation is that most juvenile crime occurs not during late-night hours, when curfews are in effect, but rather after school.

—*Phyllis B. Gerstenfeld*

See also Children's rights; Juvenile courts; Juvenile delinquency; Systematic Training for Effective Parenting (STEP).

Cycle of violence theory

RELEVANT ISSUES: Children and child development; Marriage and dating; Parenting and family relationships; Violence

SIGNIFICANCE: The cycle of violence theory was introduced to define the stages of abuse within domestic violence episodes

The concept of the cycle of violence was introduced in Lenore Walker's *The Battered Woman*

Counseling can help victims of domestic violence learn how to break out of the dangerous environments in which they live. (Ben Klaffke)

(1979). This concept was designed to describe the pattern of behaviors and attitudes that can be found within domestic violence episodes. The cycle of violence is divided into three stages: the tension-building phase; the acute battering incident; and the calm, loving respite phase.

During the tension-building phase, victims sense an oncoming episode of physical violence. The atmosphere becomes filled with anxiety, and victims may behave with extreme caution in an attempt to avoid triggering batterers' advancement to the second phase. Batterers may use emotional or minor forms of physical abuse, such as shoving or slapping, during the tension-building phase as a signal to the victims that they feel anger. If women have been victimized before, they are

likely to recognize even subtle signals of impending abuse, such as body gestures or looks.

The second phase of the cycle, the acute battering incident, is an episode of physical violence. Physical abuse may take such forms as hitting, burning, or kicking. This form of violent and dangerous physical abuse is often accompanied by verbal abuse. Batterers display irrationality and a total loss of control during this phase.

The final phase, the calm, loving respite, describes the reactions and subsequent behavior of abusers following the violent incident. Batterers desire to maintain a sense of power and control over their victims by seeking to retain the relationship. Attempts at repairing the damage of the episode may include apologies, romantic gestures, and promises never to hurt the victims again. Abuse may in fact stop for a period of time so as to give victims the illusion that the batterers are sincere and repentant. The reality of the cycle of violence, however, is that the three phases will occur over and over again in circular fashion unless some form of intervention takes place. Such intervention includes treatment programs for batterers. In fact, cycles of violence shorten and abuse intensifies over time.

The phrase "cycle of violence" refers to the potential intergenerational effect the pattern of abuse can elicit among other family members. For example, children may learn through observing their parents that anger is expressed though physical abuse and that hitting women is acceptable. This scenario creates the potential for another generation of males who will use physical violence to express their anger and another generation of females who will act submissively. These children may also be abusive toward their own children, because they have experienced abuse as a model of how to control others. Thus, without intervention, the cycle of violence repeats itself within relationships and may potentially be transmitted to subsequent generations.

—*Kimberly A. Wallet*

See also Battered child syndrome; Child abuse; Child Abuse Prevention and Treatment Act (CAPTA); Dating violence; Domestic violence; Emotional abuse; Family Violence Prevention and Services Act; Feminist sociology; Marital rape; Vengeance in families.

D

Dating

RELEVANT ISSUES: Divorce; Marriage and dating

SIGNIFICANCE: Many adults who are single because of divorce or the death of a spouse find that dating practices have changed since their youth

Divorce or the death of a spouse can unexpectedly thrust adults back into a significantly different dating environment than they experienced in their youth. People often date not only to enhance their social lives but also to find a permanent mate. Dating in this context becomes an audition for marriage, frequently creating anxiety. Expecta-

Although roughly one-third of Americans over the age of twenty-five are unmarried, many single persons have trouble finding dating partners. (James L. Shaffer)

tions often run high, and singles may be forced to examine their own imperfections at a time when their egos are especially vulnerable. Dating has also become more complicated, with fewer "rules" and an often poorly defined etiquette. Dating in the 1950's, 1960's, and 1970's usually involved a somewhat clearer understanding of who asked whom out, which party would pick up the tab, and what level of affection was appropriate on first or subsequent dates. Middle-aged and older singles now find many of these "rules" outdated or open for discussion.

Almost one-third of adults age twenty-five and over are unmarried, yet many singles have difficulty finding potential dating partners. Adult singles may also face issues that complicate dating, such as professional obligations, problems with former spouses, or the approval or disapproval of adult children. Although about 10 percent of single men and 36 percent of single women over twenty-five have been widowed, nearly one-third of adults are divorced. Approximately 15 percent of adult singles have children in the home, which may add to dating stress. Female singles may face additional challenges as they age because of the shrinking ratio of available men to women—3.5 to 1 for singles age sixty-five and older.

Initial Considerations. Before venturing out into the dating world, reentering singles should consider why they want to date. Some persons are seeking new mates, while others hope to relieve boredom and loneliness. They must also determine what personality traits they find interesting and attractive and assess their own lifestyles and stages of life. Relatively sedentary men may find athletic, active women appealing but may be unable to form a healthy relationship with them. Although women may find adventuresome men attractive, their own priorities may tend toward security and a stable home life. Issues such as the possibility of creating a second family or forming a permanent relationship with persons who have children in the home should also be thoroughly assessed. Singles who are successful in dating have a fairly clear understanding of themselves and their own needs.

Meeting Other Singles. There is no one place where eligible singles congregate. Bars and lounges are often the first place new singles go to find potential dates. Many singles congregate in such locations, but the atmosphere is usually not conducive to accurately evaluating potential dating partners' true personalities and behavior patterns. Alcohol can also impair persons' ability to make accurate value judgments.

Work may appear to be one of the best places to meet people, since most adults spend more than a third of their waking hours on the job. More relationships begin at work than in any other social setting. The job provides a natural environment for persons with similar interests and backgrounds to meet. It also allows singles to evaluate potential dating partners in familiar surroundings.

Dating in the workplace does have its pitfalls. With increased sensitivity toward sexual harassment, singles may jeopardize their careers by engaging in flirtatious behavior or asking subordinates out on dates. In addition, failed romances can seriously damage professional relationships. Employees considering dating coworkers should check company policies and avoid dating personnel within their management chain.

Many people turn to the Internet to meet other single persons. However, online chat rooms rarely provide any reliable information about potential dating partners. Without the visual and verbal cues inherent in face-to-face interaction, singles are at a severe disadvantage when trying to assess the suitability or even the stability of potential online dates. Users should never give personal information such as last names, phone numbers, and addresses over the Internet.

Singles dances and activities provide forums for interaction—usually with the assumption that those attending are interested in meeting other singles of the opposite sex. One of the pitfalls of such gatherings, however, is that participants are usually provided with little background information about one another. Some singles find such activities to be enjoyable, but many singles-only functions suffer from an air of desperation that some may find uncomfortable or depressing.

The burgeoning market for personal advertisements and dating services attests the challenges many singles face in identifying potential dating partners. A well-written personal ad can generate literally hundreds of responses, even if the quality of responses is often disappointing. Personal ads offer only the most basic demographic information about persons' age, race, and personal interests, all of which may be embellished to enhance such advertisements' success. Those who seek dates through personal ads should limit the amount of personal information they give out and always meet respondents in a public place.

Dating services have a considerably higher rate of success than many other matchmaking techniques. They have also lost much of their stigma as a last resort for "desperate" singles. Quality dating services often perform a fairly intense initial screening of members. They also rely on computer technology to match singles with similar interests. Dating services can be expensive, however, and offer few, if any, guarantees. Their success as defined by permanent or long-term relationships depends largely on volume. The more dates generated, the more chances of a "match."

Many singles find potential dating partners through friends and relatives. The advantage of this resource is that acquaintances may be aware of shared interests or similar traits among the potential dating partners. In addition, those arranging such dates usually have personal knowledge of the stability and trustworthiness of the parties involved.

Some singles consider looking up former significant others. Such efforts provide mixed results. Many people find it easy to rekindle a former romance, and those involved often know a great deal about each others' personality traits. The down side is that "old flames" may be married. Pursuing such relationships could cause significant turmoil. In addition, although former partners may have "matured," many singles find themselves dealing with the same issues that caused their relationships to fail in the first place.

Many singles find that the best places to meet other like-minded singles are at activities they enjoy themselves. Among the most successful places to establish new relationships are classes. Many singles also find special-interest organizations, such as athletic or writing clubs, single-parent support groups, political campaigns, charities, and churches, to be rich sources of potential dates. The advantage of these dating resources is that they allow singles to get to know each other in an informal, nonthreatening environment over long periods of time.

Dating Etiquette and Protocol. Perhaps no other subject creates more stress in singles' lives than trying to determine what constitutes appropriate dating behavior. Who calls whom, who pays for dinner, who initiates subsequent dates, and what level of physical affection is appropriate are just a few common concerns among singles of all ages. The location of the first date should be based on persons' knowledge of their dating partners. Singles who have met in a bar, through the Internet, or by other means that offer little information about potential dating partners should meet in well-populated locations and under circumstances that permit an easy and safe exit if necessary.

The "typical" first date traditionally consists of dinner and a movie. However, many singles find this arrangement both restrictive and unimaginative. Long dinners with clearly inappropriate persons can feel like a life sentence. Moreover, two or more hours sitting quietly in a dark theater is rarely conducive to getting to know others. Initial dates should be informal, convenient, and informative. They should also allow for a graceful and rapid exit by either party if things are not working out. Many singles find weekday lunches, a trip to the museum or zoo, or other daytime activities especially valuable, since such activities allow persons' to get to know each other in an informal setting. Simply meeting for coffee can also be effective, because the amount of time devoted to such an event can be adjusted based on the success of the date.

If the initial date is positive, subsequent dates should be arranged so that persons can gradually, but increasingly, come to know each other. Detailed personal histories provided during the first few dates can frighten off potential mates. Conversely, revealing little or nothing about oneself can interrupt the natural process of personal intimacy and relationship building. The key to healthy dating is to create situations that allow parties to get to know each other at a comfortable pace. Dates that involve too little or too much conversation impede this process.

There is no simple answer to the often-asked question: "who pays?" However, the person who makes the invitation is generally obligated to "foot the bill." Some singles may be uncomfortable with this arrangement, conforming to the tradition that men should pay. However, women who invite men out should be prepared and willing to pick

During the 1990's dating occasions tended to be much less formal than in earlier decades. (James L. Shaffer)

Despite relaxing standards in dating etiquette, some formalities are still observed. (Mary LaSalle)

up the tab. Often, men and women who date frequently take turns picking up the check or paying for other activities. The financial circumstances of the parties may also dictate who pays or how expensive dates will be.

Either party can initiate a second date. Of course, both parties should be prepared for rejection or for the possibility of taking the relationship to a more permanent or intimate level. Rejections should be made and taken gracefully without attacking the other person's tastes or personality.

Affection and Sex. Despite the media's characterization of singles as having unrestrained sex lives, most singles enter into sexual relationships cautiously and with significant consideration. Although some singles do have sex on their first dates, many wait several months or more before engaging in sexual activity. Adult singles often find holding hands or a first kiss initially awkward, and there is no "correct" time to initiate them. A gradual increase in affection is usually a more natural evolution of the physical aspects of a relationship. Rushing sex frequently complicates and impairs the natural progression of a relationship.

Most adult singles restrict affection to a brief goodnight kiss or a hug if the relationship is not exclusive. By gradually increasing the level of physical intimacy, dating partners can tactfully broach questions regarding previous sexual partners, sexually transmitted diseases, contraception, and protection, rather than going through an awkward and uncomfortable interrogation while sitting on the edge of the bed. Although the popular media would have the public believe that discussing and preparing for sex removes the romance and spontaneity of sexual relations, partners in a healthy, exclusive dating relationship should understand each other's views about sex before the relationship becomes physically intimate. Singles of all ages should be concerned about the possibility of contracting sexually transmitted diseases. Persons who even vaguely anticipate the possibility of sexual activity should keep condoms discreetly available, even if pregnancy is not an issue.

Children's Reactions. Nearly 6.6 million single women and 1.6 million single men head households with children under eighteen years of age. Single adults with children in the home face special challenges. Most dates should occur outside the home and not involve children until an exclu-

sive relationship with a strong chance of permanence develops. Once this occurs, children should be introduced to new partners slowly, with relatively little fanfare. An outing to the zoo or other daytime events are often excellent initial activities. Children of single parents should never be forced to show affection to parents' dates, and dates should not be put in the position of having to discipline their partner's children. Like the adult dating relationship, healthy relationships with children can only evolve at a natural and comfortable pace for both parties.

Although singles are entitled to show each other a moderate amount of affection such as hand-holding or an occasional brief kiss during later activities involving children, early events should simply depict a healthy friendship between dating partners. Behaviors that indicate a sexual relationship, such as spending significant amounts of time alone in the bedroom or overnight stays, should be avoided, because they send conflicting messages about appropriate sexual behavior to children and adolescents.

Adult children of mature singles may disapprove of a specific dating partner or may actively discourage all dating by their parents. Occasionally adult children may view dating by older adults as undignified or an insult to a deceased parent. In addition, they may also see the potential relationships that could result from such dating as a threat to an inheritance. In most cases, the adults involved in dating relationships are capable of making rational decisions and should gently but firmly express their right to date. Statistically, a healthy social life enhances the quality and longevity of life for men and women of all ages and should therefore be encouraged. —*Cheryl Pawlowski*

BIBLIOGRAPHY

Bhaerman, Steven, and Don McMillian. *Friends and Lovers, How to Meet the People You Want to Meet.* Cincinnati, Ohio: Writers Digest Books, 1986. Focuses on creating enjoyable dating situations and boosting self-confidence with personal action plans.

Brown, Joy. *Dating for Dummies.* Foster City, Calif.: IDG Books Worldwide, 1997. Provides information in an encyclopedia format on a variety of topics from dating anxiety to where to meet singles.

Day, Jennifer Cheeseman, ed. *Projections of the Number of Households and Families in the United States: 1995 to 2010. United States Bureau of the Census.* Washington, D.C.: U.S. Bureau of the Census, 1996. Statistical data and projections on U.S. family structures.

Gove, Walter R., and Hee-Choon Shin. "The Psychological Well-Being of Divorced and Widowed Men and Women: An Empirical Analysis." In *Journal of Family Issues* 10 (March, 1989). Compares mental illness and mortality trends between divorced and widowed men and women.

Kuriansky, Judy. *The Complete Idiot's Guide to Dating.* New York: Alpha Books, 1996. Provides strategies for meeting other singles and understanding the opposite sex in a dating situation.

Saluter, Arlene F. *Marital Status and Living Arrangements: March 1995.* Washington, D.C.: U.S. Bureau of the Census, 1995. Statistical information about the marital status and other data of the U.S. population.

Weiss, R. S. *Marital Separation.* New York: Basic Books, 1975. Examines the challenges of adjusting to marital separations and regaining an autonomous identity.

Wolf, Sharyn. *Guerrilla Dating Tactics, Strategies, Tips and Secrets for Finding Romance.* New York: Penguin Group, 1993. Arms readers with a guide to dating strategies, including innovative, step-by-step ways to meet people and a variety of case studies.

See also Couples; Courting rituals; Dating violence; Divorce; Matchmaking; Remarriage; Single life; Single-parent families; Widowhood.

Dating violence

RELEVANT ISSUES: Marriage and dating; Violence
SIGNIFICANCE: Dating violence occurs when persons in dating relationships inflict physical, sexual, emotional, or verbal injury on their partners

In the 1970's the combined efforts of the civil rights and women's movements exposed the brutality and frequency of the physical, emotional, and sexual battering with which many women live on a daily basis. Subsequent research focused on such abuse in marriage or between cohabiting partners. Dating, traditionally regarded as a time of innocence, when boys and girls or young men and women courted and tried to impress one another, was virtually ignored by early research. Dating relationships seemed safe from gender-based violence. Studies in the 1980's, however, shattered this false belief by revealing that dating and violence often go hand-in-hand. Countless adolescents and young adults cope with violence and trauma while dating that is similar to the abuse endured by adult women, and many others are victims of sexual assault during dates and at parties. Experts estimate that as many as one-third of all thirteen- to twenty-two-year-olds have experienced or will become involved in at least one violent dating relationship. Most of this violence falls into one of two general categories: date or acquaintance rape or repeated abuse in a long-term, intimate relationship.

Date Rape. Acquaintance rape poses a very real threat in both the United States and Canada. An estimated 70 to 80 percent of all rapes are perpetrated by persons victims know. Whether they live in college dormitories or in inner-city tenements, young women are especially vulnerable to sexual attack. Nearly 40 percent of rape victims are fourteen to seventeen years old; 25 percent of college women report being victims of rape or attempted rape. Studies estimate that 85 percent of these women are victimized by an acquaintance, nearly 60 percent while on a date.

More often than not, alcohol or drugs are involved. According to recent research, 75 percent of men and 55 percent of women were drinking at the time of an attack. While not causative, alcohol does lower persons' inhibitions and reduces their ability to make good judgments. Drugs are sometimes intentionally foisted on victims. In the 1990's, for example, the drug Rohypnol became known as the "date-rape" drug. When it is slipped into a drink, its tranquilizing and amnesia-inducing effects sedate potential victims.

Date rape, a term coined by researcher Mary Koss in 1982, can take place in a dormitory, a car, a party—anywhere young people socialize. Many men who force sex do not define the act as rape, believing instead that women are not really serious when they refuse sexual advances. These men believe the cultural myth that women only resist initially and must be persuaded to have sex. Young women, often naïve and trusting, fall prey to young men who may rape because they think women owe them sex on a date. At parties attacks may occur when victims are lured to a quiet spot, ostensibly to get to know their attackers better. Young men, often under the influence of alcohol, may interpret women's willingness to be alone as an invitation to have sex.

The overwhelming majority of date rapes involve men attacking women, but this pattern does not represent all such attacks. Women in lesbian relationships are also sometimes brutalized. Moreover, a small number of men are sexually assaulted by women and more are the victims of sexual violence in gay relationships.

Date or acquaintance rape often proves even more traumatic to victims than stranger rape. Not only do such assaults undercut victims' ability to trust men, but they may also easily blame themselves for such attacks. Often date rape victims find little support during their post-rape trauma. One major reason is that an estimated 75 to 80 percent of teenage rape victims do not tell their parents about attacks. Ashamed to admit to what they believe is poor judgment, fearful of losing their hard-won independence, and reluctant to involve authorities in their peer groups, they are alienated from traditional support systems. Fear of pregnancy and acquired immunodeficiency syndrome (AIDS) compounds their distress, and such victims often suffer depression and withdraw from their peers and families.

Abusive Dating Relationships. The second, and often even more insidious, kind of dating violence takes place in intimate, long-term relationships. As in most cases of spousal abuse, this violence usually escalates over time. Again, the vast majority of these cases involves the domination of men over women. Abusers, often motivated by a desire for power and control, seek young women or girls who accept traditional gender roles such as female submissiveness and who may also have a romanticized view of love. Often males gradually break their partners' will, in part by isolating them from family and friends. Males may tell them how to dress and wear their hair. Possessive and jealous, they also demand that such women account for all of their time away from them. Many young people misinterpret these controlling behaviors as signs of love. If, as is often the case, men begin to com-

pound emotional abuse with physical violence or sexual coercion, women have become too accustomed to doing whatever men dictate to effectively protest. Men may also resort to threats to further injure women or persons the women care about or to expose their sexual behavior to family and friends. Typically in these relationships, abusers express remorse after attacks and vehemently promise not to repeat such behavior. For a period of time, they are romantic and caring. Meanwhile, they may manage to make their victims believe that the latter are somehow responsible for what happened. Peer pressure may also serve to hold victims in violent and demeaning relationships. Teenagers, especially girls, face tremendous pressure to have boyfriends, to belong to someone. Several studies of teenagers have shown that many of them believe violence can be a justifiable sign of love under certain circumstances, such as for disciplining partners.

Support for Victims. Social, family, and legal support is often insufficient or unavailable to victims of date rape and abusive dating relationships. Parents, who may not be fully aware of what their daughters are experiencing or who often feel helpless in the face of their emotional withdrawal and refusal to confide in them, may hesitate to act. Many adolescents who manage to reach out instead of withdraw are rebuffed by adults—parents, teachers, police, or judges—who do not take them, their feelings, their relationships, or their injuries seriously. Most women's shelters are intended for adult victims of domestic abuse and are, therefore, unequipped to provide aid to minors. Legal protection from abuse varies by location. Canadian law broadly defines sexual assault to include any unwanted or forced sexual touching or activity. Each state in the United States decides independently how to define such acts. Often minors, who in most courts do not have legal standing, are unable to obtain restraining orders. Without these kinds of support, many teenagers find themselves with no escape from battering.

Prevention. Education and awareness are the best tools available to prevent dating violence. Parents and teenagers who are aware of its dangers and who recognize warning signs like extreme jealousy, possessiveness, and enforced social isolation are better prepared to bring relationships to

Education and public awareness are the best tools for preventing dating violence. (James L. Shaffer)

an end before they go too far. Studies show that when children learn that violence is neither appropriate nor loving, they are less likely to express or accept such behavior as adolescents.

Most successful prevention and intervention programs involve the whole community. When parents, schools, and social service and law enforcement agencies work together, deterrence is most effective. Especially successful programs include Project NATEEN in Los Angeles, the Dating Violence Intervention Program in Massachusetts, and the Minnesota School Curriculum Project, sponsored in part by the Minnesota Coalition for Battered Women. These programs use various techniques, including specially designed curricula, workshops, role plays, and support groups to reach young people.

Dating violence often begets a life of battering. When teenagers learn violent patterns, they are more likely to become abusive or abused adults. Except in rare cases, only intervention and education can help them break this cycle of violence.

—*Jane Marie Smith*

BIBLIOGRAPHY

Byers, E. Sandra, and Lucia F. O'Sullivan, eds. *Sexual Coercion in Dating Relationships.* New York: Haworth Press, 1996.

Levy, Barrie, ed. *Dating Violence: Young Women in Danger.* Seattle: Seal Press, 1991.

_____. *In Love and in Danger: A Teen's Guide to Breaking Free of Abusive Relationships.* Seattle: Seal Press, 1993.

Pirog-Good, M. A., and J. E. Stets, eds. *Violence in*

Dating Relationships: Emerging Social Issues. New York: Praeger, 1989.

Warshaw, Robin. *I Never Called It Rape: The Ms. Report on Recognizing, Fighting, and Surviving Date and Acquaintance Rape.* New York: HarperPerennial, 1994.

See also Couples; Dating; Domestic violence; Emotional abuse; Marital rape; Puberty and adolescence.

Day care

RELEVANT ISSUES: Children and child development; Parenting and family relationships

SIGNIFICANCE: High-quality day care, although it is needed by the majority of families in the United States and Canada, is not available to many working-class and poor families

The challenge of caring for children has always been shared by parents, their families, and their communities. The term "day care" refers to professional, licensed care for young children outside the home. Some day care is center-based—that is, it is provided in institutions with classrooms and large numbers of children. Other forms of day care are provided in caregivers' homes, usually with a small number of children. Home-based day care is more common than center-based care because center-based care is more expensive and less available.

Day Care up to World War II. The Industrial Revolution in Europe and North America influenced the child-care practices of both middle- and working-class families. Middle-class families increasingly relied on professional child care, including nannies, formal schooling, and boarding schools. This allowed parents to spend more time

At its best, day care provides children with environments that are not only safe but stimulating. (Cindy Beres)

supporting the family and caring for their property and social status, activities that were crucial for their economic survival. In poor and working-class families, parents and extended family had to work outside the home, leaving many younger children on their own. Infant and child mortality increased among poor children, leading in the 1830's to the founding of the Infant Schools, the first day-care centers in the United States.

The next rise in demand for day care occurred during World War II, when fathers were needed in the military and mothers were needed in factories and businesses. Day-care centers for young children were supported by the federal government in the United States, and some centers also provided meals and other family support services.

The Postwar Period. After the war, fewer mothers worked outside the home than at any time in

Deprived of time that might otherwise be spent with their parents, children in day care may find compensation in associations with other children. (James L. Shaffer)

Some day-care centers start children on skills they will need for school. (Hazel Hankin)

the twentieth century. There were several reasons for this change. First, federal policy in the postwar years was aimed at increasing employment for returning veterans. It was believed that day care encouraged women to work at the expense of veterans. Federal support was removed from day care and transferred to education and the development of part-time preschools, which would enhance child development. This type of funding eventually led to Head Start in the 1960's, a part-time preschool program for low-income children.

A second reason for the reduction in day care

during the 1950's was that wages rose and prices remained stable throughout the 1950's and 1960's, making it easier for many couples to have large families and to live on one income. Moreover, as many former working-class families aspired to join the middle class, there was substantial social pressure on women to withdraw from the workplace and on men to be the sole family wage earners, because this "traditional" family arrangement was associated with middle-class status.

Expanding Day-Care Needs. The demand for day care increased from 1970 through the 1990's

For many children day care can be an adventure. (James L. Shaffer)

in response to several social developments. First, real wages, or wages relative to inflation, stopped rising and then began to fall during this period, putting economic pressure on most families. Second, the social climate surrounding marriage and family began to emphasize individual rights and freedoms. Divorce laws became less restrictive, the culture at large encouraged people to leave abusive or unhappy marriages, and more children were born out of wedlock. In addition, child support laws did not keep pace with these social changes, making it difficult for custodial parents to collect support. The result of these factors was that more children than previously were raised by single, working parents. Third, day care grew for cultural reasons. The women's movement that began in the 1960's promoted women's right to economic independence and employment regardless of their husbands' ability to provide for them, an agenda that previous women's rights groups in the nineteenth and twentieth centuries had not pursued.

The net result of all these changes was that by 1995, 70 percent of women with children under the age of five worked outside the home. Although many women with children worked outside the home during the Industrial Revolution of the nineteenth century and during World War II, the large number of middle-class families who needed and demanded high-quality, affordable child care fueled the rise of professional day care from the 1970's through the 1990's.

Ensuring Quality and Availability. The increase in the number of children in day care prompted social concerns about the effects of day care, especially low-quality care. Several decades of research have resulted in a general consensus about the features of high-quality care: a low number of children per adult; adequate space, hygiene, and nutrition; activities and materials that are safe, interesting, and developmentally appropriate for children; staffs that are trained in child development; low staff turnover; and a high level of positive adult-child interaction.

Unfortunately, the same research often showed that high-quality care was not always the norm, especially for low-income families. One barrier to ensuring quality care in the United States was that there were no national licensing standards. The only national standards were the voluntary accreditation guidelines of the National Association for the Education of Young Children (NAEYC). Licensure was left to the states, with variable results. For example, in the 1990's just two states required one adult for every three infants, the number recommended by the NAEYC. Several states required only one adult for every *twelve* infants; and ten states had no standards at all. In Canada, there were national licensing standards, but as in the United States, the number of licensed day-care spaces was too low to meet demand.

In the 1990's the majority of families with young children in the United States and Canada used informal child care rather than licensed, center-based day care. Many families preferred day-care centers but relied on other types of care because center care was not available or flexible enough. For example, in 1990 one in five workers in the United States worked odd hours or traveled frequently for their jobs, yet there were only twelve licensed centers in the entire United States that provided 24-hour care.

The cost of day care was another problem limiting the availability of high-quality care. Parent-subsidized day care absorbed 12 to 20 percent of family income by the late 1990's. Working parents who could not afford to pay for child care received government subsidies, although the amount of money available for these subsidies decreased in both the United States and Canada during the 1990's, even as demand was growing. Middle-class parents in the United States received a tax credit for a portion of their child-care costs beginning in the 1980's. Federally-funded education programs for children of poor parents and children with disabilities served some—but not all—of the children who qualified for them.

Day-Care Controversies. Concern about the effects of nonmaternal care and the low quality of many child-care settings was most intense during the 1970's and 1980's, when some child-development experts and public figures advised women to stay home full-time rather than expose their children to the risks of out-of-home care. This concern and controversy gave rise to studies of the effects of nonmaternal child care. Many of these studies showed conflicting results, in part because their methods differed. In an effort to use consistent methods and adequate samples, the National Institute of Child Health and Human Development in the United States in the 1990's sponsored a nationwide study of the effects of child care from infancy onward. This study included more than 1,200 children in every care arrangement, including full-time maternal care. This study concluded that the majority of differences between children—32 percent—arose from family factors such as parents' education and the quality of parent-child interactions. Fewer differences—1 percent—were due to the effects of nonmaternal child care. Children were not negatively affected by high-quality day care. Children in care for many hours per week during early infancy or in low-quality care were most likely to be negatively affected by day care. The study also found that many types of informal care, which the majority of families relied on out of necessity, were high in quality, although many financial and scheduling hardships were involved. —*Kathleen M. Zanolli*

BIBLIOGRAPHY

American Academy of Pediatrics and the American Public Health Association. *Caring for Our Children*. APHA Publication Sales, 1996.

Berezin, Judith. *The Complete Guide to Choosing Child Care*. New York: Random House, 1990.

Hayes, Cheryl, John Palmer, and Martha Zaslow. *Who Cares for America's Children?* Washington, D.C.: National Academy Press, 1990.

Lusk, Diane, and Bruce McPherson. *Nothing But the Best: Making Daycare Work for You and Your Child*. New York: William Morrow, 1992.

Zigler, Edward, and Mary Lang. *Child Care Choices*. New York: Macmillan, 1991.

See also Baby-sitters; Child care; Child Care and Development Block Grant Act; Child rearing; Latchkey children; Maternity leave; Nannies; Single-parent families; Substitute caregivers; Women's roles; Work.

Death

RELEVANT ISSUES: Aging; Health and medicine; Parenting and family relationships

SIGNIFICANCE: The death of different family members has a varying impact on survivors, necessitating various strategies to cope with grief

Children's concepts of death inherently originate from their parents. So, too, do their notions of grief and mourning. Whether it be "anticipatory" grief that takes place before an actual death oc-

curs, as in the case of a prolonged illness, or grief after death, the process of grieving seems to follow a set pattern. After the initial shock and disorganization that characterizes the stage of bereavement, survivors usually release a number of different emotions, such as anger, guilt, regret, sadness, and even relief. One's emotional response to a loss is called "grief." The mourning stage occurs when the survivors begin to incorporate the death into their ongoing lives, looking toward the future rather than the past.

When a death takes place, the deceased per-

Deaths traditionally reunite families at funeral services. (James L. Shaffer)

son's entire family is bound to be affected. Not only is an integral member of the family now absent, but the family is plunged into the chaos of intense grief. The family, traditionally the source of support for a grieving person, can no longer offer that individualized attention. The intensity and manner of grief of each surviving family member is usually dictated by the person's relationship to the deceased.

Grieving for a Child. The death of a child is considered the most "unnatural" or "untimely" of all deaths. The interdependence between parents and children makes the death of a child a devastating experience of loss. Parents who suffer the death of adult children must not only deal with the "unnaturalness" of the sequence, but they also find themselves virtually alone in coping with their grief, as there are relatively few available social support resources. Older parents who survive the death of middle-aged children may have the added trauma of losing caregivers. In almost all cases, parents experience profound guilt, since their roles as nurturers and protectors have been compromised, especially in the case of the death of young children.

Miscarriage, stillbirth, neonatal death, and sometimes abortion and giving up children for adoption evoke feelings of grief that may even be more profound for parents than the deaths of children, because they mourn not only what was, but what might have been. In addition, there is virtually no societal support for parents in these situations.

There is an extremely high rate of marital discord and divorce among parents who have survived their children. Because of different "grieving styles," spouses may feel "out of synch" with each other or may judge the other's style of grief to be inappropriate. Traditionally, grieving mothers receive more outside social support than do fathers, which may also contribute to the disharmony. Psychological studies of bereaved parents show that open and honest communication is the best way of compensating for the loss.

Sudden Infant Death Syndrome. Sudden infant death syndrome (SIDS), or "crib death," usually affects children below the age of one. Since such deaths often take place at night, some believe that they are caused by asphyxiation most likely as a result of infants' sleeping position (usually on their stomach). The actual cause of SIDS is uncertain. Because of the sudden, unexpected, and uncertain nature of these deaths, parents are often consumed with a sense of guilt and anger. In addition, SIDS deaths may prompt criminal investigations, adding to parents' sense of responsibility. Because of these factors, SIDS deaths are considered "high-grief" losses, characterized by intense emotional and physical reactions. Many support groups have been formed for parents of SIDS victims.

Grieving for a Parent. The death of a parent usually signals drastic changes in children's sense of security. The emotional, physical, and psychological support upon which children would have relied has been taken from them. This, in turn, can effect a "developmental push," forcing children to mature and to no longer regard themselves as children.

The death of a mother is considered by many a more difficult loss than that of a father. This may be attributed to mothers' traditional status as the primary nurturing caregivers, or it may be that because fathers tend to die before mothers, the death of a mother may signal the end of all parenting. In dysfunctional families, a parent's death brings an end to the hope of establishing more functional relationships.

In many cases, children's grief is mixed with guilt. Because of the psychological phenomenon called "magical thinking," whereby children believe that their thoughts can make events occur, children sometimes feel that they have caused their parent's death. Perhaps in moments of anger or frustration they wished that their parents were dead. If death does occur, they feel responsible for it. In other cases, children feel as if they have contributed to their parent's death by misbehaving. It is acknowledged by virtually all child psychologists that children's grief must be expressed. One popular method is "art therapy," in which grieving children draw pictures of the deceased. A trained psychologist is often be able to discern children's deep-seated emotions and anxieties as they are revealed in their artworks.

Adult children usually suffer less intense grief for the death of a parent than young children, probably because they are involved in their own lives and families. Nevertheless, the death of a parent can have a long-term impact, as the be-

Deaths in families encourage relatives and neighbors to remember the needs of the survivors. (James L. Shaffer)

reaved child mourns the loss of the unique parent-child relationship.

Grieving for a Spouse. Intense depression is reported by spouses of all ages in the first year of bereavement. Younger spouses may be more inclined to counter their intense physical distress by some form of "escape," such as drugs. Among older couples, there is a high rate of mortality in the first years following the death of a spouse, in part because of health problems that were ignored when caring for their dying spouses and due to survivors' diminished contact with the outside world. "Broken heart syndrome" refers to the phenomenon of spouses (especially males) dying within a few years of their mates. Spousal bereavement can be further complicated by societal pressures that prescribe different "acceptable" forms of mourning for different genders or by the need of a surviving spouse to learn to manage unfamiliar role responsibilities. Since women statistically outlive men, it is estimated that three out of four married women will be widowed at some point in their lives.

Grieving for a Sibling. Even though the loss of a sibling does not necessarily represent the loss of security that the death of a parent does, it does make tangible to surviving siblings the inevitability of death and siblings' own vulnerability. Surviving siblings no longer view the universe as a safe place. Death can arrive at a moment's notice and even strike children. Because of siblings' identification with a deceased brother or sister, sibling death can be considered a "high-grief" loss. It is not uncommon for survivors of a sibling's death to profoundly question the meaning of life and the validity of their religious beliefs. While experiencing the sadness that comes with the loss of a playmate and the anxiety that comes with the loss of a possible protector, surviving siblings may also feel a sort of reluctant pleasure, because they will no longer have to share center stage with the deceased sibling for parents' attention. This mixture of emotions can produce confusion and guilt in surviving siblings.

Children look to their parents for guidance in coping with the death of a sibling and its effects on the family. Inappropriate parental behavior can initiate dysfunctional patterns in the family relationship. For example, parents may try to recreate some of the qualities of the deceased child in the surviving ones, or the mere presence of the surviving siblings may be a constant reminder of the parents' loss. In some cases, parents minimize contact with their surviving children or become overprotective of them.

Suicide in the Family. Probably no other type of death triggers as much guilt on the part of survivors as suicide. Surviving family members are plagued with such questions as, "Why didn't I recognize the severity of the situation?" and "What could I have done to prevent this from happening?" In addition, feelings of anger and resentment toward the victim are usually intensified because the death occurred by the person's own hand. Social support systems are often lacking because of the discomfort felt by those outside the

Leading Causes of Death in the United States in 1900 and 1995

1900	*1995*
1. Pneumonia and influenza	1. Heart diseases
2. Tuberculosis	2. Cancer and other malignant tumors
3. Diarrhea, enteritis, and ulceration of the intestine	3. Strokes
4. Heart diseases	4. Chronic obstructive pulmonary diseases
5. Senility (ill-defined or unknown)	5. Accidents
6. Strokes	6. Pneumonia and influenza
7. Nephritis	7. Diabetes mellitus
8. Accidents	8. HIV-AIDS
9. Cancer and other malignant tumors	9. Suicide
10. Diphtheria	10. Chronic liver disease and cirrhosis

Source: The Time Almanac 1998. New York: Information Please, 1997.

family in discussing the "unmentionable" act and because there is a tendency to hold family members partially responsible for not being able to prevent the death. The suddenness and unnaturalness of suicide and ethical or religious qualms may further intensify survivors' grief, affecting the interpersonal dynamics of the family unit.

The Hospice Movement. The roots of family-oriented holistic care of the dying can be traced to religious traditions of caring for the ill. Medieval orders established "places of welcome" ("hospitia") for pilgrims traveling to religious shrines in the quest for miraculous cures for their illnesses. These "rest" homes, established at key junctions along pilgrimage routes, provided lodging and nursing care. The Irish Sisters of Charity, under the leadership of Mary Aitkenhead, were dedicated to this type of care for the dying, establishing the first in-patient hospice in Dublin, Ireland, in 1870. As the founder of St. Christopher's Hospice, which opened in London in 1967, Cicely Saunders has been credited with introducing the concept of dispensing narcotics at regular intervals to preempt the pain of sufferers. The first hospice in the United States was opened in New Haven, Connecticut, in 1974. In Canada, Balfour Mount offered the first "palliative care" (as hospices are called in Canada) at the Royal Victoria Hospital in Montreal in 1976.

The difference between hospital and hospice care for the dying is that hospice care recognizes dying as a "natural process" with which we should not interfere. Instead, all attempts should be focused on making patients comfortable and not prolonging the dying process with invasive medical techniques. Patients' comfort necessitates pain relief, including relief from the anxiety of waiting for pain to return before being administered another dose of medication. The dispensation of narcotics before pain actually occurs is the most controversial element in hospice care. Critics have charged that the dying are being turned into drug addicts.

Other principles of hospice care include familiarity of surroundings, spiritual and emotional support for patients and family, and the participation of the family in caring for patients. Care may be given in institutional settings (hospices), in specially designated hospice-care beds or units in hospitals, or, most preferably, in patients' own homes.

Family members are trained by hospice nurses to administer pain medication. Volunteers offer physical and emotional support to families, both during illnesses and after patients' death. In this way, families as well as patients are cared for. Hospice care, which relies on heavily trained volunteers and contributions for its support, is less costly than traditional hospital care.

Death of the Elderly and the Terminally Ill. In 1900 more than half of all reported deaths involved children under the age of fifteen. By the end of the twentieth century less than 3 percent of all deaths occurred among this age group. Life-extending technologies have increased average life expectancy in North America from forty-seven years at the turn of the century to seventy-six years by the end of the century. Sophisticated machines are able to prolong the dying process, altering the way that death has been defined. With technological advances, the moral issue of when to limit their use has come increasingly to the fore.

With the introduction of life-sustaining technologies, the rise of institutionalized care, and the increase in geographical mobility, by the end of the twentieth century about 80 percent of dying patients died in institutional settings. Because of the increased life span, many adults at the end of the century found themselves part of the "sandwich generation" as they cared for their own children as well as for their elderly parents.

—*Mara Kelly-Zukowski*

BIBLIOGRAPHY

Buckingham, Robert. *Care of the Dying Child: A Practical Guide for Those Who Help Others.* New York: Continuum, 1990. Provides useful information for all involved in the care of terminally ill children and their families.

DeSpelder, Lynne, and Albert Strickland. *The Last Dance: Encountering Death and Dying.* 4th ed. Mountain View, Calif.: Mayfield, 1996. Used as a textbook for courses on death and dying, this work is a thorough treatment of all aspects of death, including cultural attitudes toward death, burial, grief, the funeral industry, cryonics, euthanasia, and suicide.

Donnelly, Katherine Fair. *Recovering from the Loss of a Child.* New York: Macmillan, 1982. Invaluable resource for bereaved parents, relatives, friends, and health care professionals that includes a list of support groups for families who have survived a loss.

Kübler-Ross, Elisabeth. *On Children and Death*. New York: Macmillan, 1983. Writing for parents who have experienced the death of a child, whether by illness, accident, or violence, Kübler-Ross offers consolation by focusing on the spiritual dimension of death.

_____. *On Death and Dying*. New York: Macmillan, 1969. Study that initiated the "study of death" (thanatology) movement and deals with the psychological stages of the terminally ill and the tendency of institutionalized care to deal with the dying.

Myers, Edward. *When Parents Die: A Guide for Adults*. New York: Viking, 1986. Examines the psychology of mourning and of parental loss, offering concrete suggestions for the medical, financial, and emotional issues surrounding death.

Schaefer, Dan, and Christine Lyons. *How Do We Tell the Children?* New York: Newmarket Press, 1993. Thorough treatment of children's attitudes toward death and practical advice for the words one should use with children of various ages.

See also Acquired immunodeficiency syndrome (AIDS); Aging and elderly care; Childhood fears and anxieties; Euthanasia; Family caregiving; Funerals; Grief counseling; Health problems; Infanticide; Inheritance and estate law; Kübler-Ross, Elisabeth; Life expectancy; Orphans; Substitute caregivers; Sudden infant death syndrome (SIDS); Suicide; Widowhood.

Desertion as grounds for divorce

RELEVANT ISSUES: Divorce; Law

SIGNIFICANCE: Desertion is a common grounds for divorce in jurisdictions that require that one married partner demonstrate that the other's fault justifies a divorce

Under "fault-based" divorce laws, which require that parties to divorce show that wrongdoing occurred by one marriage partner against another, desertion is a common grounds for divorce. When one marriage partner willfully deserts the other without consent for a specified period of time under relevant state law, the desertion will gener-

ally provide sufficient justification for a divorce. The three most prominent elements of desertion are that it occur willfully, that it occur without the other partner's consent, and that it last for a period of time specified under a jurisdiction's law as sufficient to constitute desertion, such as one year. Traditionally, when a married couple has separated, desertion can be proved when one partner offers to resume living with the other and this offer is rejected. The partner who rejects the offer to resume cohabitation will then be deemed the deserter in most cases. If, on the other hand, a marriage couple has mutually agreed to live separately, neither will be able to assert that the other is a deserter.

No-fault divorce systems do not require proof of wrongdoing by either spouse. Instead, these systems grant divorces when marriages have suffered an irreversible breakdown. However, in these systems the law commonly recognizes the separation of spouses for an extended time as evidence of such a breakdown. In this respect, separation in a no-fault system is similar in some respects to desertion in a fault-based system. Unlike desertion, however, which must be against the wishes of the partner deserted, married couples in a no-fault system can obtain a divorce as a result of a mutually agreed upon separation for the required duration.

In jurisdictions that allow desertion as grounds for divorce, it is not always the person who leaves that is the deserter. One marriage partner may make life unbearable for another, for example. Under such circumstances, courts sometimes find that this partner has "constructively" deserted the partner forced to leave. When one partner engages in conduct that provides the other with the justification to leave, the partner that engages in such conduct will be determined to be the deserter, not the partner who walks out. Sometimes, a desertion may occur even when neither partner has moved away from the other. Some courts have held, for instance, that partners who unjustifiably refuse to have sexual relations with the other has engaged in "constructive" desertion.

—*Timothy L. Hall*

See also Abandonment of the family; Cohabitation; Cruelty as grounds for divorce; Divorce; Legal separation; Marriage laws; No-fault divorce; Uniform Marriage and Divorce Act (UMDA).

DINKs

RELEVANT ISSUES: Demographics; Economics and work; Parenting and family relationships
SIGNIFICANCE: DINKs (dual income, no kids) are couples, usually married, without children

The term "DINKs" appeared in the 1980's as a new media buzzword to describe the demographic phenomenon of a growing number of couples who were electing not to have children. Its origin is unknown, although it may be a marketing term coined in an era of labels, such as "yuppies." According to a professor of marketing, there tend to be two kinds of DINKs: upper- and lower-class ones. Being a DINK couple is not necessarily a permanent situation. However, some people realize that children cost money and that by having children they place limitations on their leisure time and experience a lower standard of living.

DINKs reflect changing post-World War II economic patterns in the United States, particularly the rapid rise in female employment, especially in the professions. Although women have always worked, men tended to dominate professional employment, while the expectation of society was that women would raise children and tend to their families. The liberation of women has broken down this traditional division between men and women and has led to the rise of demographic categories such as DINKs. —*Steven R. Hewitt*

See also Childlessness; Couples; Cultural influences; Dual-earner families; Family: concept and history; Family demographics; Family economics; Family size.

Disabilities

RELEVANT ISSUES: Health and medicine; Parenting and family relationships
SIGNIFICANCE: Persons with physical disabilities have the ability and the legal right to participate fully in family and community life, but this requires that everyone make special accommodations for their unique needs

There are many definitions and types of disabilities. In the United States disability is legally defined as any physical or mental impairment that substantially limits one or more of a person's major life activities. Temporary impairment due to an illness or injury from which the person can completely recover are not considered to be disabilities. Employment, education, use of public facilities, parenting, and social contact are all major life activities that can be limited by physical disabilities unless disabled persons, families, and communities work together to remove barriers in the way of full participation. The challenges faced by persons with disabilities affect everyone not only by law, but also because of the large numbers of disabled persons. One in six Americans has a disability, and one in eight has a physical disability. Almost every nuclear or extended family in America has at least one member who is or will be affected by a disability at some point during the life span.

Types of Physical Disabilities. There are four types of physical disabilities. The first is impairment in the sensory system (vision and hearing). The most common type of all physical disabilities is hearing impairment, which affected 22 million Americans by the late twentieth century. Hearing impairment ranges in severity from complete lack of sound perception to loss of only a portion of normal hearing. Vision impairment is less common than hearing impairment. The majority of vision-impaired persons are totally blind—that is, they have no functional sight. Legally blind persons have some sight but are limited in some life activities because of their limited acuity of vision (clarity and sharpness) or field of vision (the amount of area the eye can see at one time). Many people with sensory impairments can achieve nearly normal perception with the help of hearing aids, glasses, or surgery. Even though a disability can be completely compensated for, persons are still regarded as having a disability if they need continuing medical assistance to be able to fully engage in major life activities.

The second type of physical disability is impairment of a person's ability to move or control the body. This can include loss of control over involuntary functions such as bowel, bladder, breathing, or sexual activity. Persons with motor impairments may have difficulty eating or speaking. Most people with motor impairments use some type of equipment to help them move around, including wheelchairs, canes, walkers, and orthotic devices that keep paralyzed or spastic body parts in correct alignment. The most severe motor impairments include paraplegia, or paralysis in the legs and lower body, and quadriplegia, or paralysis in the upper and lower body. The majority of motor impairments affect only some body parts and functions, leaving others completely healthy. For example, a person with paraplegia due to spinal cord damage may have no sensation or movement in the legs, but may have bowel and bladder control and normal sexual functioning. Most people with motor impairments have the same cognitive ability as others, although individuals with severe mental retardation often have both sensory and motor impairments.

The third type of physical disability is disfigurement of one or more body parts. Even if disfigurements do not cause motor or sensory impairments, they can contribute to social isolation or loss of self-esteem, presenting a barrier to many major life activities.

The fourth type of physical disability includes chronic, incurable illnesses that interfere with major life activities. Such illnesses may include epilepsy, diabetes, human immunodeficiency virus (HIV) infection, autoimmune diseases such as multiple sclerosis (which affects the nervous system) or lupus erythematosus (which can affect all body tissues), and severe respiratory problems such as asthma or emphysema. These are only considered to be disabilities if they are severe enough to interfere with daily activities.

Causes of Physical Disabilities. There are three causes of physical disabilities, each of which presents families with unique challenges. The first is congenital or developmental problems. Congenital problems are present at birth and have many sources. Some congenital problems are inherited, as is true of some types of cataracts that result in blindness and some forms of hearing impairments. Others may be the result of prenatal exposure to toxic substances, drugs, or a disease such as German measles. Congenital problems can also be the result of random genetic accidents that are not

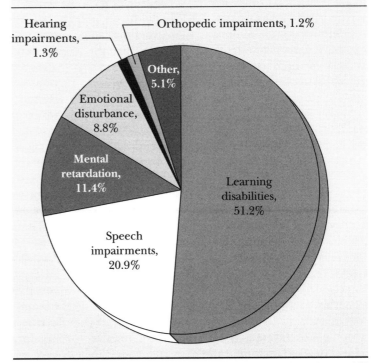

U.S. Youths with Disabilities Served by Special Programs in 1995

Hearing impairments, 1.3%
Orthopedic impairments, 1.2%
Other, 5.1%
Emotional disturbance, 8.8%
Mental retardation, 11.4%
Learning disabilities, 51.2%
Speech impairments, 20.9%

Source: U.S. Bureau of the Census, *Statistical Abstract of the United States: 1997.* Washington, D.C.: GPO, 1997.

Note: In 1995 approximately 4,859,100 persons with disabilities aged six through twenty-one were served by programs such as the Individuals with Disabilities Act. This chart summarizes their disabilities. Percentages are rounded to the nearest 0.1%.

inherited and can affect anyone, such as Down syndrome. Problems during pregnancy and childbirth, including anoxia (lack of oxygen) and illnesses contracted by expectant mothers can also create problems that lead to disabilities. Some problems start before birth, but are not apparent at birth. These often result in disabilities later in life as children grow and are called developmental problems because they appear during childhood. Many conditions that affect motor control, speech, and eating are only discovered when children fail to develop these abilities at the same time as other children of the same age.

The second cause of physical disabilities is accidental injury. Such disabilities affect adolescents and young adults more than any other group. The leading cause of motor disabilities is head injuries, which most often occur in bicycle or automobile accidents. Automobile accidents are also responsible for most cases of spinal cord injuries that result in paralysis.

The third cause of physical disabilities is physical deterioration and illnesses that sometimes accompany aging. Persons who have been healthy and unimpaired all their lives can become disabled by strokes, arthritis, chronic illnesses, and chronic pain.

Family Issues. No two individuals with a physical disability, even the same disability, are alike. No two families will face the same challenges and experiences in dealing with disabilities. How families cope and the types of support they need depend on the types of disabilities, the causes of the disabilities, and families' strengths and vulnerabilities.

Disabilities that require a great deal of physical assistance are the most time-consuming for family members, who may take time away from work and education to care for disabled persons. There are some sources of funding in the United States and Canada for in-home help, ranging from caregiving for an evening to live-in aides. Family members with the most severe motor disabilities still require a great deal of family time and planning, even with such assistance.

The causes of disabilities present different challenges to every family. Parents of children with congenital or developmental problems may blame themselves for their children's impairments. This natural tendency toward self-blame is aggravated by the difficulty, present in most cases, of identifying the problem and finding appropriate treatment and support, a process which can take many years. Parents also face the financial and emotional responsibility of providing for children who may need assistance well into adulthood. When adolescents or adults are suddenly disabled by illness or injury, the issues are different but no less difficult. Persons who have been disabled by head injuries or strokes or who take medication to control pain may undergo personality changes in addition to suffering from their physical disability. Many people who become disabled later in life feel depressed and angry for a time after being injured, which can put a strain on family relationships. Like developmental problems, it can take many years to diagnose and treat chronic illnesses, leaving families on a roller coaster of hope and disappointment.

The strongest factor contributing to family member satisfaction and the disabled person's sense of fulfillment is not the cause or type of disability, as challenging as this may be. Nor is it the family's financial status, education, or the number of family members, all of which can affect the amount of effort each member must devote to the care of the disabled. The strongest factor is the emotional climate before onset of the disability. Families in which communication has been good, the emotional climate has been positive, and family members' needs have been met before the onset of disability are best able to cope when a disability occurs. This does not mean that emotionally strong families do not experience the self-blame, depression, and anger that normally accompany adjusting to a disability. Nor does it mean that families who faced emotional problems before the onset of disability will be unable to cope. It does mean that all family members must learn to communicate and meet each others' emotional needs in order to cope with the disability when it arises.

How Families Cope with Disabilities. Many families who are faced with the challenges of disability have a strong desire to help the disabled person. Sometimes one or more family members devote all their energy and attention to the disabled person. This is a pattern of coping that does not work well either for the disabled person or for the family. Disabled children who receive too much help, attention, and pity may find it difficult to become as independent as they can be. Adults who suddenly become disabled often do not want help or extra attention; most such adults want life and family relationships to return to normal. Family members who devote all their energies to disabled relatives may feel either depleted of energy and feeling or neglected and angry.

There are ways of coping with disabilities that help disabled persons as well as their families. First, every member of the family should feel free to discuss their caregiving responsibilities, feelings, and needs openly. Second, responsibilities should be divided as equitably as possible, allowing all family members to pursue their own work and educational goals. Third, families should seek as much help as they can get—financial, practical, and emotional. Fourth, nondisabled family members can find ways to value and enjoy the company of their disabled relatives as they are, while en-

In order for persons with disabilities to enjoy full lives, barriers to their participation must be removed. (James L. Shaffer)

Much of the success that persons achieve in overcoming their disabilities is due to their refusal to accept limitations. (Betty Lane)

couraging them to pursue their own goals and achieve independence. Finally, and most importantly, disabled persons should be active parts of their families' coping processes; they should be included in any decisions that affect them or the family. By recognizing disabled persons' right to be contributing members of the family, families help the disabled to see themselves as fully capable, independent, and valuable persons.

Legal Issues. The concept of rights for persons with disabilities began with the Civil Rights movement in the United States during the 1960's. The 1964 Civil Rights Act recognized and protected women and religious and ethnic minorities from discrimination. By the 1970's many legislators began to recognize that persons with disabilities were also discriminated against. At that time, children with disabilities were not allowed to attend public

school if they could not keep up with the other children. Most of them attended special schools or lived in institutions or at home, where educational opportunities were very limited. Ninety percent of disabled adults were unemployed, even though 70 percent of them wanted to work and felt that they were able and qualified. Disabled persons in wheelchairs were unable to go shopping, ride buses, or eat in restaurants, because buildings and vehicles were not built to accommodate them.

Beginning in the 1970's civil rights laws protecting disabled persons were passed in both the United States and Canada. In 1975 all children in the United States were guaranteed free and appropriate public education in the least restrictive settings. In the next two decades, numerous state and federal laws were passed, culminating in the 1990 Americans with Disabilities Act (ADA). This act protects from job discrimination persons with a current disability, a past record of a disability, or the appearance of having a disability. It also protects friends and family members of disabled persons from discrimination because of their association with them. The law requires that public and private buildings with public facilities be accessible to all persons with disabilities. This means that buildings must be wheelchair accessible and that elevators and other facilities must provide both visual signs for the hearing impaired and tactile (touchable) signs for the visually impaired. Other government programs, including social security, supplemental security income, and medicare, provide funding for persons with disabilities, so that families do not have to absorb the full costs of disability.

Full Inclusion. For the first time in North American history, government programs and disability rights legislation from 1970 to the 1990's have shown communities how to take responsibility for protecting and accommodating the needs of persons with disabilities, resulting in many changes in the United States and Canada. In the 1990's, 26 percent of disabled adults were fully employed. Every public school classroom included children with disabilities, and every college campus enrolled students with disabilities. Persons with disabilities were represented at every level of education, income, and responsibility. Persons with disabilities, once segregated and kept out of sight, were involved in every aspect of community, social, and family life. Many problems and social barriers remained, as indicated by the large number of lawsuits filed under the ADA during the 1990's. As medical care has improved and people live longer, a result of the fact that once-fatal injuries have become only disabling, the number of families affected by disability may increase. The sharing of responsibility between families and communities may help families to cope with disability. Furthermore, research has shown that the inclusion of disabled persons in family and community life has persuaded more persons to believe that they can lead meaningful, productive lives—with or without a disability. —*Kathleen M. Zanolli*

BIBLIOGRAPHY

Albrecht, Donna G. *Raising a Child Who Has a Physical Disability*. New York: John Wiley & Sons, 1995. Written by a parent of two children with physical disabilities, this book explains how to find funding, set up a support network, navigate the medical and educational system, and how to cope with guilt and stress.

American Heart Association. *Family Guide to Stroke*. New York: Random House, 1994. Provides an easy to understand explanation of one of the most common causes of physical disability in older adults and relates anecdotes about rehabilitation and family relationships after strokes occur.

Kissane, Sharon. *Career Success for People with Physical Disabilities*. Lincolnwood, Ill.: VGM Career Horizons, 1997. Provides many strategies for persons with disabilities in selecting, training for, finding, and keeping employment.

LaPlante, Mitchell P. *Families with Disabilities in the United States*. Washington, D.C.: U.S. Department of Education, 1996. Describes in detail the facts of disability and its effect on families, with national, regional, and state breakdowns as well as descriptions of model programs for persons with disabilities.

Solomon, Marc D. *A Guide to Legal Rights for People with Disabilities*. New York: Demos, 1994. Describes in clear, understandable language the ADA and other government programs and laws affecting persons with disabilities and discusses family rights and responsibilities.

Sullivan, Tom. *Special Parent, Special Child*. New York: Putnam, 1995. Written by a visually impaired person from a unique and interesting perspective, this book relates the stories of families dealing with children's disabilities.

Tracey, William R. *Training Employees with Disabilities*. New York: Amacom, 1995. Detailed description of the legal, ethical, and training issues involved in hiring and managing persons with disabilities, pointing out that by the year 2000 the majority of the workforce, including persons with disabilities, will be protected by civil rights legislation.

See also Acquired immunodeficiency syndrome (AIDS); Alzheimer's disease; Americans with Disabilities Act (ADA); Birth defects; Child safety; Family caregiving; Genetic disorders; Health of children; Health problems; Learning disorders; Pediatric AIDS.

Disciplining children

RELEVANT ISSUES: Children and child development; Parenting and family relationships

SIGNIFICANCE: Families need disciplinary methods that will help children to take responsibility for their own actions, understand basic moral principles, and live meaningful lives, goals that are undermined by employing disciplinary measures that involve punishment, harshness, and parental anger

Discipline refers to any method parents use to teach their children to become moral, respectful, responsible people. There are many different methods of discipline. Parental use of discipline is strongly influenced by culture, religious beliefs, and moral values. Although research has shown that some methods of discipline are effective while others are harmful to children, the issue of discipline is still controversial. Moreover, not every method is equally effective for every family. Parents must therefore decide how to use discipline in raising their children.

Historical and Cultural Perspective. Parents discipline children differently in different cultures. Disciplinary methods include teaching by example, explaining the reasons for good behavior, using games and stories to illustrate principles, providing affection and encouragement, rewarding good behavior, and making rules. Punishment, such as brief isolation, scolding, criticizing, and hitting or physically hurting children, are sometimes used. Cultures also differ in the goals of discipline. In some cultures the primary goal of discipline is to teach children to be obedient and willing to sacrifice for the group. In others, conformity to strict moral rules is the goal. There are cultures in which learning complex rules of social interaction and status is important. Sometimes the primary goal of discipline is to help children develop highly valued characteristics such as contentment, compassion, academic achievement, or economic productivity.

Western history is filled with examples of very harsh methods of disciplining children. In ancient Greece boys from a very young age were expected to engage in adult endeavors, including military work. Disobedience or incompetence was punished by striking, whipping, or starving children.

Girls were expected to do housework and to be obedient to the male members of their households. Defiance could be punished by beatings or by selling the children into slavery. These methods were not considered abusive. Rather, it was believed that parents had the right to punish their children for disobedience as they saw fit, because their children were essentially their property. In the Middle Ages extreme physical punishments were also the rule. Public whippings, executions, and torture of adults, which were viewed as public entertainment, were commonly used to punish criminals in early Western cultures. Many historians believe that harsh treatment in childhood led children to accept and even enjoy watching brutality in adulthood.

In more recent history, almost every generation has included those who have recommend the use of physical punishment to discipline children. Defiance of any kind has been seen by many to be a sign that children are under the influence of the devil. Some have believed that children are born evil. Severe physical punishment and emotional abuse have been aimed at breaking children's will and have often been viewed as necessary to save their souls. Harsh punishments have frequently gone hand in hand with very high behavioral expectations. For example, in the sixteenth century six-month-old infants were toilet trained by tying them to the seat and striking them if they tried to get up. This tradition of high expectations and harsh punishment is called "authoritarianism."

Another style of discipline is "permissiveness," which was originally advocated in modern times by the French enlightenment philosopher Jean-Jacques Rousseau. Permissiveness assumes that children are essentially good, complete, and natural. It is the harsh treatment and contradictory rules of civilization that cause children to do evil. This situation can be remedied by indulging children's desires and whims, thereby allowing infallible nature to guide them from within. The most recent version of permissive discipline was the psychologist Carl Rogers's belief that parents must give children unconditional positive support, regardless of their behavior. This belief was popularized in the 1960's by practices such as hugging children after they hit someone or refraining from ever saying "no."

The "authoritative" approach is an additional

method of disciplining children. This method emphasizes parents' roles as teachers, mentors, and protectors of their children. The goal of this style of discipline is that children should learn to make choices, participate in decision making, and become productive. To achieve this, parents reason with their children, provide resources to help them achieve worthwhile goals, and give them affection and encouragement. Even during the harshest periods in history, some philosophers and social commentators recommended that love, affection, and respect should be the bases of family life and education. In the late twentieth century this approach was favored by most developmental psychologists and educators.

Discipline continued to be a controversial issue throughout the twentieth century. In some countries it is illegal to spank or otherwise hurt children. In others, children are tortured if they are suspected of criminal activity. For the most part, child health is better and the violent crime rate is lower in countries that have laws restricting the physical punishment of children. Some research suggests that children who experience harsh physical punishments are more likely than those who have not experienced such forms of punishment to become depressed or violent adults.

In the United States the majority of adults report that they were physically punished as children, and a somewhat smaller majority endorses the use of punishment for their own children. Many of those who endorse physical punishment give religious reasons for doing so, although an equal proportion of people oppose physical punishment on religious or moral grounds. Other popular methods of discipline include rules, time-outs, and loss of privileges. Moreover, parents reward their children with treats for good behavior. However, many persons equate discipline with punishment of some kind.

Research has shown the outcome of different disciplinary methods. In general, both child behavior problems and child abuse are highest among families in which parents have very high and rigid expectations for their children's behavior and use frequent or harsh physical punishments and anger to discipline them. Parents who spend relatively little time with their children, who are inconsistent in the way they respond to their children's behavior, or who allow their children to always take the lead in family life experience the second highest level of child behavior problems. Parents who have reasonable expectations based on accurate knowledge of child development and who are affectionate, calm, and assertive have children with the least behavior problems. There is no perfect disciplinary method suitable for every child, but the basic components of discipline that work for most families can be adopted by others.

Parent-Child Relationship. The emotional tone of the everyday relationship between parents and children is the strongest predictor of child behavior problems. An intimate, relaxed, positive relationship is the most important factor in discipline,

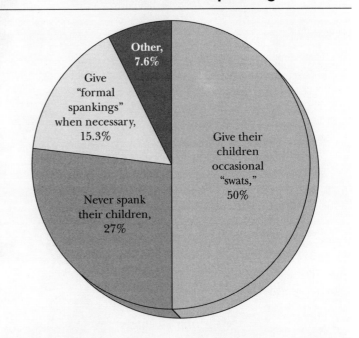

Parents' Views on Spanking

Other, 7.6%

Give "formal spankings" when necessary, 15.3%

Give their children occasional "swats," 50%

Never spank their children, 27%

Source: Parentsroom website (1998)

Note: In early 1998 Parentsroom conducted an informal poll among visitors to its website, asking them if they believed in spanking their children as a means of discipline. This chart summarizes responses. Percentages are rounded to the nearest 0.1%.

One of the most difficult tasks of parenthood is finding a satisfactory balance between strictness and leniency in disciplining children. (James L. Shaffer)

although many parents may not think of this as a disciplinary method at all. Parents can establish the emotional tone of the parent-child relationship by frequently smiling, touching, and expressing pride or pleasure when their children are happy, busy, well-behaved, or just trying to be good. If parents show their children affection, their children will be eager to be with them, imitate their actions, and listen to their instructions.

Parents must also set aside time to be with their children. During this time together, mutual involvement in activities helps the relationship to grow, providing many opportunities for parents to be mentors and teachers. For example, parents can teach children about food, money, greeting people in public, making choices, delaying rewards, and good behavior during trips to the grocery store. At least half of the activities shared by parents and children should be child focused. That is, children should choose their activities and set the rules for how they are to be done—whether they decide to play with toys or games, read stories, or play ball outside. Child-focused activities allow children to learn to make choices, decide what is fair, negotiate rules, and increase their skills. These activities also allow parents to express affection and show pride in their children's abilities.

As children get older, the parent-child relationship focuses more on talking and thinking about daily experiences. Parents should speak honestly with their children about how to cope with difficult feelings, express emotions, and understand the feelings of others. Listening and observing carefully will enable parents to know their children's personalities and understand their points of view, both of which are needed if discipline is to be a positive experience for parents and children.

Developmental Needs and Expectations. Children have different needs and abilities at different ages. Many instances of parental anger and harsh discipline occur when parents expect children to perform beyond their level of ability or when home arrangements conflict with children's developmental needs. For example, toddlers develop their cognitive abilities by exploring their environment and by touching and moving objects. They are also very active and have a great deal of physical energy to expend in developing their new motor skills. In homes containing many fragile or dangerous objects within children's reach, parents spend much time fighting their children's natural and healthy tendency to move around and touch everything. If parents expect their children to respect property or to take care of valuable objects—both concepts that are beyond toddlers' understanding—they will feel anger when their children do not live up to this expectation, even striking them in an attempt at discipline.

However, if parents arrange their homes so that their children can safely explore almost everything within reach, their children will learn a great deal about objects and spatial relationships. This experience will eventually help them to understand why certain objects are breakable and how to discriminate between objects they may handle and those that must be treated with care. Once children are able to talk with their parents about concepts of fairness and property, which usually occurs after children reach three years of age, they can then learn about respecting property without arousing their parents' anger or incurring physical punishment.

Motivation and Encouragement. Although affection should be an everyday part of the parent-child relationship, children sometimes need extra encouragement when their parents are trying to teach them difficult lessons. Parents motivate their children by employing several techniques. Feedback, or simply telling children whether their behavior is good or not, can provide information as well as motivation. If children are eager to please their parents and the task they seek to accomplish is not difficult, feedback alone may be enough to motivate them. Praising children for trying to do well and applauding their successes is even more motivating, as long as this praise is sincere and enthusiastic.

Some parents give their children small treats or reward them with special privileges when they behave well. Because such rewards clearly express parents' pleasure, they can be especially effective in dealing with very young or disabled children, who find it difficult to understand verbal praise and instructions. However, if parents use material rewards too frequently at the expense of spending time with their children or in lieu of genuine affection, the rewards may lose their effect or even have a negative impact on children's behavior. Rewards are most effective when they are small, immediate, personal, and surprising. The least ef-

Common Disciplining Mistakes

The mistakes parents often make in enforcing their time-out periods are representative of the kinds of disciplining mistakes parents make generally. Child rearing authority Sylvia Rimm summarized these common errors:

- When parents let their children go to their rooms by themselves, the children often slam their doors, prompting their parents to tell them not to, thereby reinforcing their belief that they are more powerful than their parents.

- Parents often make the mistake of letting their children lead them into arguments about how much time remains in their time-outs, thereby negating the effect of withdrawing their attention from their children during time-outs.

- When parents hesitate to lock their children's rooms and remain outside holding the doors closed, their children sense that they are winning the power struggles.

- When parents use time-outs after losing their tempers and yelling, the time-outs are not effective.

Source: Family.com website (1998).

fective way for parents to use rewards is to make big promises to their children when they face large and difficult tasks, such as promising them new computers if they get straight A's. A good rule of thumb is that large rewards promised in advance are bribes that will undermine children's desire to learn from their parents solely because they derive emotional satisfaction from doing so. Surprise rewards, especially those that have a personal meaning to children and are shared by parents and children alike, strengthen the parent-child relationship and motivate children to learn.

Sometimes parents use physical punishment, time-outs, scolding, criticism, yelling, or loss of privileges to motivate their children. Many people believe that the most upsetting or painful punishments are the most effective. Thus, if scolding a child does not work, parents may give them a time-out. If the time-out fails, they may spank them. Punishments can sometimes deter children, but only if they are used carefully. No forms of punishment will work if a positive parent-child relationship and reasonable developmental expectations are lacking. Very mild punishments—even turning away from a child for a moment—will reduce misbehavior if the parent-child

relationship is positive. Severe punishments or parental anger that frighten children are most likely to have undesired effects, leading parents to feel constantly angry and depressed or to abuse their children while causing children to hide from or attack their parents, engage in criminal behavior, or run away. Finally, it is helpful to remember that punishment does not teach children new lessons or skills; it only reduces some misbehavior. If the goal of discipline is to teach children, punishment can only play a small role in this.

Teaching and Setting Limits. Research has shown that the teaching methods used by parents are different from those used in schools, because parental teaching takes place "on the spot" and not on paper. Modeling, or teaching by example, is the method parents use most frequently. Modeling is effective because children are naturally inclined to imitate adults, as long as the parent-child relationship is positive and secure. Another effective technique is to prepare children for upcoming situations by discussing expectations and why they should behave well. If children actively participate in these discussions by offering their own ideas and examples, they will learn to decide what to do on their own. The more freedom children have to make choices and develop their own rationales for good behavior, the more likely they will be to follow through when their parents are not there to help them. When confronting questions of children's personal safety, parents should set the limits within which their children make choices and acquaint them with the challenges they will have to face alone. Parents should follow through with clear instructions and provide frequent feedback.

Combining modeling, discussion, instructions, feedback, and positive motivation will give children many opportunities to behave well. For example, before their children participate in a basketball game, parents should prepare them by explaining that following the rules and showing good sportsmanship is more important than winning. Children may recognize such behavior in their parents when the latter obey traffic laws and do not cut off other drivers. Parent may explain to their children that being good sports is more important than winning, because the rules ensure everyone's safety and allow all the players to honestly test their skills. If their children's team should lose, parents may tell their children to shake hands with the members of the opposing team and show good sportsmanship. Afterward, parents may express pride in their children's ability to follow the rules and be good sports. Once they get home, the parents can invite their children to play basketball—and let them win. —*Kathleen M. Zanolli*

BIBLIOGRAPHY

Gootman, Marilyn E. *The Loving Parents' Guide to Discipline.* New York: Berkley, 1995. Emphasizes a parent-child relationship based on mutual respect and understanding and encourages parents to plan for their children's discipline and to evaluate what works.

Greven, Philip. *Spare the Child: The Religious Roots of Punishment.* New York: Alfred A. Knopf, 1990. Gives a detailed history of physical punishment and its relationship to religious beliefs in the United States and reviews research and anecdotes on the effects of physical punishment.

Lindsay, Jeanne W, and Sally McCullough. *Teens Parenting—Discipline from Birth to Three: How to Prevent and Deal with Discipline Problems with Babies and Toddlers.* Buena Park, Calif.: Morning Glory, 1991. Argues that children's early years, which are difficult for many adults to understand, are important for establishing the parent-child relationship, preventing problems, and laying the foundation for communication and mutual respect.

Nelsen, Jane, Lynn Lott, and H. Stephen Glenn. *Positive Discipline A to Z: 1001 Solutions to Everyday Parenting Problems.* Rocklin, Calif.: Prima Press, 1993. A practical and easy-to-follow description of how to respond effectively to situations that are difficult for most parents, including information on techniques for helping children to contribute to discussions about discipline and learn to solve moral dilemmas on their own.

Williamson, Peter. *Good Kids, Bad Behavior: Helping Children to Learn Self-Discipline.* New York: Simon & Schuster, 1990. Argues that the goal of discipline is not obedience, but self-control, the ability to carry out plans, and make difficult decisions. Filled with detailed advice on how and when to set up children's schedules, use positive motivation and time-outs, and seek outside help.

Windell, James. *Children Who Say No When You Want Them to Say Yes: Fail-safe Discipline Strategies for Stubborn and Oppositional Children and Teens.* New York: Macmillan, 1996. Explains how to deal with serious behavior problems, describes the developmental needs of middle childhood and adolescence, and advocates understanding the underlying message or purpose of misbehavior.

See also Allowances; Behavior disorders; Child abuse; Child care; Child safety; Domestic violence; Educating children; Family advice columns; Family life cycle; Family life education; Parenting; Siblings; Time-out.

Displaced homemakers

RELEVANT ISSUES: Aging; Divorce; Economics and work

SIGNIFICANCE: A concept that emerged during the mid-1970's, the term "displaced homemakers" has evolved and grown in scope

The term "displaced homemakers" was coined in January, 1975, by Tish Sommers, writing in the newsletter of the Older Women Task Force of the National Organization for Women (NOW), of which she was chairperson. Legislation to assist displaced homemakers, developed by Sommers and Laurie Shields, also of NOW, was introduced in California several months later. The nation's first Displaced Homemakers Center opened in March, 1976, at Mills College in Oakland, California, with Sommers as founding director. Eventually more than one thousand centers, programs, or services were formed.

"Displaced homemaker" originally referred to any individual between the ages of 35 and 64 who worked in the home for many years, providing unpaid household services for family members. Such persons were not gainfully employed, would have difficulty securing employment, were dependent on the income of other family members but lacked support because of separation, divorce, or death. Displaced homemakers were usually

Displaced homemakers entering the job market in middle age often face both sexual and age discrimination. (Betty Lane)

women and usually too young for old-age benefits, but they did not qualify for Aid to Families with Dependent Children (AFDC) because their children were grown or would shortly become too old for such assistance. A bill to change the description of displaced homemakers to include underemployed individuals already receiving AFDC was unsuccessfully proposed in the Senate in 1995. However, the term now includes persons under thirty-five and more than sixty-four years of age.

In the 1970's it was estimated that there were four to seven million displaced homemakers. In the late 1990's this had increased to sixteen to twenty million. Divorce and widowhood still account for most displaced homemakers. Women in this group often face sexual, age, and, in some cases, racial discrimination. Older displaced homemakers tend to be underqualified, never having prepared for work outside the home, while younger women are often overqualified for the jobs that are available. Many persons must cope with traumatic emotional and psychological barriers related to low self-esteem. Displaced homemakers are called "displaced" because they are either unemployed or confined to low-paying, part-time jobs with little job stability, high turnover rates, and few or no fringe benefits.

Programs to overcome displacement are more likely than job placements themselves to offer job training, job-placement skills, and counseling. Colleges, Young Women's Christian Associations, and local agencies, some of which have emerged from the Comprehensive Employment and Training Act, are the most common sponsors of such programs.   —*Erika E. Pilver*

See also Abandonment of the family; Ageism; Alimony; Child support; Divorce; Divorce mediation; Family economics; Feminization of poverty; Remarriage; Women's roles.

Divorce

RELEVANT ISSUES: Children and child development; Law; Marriage and dating; Parenting and family relationships; Religious beliefs and practices

SIGNIFICANCE: Divorce affects families economically, socially, legally, psychologically, and spiritually

Divorce is a judicial process that dissolves marriage vows and releases marriage partners from all matrimonial commitments. This process is necessary before partners can legally marry again. Every civilized society on earth has laws governing divorce.

History of Divorce Laws. Modern divorce laws in the United States and Canada have evolved from ancient Roman and Judeo-Christian regulations for dissolving marriages. Roman society did not require formal marriage contracts. When marriages were dissolved, however, the government did ask for a written document stating the reasons for the divorce. Under Jewish law, only the husband had the right to institute a divorce. Early Roman society, in contrast, allowed either husbands or wives to initiate a divorce. In the Roman Empire, especially among the aristocracy, politics and wealth were major reasons for divorce. In 18 B.C.E. Augustus Caesar became so alarmed at the high divorce rate that he issued a series of proclamations, Julian Laws, specifically designed to punish adultery. Although these laws were directed more at women than men, even allowing a husband to kill his wife should she be caught in an adulterous act in the couple's home, there were severe financial penalties for men as well.

With the combination of the early Christian church and the Roman Empire during the Middle Ages, marriage came to be seen as a sacred institution governed by canon law that was enforced throughout the Christian countries of Europe. Roman Catholic canon law was based on Matthew 19:6, "What therefore God has joined together, let no man put asunder." Under canon law, divorce was frowned upon; however, annulment provided a way out of the marriage contract if church laws were broken. The church and the governments of Christian countries allowed and sanctioned annulments even after years of marriage, allowing either partner to legally remarry.

With the Protestant Reformation in Europe, Martin Luther defined marriage more as a secular than a religious institution and broadened the grounds and reasons for divorce. Until 1857, when the English Parliament broke away from European custom and established the Court for Divorce and Matrimonial Causes, divorce was still obtainable mainly by rich and powerful members of society who could afford the expensive court costs of individual decisions by Parliament.

Three main views on divorce and marriage divided early lawmakers in the United States. Under Roman Catholic canon law, marriage was a Sacrament of the Church and should be governed by religious doctrine, which forbade divorce. According to Protestant religious views, marriage and divorce were secular contracts to be decided by civil law. Under English law, marriage and divorce were decided by legislative actions and could be modified as new circumstances and changes arose in society.

Divorce Laws in North America. Since the U.S. Constitution did not restrict individual states' right to decide separate laws on divorce and marriage, each state began developing its own codes and regulations. The concept of migratory divorce developed as some states enacted more lenient laws making divorce easier. For example, in the 1960's Nevada became known as the divorce capital of the United States, because it was one of the first states to require a waiting period of only six weeks. Nevada also extended the grounds for divorce to include mental cruelty. Only one marriage partner's dissatisfaction with the relationship was necessary to obtain a divorce. The partner filing for divorce was required to state under oath that the marriage could not be repaired

As the United States became more urbanized, society demanded changes in divorce laws. Courts began concentrating more on the nature of the

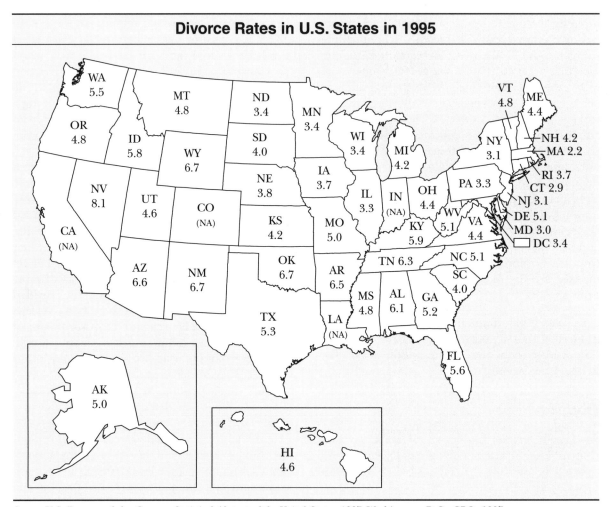

Divorce Rates in U.S. States in 1995

WA 5.5
OR 4.8
ID 5.8
MT 4.8
ND 3.4
MN 3.4
VT 4.8
ME 4.4
NY 3.1
NH 4.2
MA 2.2
RI 3.7
CT 2.9
NJ 3.1
DE 5.1
MD 3.0
DC 3.4
WY 6.7
SD 4.0
WI 3.4
MI 4.2
PA 3.3
NV 8.1
UT 4.6
CO (NA)
NE 3.8
IA 3.7
IL 3.3
IN (NA)
OH 4.4
WV 5.1
VA 4.4
CA (NA)
KS 4.2
MO 5.0
KY 5.9
AZ 6.6
NM 6.7
OK 6.7
AR 6.5
TN 6.3
NC 5.1
SC 4.0
TX 5.3
LA (NA)
MS 4.8
AL 6.1
GA 5.2
FL 5.6
AK 5.0
HI 4.6

Source: U.S. Bureau of the Census, *Statistical Abstract of the United States: 1997.* Washington, D.C.: GPO, 1997.

Note: Numbers of divorces per 1,000 residents. Figures include divorces of nonresidents (especially in Nevada). California and Indiana rates are for 1987; Louisiana rate is for 1983. The national rate for 1995 was 4.4.

Reasons for Seeking Divorce Among U.S. Couples

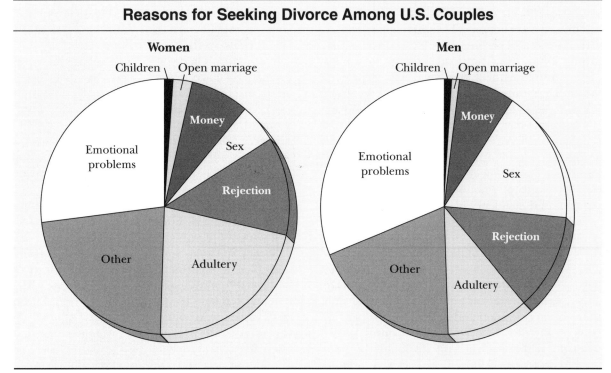

Source: The Janus Report (1993)

breakdown of the marriage relationship than on establishing grounds for divorce. Earlier laws did not recognize addictions or lack of financial support as legitimate reasons for divorce. Newer laws and interpretations of existing laws recognized such issues and also allowed couples to divorce when there was joint consent, evidenced by voluntary separation for a designated period of time. In 1969 California became the first state to institute no-fault divorce laws. Under no-fault divorce, courts recognize that no one partner is to blame for the dissolution of a marriage, but rather that both partners contribute to marital breakdowns. Since that time, almost all states permit divorce under no-fault statutes.

Canada's Constitution permits only the federal government to determine divorce law. The government's federal Divorce Act applies uniformly in all provinces of Canada. In 1986 Canada revised the Divorce Act, allowing no-fault divorce in situations where the marriage has broken down or where couples have lived apart for a year. If uncontested, the request can be a packet of information outlining issues, negotiated by both parties, such

as custody and support of minor children, spousal support, and division of physical property. Requests for financial support are classified as corollary relief and require complete financial disclosure in the application for divorce. If the application does not adequately address all pertinent issues, the petitioners then must go through a court hearing. The majority of divorce petitions in Canada do not require court debates with lawyers and mediators.

Psychological Effects. Divorce is more than a physical separation in which couples relinquish their matrimonial rights and dissolve their mutual obligations. Divorce takes place on several levels: psychological, legal, economic, social, spiritual, and parental.

Psychologically, both partners in a divorce must function without each other's emotional support and approval. If only one partner wants the divorce, the other usually suffers from feelings of rejection, anger, and low self-esteem, at least temporarily. Many people who have gone through divorce after being rejected by a marriage partner have expressed that the death of the other person would have been easier to endure. Emotionally, the divorced person must live with daily rejection, since the other partner is still alive and establishing a new life. The death of a spouse and a divorce evoke parallel emotions; both represent losses that require time to work through the grieving process, which includes shock, denial, and anger before coming to the stage of resolution and acceptance. These emotions are normal. For example, some level of anger and struggle is healthy and constructive. Anger and friction help dissolve existing bonds of emotional attachment and old patterns of dependency in a broken relationship.

Divorce forces both partners to establish a new emotional perspective toward themselves and their former spouse. Immediately following a divorce, either partner may experience depression, have to deal with forgiveness, learn to manage anger, strive to prevent bitterness, and deal with the general confusion and pain of loneliness. Psychologically, divorce forces former spouses to confront the reality that they will no longer be honored, cherished, or loved, in sickness and in health, until death do they part—as most marriage vows promise. A redevelopment of the self becomes necessary before persons come to terms with being divorced, regardless of who initiated the separation. Evolution of the self as an individual involves moving through the frightening process of emotional separation, striving to achieve a new balance as a single person, and redefining one's independence. The redefinition and redevelopment of the self is necessary to gain a sense of closure in a broken family relationship. Lack of emotional closure inhibits divorced individuals from forming new relationships and regaining self-respect and self-confidence.

Legal and Economic Effects. Legally, both divorced spouses relinquish all rights to the other person: the right to have sexual contact, the right to bear children, and the right to make decisions affecting the other person. Divorce is a judicial declaration that partners in a marriage give up their legal rights to influence each other's lives. Most divorces require lawyers, judges, and, sometimes, mediators to draw up contracts to solve legal issues resulting from decisions married couples have made for the future. These issues include, among others, investments, mortgages, property settlements, and inheritances. After a di-

vorce, both formally married partners must make legal decisions alone that would have previously been made together.

Economically, a divorce requires both marriage partners to make financial decisions that impact on each other and any children involved. In most cases, men's spendable income increases (even though they, more often than not, must pay child support and sometimes alimony), while women's spendable income decreases. In some cases, women must pay child support when their incomes are the household's primary means of support. In any event, after divorce, the total incomes must support two homes and two separate lifestyles instead of one.

Social, Spiritual, and Parental Effects. Socially, both marriage partners are affected by a divorce because they must make new friends and are often uncomfortable in the presence of old friends who knew them as a couple. Regardless of age, divorced partners are eligible for remarriage but often feel awkward entering the dating stage of developing new relationships. Typically, divorced men remarry earlier than divorced or widowed women. When children are involved, divorced couples must share the children's holidays, whereby children frequently spend major holidays alternately with each parent. Socially, children present a problem for persons who want to remarry because of the complications of blended families. Such families can be combinations of natural children, step-children, and adopted children. Managed carefully and with advanced planning, blended families can survive the challenges of shared holidays, summer vacations, and family reunions.

Spiritually, some divorced couples suffer disengagement from the church if the church does not sanction or approve of divorce. Also, after a divorce spiritual development and growth no longer include activities with the divorced spouse, such as church attendance, receiving the sacraments, and participating in church activities together. Divorce requires that individuals come to terms with major spiritual issues such as dealing with the guilt of a failed marriage, receiving grace to continue personal growth, offering forgiveness to all parties involved in the divorce proceedings, and deciding whether or not to remarry.

When families involve children, part of the legal

A popular film about divorce, Kramer vs. Kramer *(1979), dramatized the struggle of a father (Dustin Hoffman) seeking custody of his son (Justin Henry).* (Museum of Modern Art, Film Stills Archive)

decree of the divorce stipulates who will retain minor custody. Most often, children remain with the mother while the father is granted visitation rights. Sometimes, when parents cannot decide where minor children will live and who will care for them, family courts award joint custody. This often involves children living with each parent alternately for a specified amount of time. In the late twentieth century, however, more and more fathers assumed primary custody and daily responsibility for minor children after a divorce. This situation is especially suitable when mothers have other goals and are simply willing to grant full custody to fathers. Although not supported by research, courts and society still generally assume that minor children are better off in the care of their mothers. Whoever retains primary custody of minor children must face the challenges of being a single parent. Usually, divorced parents must deal with the developmental stages of their children's lives alone, since most divorces do not end with positive or frequent communication between parents.

Effects of Divorce on Children. Regardless of their age, children usually blame themselves when their parents divorce. Young children are egocentric: They have difficulty understanding issues from others' viewpoints. They think that almost everything that happens has something to do with them, how they have behaved, how much they loved their families. This kind of thinking is normal for young children. Because they assume blame and responsibility, especially for negative events in their lives, young children need reassurance that both parents still love them, that they have not done anything wrong, and that they have not done anything to cause their parents' separation and divorce.

Most children fare well if they develop positive self-esteem, self-confidence, and self-worth when growing up in a dual-parent home. Since divorce is such a traumatic event in children's lives, parents need to pay special attention to their feelings and their behavior during the divorce process. When parents continue to fight, refusing to resolve conflicts arising from the marriage, children suffer short-term and long-term problems. Short-term problems can include depression, poor academic performance, rebellion, and even physical illness. Long-term problems can include trouble estab-

lishing and maintaining loving relationships and difficulty developing trust.

When parents refuse to negotiate problems, children are often caught in the middle, unsure about how to respond emotionally to either parent. Children of any age have difficulty expressing hurt feelings and sadness to parents who are themselves angry and grieving. Responsible parents, no matter how much they are hurting, will develop a parenting plan that coordinates visitation, maintains financial obligations, and takes time to deal with children's feelings in each stage of the divorce process.

—*Thomas K. McKnight*

BIBLIOGRAPHY

Everett, Craig, and Sandra Everett. *Healthy Divorce.* San Francisco, Calif.: Jossey-Bass, 1994. Extended discussion on how to maintain emotional and psychological stability, redefine a sense of security, begin the process of personal renewal, and even prosper as an individual while going through the divorce process.

Garrity, Carla B., and Mitchell A. Baris. *Caught in the Middle: Protecting the Children of High-Conflict Divorce.* New York: Macmillan, 1994. Discusses how to understand the real issues of conflict during a divorce and details the development of family therapy strategies that benefit parents and children.

Popenoe, David. *Life Without Father.* New York: Simon & Schuster, 1996. Uses historical, economic, social, and scientific data to develop a case for the negative impact of divorce on children and asserts that children who grow up in homes without fathers are statistically more prone to drug and alcohol abuse, teenage pregnancy, poverty, welfare dependency, juvenile delinquency, and many other social and personal problems.

Textor, Martin, ed. *The Divorce and Divorce Therapy Handbook.* Northvale, N.J.: J. Aronson, 1994. A wide selection of authors and therapists who discuss each stage of the divorce process, this book elaborates on various approaches to divorce therapy and addresses the needs of children and adults.

Weiner-Davis, Michele. *Divorce Busting: A Revolutionary and Rapid Program for Staying Together.* New York: Simon & Schuster, 1992. Believes that divorce is not the answer to most marriage problems and describes achievable strategies and techniques for restoring communication, changing destructive habits and patterns of interaction, solving problems, resolving conflict, and understanding each partner's point of view.

See also Adultery; Alimony; Annulment; Cruelty as grounds for divorce; Desertion as grounds for divorce; Displaced homemakers; Divorce mediation; Dysfunctional families; Family law; Legal separation; Marriage; Marriage counseling; No-fault divorce; Prenuptial agreements; Uniform Marriage and Divorce Act (UMDA).

Divorce mediation

RELEVANT ISSUES: Divorce; Parenting and family relationships
SIGNIFICANCE: Divorce mediation is an alternative, more amicable divorce process than the traditional adversarial process conducted in lengthy, often embittered court proceedings

Divorce mediation is a process that assists couples in dealing with the problems that arise during separation and divorce. The process is a means of resolving partners' differences by bringing them to the same conclusions without the typical costs, time, and emotional injuries associated with traditional court proceedings. With a sharp increase in divorce in the United States from the mid-1960's to the 1970's, increased awareness and concern developed over the effects that divorce was having on affected families, especially their children. Consequently, during the early to mid-1980's major bar associations in the United States formed special committees to study alternative approaches to litigation as the primary means of solving divorce disputes. Thus, divorce mediation emerged as a mental-and emotional-health response to divorce. Its popularity increased significantly during the late 1980's and early 1990's.

Divorces settled through an adversarial court system tend to create long-lasting, bitter disputes, because couples in such a system typically do not work together to manage their problems. In contrast, mediation provides couples with the opportunity to take control of the divorce as a team through cooperative problem solving and to significantly reduce the psychological and social pressures that create stress and depression for them and their children. Since children typically develop an intense loyalty to their family structure, divorce can cause a painful disruption of their lives. Children can become very sad and vulnerable, because they sense the loss of continuity in their relationships with both parents. Divorce mediation focuses on maintaining the identity and self-esteem of the children involved.

Divorce-mediation services include both private and public programs. Mediators consist of divorce professionals, including attorneys, family therapists, and psychologists, who are hired by couples to assist them in formulating agreements about their problems. Private mediation programs are not directly associated with the courts, while public mediators serve courts and receive referrals from judges for official legal action.

Divorce mediation is typically activated when parents are involved in a dispute over the issues of finances, debts, property resolution, child custody and visitation rights, parental responsibilities, and child support. Although different mediators approach the process with different strategies, the mediation process focuses on helping couples to develop insights that will provide breakthroughs in negotiating the psychological, social, and legal terms of their divorce. The process provides an opportunity for couples to discuss grievances and deal with the relevant issues, emphasizing the needs of their children. Divorce mediation is especially recommended for couples who are prepared to put the past behind them and focus on the future. Such couples are ready to listen to each others' interests, to separate and still be friends, and to recognize their children's development as the top priority.

—Alvin K. Benson

See also Alimony; Child custody; Child support; Divorce; Family therapy; Marriage counseling; No-fault divorce; Prenuptial agreements; Visitation rights.

Domestic partners

RELEVANT ISSUES: Economics and work; Health and medicine; Law; Parenting and family relationships
SIGNIFICANCE: Although the nuclear family has been the standard family form in North America in modern times, "families" may also consist of legally unmarried partners

The marriage certificate is a relatively late phenomenon, and European persecution of nonheterosexuals began only in the thirteenth century. For millennia, families have consisted of many combinations of persons who share together in the same domicile, including opposite-sex, same-sex, polygamous, and polyandrous relationships. Some, but not all, of these relationships have involved sexual relations. An elderly widow and an unmarried son, for example, can constitute a domestic partnership by living together in a committed two-person household, sharing financial resources and domestic responsibilities but not engaging in sexual relations. By the 1990's at least five million Americans lived in households containing unrelated persons. Whereas divorce and single-parent families are increasingly common and the traditional nuclear family is declining in percentage terms, many gay men and lesbians place great emphasis on the institution of marriage and want their relationships to be accorded equal status with heterosexual marriages.

Married couples enjoy far more rights than unmarried domestic partners. The former are assured some four hundred rights conferred only on legally married couples. These include favored immigration status, jail and hospital visitation rights, reduced-cost club memberships, the ability to file joint income-tax returns, exemption from gift taxes, estate tax deductions, extension of health benefits, the right to sue for loss of consortium (the right of a spouse to the company of, affection from, and sexual relations with another spouse), the right to sue for wrongful death, the privilege not to testify against a spouse, the ability to own property as tenants in entirety, and entitlement to spousal survivor benefits.

Domestic Partners Begin to Seek Recognition. The need to give legal recognition to domestic partners lacking marriage certificates gained im-

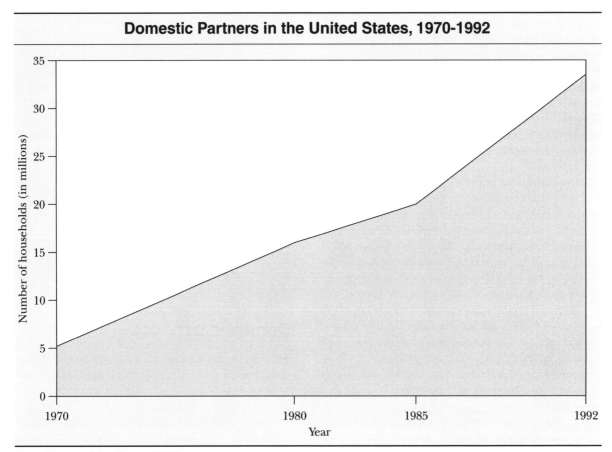

Domestic Partners in the United States, 1970-1992

Source: Bureau of the Census (1992)

petus when actor Lee Marvin was sued for "palimony" by Michelle Triola Marvin, a female domestic partner who lived with him in an unmarried state for seven years. Claiming that there was a verbal agreement to pool financial assets, she asked for half the actor's earnings over the years of the apparent common-law marriage (in other words, a cohabiting relationship that was not legally sanctioned). In 1976 the California Supreme Court ruled in *Marvin v. Marvin* that an unwitnessed verbal agreement had no legal standing, although Michelle Marvin was awarded a small sum for rehabilitation.

An urgent problem arose in the 1980's when gay males were hospitalized for acquired immunodeficiency syndrome (AIDS). Medical authorities often barred gay males from visiting their sick partners in the hospital, because they were not immediate family members. As treatment for AIDS was extraordinarily expensive, gay males with health insurance sought in vain to have their lovers covered in the same manner as legally married heterosexual couples. The term "domestic partners" then arose as a concept to which legal responsibilities and rights could be attached.

Legal Innovations. In 1975 two gay men were issued a marriage license by the city of Boulder, Colorado, in an effort to reclassify one of the partners, an Australian, as an "immediate relative" of the other for purposes of immigration. Although immigration authorities did not accept the reclassification (*Adams v. Howerton*), the license was never revoked. In 1983 the California Workers' Compensation Appeals Board ruled that a gay man was entitled to benefits after the job-related suicide of his lover, because the two belonged to the same household (*Donavan v. Workers' Compensation Board*). In 1985 the newly incorporated city of West Hollywood, California, passed a domestic partnership statute allowing same-sex couples to register even if they lived elsewhere. In 1988 Madison, Wisconsin, followed suit, and in the 1990's more than ten American cities adopted similar laws. In 1990 the state of California agreed to accept registration of families as unincorporated nonprofit associations, although with no specific economic benefits or legal rights.

In 1989 the highest court in New York State ruled, for the purposes of determining succession in rent-controlled apartments in New York City,

that a family can include "two adult lifetime partners whose relationship is long-term and characterized by an emotional and financial commitment and interdependence" (*Braschi v. Stahl Associates*). In 1991 a ruling established that a member of a same-sex couple was to be covered by Ohio's Domestic Violence Act. In Minnesota one woman in a same-sex relationship was assigned guardianship over the other when the latter was disabled by a serious accident because, the judge ruled, the two constituted a family.

In 1993 the Hawaii Supreme Court ruled that the state health department could not deny marriage licenses to gays and lesbians unless the department could prove that there was a compelling state interest in denying such licenses (*Baehr v. Lewin*). In 1996, when the state was unable to demonstrate in a lower court a compelling state interest in denying same-sex marriage, the ruling was appealed to the Hawaii Supreme Court.

Outside the United States, an inmate of a Canadian prison in 1989 was allowed a conjugal visit by a same-sex partner (*Vesey v. Commissioner of Correctional Systems*). Subsequent rulings by Canadian administrative bodies conferred permanent residency to an alien same-sex partner, unemployment insurance benefits when one partner was transferred by a company to another city, and spousal benefits of various sorts, including family-care leave. In 1990 the Yukon voted to recognize domestic partnerships. Three Canadian provinces soon adopted similar statutes. Sweden in 1987 extended property rights to include unmarried cohabitants who lived together for at least five years. In 1989 Denmark passed the Registered Partnership Act, which conferred most of the benefits and obligations of heterosexual marriages on gay and lesbian couples. Norway followed suit in 1993.

Recognition of Domestic Partners. Since 1968 the Universal Fellowship of Metropolitan Community Church, an ecumenical Protestant denomination, has provided "holy union" as a religious sacrament for same-sex partners. As historian John Boswell has documented, the practice of blessing same-sex partners started more than one thousand years ago within certain Christian churches in the Mediterranean area.

Domestic partnerships can acquire legal status in two forms. Governmental entities can issue a document that gives public recognition to two

*In 1991 San Francisco began allowing homosexual couples to **register as domestic partners**.* (AP/Wide World Photos)

partners, much in the manner of a marriage certificate between opposite-sex couples. However, such documents can be kept confidential. Regulations vary concerning registration, but the same requirements for marriage are often applied: Parties must be at least eighteen years old, be mentally competent, not be related by blood ties, not already be married or have a domestic partner, and must have two witnesses and a notarized statement. Some ordinances impose more stringent requirements: that domestic partners be asked to affirm that they live together, to affirm that they live in the city of the ordinance, to demonstrate that they are involved in a committed relationships, or to assume an obligation for the basic living expenses of the other partner.

A second form of recognition is for employees to list a domestic partner on a form supplied by an employer in order to extend to the other partner fringe benefits—usually health benefits, sick leave, and bereavement leave. Several dozen employers, both public and private, extend these fringe benefits to domestic partners. In addition to the municipalities and Canadian provinces that provide formal recognition to domestic partnerships, a few dozen corporations now offer such an option. Advocacy organizations, computer companies, entertainment businesses, health organizations, and universities are most prominent. It has been reported that the additional amounts paid into health funds are greater than the amounts spent on health benefits.

Generally, same-sex couples are more likely to register, but opposite-sex unmarried couples are more frequent among those claiming domestic partners for purposes of obtaining health and related fringe benefits from employers. Termination of domestic partnerships are effected by written statements.

Backlash. Fearful that gays and lesbians might go to Hawaii to marry and then return home to another state to claim new rights, more than a dozen states have passed laws refusing to honor such unions as marriages. In 1996 Congress passed the Defense of Marriage Act, which confers the right of nonrecognition of gay marriages to all states. Within Hawaii, a reciprocal beneficiaries law was passed in 1997 to offer nonmarried couples a few of the benefits that accrue to married persons. —*Michael Haas*

BIBLIOGRAPHY

Becker, Lewis. "Recognition of Domestic Partnerships by Governmental Entities and Private Employers," *National Journal of Sexual Orientation Law* 1 (1995).

Berger, Vada. "Domestic Partnership Initiatives." *DePaul Law Review* 40 (Winter, 1991).

Boswell, John. *Same-Sex Unions in Premodern Europe.* New York: Villard, 1994.

Eskridge, William N., Jr. "A History of Same-Sex Marriage." *Virginia Law Review* 79 (October, 1993).

Rusk, Peter. "Same-Sex Spousal Benefits and the Evolving Conception of Family." *University of Toronto Faculty of Law Review* 52 (Winter, 1993).

Sanders, Douglas. "Constructing Lesbian and Gay Rights." *Canadian Journal of Law and Society* 9 (Fall, 1994).

Valdes, Frances. "Unpacking Hetero-Patriarchy: Tracing the Conflation of Sex, Gender, and Sexual Orientation to Its Origins." *Yale Journal of Law and the Humanities* 8 (Winter, 1996).

See also Acquired immunodeficiency syndrome (AIDS); Alternative family types; Americans with Disabilities Act (ADA); Bonding and attachment; Cohabitation; Common-law marriage; Couples; Death; Family: concept and history; Family economics; Gay and lesbian families; Health problems; Inheritance and estate law; Marriage; Marriage laws; Persons of opposite sex sharing living quarters (POSSLQ); Prison inmates.

Domestic violence

RELEVANT ISSUES: Divorce; Marriage and dating; Parenting and family relationships; Violence

SIGNIFICANCE: Domestic violence is a serious threat to the health and well-being of women and children and has contributed to the development of family courts

Many names have been used to describe the problem of domestic violence, including "wife beating" or "battering," "family violence," and "spousal abuse." While some authors have used the term "domestic violence" to describe any abuse that occurs within the family (including child and elder abuse), it is most often used to refer to the violence that occurs between adult partners. Most victims of domestic violence are women, although it is possible for men to be victimized in relationships.

In The Man with the Golden Arm *(1955) Frank Sinatra played a man whose drug addiction drove him to violence.* (Museum of Modern Art, Film Stills Archive)

The abuse which constitutes domestic violence may be emotional, physical, or sexual. Emotional abuse consists of behaviors intended to mentally hurt other persons. This may include such behaviors as name calling, suggesting that spouses are worthless, flaunting infidelity, and attempting to control spouses by withholding love, affection, or money. Emotional abuse always accompanies physical abuse and, in many cases, precedes it. Physical abuse is the infliction of physical injury on victims. It may begin nonviolently with the neglect of victims' needs, proceed to pinching and squeezing, and eventually progress to the point at which victims incur serious physical injury. Physical abuse often leads to victims' deaths if it is left unchecked. Marital rape is the form of sexual abuse that is most commonly discussed. However,

this form of domestic violence also involves any sexual behavior that is unwelcome to women and includes forcing women to make reproductive decisions that are contrary to their wishes.

Nature of the Problem. Domestic violence follows a cyclical pattern. First there is a stage of tension-building, during which abusers express increasing irritation for various reasons. During this stage, abusers are hostile and dissatisfied. They may express their feelings in ways that demean women, who try to appease them in order to prevent the situation from becoming violent. The explosion stage occurs when the tension builds to the point that abusers can no longer contain their temper. Their rage may be expressed as verbal, emotional, or physical abuse. While this stage usually lasts only a brief time—from a few minutes to twenty-four hours, it is the most dangerous time for victims. It is at this point that they are most likely to be seriously injured. After abusers calm down, couples enter a honeymoon period, during which abusers are likely to apologize for their behavior and swear it will never happen again. They may bring gifts or be especially kind, leading women to believe that they will change and persuading them to remain in the relationship. The honeymoon phase may be short or long; however, the cycle eventually begins again.

The cyclical nature of domestic violence partially explains why many women remain in abusive relationships for extended periods of time. They convince themselves that their spouses really will change their behaviors and that abuse will not reoccur. A second reason was identified by Lenore Walker, who suggested that victims of domestic violence suffer from psychological trauma as a result of the violence they have experienced. She called this condition the "battered woman syndrome." Women who suffer from Battered Woman Syndrome are depressed and have come to believe that they are helpless to alter the situation. They may lack energy and motivation. They feel powerless to change their lives and are unable to perceive options which might free them from abusive relationships.

There are also practical reasons why women stay with abusive men. Because abusers often do not allow their spouses to work, women may not be able to financially afford to leave. This may be particularly true for women with children. In many cases, abusers isolate their wives from family and friends, leaving them nobody to turn to for support. In addition, victims of domestic violence may fear retaliation or that they will lose custody of their children if they leave a relationship.

Prevalence and Consequences. Domestic violence is a serious problem. Approximately 28 percent of all violent victimizations against women were committed by intimates, such as husbands and boyfriends, while intimates accounted for only 5 percent of violent crimes against men. Compared to males, females in the late twentieth century experienced more than ten times as many incidents of violence by intimates each year. It has been estimated that 7 percent of married or cohabiting women in the United States are physically abused by their partners each year, while 37 per-

cent are verbally or emotionally abused. One study found that more people have witnessed an incident of domestic violence than have witnessed muggings and robberies combined. According to a national survey, an incident of domestic violence occurs every nine seconds in the United States. Each year at least 1,500 women, or 42 percent of all murdered women, are killed by a current or former husband or boyfriend.

The physical abuse of women has serious consequences. The financial costs generated by this problem are staggering. Each year medical expenses incurred from domestic violence total at least $3 to $5 billion. Approximately 30 percent of women treated in hospital emergency rooms are identified as having injuries caused by battering. Of those women, 28 percent have required hospitalization, and 13 percent have required major medical treatment. Since domestic violence is repetitive in nature, many women visit hospitals on more than one occasion for the treatment of injuries sustained because of family violence.

Businesses also incur the costs of domestic violence. It is estimated that 25 percent of all workplace problems are attributed to domestic violence. Businesses lose $100 million annually in the form of lost wages, sick leave, absenteeism, and nonproductivity. Seventy-four percent of abused women who work outside the home are harassed by their abusers at work. More than half are late for work three times a month or more because of their abusers, and 20 percent lose their jobs because of abuse. It has been estimated that more women leave the workforce permanently because of domestic violence than leave to raise children.

There are also social costs associated with domestic violence. Research suggests that children who witness domestic violence may be harmed in several ways. They may suffer from low self-esteem, do poorly in school, and act out. Perhaps the most harmful consequence of domestic violence is that children who see their parents fight, especially boys, may be more likely than other children to engage in domestic violence when they become adults, thus continuing the cycle of violence. In addition, violence is responsible for 22 percent of all divorces in the United States.

History of Domestic Violence. Domestic violence has not always been recognized as a social problem. This is not to say that family violence did

Canadian poster denouncing abuse in the languages of its many ethnic communities. (Dick Hemingway)

not occur, but it was considered to be a private issue best resolved among family members. In fact, only the most egregious assaults were prosecuted. The primary reason for this lies in the way in which married couples were perceived under the law. Women were not legally considered to be full human beings. Thus, upon marriage husband and wife became one person: the husband. Since a husband could be held liable for his wife's actions, it was his right and duty to impose discipline when her actions warranted punishment. Short of killing her, he was not restricted in his use of force. For instance, common law permitted husbands to hit their wives with sticks but required that the sticks be no thicker than a husband's thumb. Even

when a beating did result in death, offenders were often not severely punished.

In the United States the issue of domestic violence first received national attention during the late 1840's when the temperance movement suggested a connection between alcohol abuse and wife beating. The temperance movement involved women in political activism in ways that were previously unknown, giving rise to new ideas about women's rights and efforts to protect them from abuse. These new activists organized efforts to inform the citizenry of the violence faced by many women, brought cases to the attention of the courts, and attempted to have legislation passed that would ensure the punishment of wife beaters.

Canadians marching to protest violence against women in 1995. (Dick Hemingway)

Their efforts were successful to the extent that family courts designed to deal with the issues of family violence were established across the country in the early 1900's. However, the courts still did not perceive domestic violence to be a criminal offense. Rather, they viewed the problem to be one of family dysfunction that should be resolved privately.

Societal reluctance to interfere in the private lives of families was so strong that it was not until the late 1970's that the prosecution of men who assaulted their spouses became a common event. By 1980 all but six states had enacted laws concerning the abuse of wives, providing funding for shelters and improved reporting procedures. These laws also repealed statutes which prevented spouses from suing each other for damages and established more effective criminal procedures.

Several sensational cases kept the issue of domestic violence in the national headlines throughout the 1980's and 1990's. In 1984 the U.S. Attorney General established the Task Force on Family Violence to examine the scope and nature of the problem. The findings were instrumental in the efforts of grassroots organizations that lobbied for the successful passage of the Family Violence Prevention and Services Act, which provided funding for programs serving victims of domestic violence. By July 5, 1993, all fifty states had passed laws making marital rape a punishable offense. However, thirty-one states still provided exemptions from prosecution under certain circumstances. The following year the Violence Against Women Act was enacted on the federal level. This law expanded the funding available for victim-services programs, allowed interstate enforcement of protection orders, provided training for state and federal judges and funded school-based rape education programs. It also contained a civil rights component that defined domestic violence as an assault based on gender, making it possible for victims to file discrimination suits against their abusers.

Help Available to Battered Women. There are three basic sources of assistance available to victims of domestic violence: shelters, the police, and the health care system. Each provides a different form of help.

A shelter is a temporary residence for women who have fled a violent home. The most important service provided by a shelter is safety. Women who have left a violent marital situation are often in great danger from their spouses. In order to ensure women's safety, many shelter programs keep their locations confidential, and other agencies and may hire security officers. Most programs also educate residents about domestic violence and the resources available to them as they begin to rebuild their lives. Often shelters provide peer support groups so that victims can see that others have had similar experiences and that they are not to blame for the violence they have suffered. Many programs also have connections to legal advocates and other forms of professional support.

The first modern shelter in the United States was Haven House, located in the San Gabriel Valley, California. It opened its doors in 1964 to abused families with alcoholic husbands. However, it was not until 1974 that the shelter movement gained momentum with the opening of Women's House in St. Paul, Minnesota. By the end of 1976 there were 20 shelters in the United States. There were 300 by 1982 and approximately 1,200 in 1994. While the number of shelters has grown tremendously, there are still not enough to serve the number of victims who require assistance each year. Women who live in rural areas are particularly disadvantaged when it comes to the availability of shelters.

Prior to the early 1980's police were hesitant to intervene in instances of domestic violence. If the police intervened at all, the common practice was to separate husbands and wives to provide a cooling off period. The assumption was that once the parties had calmed down, they would be able to settle their differences in a more rational manner. In 1984, however, a study of police responses to domestic violence calls in Minneapolis, Minnesota, found that arresting aggressors was the most effective way to prevent future violent incidents. As a result of this study, police departments across the nation began to take domestic violence more seriously and have developed improved policies governing the way in which such incidents are handled.

The health care system is frequently the first provider of services to battered women, since many such women require medical treatment for their injuries. Unfortunately, few victims of domestic violence report the true cause of their injuries,

Some communities have found that arresting offenders is the most effective way to reduce domestic violence. (James L. Shaffer)

making it difficult for health care providers to accurately identify the problem. In addition, some physicians are hesitant to talk to women about violence, because they are concerned about offending patients, they lack adequate time to deal with complicated issues, and they fear taking on more than they can reasonably handle. Since the 1970's more training has been offered to physicians in order to help them ask the right questions, identify symptoms, make referrals to appropriate agencies, and avoid placing women in dangerous situations. —*AnnMarie Kazyaka*

BIBLIOGRAPHY

Berry, Dawn Bradley. *Domestic Violence Sourcebook.* Los Angeles: Lowell House, 1995. Overview of the problem of domestic violence, its causes and consequences, including practical information for women who are abused.

Browne, Angela. *When Battered Women Kill.* New York: Free Press, 1987. Focuses on the patterns of violence in relationships involving the physical abuse of women by their male partners and the unfolding of events that lead to homicide committed by women victims.

Jones, Ann. *Next Time She'll Be Dead: Battering and How to Stop It.* Boston: Beacon Press, 1994. Analyzes the attitudes and institutions in society that contribute to domestic violence and includes chapters on barriers to protecting women in the legal system, how language contributes to blaming women, and what can be done in society to eliminate the problem.

Kilgore, Nancy. *Every Eighteen Seconds: A Journey Through Domestic Violence.* Volcano, Calif.: Volcano Press, 1992. Written as a series of letters to her son, this book explains Kilgore's abusive relationship with her husband.

McCue, Margi Laird. *Domestic Violence: A Reference Handbook.* Santa Barbara, Calif.: Contemporary World Issues, 1995. Overview of the problem of domestic violence, focusing on its development as a recognized social problem and the legal issues surrounding it.

Walker, Lenore. *The Battered Woman.* New York: Harper & Row, 1979. Explores the myths and realities about battered women, including a discussion of the cycle of violence and the dynamics of learned helplessness.

_____. *The Battered Woman Syndrome.* New York: Springer, 1984. Update of Walker's 1979 book that includes psychosocial characteristics of battered women and their abusers, the impact of domestic violence on children, and the role of drugs and alcohol in cases of abuse.

See also Alcoholism and drug abuse; Corporal punishment; Cruelty as grounds for divorce; Cycle of violence theory; Dating violence; Disciplining children; Dysfunctional families; Elder abuse; Family Violence Prevention and Services Act; Gangs; Infanticide; Marital rape; Shelters; Vengeance in families; Violence Against Women Act.

Dowry

Relevant issue: Marriage and dating

Significance: Dowry is a cultural or socioeconomic marriage practice in which brides give money or property to grooms or grooms' families

A dowry is part of a series of exchanges of money or property negotiated between families whose children are marrying. The exchanged property may take the form of land, animals, buildings, or personal possessions. Brides' families give dowries to grooms or grooms' families, who often respond by paying a bride-price. These exchanges cement the ties between families and consequently bring them social, economic, or political advantages.

The practice of dowry dates back to early tribal societies and still exists in various tribal and ethnic groups worldwide. In Europe, the practice evolved from Celtic, Roman, and Greek customs, which also guaranteed brides financial support in the event that their husbands died or divorced them. In North America, with the exception of French-influenced Quebec and Louisiana, the use of dowries largely followed British customs and generally allowed grooms to enjoy all the rights and privileges of the dowry during their lifetimes. Changes in U.S. law after 1839 protected brides' dowries from misuse. After 1870 such misuse was halted in Canada after Britain passed a similar act. In North America in the 1990's the practice of providing dowries for brides continued among some strongly traditional ethnic groups with roots in Asia, India, the Middle East, the Caribbean, and Mexico.

—*Kristin L. Gleeson*

See also Bride-price; Courting rituals; Hinduism; Matchmaking; Muslims; Son preference; Weddings.

Dual-earner families

Relevant issues: Economics and work; Parenting and family relationships

Significance: Once a family form reserved for the poor, two-income families became commonplace for middle-class North Americans in the late twentieth century, affecting family behavior, member interaction, and public policy

By the late 1970's a combination of social and economic factors had led to a demographic shift from the predominance of single-earner to dual-earner families. In 1940 less than 10 percent of all families in the United States maintained two incomes. By 1992 that percentage had risen to more than 40 percent—a fourfold increase. The shift is generally attributed to economic need. In an attempt to maintain middle-class aspirations of prosperity, which included home ownership, multiple vehicles, and keeping up with changes in domestic technology while facing inflation and stagnant wages, many families were forced to seek additional sources of income. Inflation, which surpassed double-digit levels during part of the 1970's, led to a significant erosion in purchasing power. In addition, from the 1970's through the early 1990's average real wages, or income adjusted to reflect cost-of-living increases, was flat, further eroding purchasing power in the face of expanding needs. Social forces were also at work. The greater acceptance of women as equal and competent employees in the workplace created more opportunities for women to find gainful employment.

Decline of Separate Spheres. North American society in the nineteenth and twentieth centuries has often been characterized as heavily middle class. Through much of the twentieth century, the roles of middle-class women were largely influenced by the norms of the "cult of domesticity" that had emerged out of the industrial revolution. As the economy transformed from agrarian-centered to production-centered, work life took on a dual existence. There was a separation of domestic work from paid labor that had not been previously so clearly demarcated on farms. In many cases, the doctrine of separate labor spheres was supported by company rules that prohibited the hiring of married women. Men's labor was a public affair that resulted in monetary compensation and the emotional rewards of title and promotion. Women's work revolved around the home and child rearing, which resulted in no income and no titles. Often women worked outside the home only if their families were poor or if they wished to earn extra for luxuries—sometimes referred to as "pin money." The separate spheres of labor—public for men and private for women—went largely unchallenged until World War II.

Because male troops were required to fight overseas while the economy expanded to accommodate war needs, the need was created for women to enter the paid workforce, despite social norms to the contrary. A national campaign was launched to draw women out of the home and into the workplace. The effort was successful as the economy geared up for war production. The end of the war, however, brought widespread layoffs of women, as men returned from overseas service to reclaim their jobs. Nevertheless, the social upheaval left a lasting impact. The myth that women could not be productive wage workers was dispelled. The number of families with a sole male breadwinner declined from almost 70 percent in 1940 to less than 20 percent in the 1990's.

Division of Labor in the Family. The relatively rapid rise of dual-earner families in the twentieth century aggravated the tensions between traditional and modern family roles. Men in dual-income families have continued to be responsible for paid labor, while being asked to play larger roles in domestic labor and child raising. Women have continued to be viewed as the primary caretakers of children; however, in two-income families they have also become wage earners. Statistics suggest that men were slower to adapt to their changing roles than were women. By the mid-

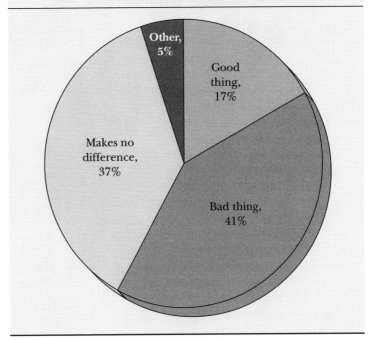

Women's Attitudes on Working Mothers

Other, 5%

Good thing, 17%

Makes no difference, 37%

Bad thing, 41%

Source: The Pew Research Center (1998)

Note: A cross-section of American women were asked if the trend of more mothers working outside the home was a good or bad thing for society.

In dual-earner families both parents usually share domestic responsibilities. (James L. Shaffer)

Percentage of Household Chores Done by Wives Who Earn More than Their Husbands

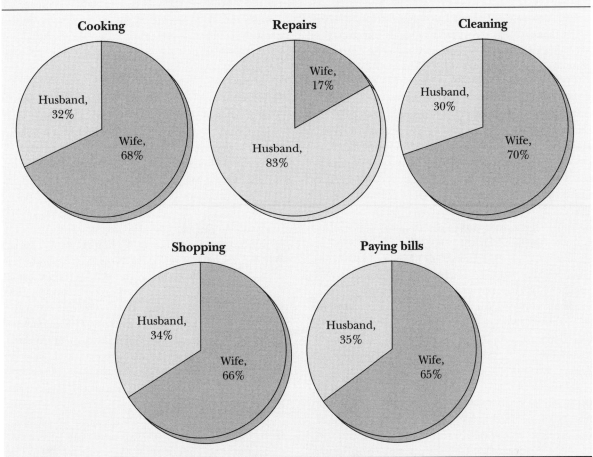

Cooking

Husband, 32%

Wife, 68%

Repairs

Wife, 17%

Husband, 83%

Cleaning

Husband, 30%

Wife, 70%

Shopping

Husband, 34%

Wife, 66%

Paying bills

Husband, 35%

Wife, 65%

Source: Christian Science Monitor (July 15, 1997)

1990's typical mothers worked seven to ten additional hours per week in performing paid and domestic labor.

Family and work changes gave rise to a new vocabulary to describe dual-earner families. For example, women caught between the desire to replicate their mothers' standards of housekeeping and child rearing, while simultaneously competing with men at the workplace, have been labeled as suffering from the "superwoman syndrome," which results from wanting to succeed on all fronts. The expectation—sometimes internally and sometimes externally imposed—that women are responsible for all domestic labor after completing a full day of paid labor has been called the "second shift." These terms reflect the pres-

sures on women during a period of changing social standards. Men have also adjusted to new roles, including the ego adjustment that comes with not being the sole income providers for their families.

A dual-earner family is not necessarily an equal-earner family. By the mid-1990's a wage gap of about 30 percent remained between husbands and wives; on average, women in the United States earn 70 cents for every dollar that men make. At the same time, a glass ceiling has continued to persist, with more men being promoted to upper levels of management than women. Even in dual-earner families, men's jobs have often been viewed as more significant than women's, because men earn more or occupy higher positions. Men have therefore often dictated many family decisions, such as those pertaining to relocations or job priorities.

Child Rearing. Part of the family values debate of the early 1990's revolved around whether the time pressures placed upon dual-earner families shortchanged the care of children. Two-income families were sometimes accused of seeking material well-being over the best interests of their children. The term "DINK," an acronym for dual income, no kids, has often been applied pejoratively to working couples who seek upper-middle-class lifestyles. Some conservative religious organizations have decried the practice of dual-earner families, while some women have felt left out of the women's movement because of its focus on gaining rights for women at the workplace. Despite strong feelings on both sides of the issue of the impact of dual-earner families on children, research has been inconclusive on this point. No evidence has been found indicating significant differences between the happiness and development of children from single- versus dual-earner families. Ultimately the question may be moot, because women work outside the home, primarily for economic reasons.

Economics plays a major role in the decision of dual-career couples to have children. With the advent of affordable and effective birth control as well as new reproductive technologies, families in modern industrialized countries can confidently decide when to have children and how many children to have. Couples' ability to plan parenthood allows economics to enter into the decision-making process. Studies indicate that it cost a middle-class American family in the mid-1990's between $160,000 and $300,000 to rear a child up to its eighteenth birthday. This figure is significant, as couples factor their financial standing into their projected quality of life and that of their offspring. Live births in the United States declined from approximately 55 per 1,000 persons annually in 1820 to 25 per 1,000 in 1950 and 20 per 1,000 in 1990. In the 1990's American couples had fewer children and delayed their births, in part because of career and financial considerations.

Policy Adjustments. As worker demographics in the United States shifted, policy changes took place at the corporate and national levels to accommodate the middle-class transformation to the dual-earner norm. At the corporate level, more companies made decisions based on the needs of dual-earner families. A small but growing number of companies have provided financial assistance for child care, and a few have offered on-site child care. Many companies have adopted policies that assist relocated workers in finding work for their spouses, thus recognizing that most professionals have wives or husbands who also have careers. Some universities have advertised policies geared to assisting dual-career couples in higher education. Flexible scheduling has also been employed by some firms to assist dual-income families in taking care of many of the routine responsibilities that stay-at-home adults have previously undertaken.

Perhaps just as significant as these policy changes have been cultural changes at the workplace. Greater tolerance for both men and women who need to take time off to address family issues has emerged. It can no longer be assumed that housewives stay home to perform domestic chores. Meanwhile, some men and women have become so frustrated with family-unfriendly policies that they have struck out on their own by starting businesses. By the middle of the 1990's women had surpassed men in the number of entrepreneurial start-ups.

At the national level, labor laws have evolved from the assumption of single-earners to the recognition of the needs of dual-earner families. The Family and Medical Leave Act, signed into law by President Bill Clinton in 1993, allowed for unpaid, twelve-week pregnancy leaves and unpaid leaves from work by both fathers and mothers for family emergencies. Canadian law provided for between seventeen and forty-one weeks of pregnancy leave for mothers at 60 percent of their full salaries for the first fifteen weeks. While the United States has inaugurated no national child-care policy or program, it has provided certain tax breaks for child care based upon parents' economic need. These policies reflect the cultural shift to dual-earner families as the norm.

Time as a Valued Commodity. With the growing prosperity of the 1990's, some research has indicated that strains on dual-earner families placed greater emphasis on the availability of discretionary time. A growing number of paid workers were willing to forgo a certain amount of additional compensation and promotions for fewer work hours. Some legislators and labor representatives in the United States have sought to give employees the option of choosing compensatory time off in lieu of accepting overtime pay for work that exceeds the usual forty hours per week. Ironically, time pressures have placed additional stress on home life. Parents in dual-earner families are often frustrated by the lack of time and autonomy at home (particularly given the demands of child raising). This phenomenon has led some to view the workplace as a kind of sanctuary away from the stresses of home life.

Technological Fixes. In the search to find methods to overcome the stresses of dual-earner families, some families turned to technological answers. Since the 1980's, the growing availability of fax machines, personal computers, modems, and the Internet has made it possible for more workers to spend some or all of their time at home and remain productive. However, a number of psychosocial issues accompany "telecommuting." While a parent can be present to care for, or greet children after school, it is sometimes difficult to avoid interruptions and stay focused on work responsibilities. Moreover, some people find a psychological barrier in the idea of working at home. In addition, disruptions and the temptation for disruption can be greater. The loss of direct social contact with other employees, superiors, and clients can also be an issue. Nevertheless, the turn to technology is indicative of the motivation and creativity that dual-earner families are willing to employ to garner the benefits from both working careers and families. —*Maurice Hamington*

BIBLIOGRAPHY

Barrett, Rosalind C., and Caryl Rivers. *She Works/He Works: How Two-Income Families Are Happier, Healthier, and Better Off.* New York: HarperCollins, 1996. Based largely on a study funded by the National Institute of Mental Health, this book mixes report findings and extended case studies to dispel conventional wisdom that the family unit is deteriorating under the strain of the need for dual earners.

Coontz, Stephanie. *The Way We Never Were: American Families and the Nostalgia Trap.* New York: Basic Books, 1992. Analyzes myths and traditions surrounding families, including lingering romanticization of the single-earner families of the 1950's.

Gilbert, Lucia Albino. *Two Careers/One Family.* Newbury Park, Calif.: Sage Publications, 1993. Brings together data that confirm how dual-earner families have come to characterize the middle class, while demonstrating how dual-career norms are in turn influencing the spectrum of social relationships.

Hochschild, Arlie. *The Time Bind: When Work Becomes Home and Home Becomes Work.* New York: Metropolitan Books, 1997. Reports on a three-year study of working parents at a large corporation and finds that time pressures alter family behavior and interaction. Hochschild advocates reducing the hours in the standard workweek to accommodate changes in modern working conditions.

Hochschild, Arlie, with Anne Machung. *The Second Shift: Working Parents and the Revolution at Home.* New York: Viking, 1989. Seminal work in the study of the impact of two wage earners on the family, focusing on the difficulties in, as well as the positive impact on, raising children.

Lee, Deborah, et al. *Having It All/Having Enough.* New York: American Management Association, 1997. Recognizing that balancing work and family life is a vexing issue for dual-income families, Lee uses interviews with working couples to offer methods for addressing the multiple demands made upon employees.

Parcel, Toby L., and Elizabeth G. Menaghan. *Parents' Jobs and Children's Lives.* New York: Aldine de Gruyter, 1994. Reports the findings of various sociological studies on the impact of working parents on the lives of children, paying particular attention to issues of gender.

Schwartz, Felice. *Breaking with Tradition: Women and Work, the New Facts of Life.* New York: Warner Books, 1992. The founder and president of Catalyst, an organization dedicated to improving business policy for women, Schwartz addresses the problems dual-earner families face and provides strategies to overcome the stress created by trying to achieve multiple goals.

See also Corporate families; Cult of True Womanhood; DINKs; Equalitarian families; Family demographics; Family economics; Gender inequality; Mommy track; Second shift; Women's roles; Work.

Dysfunctional families

RELEVANT ISSUES: Divorce; Parenting and family
relationships; Sociology; Violence

SIGNIFICANCE: Dysfunctional families are those in
which particular functions become excessively
disruptive or counterproductive

Adapted from classical functionalist sociology, the
concept of "dysfunctionality" has been widely applied and at times misapplied to a considerable
variety of familial problems in ways that at times
depart from the original theoretical context.
When using the term "dysfunctionality" both the
original context and the modern expanded meaning should be carefully taken into account.

Original Theoretical Context. The concept of
dysfunctional families first arose from the theoretical framework of functionalist sociology, as found
in the works of Robert Merton (1949), Talcott
Parsons (1955), and William Goode (1964). According to the functionalist perspective, every social institution, indeed every social activity occurring in an institutional context, performs a variety
of positive and negative social functions within the
broader social arena, just as each individual performs a variety of institutionally conditioned social
roles in the same arena. The family is thus perceived as one of the key institutions providing
structure, continuity, and meaning to society. Ideally it should collaborate smoothly with schools,
churches, government agencies, neighborhood
groups, and other institutions to transmit and sustain the shared values on which a civil society is
said to be based, assisting in the development of a
productive citizenry who perform constructive social roles. According to Merton, functions may be
either manifest, with intended consequences, or
latent, with unintended consequences. Most social
institutions, including the family, perform a combination of manifest and latent functions.

When all these roles and functions are performed effectively and compatibly, a condition of
solidarity is said to exist in society, which functionalists often describe by drawing an analogy to an
organic whole with harmoniously interadaptive
components. When particular activities or institutions become excessively disruptive or counterproductive, either toward their own perceived ends or
toward those of the larger social system in which

they are structurally embedded, they are sometimes said to be dysfunctional. The family and its
activities are among the most frequent social realities to which the latter term has been applied.

General Applications to the Family. As a historically viable social institution which has long been
the nexus of many important social activities, the
American family has come under increasingly
critical social, political, moral, and religious scrutiny. Its various manifest and latent shortcomings
have often been identified as dysfunctions. Families with allegedly excessive failings, including acknowledged social problems such as domestic violence or substance abuse, have increasingly been
identified as dysfunctional. The phrase "dysfunctional family" has thus become a generic term for
families with internal problems, much as the term
"broken home" was once used somewhat more
pejoratively as a generic term for families whose
problems had already torn them apart, even if
such breakups were ultimately beneficial to the
persons involved. The main difference between
dysfunctional families and broken homes is that a
certain degree of dysfunctionality exists in almost
all intact families, given the large variety of manifest and latent functions they are expected to perform in a complex modern society. No family can
perform all its perceived functions equally effectively, and despite increasing rates of divorce and
separation most families that stay together have a
somewhat mixed record of functionality and dysfunctionality. Thus, it is not just the potentially
broken homes, but also a considerable variety of
the unbroken ones, that are often described as
dysfunctional.

Ironically, this generic usage of dysfunctionality
in relation to the family has become commonplace during a period when the functionalist view-
point itself, including its candidly conservative institutional perspective on the family, has been
under persistent critical attack. It has come under
attack particularly from conflict theorists using the
paradigm dating from C. Wright Mills (or more
radically Karl Marx), interactionists in the tradition of George H. Mead, feminists such as Jessie
Bernard, postmodernists, and other thinkers
within the sociological profession. Parsons's over-
simplified emphasis on the provider role of fathers
and the nurturer role of mothers is no longer
ideologically acceptable to many sociologists, and

In the 1955 film Rebel Without a Cause, *James Dean played a teenager whose alienation from his parents exposed the family's fundamental dysfunction.* (Museum of Modern Art, Film Stills Archive)

the role of parents in the socialization of children is now seen to be quite complex, even by neoconservatives who still insist that this function is the litmus test of the family as a social institution. Symptomatic of modern ideological uncertainties about the family is the work of Arlene Skolnick (1991), who has joined the growing call for a new research agenda on family issues, starting with a redefinition of the very concept of a family and its functions.

Specific Variations and Examples. In order to determine whether particular families are actually dysfunctional, one does not merely list their possible functions, enumerate their failings, and compare mathematically. This would only be possible if there were a canonical list of positive family

functions (some might call them "family values") by which to make such a comparison. The unavailability of a clear-cut operational definition of familial dysfunctionality is primarily attributable to the change and diversification the family itself is undergoing as people move toward increasingly complex modern and postmodern lifestyles.

For example, in simpler agrarian times it was imperative for families to produce numerous healthy offspring to perform the duties of the homestead and guarantee the survival of the family's name and claims through the next generation. Modern urban couples have a greater variety of options, including childlessness, which they might decide to pursue as a way to avoid the expenses of cars and college while seeking pleasure, companionship, sexual gratification, economic opportunity, or personal fulfillment. In the first type of household, the obligatory presence of children favors the classical concepts of familial functionality and social solidarity. Dysfunctionality, if present, would thus be relatively easy to define or determine within the traditional parameters of the household. In the second type of household, the mere presence of children might actually increase the likelihood of dysfunctionality, and unless or until children arrive, some of the latent functions of the family might replace some of the manifest functions. Dysfunctionality, if present, might thus be harder to define or determine, but upon its emergence it would be harder to ignore without the children to "hold the family together."

Traditionalists would say that the second household is not yet a family until it produces children, while modernists and postmodernists might blur the traditional concepts of marriage and family by subsuming them into the more inclusive concept of a household. Until the basic functions of a modern household are clearly articulated, the concept of a "dysfunctional household" is unlikely to appear in the sociological literature. Meanwhile, some allegedly dysfunctional families may in fact be functional or marginally functional households of another as yet unidentified or undefined sort. Some single-parent households are now recognized as more functional than they were once thought to be, although there is a general consensus that two compatible parents can usually do a better job than one overextended parent.

It is not merely the high frequency of divorce, separation, and single parenting that is often taken to be indicative of increasing familial dysfunctionality. Multiple career households, latchkey households, domestic-violence statistics, illegitimate births (especially to teenage mothers), and the declining role and status of the extended family are also cited by family values advocates, academicians, and various others as symptoms of growing troubles on the domestic scene. Blended or reconstituted families are increasingly prevalent and often have unique problems of their own in addition to the types of problems they tend to share with nuclear families. At the same time, the high remarriage rate in itself is fairly persuasive evidence that despite its frequent failings the family is likely to persevere in some viable form(s) as a social institution. Other adjustments and accommodations, such as the increasing ages of both parties in first marriages, the willingness to defer childbearing, and the decreasing number of children per household tend to support this claim.

Social Changes and Awareness. Whether alternative familial structures will become the social equals of the nuclear family remains to be seen, but there is clear evidence of a trend in that direction. Thus, the neofunctionalists may ultimately prevail on familial issues, after assimilating the highly relevant criticisms of their opponents.

To say that the family is successfully enduring a period of rapid social change and adaptation is not to say that it is never dysfunctional. Highly abusive, disruptive, or exploitative relationships in which spouses, children, stepchildren, or elderly relatives are routinely victimized are quite clearly dysfunctional in many cases. Alcohol and other drugs frequently aggravate the situation. In some cases the best solution both for the participants and for society is to dissolve the original domestic unit, a consequence which the structural functionalists of the 1950's were somewhat unprepared to accept. Not all broken homes are healthy enough to repair, and researchers have come to realize that the tendency toward the abuse of people and substances, toward exploitation, and toward people's susceptibility to intrafamilial victimization are personal characteristics that can often pass from generation to generation by way of negative role models.

In many cases children who grow up believing that adverse behavior patterns are perfectly "normal" replicate the dysfunctional family settings of previous generations. However, certain familial behaviors that were once widely tolerated or routinely denied have gradually been relabeled as socially deviant, and the resulting social awareness may ultimately help reduce their incidence. Meanwhile, many stigmatized behaviors still persist with alarming frequency, and only the most extreme or perverse can clearly be categorized as aspects of dysfunctional families per se rather than as deviant behaviors which often happen to occur in family settings.

Signs for the Future and Reflections on the Past. As the family redefines itself in the crucible of social change, it remains remarkably durable and functional despite premature reports of its impending demise. Some of its flaws endure as well. Yet changing sex roles, receding gender stereotypes, declining paternalism, greater marital egalitarianism, and the emergence of a new sensitivity to the rights and needs of children are all optimistic signs for the future. To avoid the vacuous tautology that "every modern family is somehow dysfunctional," the overly sloganized phrase "dysfunctional family" should thus be applied primarily to extremely adverse cases of abuse and exploitation. Codependency is another highly symptomatic characteristic that is often found in dysfunctional families, and upon careful analysis it is probably found to some extent in almost all families. Yet it would be equally uninformative to say that "all family members are codependent." Thus, this label, too, should usually be saved for the obvious extreme cases.

Whatever terminology is used to describe the problems of the modern family and its various nontraditional analogues, it should be frankly admitted that the perfectly functional nuclear family of the *Ozzie and Harriet* era was largely a nostalgic cultural myth, whose latent functions if fully realized might have been just as dysfunctional as its manifest functions were thought to be functional at the time. Family processes are now taken to be just as indicative of social health as family structures were once thought to be. Diversity has joined functionality as a dominant cultural theme, but a clear trade-off between the two has yet to emerge.

National Issues Forums on Troubled Families. In 1995 the National Issues Forums selected "The Troubled American Family" as a special topic for discussion in focus groups and public forums. With the assistance of the Public Agenda Foundation, the forums identified three fundamental choices that have had significant social support: the revival of traditional values, the promotion of parental responsibility, and the expansion of socie-

In the Oscar-winning film Ordinary People *(1980) an ostensibly happy and successful American family was torn apart by dysfunction.* (Museum of Modern Art, Film Stills Archive)

tal responsibility. Each of these choices appeals to a somewhat different constituency, but there is also considerable overlap, particularly in their strong concern for the welfare of children. The National Issues Forum booklet *The Troubled American Family* remains one of the most balanced and readable summaries of the modern discussion of familial issues.   —*Tom Cook*

BIBLIOGRAPHY

Bernard, Jessie. *The Future of Marriage.* New York: World, 1972. Frequently cited feminist critique of the institutions of marriage and family, emphasizing the divergent perspectives that males and females bring to these institutions.

Goode, William. *The Family.* Englewood Cliffs, N.J.: Prentice-Hall, 1964. Standard structural functionalist account of the family in all its relevant aspects, written just after the high point of functionalist ascendancy on such topics.

Merton, Robert. *Social Theory and Social Structure.* Glencoe, Ill.: Free Press, 1949. Classic source of structural functionalist theory, including the fundamental distinction between manifest functions and latent functions of social institutions and activities.

National Issues Forums. *The Troubled American Family.* Dubuque, Iowa: Kendall/Hunt, 1995. Balanced modern account of the family and its problems, with three alternative choices and additional bibliography for each choice.

Parsons, Talcott, and R. F. Bales, eds. *The American Family: Its Relation to Personality and Social Structure.* Glencoe, Ill.: Free Press, 1955. Collection of typical functionalist writings on familial issues, including Parson's classic essay on "Family Socialization and Interaction Processes," which is frequently anthologized elsewhere.

Skolnick, Arlene. *Embattled Paradise: The American Family in an Age of Uncertainty.* New York: Basic Books, 1991. Modern sociological account of familial issues, stressing the need for a flexible outlook and redefinitions of key basic concepts.

_____, et al., eds. *Family, Self, and Society: Toward a New Agenda for Family Research.* Hillsdale, N.J.: Lawrence Erlbaum, 1993. The final chapter written by Skolnick and several others in this anthology explores many key issues related to family functionality and family issues.

See also Alcoholism and drug abuse; Behavior disorders; Bradshaw, John; Child abuse; Codependency; Domestic violence; Family counseling; Family crises; Family therapy; Incest; Mead, George H.; Recovery programs.

Earned income tax credit

DATE: Enacted on February 18, 1975, as part of the Tax Reduction Act of 1975
RELEVANT ISSUES: Economics and work; Law
SIGNIFICANCE: The earned income tax credit, an attempt to use the tax system as a method of social policy, provided for government cash payments to lower-income families with children

The earned income tax credit is traceable to the early attempts to reform the nation's welfare system. In 1969 President Richard M. Nixon proposed a guaranteed annual income as part of his Family Assistance Plan. Under this plan, the government was to establish a minimum income level, and Americans, whether employed or not, would have been eligible for coverage. No American family would have been permitted, under Nixon's proposal, to fall below a certain income level. Nixon's Family Assistance Plan was controversial and was opposed by both Democrats and Republicans. Although it was passed by the House of Representatives, it was defeated in the Senate. Nevertheless, the concept, in a much-revised format, became the earned income tax credit.

The earned income tax credit became part of American public policy in 1975, when Congress passed a new tax law. One component of this law provided for government cash payments to lower-income families with children. While not as far-reaching in scope as Nixon's plan, the earned income tax credit has become an important part of American social welfare policy. During the 1980's the administration of President Ronald Reagan supported increases in the program, and in 1993 the administration of President Bill Clinton supported an expansion of the program.

—*Michael E. Meagher*

See also Child and dependent care tax credit; Family demographics; Family economics; Tax laws; Work.

East Indians and Pakistanis

RELEVANT ISSUES: Parenting and family relationships; Race and ethnicity
SIGNIFICANCE: Immigrants to North America from the Indian subcontinent attempt to maintain their cultural identities while striving to integrate successfully into mainstream American culture

The 1990 U.S. census counted 1.4 million East Indians and a half million Pakistanis and Bangladeshis. Even though the United States has far fewer immigrants from the Indian subcontinent than from several other Asian and Middle Eastern countries, the former became the fastest-growing immigrant group in the 1990's. The Indians and Pakistanis who have migrated to the United States and Canada since the 1960's represent a highly professional and educated class. Some 62 percent of them have earned undergraduate and graduate degrees. South Asians are concentrated primarily in several large urban centers, such as New York, Los Angeles, San Francisco, Philadelphia, and Chicago, although sizable numbers also live in smaller cities. Evidence has suggested that permanent communities of South Asians have established themselves in several big cities.

Family Size. The size of the average East Indian and Pakistani family in the United States is small: 3.2 people per household. Families are usually nuclear, with parents and children living by themselves. However, groups of close relatives may live in the same area and maintain frequent contact with one another. Parents of Indian couples living in the United States quite commonly visit their children for several months, but they face relative isolation because they lack social contacts with persons with similar backgrounds.

Within families from the Indian subcontinent, husbands have remained the authority figures even in homes where wives have professional careers. Wives must often contend with the pressures of the "second shift" and their husbands' continuing demands for special privileges. Divorce has continued to be rare among all groups of South Asians. Only 4.5 percent of East Indian and Pakistani households lack husbands and only 1.3 percent are headed by unmarried couples. While these immigrants have a higher per-capita income than other Americans, they consume less than those in the same income brackets. They put a great premium on savings and investment.

East Indian food consumption has been highly resistant to change. Most Indian Hindus avoid beef and pork, while Pakistanis avoid pork and alcoholic beverages. In households with children, American style meals have become more frequent, but traditional Indian meals predominate.

Community Relations. India is a culturally diverse country with sixteen major languages and several main religions. First-generation immigrants from the Indian subcontinent maintain the traditional values and rituals handed down to them as a way of preserving their identity. Most of them participate in organizations with others from their places of origin who speak the same language, practice the same religion, and eat the same foods. Visiting friends and entertaining guests from similar backgrounds are major leisure-time activities among Indians and Pakistanis. Preparing lavish feasts for guests is a common traditional practice, and anything less is considered bad manners. Among those who practice Islam, regular Sunday schools exist in which children are taught to read the Qur'an and how to pray. Among Hindus, religious practice is less rigid and the major Hindu festivals are conducted in temples, usually presided over by priests.

Children. South Asian children, both male and female, are usually indulged for the first five years of their lives. The age of five marks a transition in their lives; by then, they are expected to adhere to socially appropriate standards of behavior and to advance academically. The transition is more abrupt for boys than for girls. Indian and Pakistani immigrants' attitudes toward raising children have remained traditional. Rigidly defined sex roles are taught and reinforced by adults. Girls are expected to become proficient at housework, take care of younger siblings, and be sensitive to social cues, while boys are expected to be strong and academically successful. Families from the Indian subcontinent have not emphasized athletic competence as much as other American families. Such

attitudes have often been a source of conflict for young boys, whose parents have often not been willing to spend time or money in developing their children's athletic capacities to match those of their school peers.

Indian and Pakistani adolescents are expected by their families to excel in the sciences and enter science careers (preferably high-status and high-paying ones). Since mainstream American society places great emphasis on education, there is no conflict in this area. Yet, South Asian immigrants have not viewed education as the free, individualistic enterprise that the host society considers it. Children's educational achievements are regarded as contributing to families' social prestige.

Dating and Marriage. Children of South Asian immigrants, especially when they reach adolescence, face immense conflicts between parental values and peer pressure to conform to American customs, conflicts that have been especially pronounced in dating and marriage. Dating is usually forbidden, and arranged marriages are the preferred norm in most families. Girls are expected to remain virgins until they are married, and chastity is highly valued among Indian and Pakistani families when choosing brides for their sons. Parents consider sexual contact before marriage to be immoral and corrupt. There have been several reported cases in which lovers have eloped, married secretly, or even committed suicide because their relationships were unacceptable to their parents.

Most men and women from the Indian subcontinent prefer to return to their homelands for arranged marriages. Relatives back home establish ties with several prospective partners and their families. Eventually, immigrant sons and daughters go to South Asia for short visits in order to select from among the chosen candidates and marry. Muslim parents usually tolerate interfaith marriages for boys, since offspring are expected to follow the father's faith. Daughters' choices are more limited, because children of daughters could lose their Islamic affiliation.

Religion and Religious Holidays. When South Asians arrive in the United States and Canada, their religious attitudes become more lenient. Most Hindus fervently participate in religious activities, worshiping at home or at temples. Families with children practice their religions more often than families without children as a way of main-

Many East Indian Americans live lifestyles that differ little from those of other Americans. (Ben Klaffke)

Sikh family celebrating a traditional holiday in Toronto. (Dick Hemingway)

taining their children's sense of traditional consciousness.

Hindu and Muslim families celebrate most of their religious holidays as a way of keeping the heritage alive for their children. At such times, families renew social bonds and meet to discuss issues pertinent to their communities. East Indian children learn forms of classical (Indian) music and dance, and religious functions are a medium to display children's talents and skills. Hindu and Muslim schools have been opened in all areas with significant South Asian populations. Such schools are open on weekends and in the evenings to teach children basic religious practices.

A principal Hindu holiday is the Diwali, or the festival of lights, which celebrates the day Krishna, one of the principal gods in the Indian pantheon, killed the demon Kamsa. In India, streets and homes are usually lit up with oil lamps a month before the holiday. The night before the festival, firecrackers are lit and effigies of the demon Kamsa are burnt on street corners, while people sing praises to Krishna. The festivities continue the next day with more firecrackers, while friends and families exchange sweets and feast together.

Muslims' main holidays are Ramadan and aftar (breaking the fast at sunset). Prayers are held every evening followed by *taravih* (recital of

Newly arrived East Indian immigrants bring with them modes of dress that they are initially reluctant to shed. (Ben Klaffke)

Qur'anic verses). Devout Muslims begin fasting a month before Ramadan. Adults and children refrain from eating or drinking water from sunrise to sunset. Special prayers are offered at Eid-ul-Fitr (marking the end of the month of Ramadan) and Eid-ul-Adha (commemoration of the pilgrimage to Mecca). After prayers, families often gather together for feasts. —*Gowri Parameswaran*

BIBLIOGRAPHY
Aswad, Barbara, and Barbara Bilge. *Family and Gender Among American Muslims.* Philadelphia: Temple University Press, 1996.
Kurian, George, and Ram Srivastava. *Overseas Indians.* New Delhi, India: Viking, 1993.
Light, Ivan, and Parminder Bhachu. *Immigration and Entrepreneurship: Culture, Capital and Ethnic Networks.* New Brunswick, N.J.: Transaction Publishers, 1993.
Ng, Franklin, ed. *Asian American Encyclopedia.* 6 vols. New York: Marshall Cavendish, 1995.
Pyong Gap Min. *Asian Americans.* Thousand Oaks, Calif.: Sage Publications, 1995.
Saran, Parmatma. *The Asian Indian Experience in the USA.* New Delhi, India: Vikas Publishing House, 1985.
Vaidyanathan, Prabha, and Josephine Naidu. *Asian Indians in Western Countries: Cultural Identity and the Arranged Marriage.* Amsterdam, the Netherlands: Swets & Zeitlinger, 1991.

See also Chinese Americans; Filipino Americans; Hinduism; Holidays; Japanese Americans; Middle Easterners; Muslims; Southeast Asian Americans.

Eating disorders

RELEVANT ISSUES: Children and child development; Health and medicine; Parenting and family relationships

SIGNIFICANCE: As eating disorders are a manifestation of problems in a family or substitute family, treatment must thus include a family component in order for persons to completely recover

The decision to diet, or restrict one's eating, begins as an attempt at self-improvement. Because the American culture of the late twentieth century has promoted thinness as being healthy and beautiful, persons' decision to diet is supported by friends and family. It is not well understood what turns a decision to diet into an eating disorder, but that decision affects friends and family as long as the eating disorder continues.

Three Forms of Eating Disorders. Eating disorders take one of three forms: anorexia nervosa, bulimia nervosa, and binge eating disorder. The prevalence and demographics vary between them. The least prevalent eating disorder is anorexia nervosa, in which persons act to achieve marked weight loss and have a morbid fear of fatness. This disorder normally begins around puberty. Only 4 percent of sufferers contract the disorder when they reach college age or adulthood.

Bulimia nervosa is diagnosed about four times as often as anorexia nervosa, and there is an even larger subgroup that displays some of the behaviors of the disorder but that is not diagnosed as suffering from it. Because the onset of bulimia nervosa occurs during late adolescence or early adulthood, families are not always the first to notice it. Bulimics have a powerful urge to overeat, and their response to their feelings of self-loathing over their lack of control results in purging to expel food. This purging is accomplished most often by vomiting, but diuretics, laxatives, or excessive exercising is also used.

Recommended Weights for Women Aged 25+			
Height (in inches)	**Weight (in pounds)**		
	Small Frame	*Medium Frame*	*Large Frame*
4'10"	96-104	101-113	109-125
4'11"	99-107	104-116	112-128
5'0"	102-110	107-119	115-131
5'1"	105-113	110-122	118-134
5'2"	108-116	113-126	121-138
5'3"	111-119	116-130	125-142
5'4"	114-123	120-135	129-146
5'5"	118-127	124-139	133-150
5'6"	122-131	128-143	137-154
5'7"	126-135	132-147	141-158
5'8"	130-140	136-151	145-163
5'9"	134-144	140-155	149-168
5'10"	138-148	144-159	153-173

Source: Metropolitan Life Insurance Company

Despite her great success as a singer, Karen Carpenter (pictured with her brother, Richard Carpenter, and producer Herb Alpert) died at thirty-two of a heart attack brought on by anorexia nervosa. (AP/Wide World Photos)

Bulimics, with their cycles, often maintain a near normal weight, so that friends and family may praise them for doing so well with their diets. Ten times more females than males suffer from both anorexia nervosa and bulimia nervosa. High-risk groups for both disorders involve populations in which there is either a perceived or real need to maintain low weight or a specific weight. Common examples of sufferers include models and athletes. There is a subpopulation of athletes with anorexia athletica, those who lose enough weight to affect performance but cannot stop such behavior. In females, this can lead to the female athlete triad, a group of symptoms that begins with an eating dis-order leading to amenorrhea, lack of menstrual cycles, loss of estrogen and, if continued for at least six months to a year, a potential significant loss of bone structure that can cause osteoporosis (decrease in bone density leading to the disintegration of the bones).

The third eating disorder, binge eating, is much more common than anorexia nervosa and bulimia nervosa. It occurs in 5 to 8 percent of the obese population, or among approximately two and a half million people. The ratio of female to male incidence is about three to two, and the age of onset is twenty to fifty years. It has a very similar diagnosis as the bingeing of bulimics, but patients do not purge, resulting in weight gains that usually are not treated until patients reach the point of obesity, or normal weight exceeded by at least 20 percent. Treatment is often sought because patients suffer from secondary illnesses that have a strong link to obesity, such as hypertension or diabetes. Thus, treatment includes controlling eating. As with anorexia nervosa and bulimia nervosa, binge eating has a psychological component that is either part of the cause of the disorder, such as low self-esteem, or its result, such as depression or disgust.

Self-Control and Eating Disorders. Many professionals treating patients with eating disorders feel that such disorders are only a manifestation of other problems. Problems can include interaction with family or family substitutes during periods of conflict or stress, which patients handle by controlling eating, a part of life over which they have total control. Because persons with eating disorders have problems with control and autonomy with regard to food, these disorders can only occur where food is available in abundance. Poor people in Third World countries have no eating disorders, and obesity may even be considered a status symbol. The problem of control arises when persons receive contradictory signals. While advertisements for high caloric foods abound in the media, the same media preach the desirability of slimness and fitness, requiring self-control, dieting, and self-constraint. Although all women are exposed to these signals, only a small, but growing, percentage present clear-cut symptoms that make them diagnosable as having eating disorders.

Eating Disorders and Individuation. Families are involved in eating disorders, because whatever society has to offer in the way of values, expectations, and contradictions are conveyed through families in a filtered and modified form. Self-esteem, expectations, rights and duties of individual family members are internalized, perpetuated, or modified by the family situation. Professionals adhering to the Family of Origin model of treatment have coined the term "related individuation." They feel that family members with eating disorders attempt to put up walls in the family system that nonetheless remains united. Different family dynamics contribute to producing anorectics or bulimics, but they develop over generations and inhibit patients from becoming individuals.

Family histories are systems of stages that change constantly. In order to remain part of a family, all members must react to and come to terms with the family changes that affect their individual development, reshaping their relationship to the family. Family members with eating disorders do not experience the process of individuation, including understanding and drawing boundaries between their own self-perceptions and personal rights and those of other family members or of society at large; becoming independent of the family; being able to accept criticism; and, most important, being willing and able to assume responsibility for one's own behavior. Although becoming an individual is not meant to exclude the relatedness of families, all family members must change in order to maintain relatedness. They have to remember that conflict may be a part of the process, and they must be able to develop a plan to work out disagreements, even if this includes some separation. Parents must teach their young children the values they need to develop. As children get older, parents must be willing to negotiate with them rather than dictate.

Anorectic and Bulimic Families. There are subtle differences between anorectic and bulimic families. The anorectic eating disorder most often manifests itself around puberty. The physical changes associated with puberty may occur before young people are emotionally ready and at a time when adolescents are attempting to separate from the family. Peer pressure may encourage adolescents to question family values, which is interpreted as a threat to the family unit.

Eating disorders may develop as a way for girls to prove their autonomy both against their parents and their own bodies. Girls report feelings of triumph and gratification when they exercise control over their eating, leading to a distortion of reality and the insistence that their skeletal thinness is normal, healthy, and even aesthetically pleasing. They never triumph completely, however, because the preoccupation with food continues to dictate many of their actions. Families that are inflexible are often ill-equipped to deal with separation, leading to familial stress. Other causes of stress may include tragic events such as family deaths.

Families with members suffering from bulimia nervosa generally experience the onset of the disorder when children approach adulthood. The physical separation that often occurs when young family members go to college or begin employment may serve as a catalyst for bulimia nervosa. Bulimics may also belong to substitute families, such as living groups or sports teams. In such cases, their actual families may not be directly involved in the eating disorder. As in anorexia nervosa, control is also an issue in bulimia nervosa, but it may be an external factor, such as inappropriate achievement goals, chaotic lifestyles, or separation anxiety. Bulimics engage in a constant power struggle; they are out of control while bingeing and in control while purging, which may be perceived as a loss of control if it becomes automatic.

Economic Impact. The economic impact of eating disorders on families can be enormous. Often treatment requires that patients stay for extended periods at care facilities. Insurance companies recognize eating disorders, but because they lack standards of care, patients may be forced to pay significant out-of-pocket expenses. For optimum care, treatment teams of physicians, therapists, and registered dietitians must work together with families of patients with eating disorders. Treatments that begin when family members show only a tendency for abnormal eating behaviors have a greater chance of success than treatments that deal with diagnosed eating disorders. About 20 percent of anorexics and a smaller percentage of bulimics die from their disorders. Efforts must be made to help young people at critical stages in their lives develop positive self-images, including realistic body images and ways to handle the stress of becoming independent. —*Wendy E. S. Repovich*

BIBLIOGRAPHY

American Psychiatric Association. *Diagnostic and Statistical Manual of Mental Disorders.* 4th ed. Washington, D.C.: American Psychiatric Association, 1994.

Boskind-White, Marlene, and William C. White. *Bulimarexia: The Binge/Purge Cycle.* New York: W. W. Norton, 1983.

Brownell, Kelly, and John Foreyt, eds. *Handbook of Eating Disorders.* New York: Basic Books, 1986.

Lemberg, R., ed. *Controlling Eating Disorders with Facts, Advice, and Resources.* Phoenix: Oryx Press, 1992.

Liu, Aimme. *Solitaire: A Young Woman's Triumph over Anorexia.* New York: Harper & Row, 1980.

Pipher, Mary Bray. *Reviving Ophelia: Saving the Selves of Adolescent Girls.* New York: Putnam, 1994.

See also Child molestation; Codependency; Eating habits of children; Emotional abuse; Family counseling; Family therapy; Foodways; Health problems; Mealtaking; Recovery programs.

Eating habits of children

RELEVANT ISSUES: Children and child development; Health and medicine

SIGNIFICANCE: Developing good eating habits in infants and young children prepares them for good physical, mental, and social development and may prevent future health problems

Developing good eating habits in children begins before birth. Parents, grandparents, siblings, and other caretakers should have good eating habits, because they serve as role models for children.

Infant Feeding. Breast milk is the preferred food for newborns. It provides the proper proportion of nutrients and the antibodies infants need. Furthermore, there is a reduced risk of allergies in the breast-fed child. This is especially important in families in which a history of allergies is present. In addition to strong bonding between mothers and infants, breast-feeding promotes the proper development of jaws, teeth, and subsequent speech patterns. When an infant is breast-fed, there is less possibility of overfeeding. It is also rare for breast-fed infants to develop baby bottle tooth decay, which often occurs when bottle-fed infants are put to bed with formulas or other liquids containing sugar.

If mothers cannot or do not want to breast-feed their infants, formula feeding is a good option. It allows others to feed the infants and to make eating an enjoyable experience for them. To ensure this, babies should always be held when fed, and adults should interact with them. They should watch for cues that the infants are full and guard against overfeeding, which may lead to poor eating habits in the future. Solids, fruit juices, or other sweetened beverages should never be put in an infant's bottle. Solid foods should be offered with a spoon, because one of the reasons for feeding solids is to teach children how to eat them and to develop the appropriate muscles. Liquids other

Playing with food is common among young children. (Long Hare Photographs)

than formulas and water should be introduced from a cup when babies are about seven to ten months old.

Infants respond positively to sweet tastes. As caretakers observe this satisfaction in infants, they often promote it by adding other sweets to the diet. Because infants respond negatively to bitter and sour foods, adults often avoid them. When solids are generally added to infants' diets when they are four to six months old, infants show a preference for salty foods. Because adults often prefer salted foods themselves, they may add salt to babies' food, thereby increasing infants' desire to consume it. The taste for salt increases in pro-

portion to the amount consumed. Thus, the habit of adding salt to food, often before even tasting it, is encouraged at an early age.

When infants first begin to consume solid foods, it is most appropriate to begin with iron-fortified infant rice cereal. Caregivers may follow up with single-ingredient vegetables and fruits. Infants may accept sweet potatoes and carrots more readily than other foods because they are sweet. Only one new food should be introduced at a time, and it should be continued for three to five days before another new food is added. This procedure allows infants to accept new foods, while allowing providers to determine if infants are allergic to them.

Familiarity is as important as taste in determining children's food preferences. When children's first teeth begin to emerge, it is time to add slightly lumpy foods so that they can learn to chew. As soon as infants can grasp, they may be given soft finger foods such as cooked carrots, peaches, or soft fresh bananas. It is important to add foods at appropriate times so that children begin to like them and can develop their eating habits, just as they develop in other ways.

Sweet desserts and fruit-flavored beverages should be avoided, as they provide calories and few other nutrients. They may increase the desire for sweets, thus reducing infants' capacity for other, more nutritious foods. Egg whites should not be given to infants until they are twelve months old because of the possibility of allergies. Foods such as popcorn, whole grapes, nuts, hot dogs, and raisins should be avoided, because infants or young children may choke on them. They should not be given gravy, fried potatoes, or other fried foods. Such foods increase their fat intake and may also reinforce their desire for other foods that are high in fat. Honey should never be given to infants because of the risk of botulism.

Feeding Toddlers. Infants grow rapidly and usually eat well, often doubling their birth weight at four months and tripling it at twelve. Because toddlers often show less interest in food and grow at a slower pace than infants, many parents and caretakers begin to worry unnecessarily. One method of avoiding this concern is to weigh and measure children periodically and to record the measurements on growth charts. The growth charts most commonly used are those developed by the National Center for Health Statistics. They are available for both boys and girls from birth to thirty-six months of age and for children aged two to eighteen. In using these charts, it is essential that children be measured accurately, that the measurements be recorded correctly, and that the records be properly evaluated. Because children grow at different rates, growth spurts or periods of slow growth should be expected. If spurts or slow growth continue, the children should be taken to a physician. Regular increases in weight and height usually indicate that children are eating well and growing appropriately.

Preschoolers usually prefer plain foods served at moderate temperatures. Appropriate foods include milk, tender meat, fish, poultry, vegetables, fruits, breads, and other grains. Occasionally, puddings, custards, gelatin, ice milk, or cookies may be served. In general, if children are offered suitable nutritious foods, they will eat adequate amounts. Their intake may vary from day to day depending on appetite, but over several days it will average out. At this age, children should be provided the right kinds of foods by caretakers, but it is children's option to determine how much to eat. Most toddlers need to eat five to six times a day. These meals and snacks should be planned and served on a regular basis, and uneaten food should be removed. No other food should be offered to toddlers until the next meal or snack time. As a rule of thumb, portions should be about one tablespoon of food per year of life. Thus, a two-year-old might eat two tablespoons of meat, vegetables, and fruit, half a slice of bread, and about half a cup of milk. It is better for children to have the option to ask for seconds rather than to discourage them from eating by overloading their plates. One should never encourage the "clean plate club" by forcing children to eat everything they are served. This can lead to overeating in the future.

Nutrient Intake. If children eat well, vitamin and mineral supplements are not necessary. The best source of nutrients is food. Children can confuse some vitamin and mineral supplements for candy and eat them like snacks. Consuming too much iron and vitamins A and D can be dangerous to children's health. Most children meet their needs for calories, protein, vitamins, and minerals. The nutrients most often lacking in children's diets are iron, calcium, and zinc. An iron deficiency may result in poor growth and development, decreased attentiveness, and decreased learning ability. Sources of iron include meat, poultry, enriched and whole-grain cereals, legumes, and nuts. Iron from animal sources is better utilized, but the absorption of iron from vegetable sources can be improved by including vitamin C in children's meals. For example, orange juice can be served with an iron-fortified cereal or with a peanut butter sandwich. Another source of iron is provided by cooking in iron pots. Calcium is essential for the growth of strong bones and teeth. Milk, cheese, yogurt, and calcium-fortified orange juice are all good sources of calcium. Zinc is essential

for building proteins, developing a good appetite, and proper growth. Sources of zinc include meat, dairy products, and whole-grain cereals.

Health Problems. Excessive consumption of total fats, saturated fats, and sodium is more of a problem in the United States than specific nutrient deficiencies. Obesity is on the rise. Decreased physical activity is more frequently the cause of obesity than high caloric intake. The consumption of calories has remained stable, but physical activity has decreased over the years. In general, the more television children watch, the more likely they are to be obese. Food insecurity, which is defined as a lack of enough kinds and amounts of food, a lack of the kinds of food desired, or insufficient food, exists in some homes. This can also lead to future obesity, as persons who fear not having enough to eat overcompensate by eating too much.

Lead poisoning in children may cause poor growth and damage the nervous system, resulting in lowered intelligence quotients (IQ) and in

Aversion to vegetables is common among children. (James L. Shaffer)

Early instruction in proper dental care is an important corollary to proper nutrition. (Long Hare Photographs)

learning disabilities. Common sources of lead are old lead water pipes and lead-based paint. Regular meals that are high in iron, calcium, and zinc can hinder the absorption of lead. Dental cavities may be decreased by the regular use of fluoridated water, infrequent use of concentrated sweets, and regular brushing and flossing.

Constipation caused by lack of dietary fiber and water in the diet may be a health problem for some children. Dietary fiber may be increased by consuming more fruits, vegetables, whole-grain cereals, and bread. Fiber may also reduce the risk of heart disease, some cancers, and adult-onset diabetes in later life. The consumption of fruit

juices should be limited, because they may replace milk consumption, they are high in simple sugar, and they do not have as much fiber as fruits.

Feeding Concerns and Food Allergies. Children often go on food jags, eating only peanut butter sandwiches, hamburgers, or hot dogs for several days. Usually, if these jags are ignored or casually accepted, they will stop before long. If children refuse to eat meat, caretakers may substitute peanut butter, tuna fish, chicken, or eggs. If they refuse vegetables, they may be offered raw or slightly cooked vegetables that have been prepared in a microwave oven or steamed to retain their color. Fruit can also be served more frequently. If chil-

Between-meal snacking disrupts the eating habits of many children and adults. (James L. Shaffer)

dren refuse to drink milk, powdered milk can be added to mashed potatoes, meat loaf, or hot cereals. Yogurt, cheese, or pudding are appropriate nutrient substitutes for milk. Children may also drink milk more readily if they are allowed to pour it from a small pitcher.

Small amounts of new foods should be introduced with familiar foods. If children refuse one or two foods, adults should not be concerned; usually another equally nutritious food item can be substituted. Also, review the food habits of caretakers, parents, peers, and siblings to ensure that they are setting a positive example for children.

Eggs, milk, nuts, wheat, soy, and shellfish are the most common food allergens, although children may also be allergic to such foods as citrus fruits and strawberries. Caution must be taken if children are allergic to foods, because they may cause multiple symptoms. Most children outgrow allergies to milk and soy as they get older. Food intolerances may be caused by proteins, sugars, fats, toxins, or food additives. If food allergies or intolerances are numerous, children's diets should be evaluated for adequacy.

Eating Can Be Fun. Meal time should be a social time. At home parents should serve as role models and eat with their children. Both adults and children should enjoy family-style meals together in child-care centers. Socialization is important and both adults and children should talk with each other. Most important, eating should be a pleasant experience. If a wide variety of nutritious food is offered in a pleasant environment, children will usually select the amount of food they need to grow into healthy, happy, productive adults.

—*Margaret Ann McCarthy*

BIBLIOGRAPHY
Birch, Leann L. "Children's Food Acceptance Patterns." *Nutrition Today* 31 (1996). Describes the effects of early learning and experience on children's acceptance of food.
Constable, George, et al., eds. *Food and Your Child.* Alexandria, Va.: Time-Life Books, 1988. Colorfully illustrated book that presents nutrition information for infants and children up to the age of six and includes hints on how to involve preschoolers in nutrition education, food preparation, and meal planning.
Evers, Connie L. *How to Teach Nutrition to Kids.* Tigard, Oreg.: Carrot Press, 1995. Presents information on nutrition education for children aged six to ten and includes such topics as the food pyramid, nutrition labeling, childhood obesity, eating disorders, and exercise.
Kennedy, Ellen, and Jeanne Goldberg. "What Are American Children Eating? Implication for Public Policy." *Nutrition Reviews* 53 (1995). Describes surveys and studies of children's diets in the United States and Canada and includes suggestions for developing public policy to counteract poor eating habits by stressing a healthful diet and increased physical activity.
Lin, Biing-Hwan, and Joanne Guthrie. "Nutritional Quality of American Children's Diets." *FoodReview* 10 (January-April, 1996). Reviews data from the U.S. Department of Agriculture's 1989-91 Continuing Survey of Food Intakes by Individuals, focusing on food intake by children and adolescents between the ages of two and seventeen.
Satter, Ellyn. *Child of Mine: Feeding with Love and Good Sense.* Palo Alto, Calif.: Bull, 1991. Utilizes the knowledge gained from the fields of dietary science, social work, and parenting to guide parents through the important early years of developing good food habits in their children.
Tamboriane, William V., ed. *The Yale Guide to Children's Nutrition.* New Haven, Conn.: Yale University Press, 1997. Presents a comprehensive guide to childhood nutrition for parents and discusses normal growth and development of children, common nutrition concerns of parents, and nutrition under special conditions.
Trahms, Christine M., and Peggy L. Pipes, eds. *Nutrition in Infancy and Childhood.* 6th ed. New York: McGraw-Hill, 1997. Presents an overview of growth and development in infants and children and includes comprehensive coverage of the nutritional needs of both healthy and sick children from infancy through adolescence, the development of food habits, and the prevention of chronic diseases through dietary intervention.

See also Breast-feeding; Eating disorders; Foodways; Gray, John; Mealtaking; Supplemental Nutrition Program for Women, Infants, and Children.

Echo effect

RELEVANT ISSUES: Demographics; Health and medicine
SIGNIFICANCE: As the female members of the baby-boom generation reached their prime childbearing years, a second baby boom was created as an "echo" of the first

The term "echo effect" was used by demographers from the late 1970's through the early 1990's to refer to the situation in which a large number of American women belonging to the baby boom generation had reached the age at which they were most likely to bear children. The increase in the number of children born during these years was not the result of an increase in the fertility rate but was simply an inevitable result of the large number of women in their twenties and thirties. This second baby boom was also known as the "echo boom" or the "baby boomlet."

The baby boom began after World War II, when the number of births in the United States increased from 2.9 million in 1945 to 3.4 million in 1946. The boom lasted nearly twenty years, until the number of births dropped from four million in 1964 to 3.8 million in 1965. The number of births remained relatively low between 1965 and 1976, reaching its lowest point in 1973 with 3.1 million births. In 1977 the number of births began climbing again, reaching a peak of 4.2 million in 1990. The number of births remained above four million until 1994, the last year of the second baby boom.   —*Rose Secrest*

See also Baby-boom generation; Baby boomers; Family demographics; Generation X.

Edelman, Marian Wright

BORN: June 6, 1939, Bennettsville, S.C.
AREAS OF ACHIEVEMENT: Children and child development; Education; Health and medicine; Law
SIGNIFICANCE: In her career as an advocate for disadvantaged youth, Edelman created the Children's Defense Fund (CDF) to collect data and promote legislation

Influenced by her Baptist minister father, Marian Wright learned the importance of community service at a young age. As a student at Spelman College in Atlanta, Wright won a Merrill Scholarship and spent her junior year abroad. She spent a summer in Moscow under a Lisle Fellowship and considered pursuing a diplomatic career. Her dedication to civil rights, however, led her to pursue a career in the field of law.

In 1963 Wright graduated from Yale Law School. After graduation she became a staff attorney for the Legal Defense and Educational Fund of the National Association for the Advancement of Colored People (NAACP) in New York City. In 1964 she became the director of the NAACP office in Jackson, Mississippi, and was the first African American woman admitted to the Mississippi state bar. Wright testified before a U.S. Senate subcommittee at a public hearing in Jackson to inform national leaders about the poverty in Mississippi resulting from the mechanization of the cotton industry. In 1967 she took Senator Robert Kennedy and his legislative assistant, Peter Edelman, to the poorest communities in the Mississippi Delta, visiting families in houses without heat, light, or running water. Wright also helped to obtain federal funding for a Head Start antipoverty program to assist underprivileged children to prepare for elementary school.

Wright moved to Washington, D.C., in 1968 and married Peter Edelman. She soon founded the Washington Research Project, a public interest law firm that investigated the effectiveness of laws designed to help minorities and the poor. She became a liaison for the Poor People's Campaign in the summer of 1968. From 1971 to 1973 she served as director of the Center for Law and Education at Harvard University.

Marian Wright Edelman in 1996. (AP/Wide World Photos)

Returning to Washington, D.C., in 1973, she created the Children's Defense Fund (CDF), a nonprofit organization supported entirely by private foundations. The CDF works as an advocate for children, documenting conditions that affect them and lobbying intensively for legislation that would improve their lives. This organization challenges leaders to consider children when making crucial budget and policy decisions. In 1984 the CDF successfully lobbied for increased Medicaid coverage for poor children, with Edelman arguing that such coverage was a "preventive investment." In 1989 the CDF supported the Act for Better Child Care to provide child care for millions of families. The goals of the CDF have included the development and adequate funding of Head Start programs, foster care reform, programs for childhood immunization and prenatal care, family economic security, nutrition programs for poor women and children, and teenage pregnancy prevention. The CDF launched the 1996 Stand for Children movement to combat the political pressure for welfare reform, which Edelman considered harmful to children's interests.

Edelman has received more than 100 honorary degrees and a variety of other awards, including the Albert Schweitzer Humanitarian Prize. She wrote *Families in Peril: An Agenda for Social Change* (1987) and the best-seller *The Measure of Our Success: A Letter to My Children* (1992). She and Peter Edelman have three sons.

—*Kathryn Dennick-Brecht*

See also Child Care and Development Block Grant Act; Children's Defense Fund (CDF); Children's rights; Head Start.

Educating children

RELEVANT ISSUES: Children and child development; Demographics; Race and ethnicity; Religious beliefs and practices

SIGNIFICANCE: Since the last decades of the nineteenth century, education has been regarded as a universal right of all citizens and a critical element in the achievement of self-development and prosperity

During the early nineteenth century parents considered education as a means of developing those skills needed by children to lead moral lives. In the late nineteenth century, however, parents began to see education as essential for children to lead productive, successful, and profitable lives. The belief that a sound education was essential for people to obtain rewarding jobs and achieve personal goals was the basis of the movement to ensure that all children receive free public education. During the twentieth century, this conviction led to the passage of legislation that defined the educational rights of children with disabilities.

Many educators have turned to the public in order to gain political leverage for their approaches to instruction. Parents have responded emotionally to warnings that education has allegedly gone in an erroneous direction. Confrontational disputes were evident during the first half of the twentieth century among progressive educators, who supported child-centered approaches to instruction that considered textbooks dispensable, and traditional educators, who supported the use of precisely developed curricula that emphasized the acquisition of skills through textbooks. The responses of these two groups were predictable when innovations in emerging technology, vocational education, and changes in the format and content of textbooks were introduced. Progressive educators supported such innovations only to the extent that they could be incorporated into their child-centered philosophies. In a parallel fashion, traditional educators supported such innovations only to the extent that they did not disrupt the curriculum-focused approach that they judged to be essential to effective education.

Assessment. Few innovations have had as great an impact on education as assessment. At the beginning of the twentieth century testing was conducted by teachers to assess those aspects of instruction which they personally judged to be important to their students. However, standardized assessment emerged as a prospect during the early 1900's, when elementary and high school curricula became progressively standardized. One of the factors contributing to this movement was the publication of uniform textbooks, in which common sets of critical information were presented. Not only was information presented in such textbooks, but it was also arranged in the sequence that students were expected to learn it. Information was sequenced because it was thought that certain types of information were

For most children formal education begins in kindergarten around age five. (Don Franklin)

simpler to learn than others and that the mastery of simpler information could facilitate the learning of more advanced concepts.

Once a common curriculum had been established and the grades identified by which students should have mastered specific materials, students could be evaluated not only in their classrooms, but also in their schools, districts, states, and nationwide. Edward Thorndike, a Columbia University professor during the early 1900's, devised procedures that fostered the development of standardized tests. Standardization was a statistical procedure to ensure that all persons taking a test would have the identical opportunity to demonstrate their knowledge of the materials under examination. Although standardized tests were used before World War I, they became extremely popular when they were used to massively test soldiers during the war. Not only standardized tests, but also informal, diagnostic tests by teachers and aux-

iliary specialists in the schools were increasingly administered. Authors of books on assessment written in the early 1930's estimated that more than 500 standardized tests had been developed and were being used in the schools.

One reason that tests were controversial was that their results did not always present a positive view of the schools. In the case of reading, testing revealed that the number of illiterate or marginally literate persons was much greater than generally suspected. During the 20-year period from 1930 to 1950, studies indicated that as many as 40 percent of students in the schools were not learning to read effectively. Annual testing of high-school seniors preparing to enter college during the 1960's and 1970's indicated that their reading ability continued to decline. Tests in other academic areas revealing students' inadequate knowledge of history, government, geography, and mathematics alarmed the public.

Critics pointed to incompetent teaching, poor administration of the schools, and the development of inappropriate curricula as factors responsible for the problems revealed by tests. Other critics, however, assaulted the tests themselves and questioned the validity of their results. Some who lacked confidence in standardized tests suggested that low scores were the results of testing biases that penalized certain types of students. For example, critics pointed to cultural, linguistic, and gender biases that unfairly penalized some learners.

Although assessment tests have revealed controversial data, they have been double-edged swords. Some persons who have scored poorly have complained that they were assessed unfairly, while others have looked to tests to validate their genuine knowledge. Students who have not completed high school but who pass tests to indicate their equivalent knowledge, or college students who have passed tests as an indication that they should not have to take certain university courses, have seen tests as opportunities as well as potential obstacles. Because assessment is controversial, a movement in the schools has developed to replace or supplement standardized tests with alternative forms of assessment. Portfolios, or files containing samples of learners' classroom work, diaries, observations by teachers, tape recordings of oral reports or readings, projects, and writing samples, may be the most popular example of alternative forms of assessment.

Home Schooling. Home schooling has always been an option available to individuals who lacked confidence in the public schools. Although there may be many reasons why parents choose to school their children at home, home schooling has been traditionally viewed as a haven for conservative Christians dissatisfied with secular public-school curricula. In 1980 less than 15,000 students received home schooling. By the middle of the 1990's this number had increased to more than a half million.

Home schooling has been legal in every state in the union and the District of Columbia. Yet, parents' ability to arrange home schooling has varied widely. In some states only parents who are certified teachers are permitted to manage home schools, while in others officials regularly inspect home schools to ensure that parents are following prescribed procedures. In some states parents need only notify officials that they intend to teach their children at home.

New Instructional Techniques. The most influential educator in the first half of the twentieth century was John Dewey. Together with his wife and several colleagues at the University of Chicago, Dewey established an experimental school in 1896. Although he maintained the school for only five years, it was the model for a highly popular approach to instruction that centered on the needs and aptitudes of individual learners rather

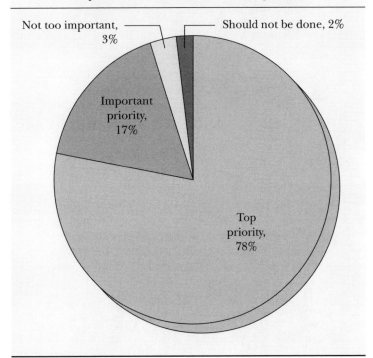

U.S. Public Opinion on the Need to Improve the Educational System

Not too important, 3%

Should not be done, 2%

Important priority, 17%

Top priority, 78%

Source: The Pew Research Center

Note: In early 1998 the PEW Research Center conducted a nationwide survey in which 1,200 adults were asked how high a priority improving the educational system should be for the federal government in the coming year. This table summarizes responses.

Despite advancements in learning technologies, teachers remain central in educating children. (James L. Shaffer)

than on textbooks or standardized curricula. Although the instructional strategies that Dewey's movement inspired went by different names, they were identified with the movement for progressive education that increased in popularity until the 1920's and waned during the 1930's and 1940's. Even after the demise of the progressive education movement, spontaneous, individualized approaches to learning similar to those used by progressive educators continued to be employed.

Instructional strategies similar to those recommended by progressive educators have more recently been characterized as holistic, implying that they were intended to teach the whole child and that they were distinct from the skills-based strategies opposed by progressives. The advocacy of holistic strategies during the 1970's and 1980's was particularly evident in the areas of reading, writing, and mathematics. The confrontation between proponents of holistic instructional strategies and the proponents of traditional instructional programs has filled professional journals and popular magazines and newspapers. Proponents of holistic instruction have claimed that their approaches have been built on the natural learning aptitudes exhibited by children in their out-of-school activities, whereas traditional programs require children to rely on artificial sets of learning skills. Proponents of traditional instruction have retorted that students who have learned through alternative approaches have lacked basic skills such as phonics in reading, spelling and grammar in writing, and calculation in mathematics.

Multicultural Education. During the early years of the twentieth century, some educators wrote about the need to ensure that immigrants in the United States quickly and efficiently learn to speak English. Conservative educators feared that non-English-speaking children threatened the development of a unified population committed to common values and political beliefs. However, even during this early period some educators disagreed that it was necessary to encourage children to abandon their native languages and familial customs. Roman Catholic schools were established in the Midwestern and Western states, in which not only religion, but also languages other than English and European customs were inculcated in students. The debate about the degree to which students in American schools should be taught a homogeneous language and curriculum became particular fervid during the late twentieth century, when some educators suggested that the dialect of African Americans should be treated as a separate language. In Canada, disputes about the advantages and disadvantages of French- and English-based schooling emerged as a central issue in educational forums.

The debates about multicultural and bilingual education have often focused on highly political rather than pedagogical issues. Conservative critics of multicultural and bilingual education have charged that all children in Western countries should be accountable for a common core of cultural information. During the 1930's persons holding this view referred to themselves as "essentialists." Proponents of multicultural education, on the other hand, have responded to nationalistic educators that learners' knowledge of their native languages and their ethnic identity is indispensable in diverse societies. As an indication of increasing social diversity in the United States, nonwhite, minority children will make up more than 40 percent of the school population during the initial years of the twenty-first century. Convinced that the United States and other Western countries are on the road to becoming "minority-majority" countries, some proponents of multicultural education have counseled that schools should implement special multicultural and multilinguistic curricula that will prepare learners for successful lives in a multicultural society. The types of programs that they have endorsed would enable all students to see themselves as capable of achieving their full potential. Ideally, such programs would develop learners' knowledge not only of their own group identity, but also of that of learners from other distinct backgrounds.

Education of Students with Special Needs. Most public schools at the beginning of the twentieth century did not accept responsibility for educating disabled learners. Early schools were segregated institutions at which learners with disabilities did not associate with their nondisabled peers. Additionally, these schools typically focused on children with a single disability, such as a hearing or visual disability. During the early 1900's educators spoke out about the needs of a full range of learners, including those with mild and severe disabilities. Many of these newly identified learners with disabilities were enrolled in the public schools but did not receive special education. By the 1920's the individualized instruction of learners with mild and moderate disabilities had expanded to many schools. In fact, the individualized instruction used in special education classes was so successful that educators began to ask whether an individualized approach relying on assessment should not be generalized to regular education as well.

During the 1930's and 1940's psychologists conducted research on the mild learning problems that eventually were referred to as learning disabilities. The most well-publicized of these learning disabilities was dyslexia, which was described as a specific inability to read by persons who exhibited normal and possibly even superior intelligence. Educators had been aware of such learning problems since the nineteenth century but had assumed that they had their origin in gross neurological or perceptual irregularities. Influenced by the research of psychologists, educators assumed that learning disabilities might be cognitive processing disorders similar to those that had been demonstrated among patients with brain lesions. Although specific learning disabilities in such areas as reading, writing, mathematics, and speech had already been probed by educators, it was not until the 1960's that special educators and the public became generally aware of them. The number of persons in the schools who had been diagnosed with learning disabilities increased geometrically year after year. By the 1980's learning disabilities were the primary reason that children were being admitted to special education classes.

Special education has been distinguished from regular education by a series of legislative initiatives and court cases that defined the rights of individuals with disabilities. Some pieces of legislation dealt with disabilities in the schools while others dealt with disabilities in the areas of employment and recreation. The Individual with Disabilities Education Act (IDEA), originally passed in 1975, precisely specified the rights of students with disabilities and ensured that all children, regardless of their degree of disability, would receive free, appropriate, public education in the least restrictive environments. If learners were to be placed in programs segregating them from their nondisabled peers, the appropriateness of this measure would have to be demonstrated. Nonsegregation was referred to popularly as "mainstreaming" and "inclusion." IDEA guaranteed that the rights of parents would be respected and that testing, conducted in a nondiscriminatory fashion, would be a component of special education.

Vocational Education. Vocational education was supported in the early 1900's by both progressive and conservative educators. Progressive educators applauded vocational education as a means of divesting the schools of curricula that they viewed as obsolete and incapable of preparing youth for the problems that they would confront on the job. They recommended that all children be exposed to the manual skills emphasized in vocational training. Many conservative educators who supported vocational education thought that two separate curricula should be available in the schools. Unlike progressive educators, conservatives recommended reserving a traditional liberal arts education for the brightest students while preparing the academically less talented for jobs in commerce and industry. These differences of opinion created an intellectual division that persisted into the late twentieth century. Debate still continues about whether vocational education should be an alternative to academic learning, typified by such subjects as reading, writing, mathematics, and social studies, or whether it should be taught in conjunction with traditional academic skills.

Technology Education. Although technology in education has been associated by many with computers, the role of technology in education has been discussed throughout the twentieth century. In the 1920's and 1930's educators debated the advantages and disadvantages of emerging technology such as radio, cinema, and television. Some saw an advantage in using media that seemed to motivate learners more than books. Others saw a disadvantage in the expense of purchasing and maintaining technology, the rapidity with which technology became obsolete, the shortage of teachers trained to use new technology, and the scarcity of educational programs designed for new media that were superior to traditional educational practices. Many educators were excited about the prospects of using television for closed-circuit, custom-designed educational programs. Generally, such prospects were too optimistic.

By the 1990's computers were finding their way into classrooms at all age levels. (James L. Shaffer)

Educators and the general public were disappointed by the failure of televised education to achieve the goals that had been set for it. They were particularly disappointed by many "talking-head" televised educational programs.

Although computers had been used for administrative purposes in the schools during the 1960's, computers became increasingly available for instructional purposes in the early 1970's. At this time the personal computer emerged, making computerized technology affordable and transportable into the classroom. Only limited software, however, was available for educational applications. Many software programs were referred to derisively as "drill and skill" programs or "electronic worksheets." Truly interactive computer

programs were eventually developed that employed ingenious techniques to foster higher-order problem-solving skills. As software became more sophisticated, teacher demand for computers increased correspondingly. From 1985 to 1995 the ratio of computers to learners in U.S. schools increased from less than one for every 125 students to approximately one for every 10 students.

Although a full range of programs has been devised for computerized education, a breakthrough occurred in the early 1990's when computers were used increasingly for communications-based activities. This breakthrough was facilitated by the availability of fast, low-priced communications hardware and the development of the Internet and the World Wide Web. The World Wide

Elementary schools often foster links with the home through exercises such as having children write letters to their parents. (Ben Klaffke)

Web used special software that made it possible to organize the Internet with text, graphics, sound, and video. By 1996 the World Wide Web contained conduits through which more than half of the information on the Internet was transferred to more than 20 million users. The amount of information available to teachers and students through the World Wide Web has become virtually limitless. In addition to having access to encyclopedias, special documents, and unique collections of information, students have been able to take electronic field trips and immerse themselves in formerly inaccessible resources. They have been able to correspond with others through electronic bulletin boards used for posting information, responding to notices posted by others, and collaborating on educational projects.

Textbooks. Although articles in newspapers have concentrated on electronic media, textbooks have continued to be the most popular educational medium. For the past one hundred years, textbooks have dominated education. However, they have also been challenged regularly. At the beginning of the twentieth century, critics contended that textbooks had effectively replaced classroom teachers because of the extent to which they relied on them. Teachers continued to rely on textbooks throughout the twentieth century, even after their qualifications had increased dramatically. During the communism scare in the United States between 1920 and 1990, textbooks were frequently attacked by conservative educators. Whereas progressive educators challenged textbooks for restricting teachers' creativity, conservative educators focused their attention on politically liberal textbooks, which they thought were undermining the morals and values needed in a democratic society. Such criticism was extended to the instructional methods reflected in textbooks that did not stress the rigorous learning of fundamental skills such as reading, writing, and mathematics.

Disputes about which textbooks to adopt became so contentious that many states adopted special procedures in which potential textbooks had to be selected from approved state lists. Populous states such as California and Texas represented critical markets, forcing textbook companies to ensure approval of their materials. Because publishers have tailored their materials to gain such approval, teachers in less populous states have complained that the larger publishing houses have developed a homogenized content and format based on the criteria of adoption committees in the populous states.

Sex Education. The degree to which moral education should be a component of public education has been controversial, because many parents believe that they, rather than the schools, should be responsible for teaching morality and ethics to their children. In a similar fashion, it may be inevitable that disputes would arise about the degree to which sex education should be introduced into school curricula. Many parents believe that sex education is a personal matter that should be taught how and when they prescribe it. Some parents also feel that information about sex, if not presented in the most careful manner, can actually increase, rather than restrict, sexual promiscuity. Pointing to numerous teen pregnancies, some educators have challenged the rights of parents to determine whether sex education shall be taught in the schools. Additionally, the high incidence of sexually transmitted diseases, including acquired immunodeficiency syndrome (AIDS), has been a significant factor influencing support for mandatory sex education within the public schools. Because of the prevalence of such diseases in large urban areas, some school districts have adopted policies in which they not only inform students about sex and how to avoid sexually transmitted diseases, but they also provide high-school students with birth control devices. In some school districts, such devices have been administered to students only with parental consent, while in others they have been distributed to students without parental consent. —*Gerard Giordano*

BIBLIOGRAPHY

Baker, Colin. *A Parents' and Teachers' Guide to Bilingualism.* Philadelphia: Multilingual Matters, 1995. In addition to questions about language acquisition, speech, and bilingualism, the author of this book answers questions about personal, scholastic, and familial issues on which bilingualism can impact.

Cannings, Terrence R., and LeRoy Finkel, eds. *The Technology Age Classroom.* Wilsonville, Oreg.: Franklin, Beedle & Associates, 1993. This book contains a comprehensive set of articles on the educational opportunities offered through computers and other technologies. The book contain reports and discussion about emerging technologies, educational benefits of technology-based education, and the future for technology in education.

Heward, William L. *Exceptional Children: An Introduction to Special Education.* 5th ed. Columbus, Ohio: Merrill, 1996. This well written textbook provides a complete overview of students with disabilities such as mental retardation, learning disabilities, emotional problems, communication disorder, deafness, and visual impairment. It includes a chapter on parents and families of learners with disabilities.

Kaplan, L., ed. *Rebuilding the Schoolhouse: Views and Issues in Education.* Boston: Allyn & Bacon, 1994. This edited anthology contains articles that appeared originally in *The Washington Post.* Chapters review controversial topics such as technology, sex education, religion in the schools, vocational education, multicultural issues, school choice, home schooling, and new teaching methods.

McGilp, Jacqueline, and Maureen Michael. *The Home-School Connection: Guidelines for Working with Parents.* Portsmouth, N.H.: Heinemann, 1994. The authors clearly identify the critical contribution that parents can make in supporting the education that their children are receiving in the schools. This book would be useful to both parents and teachers.

Oakes, Jeannie, and Martin Lipton. *Making the Best of Schools: A Handbook for Parents, Teachers, and Policymakers.* New Haven, Conn.: Yale University Press, 1990. This is a precisely written exposition of the diverse aspects of education about which parents are likely to have questions. Among the topics reviewed are testing, basic skills, tracking of learners, children with special needs, and the contribution of the home to learning.

Paciorek, Karen M., and Joyce M. Munro, eds. *Annual Editions: Early Childhood Education, 97198.* Sluice Dock, Conn.: Dushkin/McGraw-Hill, 1997. This book contains a sampling of stimulating articles about early childhood education. In addition to general articles, sections highlight the needs and responsibilities of families, educational practices, and emotional and moral guidance of young children.

Schneider, Barbara, and James S. Coleman. *Parents, Their Children, and Schools.* Boulder, Colo.: Westview, 1993. This comprehensive set of essays explores topics about education of interest to parents. Sections are included on the effects of parent involvement, public and private school choice, and the different formats for parent involvement in the schools.

See also Bedtime reading; Disciplining children; Educating children; Education for All Handicapped Children Act (EHA); Head Start; Home schooling; Learning disorders; Moral education; Private schools; Schools; Sex education.

Education for All Handicapped Children Act (EHA)

DATE: Proposed in Congress as Public Law 94-142 and enacted on November 29, 1975
RELEVANT ISSUES: Education; Law
SIGNIFICANCE: Signed into law by President Gerald Ford, this legislation ensured all handicapped children in the United States access to "free appropriate public education" that would meet their individual needs

Several years of congressional hearings revealed that the educational needs of millions of disabled children were not being met. Often families of students with special needs had to educate their children at their own expense. The Education for All Handicapped Children Act (EHA), which became effective in 1977, reshaped American education. All handicapped students were ensured an appropriate educational setting.

Specific learning disabilities and related services were clearly defined under the law. States were required to submit plans and procedures designed to meet the needs of handicapped persons between the ages of three and twenty-one. When necessary, the act allowed for the provision of services in private educational settings at public expense. It stated that students should receive special education and related services in the "least restrictive environment commensurate with their needs."

Safeguards were established to protect the rights of all concerned. These included provisions for assessment, detailed individualized education

In the early twentieth century children with disabilities were relegated to "crippled children's schools." (Library of Congress)

programs, and timetables for achievement of stated goals. Parental involvement in the educational process was strongly supported. Annual reviews of students' progress were mandated. A procedure for fair hearings was established to resolve disputes concerning educational placement. Failure to comply with the law would result in denial of federal funding. —*Kathleen Schongar*

See also Disabilities; Educating children; Health of children; Learning disorders.

Elder abuse

RELEVANT ISSUES: Aging; Parenting and family relationships; Sociology; Violence

SIGNIFICANCE: Abuse of older family members has increasingly become the concern of social scientific research, legislation, and social service and law-enforcement agencies as it has developed into a major social problem in America

Social gerontologists and other professionals who study and work with older persons report that the prevalence of elder abuse is much greater than was previously realized and that it takes multiple forms. Neglect and verbal, psychological, physical, economic, and sexual abuse do not typically occur at the hands of strangers or in unfamiliar surroundings. More often the perpetrators of elder abuse are the primary caretakers or neighbors of the victims, and the setting is the victims' own homes, neighborhoods, or institutions charged with their care. Researchers, social workers, medical professionals, and law-enforcement officials have agreed that documented cases of elder abuse

Decreasing physical ability and solitary lifestyles make older persons more vulnerable to abuse. (AP/Wide World Photos)

represent a small proportion of all such incidents, which are increasing in frequency.

Abuse by Family Caretakers. The phrase "graying of America" alludes to the fact that the fastest-growing American age group is the sixty-five-and-over population and that the category of Americans older than eighty-five has the fastest growth rate of all. As Americans become ever older, the probability of their experiencing a degree of physiological or cognitive dysfunction that makes them dependent on others for their care increases. Members of any age group who depend on others for survival are the most likely targets of domestic abuse. The infirm elderly are the most often abused; they typically become more submissive to protect themselves from abandonment by their family caretakers.

Although the prevalence of elder abuse, as with other forms of domestic violence, is impossible to assess accurately, of greatest concern are cases involving perpetrators closely related to the victims.

Not only is the specter of abuse by a family member, as opposed to a stranger, especially disturbing, but a majority of incidents occur in domestic settings. The number of documented cases of domestic elder abuse, a mere fraction of real existing instances of the problem, is increasing geometrically. Between 1986 and 1994 officially reported cases steadily increased from 117,000 to 241,000. Most cases go unreported, and 70 percent or more of documented cases are reported by someone other than the victim. Estimates of the actual number of such cases range between one and two million annually.

Data from the 1990's show that substantiated cases of reported domestic elder abuse took every form imaginable. Neglect accounted for 58.5 percent of these cases, physical abuse 15.7 percent, financial exploitation 12.3 percent, psychological and emotional abuse 8.1 percent, and sexual abuse 0.5 percent. These same data indicate that close relatives of the victims are responsible for two-thirds of the cases. Perpetrators were victims' adult children in about 38 percent of the reports, spouses in about 14 percent, and other family members in about 15 percent.

Sociologists assert that, given the strong cultural normative prescriptions for intergenerational support and affection, domestic elder abuse constitutes a violation of a social taboo—the most serious category of social infractions. This form of deviant behavior is difficult to analyze because of the complexity of its causes. Researchers who attempt to understand such dysfunctional behavior in family settings contend that—like all forms of domestic violence—the causes involve a combination of psychological, social, economic, and health-related characteristics of the perpetrators and the victims.

In some cases the stress associated with caring for an infirm elderly family member may lead to abuse, especially if the caregiver perceives the demands on time, energy, and financial resources as excessive or if the caregiver is not well prepared for the task. Some studies have found that the incidence of abuse increases when the continued physical or mental decline of the older person heightens the caretaker's responsibilities. Some domestic elder abuse is related to the perpetrator's personal problems, such as chronic financial difficulties, pathological emotional or mental conditions, or addiction to alcohol or other drugs. In these cases, the abuser is often dependent on the victim for financial support and housing, and the frustration of failing to function as an independent adult manifests itself in abusive episodes. Furthermore, some researchers report that abusers who have experienced or witnessed domestic violence in their households as children may have learned to abuse in response to conflicts or stress, resulting in an intergenerational transfer of violence. Complex combinations of these and other possible factors underlie each individual case of domestic elder abuse.

Abuse in Institutional Settings. Although only about 5 percent of older Americans reside in nursing and convalescent homes, they represent half of the long-term-care patients. As the eighty-five-and-over population continues to increase, the population of institutionalized older Americans is projected to grow from 1.5 million in 1990 to 2.6 million in the year 2020. The risk of abuse is especially high for this group of elderly Americans. Physicians have often recommended institutionalization as a way to prevent or stop abuse, but a potential for serious abuse in these settings has been demonstrated.

Assessing the prevalence of elder abuse in health-care settings is difficult. However, studies in which nursing home staff were assured of confidentiality and anonymity have shown that a problem does exist. In one such study involving almost six hundred nursing home workers, 45 percent said that they had yelled, cursed, or threatened residents; 10 percent admitted physically abusing patients by hitting, pinching, or violently grabbing them; another 3 percent stated that they had hit patients with objects or thrown objects at them; and 4 percent had denied patients food or privileges. Such research efforts have probably underestimated levels of abuse by paid caregivers, and none are likely to produce reliable results regarding sexual abuse and theft.

Adult Protective Services. A number of public agencies include elder abuse among their concerns: police and sheriffs' departments, district attorneys' offices, acute-care licensing and certification agencies, and State Long-Term Care Ombudsman's offices, which were created by the federal Older Americans Act of 1965 and organized under State Agencies on Aging to investigate elder abuse in nursing homes. However, the agencies most responsible for investigating, intervening in, and resolving cases of domestic elder abuse in most states are Adult Protective Services (APS), which are usually part of the county departments of social services. Although APS offices deal with abuse of anyone older than eighteen, 70 percent of their cases involve elder abuse.

APS responses to elder abuse have varied according to the severity and nature of the abuse. The problem is often addressed by APS case workers with a plan to provide assistance to family caregivers by linking them to public service, volunteer, and church-related agencies that assist in caregiving functions and even counsel abusive family caretakers. Case workers monitor caregiving plans to determine their effectiveness and the need for adjustments. In the most severe cases, the APS offices take more drastic measures, such as institutionalizing elderly persons or calling in law-enforcement agencies. In cases requiring institutionalization, the State Long-Term Ombudsman program is often called upon to monitor the safety of abuse victims.

APS faces great challenges in its attempts to prevent future abuse and improve the quality of life of abuse victims. Investigators' interactions with family members are usually tense at best, because elder abuse, like spousal and child abuse, is often a well-kept family secret. Furthermore, case workers are prohibited from revealing the identities of the persons who report abuse, which often frustrates the families, and the interventions sometimes confuse the victims because they seldom report the abuse themselves.

Not all APS elder abuse cases are successfully resolved. Agency intervention in cases involving chronic domestic violence, regardless of the victims' ages, is especially difficult. Moreover, elder abuse intervention is often thwarted because older persons, unlike children, are beyond the age of majority and can thus refuse assistance if they fear institutionalization, abandonment, or retribution. APS case workers must be able to investigate cases, assess victims' physical and psychological health, know about available elder services, work within the criminal justice system, deal with crisis situations, and protect themselves from violence at the hands of abusers. There are only a few thou-

In 1990 this seventy-five-year-old man testified before the U.S. House Select Committee on Aging on the physical abuse he had endured at the hands of the son entrusted with his care. (AP/Wide World Photos)

sand APS investigators in the United States, and their large caseloads are growing constantly.

Crime. Although most forms of elder abuse, including willful neglect in many states, are illegal, crimes against elderly victims committed by non-caretakers are of growing concern to law enforcement officials and older persons. Conventional analyses of crime statistics have indicated that the elderly have been far less victimized than the general adult population. There is a growing consensus, however, that these statistics have grossly underestimated the magnitude of elderly victimization. Older Americans appear to be the targets of certain types of crime, and the incidents most often occur in the victims' homes or neighborhoods. Most victims of con artists, for example, are older persons. Con games take many forms, including phoney insurance schemes, hearing-aid scams, medical quackery of all types, real estate swindles, and investment frauds. Moreover, elderly persons are the main victims of purse snatchers, pickpockets, and petty thieves, whereby the victims are often assaulted. The perpetrators of these attacks are most often young males who live in their victims' neighborhoods.

Another form of crime-related elder abuse stems from older persons' fear of crime, which research has indicated is the greatest single concern among older Americans. Although crime statistics indicate that the elderly are less likely than younger adults to be victims of most violent crimes, the consequences of physical abuse can be especially devastating to the aged. Young or middle-aged persons might sustain minimal injuries during an assault that would cripple older victims. Even a purse snatching can result in an older person requiring hip-joint replacement surgery or long-term medical care for internal injuries. In addition, larceny can significantly affect the economic independence of older persons with limited and fixed incomes. Fear of crime itself compromises the quality of life of many older Americans, causing them to live reclusively, afraid to leave their homes. Furthermore, some studies have concluded that few crimes against the elderly are reported, because the victims fear retribution by neighborhood criminals and pressure from family and friends to give up living independently because of their limited ability to protect themselves.

Elderly Homelessness. Some authors have contended that homelessness among the elderly in North America represents a serious and increasing form of abuse. Although the perpetrators are more difficult to identify and profile, there is no question that homeless older persons suffer most severely from every type of elder abuse. They experience constant absolute neglect and face daily threats of violent attacks and theft of their meager belongings. Recent studies have documented the brutality of their lives. Their first priority is the search for a place to sleep that is safe from attack, harassment, and the elements. Older homeless Americans have no dependable source of sustenance. They eat out of garbage cans or at soup kitchens, wherever they exist. They largely lack health care and suffer from high rates of debilitating and chronic ailments.

There are many causes of elderly homelessness in America, and the list has grown. Some researchers have pointed to family abandonment; the refusal of older persons to accept the loss of their independence represented by institutionalization, opting instead for life on the streets; and mental illness and alcoholism. Other authors have asserted that it is insufficient to blame the victims or the breakdown of principles of intergenerational reciprocity. They argue that society itself is responsible because of its unwillingness or inability to alleviate the problem socially. The failure of the economic system to stem the growth of impoverishment has played a part, as have government domestic policy changes that have cut back or eliminated funding for low-income housing, anti-poverty programs, and the care of the mentally ill. These changes have left many confused, "deinstitutionalized" older persons with few residential options. Another factor is the lack of comprehensive government policies to eradicate homelessness. The official response in many cities has been to clear the streets of the homeless by forcing them to move on or arresting them for vagrancy and public drunkenness.

The face of elderly homelessness has changed in modern America. Older homeless people are of every gender, race, ethnicity, and socioeconomic background; many experience poverty for the first time in their older years. One author has commented that history will judge societies more by how they care for their helpless and vulnerable citizens than by any other criteria. —*Jack Carter*

BIBLIOGRAPHY

Baumhover, Lorin A., and S. Coleen Beall, eds. *Abuse, Neglect, and Exploitation of Older Persons: Strategies for Assessment and Intervention.* Baltimore: Health Professions Press, 1996. Collection of essays focusing on the causes and nature of elder abuse, with an emphasis on responses to the problem by health-care professionals.

Byers, Bryan, and James E. Hendricks, eds. *Adult Protective Services: Research and Practice.* Springfield, Ill.: Charles C Thomas, 1993. Papers by social scientists from several disciplines examining elder abuse, highlighting the challenges facing government agencies.

Filinson, Rachel, and Stanley R. Ingman, eds. *Elder Abuse: Practice and Policy.* New York: Human Sciences Press, 1989. Contributors discuss the problem, focusing on federal and state policy responses to it.

Lustbader, Wendy, and Nancy R. Hooyman. *Taking Care of Aging Family Members.* New York: Free Press, 1994. Discusses neglect and abuse and the caregiving stress that can lead to it.

O'Connell, James J., Jean Summerfield, and F. Russell Kellogg. "The Homeless Elderly." In *Under the Safety Net: The Health and Social Welfare of the Homeless in the United States,* edited by Philip W. Brickner, et al. New York: W. W. Norton, 1990. Essay examining the demographics of elderly homelessness, the problems that plague these people, and the programs designed to help them in several large American cities.

See also Ageism; Aging and elderly care; Alcoholism and drug abuse; Domestic violence; Emotional abuse; Homeless families; Nursing and convalescent homes; Older Americans Act (OAA).

Electra and Oedipus complexes

RELEVANT ISSUES: Children and child development; Parenting and family relationships

SIGNIFICANCE: Sigmund Freud's theory of the Electra and Oedipus complexes revolutionized psychology by explaining family relationships in terms of repressed sexual attraction

The Electra and Oedipus complexes are fundamental concepts in the Freudian tradition of family psychology. Sigmund Freud (1856-1939) was a highly influential Austrian psychologist who founded the discipline of psychoanalysis. Freud asserted that the mind consists of both a conscious component and a much broader unconscious component and that the unconscious is the key to the behavior of the individual. Psychoanalysts attempt to penetrate the unconscious (the content of which is unknown even to patients) under controlled conditions. Psychoanalysts employ a variety of methods to probe the unconscious, such as the interpretation of patients' dreams, dialogue with them, hypnosis, and word-association tests. Once these methods succeed in revealing the nature of patients' psychological problems, psychoanalysts treat them using psychotherapy.

Freud coined the terms "Oedipus complex" and "Electra complex" in his 1910 essay "Contributions to the Psychology of Love." He borrowed the figure of Oedipus from Greek mythology to refer to the relationship between male children and their mothers. According to legend, Oedipus was a king who had been separated at birth from his parents and who later unwittingly killed his father and married his mother. Freud held that at an early age male children develop a sexual attraction to their mothers (the Oedipus complex) and that female children develop an attraction to their fathers (the Electra complex). As a result of the incest taboo that virtually all human societies observe, children cannot express this sexual attraction; thus, they must repress it into the unconscious. Freud concluded that in developing this attraction, children react to signals from their parent of the opposite sex, who also shows a preference for children of the opposite sex because of repressed sexual attraction.

Freud's theory has a number of implications for the psychology of the family. It implies that male children would like to replace their fathers, since fathers are competitors for the attention and affection of their mothers. Similarly, female children would like to take the place of their mothers. These wishes are repressed and may produce negative consequences later in life. Freud maintained that to lead a healthy mental life, children must at some point successfully transfer the repressed wish for the parent to another, socially legitimate sexual object. Most individuals make this transition, but those who do not suffer neuroses (mild to moderate mental disorders). The task of psychoanalysis is to identify and treat these disorders.

Freudian theory dominated psychology throughout the first half of the twentieth century, but its influence has since declined. Critics have attacked Freud for his narrow focus on sexuality as an explanation for behavior and mental life. Family psychologists continue to draw upon Freud's work as just one of many sources of insight into the dynamics of the family. —*Aristide Sechandice*

See also Father-daughter relationships; Freudian psychology; Mother-son relationships; Parenting.

Ellis, Albert

Born: September 27, 1913, Pittsburgh, Pa.
Area of achievement: Psychology

Significance: Albert Ellis, a psychologist and author of many books, treated patients by offering them advice and interpretations of their conditions

Albert Ellis's parents' divorce when he was twelve led Ellis to work on understanding other people. After earning his master's and doctorate degrees at Columbia University, he became a psychoanalyst. He taught psychology at Rutgers University and New York University. Ellis's faith in psychoanalysis crumbled, because his clients improved faster when he played an active role by interjecting advice and interpretations instead of using passive psychoanalytic procedures. As propounded by Ellis, rational emotive behavior therapy provides advice as it concentrates on changing people's be-

Albert Ellis speaking at a Mensa meeting in 1973. (AP/Wide World Photos)

havior by confronting them with their irrational beliefs and by persuading them to adopt rational ones.

Since he worked through many of his problems by reading and practicing the teachings of the Greek stoic philosopher Epicetus, the Roman emperor and stoic philosopher Marcus Aurelius, the seventeenth century Dutch philosopher Baruch Spinoza, and the English mathematician and philosopher Bertrand Russell, Ellis taught others those principles. Ellis frequently quoted Epicetus: "What disturbs people's minds is not events but their judgments on events." Ellis published fifty-four books and more than six hundred articles. He is the coauthor of such books as *A Guide to a Successful Marriage* (1977) and *How to Raise an Emotionally Healthy, Happy, Child* (1981). He is president of the Albert Ellis Institute in New York, a nonprofit humanistic educational organization that emphasizes persons' capacity to create their emotions, change and overcome the past by focusing on the present, and implement satisfying alternatives to modern patterns.   —*Marian Wynne Haber*

See also Childhood fears and anxieties; Couples; Marriage counseling; Sex education.

Emotional abuse

RELEVANT ISSUES: Children and child development; Parenting and family relationships
SIGNIFICANCE: Emotional abuse is a form of maltreatment toward family members that has complex psychological effects

Emotional abuse is an important subject, but because a generally agreed upon definition is not available, its prevalence cannot be accurately documented. The complexity of the subject and the fact that it is a topic of concern to a range of caring professionals, from social workers and psychiatrists to citizens, politicians, and scholars, accounts for much of its lack of definition. Emotional abuse is complex because it may be studied from different vantage points and deals with human subjectivity, feelings such as love and hate, and positive and negative self-esteem—notions that are easy to discuss but difficult to accurately define and measure.

Emotions may be variously interpreted by individuals experiencing them and those striving to understand what others mean when they say they have experienced something like emotional abuse. What may constitute emotional abuse to one person may not to another. To resolve such difficulties one cannot rely on prevailing norms or customs, because they are subject to change. What one generation might regard as family abuse of any kind may not be so regarded by another. Changing customs and traditions often account for the fact that many abused as children do not realize it until they are adults. Despite the lack of a clear consensus as to what exactly constitutes emotional abuse, information concerning its perpetrators, victims, and consequences as well as some general definitions of the term are available.

Perpetrators of Abuse. Within the family the primary perpetrators of emotional and other types of abuse are those with the most physical strength and power: husbands versus wives, parents versus children, and grown children versus elderly parents. This is the case regardless of factors such as social class, ethnicity, and race. Definitions of emotional abuse tend to focus on types of victims—above all, children. Thus, to The American Humane Association, emotional abuse is "active, intentional berating, disparaging or other abusive behavior toward the child which impacts upon the well-being of the child." The National Center on Child Abuse and Neglect defines it as "acts (including verbal or emotional assault) or omissions that caused or could have caused conduct, cognitive, affective, or other mental disorders."

Unfortunately, the generality of such definitions provokes as many questions as answers. Who, for example, is the implied abuser? May the perpetrator be anyone, a parent or another adult, or even another child? Furthermore, are single instances of "berating or disparaging" remarks and conduct or "verbal or emotional assault," assuming we know what these terms mean, sufficient to constitute abuse? Most experts agree that to constitute emotional abuse, any act or effort, whether direct or indirect, must represent a repetitive pattern motivated by factors such as the desire to dominate and control another by nonphysical means. Although abusive acts may be perpetrated by virtually anyone, they are most often perpetrated by those on whom victims are dependent or to whom they are obligated by birth, marriage, or employment. As family relations are the most enduring

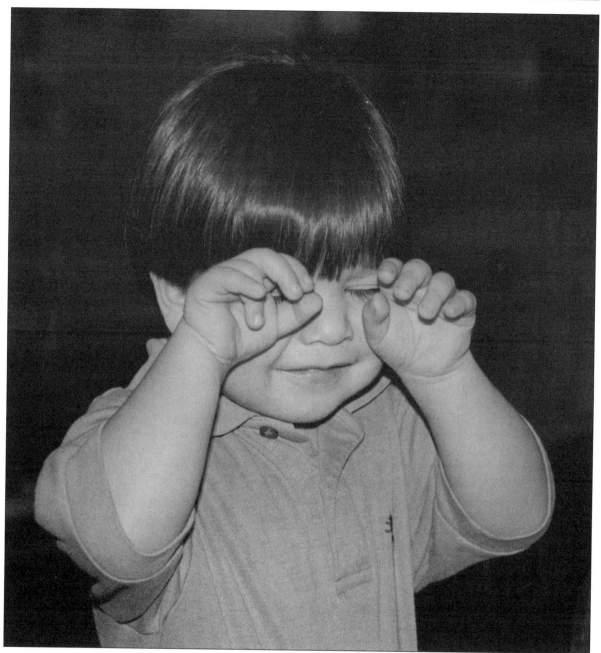

What constitutes emotional abuse is a question redefined by each generation. (James L. Shaffer)

and difficult to dissolve, they tend to be central breeding grounds of emotional and other forms of abusive patterns.

Definitions. Contributing to the definitional problem is the tendency of psychologists to refer to emotional abuse as either "psychological abuse" or "psychological maltreatment." In the Report of the American Psychological Association Task Force on Violence and the Family, psychological maltreatment is defined as "the willful infliction by a parent or other caretaker of mental, emotional, or psychological harm or anguish." It goes on to say that such maltreatment may be called psychological abuse, which can be inflicted directly by "parents, siblings, other family members, and care-takers" or indirectly as in the case of children witnessing the abuse of one parent by another. Psychological maltreatment is described as an interactive pattern involving "terrorizing, threatening, isolating, exploiting or corrupting, spurning, rejecting, denying emotional responsiveness, or neglecting mental health, medical, or educational care."

Among adult victims of psychological abuse, women and the elderly have been of primary concern. Definitions of adult psychological abuse stress the use of verbal means by perpetrators to dominate and control their victims. With wives uppermost in her thinking, Valerie Nash Chang states that "this nonphysical form of abuse is characterized by exploitative or excessive expressions of power and dominance that demean, belittle, undermine, control, define, and criticize an individual in order to create submission." She considers psychological abuse as any type of persistent nonphysical behavior aimed at controlling another by means of fear, humiliation, and verbal assault.

The conception of elderly psychological abuse also reflects concern with these same basic ideas. To R. S. Wolf and K. A. Pillemer, for example, elderly psychological abuse is "the infliction of mental anguish" by means of humiliation (ridicule, rejection), harassment (insult, intimidation), and manipulation (withholding and falsifying information).

"Emotional abuse," therefore, may be referred to as "psychological abuse" or "psychological maltreatment." All three terms refer to the mentally destructive effects imposed on victims in a patterned and persistent manner by nonphysical means that may, as Marti Tamm Loring points out, be overt (belittling, name-calling, criticizing) or covert (discounting, negation, threatening abandonment). It is important to emphasize that emotional problems are the essential effect of all forms of persistent abuse. Emotional abuse may cause emotional problems and emotional problems may be the effect of other forms of abuse. As in other types of abuse, emotional abuse is not confined to any one social class, ethnic group, or race.

Emotional Abuse of Children. The consequences of emotional maltreatment of children have not yet been precisely determined. What is known is that these consequences may be diverse and serious. Compared to nonverbally abused children, for example, verbally abused children have been found to be more physically aggressive, as indicated by attitude tests and rates of juvenile delinquency. The range of effects associated with all forms of child abuse include low self-esteem, withdrawal, depression, poor peer relations, drug and alcohol problems, exaggerated or irrational fears, lack of trust, anxiety disorders, eating disorders, poor concentration, health problems, and suicidal feelings. Failure to develop the self-confidence necessary to develop and maintain positive relationships with others is a major general consequence of such effects. Attention-span deficiencies that influence persons' ability to learn and become successful, mature adults are a related and commonly noted outcome of childhood emotional abuse. Nonetheless, studies show consistently that not all children who suffer emotional abuse evidence major emotional effects and long-term behavioral problems.

Adult Emotional Abuse. With some important differences, the effects of psychological abuse on adults are similar to its effects on children. Emotionally and physically abused women have been found to exhibit a range of serious emotional effects: fear and terror, low self-esteem, concentration difficulties, difficulties related to trust and intimacy, anxiety, memory problems, depression, anger and irritability, shame and embarrassment, nightmares, numbing, and avoidance.

Historically, largely because of antidivorce customs and the economic dependence of wives on their husbands, women had to endure abuse. Complicating the ability of women to simply leave an abusive mate is what psychologists identify as the "codependency" problem, the strong tendency of some abused victims to feel bound to their abusers. Major consequences of emotional abuse such as social isolation and loss of self-confidence promote in some abused victims an overwhelming sense of dependency on abusive relationships. As Loring puts it, "disconnected from both herself and the community, the traumatized victim feels that she has no choice but to cling desperately to the partner, no matter how abusive he is." Two themes that emerge from Loring's interviews with women charged with murdering their abusers are a failed effort to establish loving responsiveness immediately before committing murder and "fear of losing the partner."

The effects of emotional abuse on the elderly combine those evident in child and female victims. They range from infantile-like reactions such as sucking, biting, and rocking to more adultlike patterns such as sleep and speech disorders. Peter Decalmer and Frank Glendenning describe the elderly victim of psychological abuse as feeling lonely, fearful, and roleless, and in extreme situations even "cowering when approached." However, among the victims of emotional abuse, the elderly have been the least studied and examined by psychologists and others.   —*Calvin J. Larson*

BIBLIOGRAPHY

Chang, Valerie Nash. *I Just Lost Myself: Psychological Abuse of Women in Marriage.* Westport, Conn.: Praeger Publishers, 1996.

Decalmer, Peter, and Frank Glendenning, eds. *The Mistreatment of Elderly People.* Thousand Oaks, Calif.: Sage Publications, 1993.

Loring, Marti Tamm. *Emotional Abuse.* New York: Lexington Books, 1994.

The long-term effects of emotional abuse on children are not fully understood but are known to include distrust. (James L. Shaffer)

Report of the American Psychological Association Presidential Task Force. *Violence and the Family.* Washington, D.C.: American Psychological Association, 1996.

Wiehe, Vernon R. *Working with Child Abuse and Neglect: A Primer.* Thousand Oaks, Calif.: Sage Publications, 1996.

Wolf, R. S., and K. A. Pillemer. *Helping Elderly Victims: The Reality of Elder Abuse.* New York: Columbia University Press, 1989.

See also Alcoholism and drug abuse; Battered child syndrome; Child abuse; Child Abuse Prevention and Treatment Act (CAPTA); Child molestation; Childhood fears and anxieties; Cycle of violence theory; Elder abuse; Mental health.

Emotional expression

RELEVANT ISSUES: Children and child development; Parenting and family relationships

SIGNIFICANCE: Healthy emotional expression in families is crucial in shaping a healthy personality and self-concept in children, and parental influence is an important part of the larger process of socialization

Parents and siblings serve as models for children who need to learn socially acceptable ways of expressing feelings. The family provides the major training ground for understanding social relationships. Children must first guess and make assumptions about what others are feeling, thinking, or intending. Children who hear their mothers laughing assume that they are happy. Children who see a sad face on adults assume that this sadness has to do with them. Children model a wide range of behaviors on what they learn in the family environment, and they require help to deal with thoughts, feelings, and emotions in an appropriate way.

Basic Parenting Styles. Parents shape the emotional health of their children by being good role models for the expression of emotion. Some general parenting dimensions have been identified, including authoritarianism, permissiveness, and authoritativeness. Authoritarian parents tend to have very strict rules, exert much control, and have very high expectations of family members. Children of authoritarian parents tend to be withdrawn, discontented, and distrustful. Permissive parents tend to be indulgent and sometimes neglectful. Children of permissive parents have been shown to be the least self-reliant, exploratory, and self-controlled of all children. Authoritative parents tend to have warm and supportive rules that are agreed upon by both parents and children, and their children tend to be confident, independent, and socially outgoing.

Each parenting style may vary in its expression of emotions. However, authoritarian parents generally discourage open displays of affection, sadness, or even exuberant happiness by children. Their children learn to keep their feelings inside and may become withdrawn, self-punishing, or depressed. Permissive parents may allow their children any open expression of feelings, including anger and destruction. Such children learn to be manipulative and aggressive and may be antisocial. Authoritative parents believe in letting children show feelings such as anger, but they help them to distinguish between the emotions they experience and do not allow their feelings to become destructive. Children who feel angry over the destruction of a toy by playmates are helped to recognize that they are also sad that they no longer have the toy.

Temperament. Since 1956 Stella Chess and Alexander Thomas, psychiatry professors at the New York University School of Medicine, have studied the relationship between children's temperament and mental health. They found that children are of three basic temperament types—difficult, easy, or "slow to warm up." The identification of these types was significant, because it was found that parents as a general rule did not relate well to children whose temperaments differed from their own. Children with different temperaments must be handled differently, and the rules set for one child may need to be modified for others with different temperaments. Anne Roe, who trained as a clinical psychologist in the 1950's, determined that people are oriented either "toward other people" or "not toward other people." Parents who are warm, accepting, and "toward other people" are more likely to encourage outward expressions of feelings, while parents who are "not toward other people" may discourage any show of emotion in children.

Family Rules. Every family operates within a set of rules that are either out in the open or hidden. In families with open rules, all members know

Much of what children know about emotional expression they pattern on adult behavior. (James L. Shaffer)

Parents generally treat their children the way their own parents treated them. (James L. Shaffer)

what is expected of them, because the rules are verbalized. In families with hidden rules, members are expected to know what to do even though no one talks about specifics. When rules are covert, children receive mixed messages about what is right or wrong. In overt-rule families, rules may be rigid or unrealistic, but at least they permit family members to be consistent. Covert-rule families generally have unhealthy rules that convey to members that it is not acceptable to talk about feelings, that everything must be perfect, that it is not alright to have fun or be spontaneous, that family members should not lose control of their emotions, and that conflict is to be avoided. Such rules interfere with healthy emotional expression and development. Children brought up under such rules learn to suppress their true feelings and seek to avoid pain or seek pleasure. When needs are consistently left unsatisfied, children lose their ability to express appropriate emotions and internalize their deep feelings.

Emotionally Healthy Parents. Few parents intentionally inflict physical or emotional harm on their children. In general, parents treat their children the same way their parents treated them, except in cases where parents had abusive parents and they make a deliberate effort to change the family pattern. Emotionally healthy families do not make children feel responsible for making parents happy or set unrealistic standards for their children. When children become mildly frustrated, emotionally healthy parents help them verbalize their feelings and find ways to defuse situations. They do not allow children to repress anger or sadness but help them to understand what they are feeling by asking key questions, talking about their feeling, and not invalidating what they state they are feeling. Parents who belittle or make fun of their children for their fears or who try to scare them intentionally help create neurotic, pessimistic children who will find no joy in their experiences. If children are punished for aggressive or dependent behavior, they often learn to feel anxious about the behavior and about the angry feelings that accompany them. Punishment can be useful in certain situations, but it must be closely related to the behavior that is being punished and should be carefully administered.

Gender Differences in Emotional Expression. David Stoop and Stephen Arterburn argue in *The Angry Man: Why Does He Act that Way?* that much of the anger affecting men is caused by the lack of influence of fathers during their childhoods. Some of their anger is manifested as social immaturity, lack of control, unrealistic expectations, low self-worth, guilt, and role confusion. Young boys see these traits in their fathers and mimic them. Men and boys believe that they are not supposed to cry or show sadness but that it is socially acceptable for them to show anger. Women and girls have been discouraged from openly expressing anger, because to express anger has been condemned as unladylike, unfeminine, unnatural, or irrational.

Both sexes can learn to tune in to the real emotion behind feelings of anger and learn to communicate their needs in healthy ways. Children of both genders must learn that it is alright to display all emotions, not just anger. Families that encourage open displays of emotion and have open patterns of communication spend quality time together discussing the origin of different emotions and how to appropriately express them. Dysfunctional families may need guidance in learning to break family patterns of inappropriate, destructive anger and in learning to openly express love, sadness, and fear—the underlying emotions.

—*Stephanie G. Campbell*

BIBLIOGRAPHY

Berger, Kathleen Stasson. *The Developing Person.* New York: Worth, 1994.

Craig, Grace J. *Human Development.* Englewood Cliffs, N.J.: Simon & Schuster, 1989.

Hamner, Tamie J., and Pauline H. Turner. *Parenting in Contemporary Society.* Needham Heights, Mass: Allyn & Bacon, 1996.

Lerner, Harriet G. *The Dance of Anger.* New York: Harper & Row, 1986.

McGee, Robert S., Jim Craddock, and Pat Springle. *The Parent Factor.* Houston, Tex.: Rapha Publishing, 1989.

Stoop, David, and Stephen Arterburn. *The Angry Man: Why Does He Act That Way?* Dallas: Word Publishing, 1991.

See also Bonding and attachment; Bradshaw, John; Childhood fears and anxieties; Death; Dysfunctional families; Emotional abuse; Family advice columns; Freudian psychology; Gray, John; Parenting; Separation anxiety.

Employee Retirement Income Security Act (ERISA)

Date: Enacted on September 2, 1974
Relevant issues: Economics and work; Law
Significance: Signed into law by President Gerald Ford, this act protects retirement benefits of private employees

The Employee Retirement Income Security Act of 1974 (ERISA) applies to all employee benefit plans, including pension plans, profit-sharing plans, employee stock-ownership plans, and sick-pay plans. If a plan meets the requirements of ERISA, employer contributions to the plan are tax deductible. The plan pays no tax on its investment income. Employees pay a tax only when money is taken out of the plan, which is usually at retirement.

Congress passed ERISA for a number of reasons. Many employee benefit plans contained unsound investments. Employees often had to work for many years for a single employer before receiving any benefits at all and could lose their entire benefit plan if they quit or retired early.

ERISA requires that all plans be operated by trustees who are subject to strict fiduciary duties. Employees are entitled to full information about the plan and their benefits. They must be entitled to an increasing percentage of their benefits the longer they work for an employer and normally may keep all the money if they work ten years. When employees retire, they can choose a joint and survivor annuity instead of an immediate payout from the plan. The annuity guarantees a fixed income for the life of retirees and retirees' spouses.

ERISA has made it more likely that retirement money will be available from private benefit plans. Unfair rules on how long employees must work before receiving benefits have been limited. The joint and survivor annuity covers spouses in addition to employees. —*David E. Paas*

See also Aging and elderly care; Retirement; Social Security; Wealth; Work.

Empty nest syndrome

Relevant issues: Aging; Parenting and family relationships; Sociology

Significance: Once thought to be an important problem for married couples after their children left home, the concept of the empty nest syndrome has been used to describe those married couples who need support in adjusting to the absence of their mature children—a normal phase of the life cycle

The empty nest syndrome refers to the emotional problems experienced by some parents when all their children have grown up and left the home. Initially, the term referred to mothers, but it was later expanded to include fathers who experienced the same symptoms. The concept of the empty nest was very popular in the 1950's and 1960's and was coined by professional therapists who feared that mothers would have a difficult time adjusting to the departure of their children. It was reasoned that when women become mothers, their role would be heavily influenced by their duties and responsibilities toward their children. These roles would dominate a significant portion of their married lives.

Increasing Longevity. By 1950 average Americans were expected to live into their sixties, which meant that a significant demographic change was taking place in the population as a result of medical advances and better health. The majority of parents had an excellent chance of raising their children and living ten to fifteen years after their last child left home. Before the 1950's one or both parents commonly died before their last child left home. For example, one demographic study found that Quaker women born before 1786 were at a median age of 50.9 years when their first spouse died and 60.2 years when their last child married. By 1960 the average American woman's first spouse died at an average age of sixty-seven, while her last child left home when she was in her midfifties. Thus, for the first time in U.S. history women continued to live with their spouses long after their last child left home.

As longevity has continued to increase among Americans, it has become common for people to live into their seventies. U.S. census data has indicated that with increased longevity, marriages enjoy a new stage in the family life cycle between the departure of the last child from the home and parents' retirement from the workforce. Therapists previously warned that when parents were

Medical advances that have increased average lifespans have also increased the years in which parents live without children in their households. (James L. Shaffer)

relieved of their significant child-rearing roles, a vacuum would form that would be difficult for parents to fill. Because husbands in this phase of the family life cycle continued to be primary breadwinners, their major role change did not occur until they retired. Wives, on the other hand, faced a major role change when they were relieved of the primary care of their children. To com-

pound the problem, such women experienced this phase while they were undergoing the menopause.

Concern over the Empty Nest. The concern over empty nest syndrome was overemphasized by therapists and the popular media, who foresaw a dismal period for women as they struggled to adjust. A small percentage of parents become severely depressed and lonely when their children leave home, but researchers have discovered that there are also parents who make this phase a stressful time for both themselves and their children. However, most parents have not experienced empty nest syndrome or undergone a stressful period upon the departure of their last child. The "empty nest syndrome" gripped public attention until the first studies began to appear in the early 1960's. Couples reported feeling relieved from the strains of child rearing and said that this was "the best time of their lives." Evidence indicated that when child-rearing roles were carried into midlife, mothers felt the impact of the empty nest less strongly.

In the 1990's the employment, educational, and family choices open to women provided them with new opportunities for making a successful transition to a new period of the family life cycle. Wives have been able to resume the plans and projects they postponed during parenting. Most importantly, such women have asserted that they have pursued such activities because they want to, not because they wish to escape from loneliness. Parents have also reported that with the departure of their last child they have had increased time for shared activities with each other. It is not uncommon to observe middle-aged couples enjoying each other's company and getting reacquainted after the pressures of parenting.

Positive Changes. Couples have reported that marital conflicts subside to their lowest level after their last child has left the home, a situation that is most common among couples who have been married for twenty-five to thirty years and have developed teamwork, problem-solving skills, and the understanding that comes from cooperative effort over a long period of time. Evidence suggests that husbands and wives resume the provider and domestic roles that prevailed in their marriages before their children were born, with greater earning power and experience to take advantage of their time alone together.

One carefully researched study of middle-aged couples in the mid-1970's found that women's personal happiness increased after their children left home and that both men and women reported greater marital happiness during this stage. Couples reported that they were relieved to switch from the parental role of rulegivers and enforcers to the role of advisers to their grown children. In this phase of the family life cycle, couples have the resources to make improvements in their lives; many children are distressed to find that the parental home has been remodeled or refurnished and that their mothers and fathers are not available because they decided to "get away for a few days." The developmental tasks that are important for couples at this stage include adjusting to the departure of their children, dealing with the realities of aging, deciding if this stage will be one of stagnation or one of recreating and improving life, and taking stock of how family relationships have changed because of the changed roles that men and women play at this stage of the life span.

Potential Areas of Concern. Some couples decide to get divorced when their last child leaves the home, but the percentage of divorces among couples in the "empty nest" age group is small. A small percentage of persons discover that, as marital partners, they have grown apart and have little in common with each other. Getting reacquainted again can be a difficult process and may not seem to be worth the effort. Parents may identify too closely with their children, but the social norm requires that parents raise their children to be independent. Parents who overidentify with their children may feel lonely and abandoned.

There is much discussion about the sexual relationships of couples at this stage of life, since men and women undergo similar midlife changes. Men report that they experience many of the same menopausal changes that women experience. At this stage, persons slow down and lose interest, but most research has reported that these changes are easily accommodated once couples understand what to expect. While a small number of midlife couples visit therapists because of sexual dysfunction, such complaints reflect a long-term pattern of dysfunction during the course of marriage. Couples in their middle years usually take these changes in stride. Women have generally reported being more responsive sexually after the menopause because the concern of pregnancy has ceased.

In general, the empty nest syndrome or the period of "midlife crisis" seems to have been exaggerated by the general public. The reporting of a few dramatic cases as examples of the problems of the empty nest may catch the public imagination, but the facts do not warrant the conclusion that it is a significant problem for most married couples.

—*Robert Christenson*

BIBLIOGRAPHY

Duvall, Evelyn. *Marriage and Family Development.* 5th ed. Philadelphia: J. B. Lippincott, 1977.

Glenn, N. "Psychological Well-Being in the Post-Parental Stage: Some Evidence from National Surveys." *Journal of Marriage and the Family* 37 (1975).

Sheehy, Gail. *New Passages: Mapping Your Life Across Time.* New York: Random House, 1995.

_____. *Passages: Predictable Crises of Adult Life.* New York: E. P. Dutton, 1974.

See also Family life cycle; Full nest; Home ownership; Menopause; Midlife crises; Retirement; Sandwich generation; Sheehy, Gail; Volunteerism.

Enculturation

RELEVANT ISSUES: Children and child development; Race and ethnicity; Religious beliefs and practices

SIGNIFICANCE: Enculturation ensures that a society will transmit its working knowledge from one generation to the next

Enculturation is the acquisition and internalization of working knowledge within a defined group. Some elements are transmitted explicitly through rituals, and others are internalized in the discipline of daily life.

Children are neophyte societal members. They quickly learn that some actions bring approval from experienced elders, and they differentiate between appropriate and alienating behaviors. Within their families, they acquire a common

Children learn from an early age what kinds of behavior win approval from their parents. (James L. Shaffer)

ground of shared operative knowledge. As children mature, their cultural affiliations intensify. They develop self-identity versus other-identity. If they perceive nongroup members as hostile, they learn to defend their boundaries with prejudices, which become working principles for their particular cultural worlds.

Historical conquests have threatened family enculturation. The Ottoman Empire removed Greek children from their homes, forbidding their language, art, or rituals and reeducating them in the Janissary Corps. In the United States, Native American children in boarding schools were disciplined harshly for practicing their traditions. During World War II, the German government implemented a human breeding program called *Lebensborn*, in which elite officers impregnated selected women, intending that the children of such unions would be eugenically and culturally designed to Nazi perfection.

Many modern families criticize prevailing culture. Families are no longer insular, and children have greater access to unsettling information. The business of daily life supersedes cultural learning. Enculturation has become a difficult family mandate. —*Brenda E. Reinertsen Caranicas*

See also Cultural influences; Family: concept and history; Family values; Mealtaking; Myths and storytelling; Religion; Rites of passage.

Endogamy

Relevant issues: Kinship and genealogy; Marriage and dating
Significance: Endogamy is the practice of marrying within one's group, however that group is defined

Endogamy flourishes in contexts in which the distinctive characteristics of a group are threatened and may be lost. Kinship endogamy tends to divide societies into distinct segments or to reinforce such divisions that may exist. Saint Augustine pointed out in his *City of God* that in biblical times it was necessary for Jews to practice kinship endogamy. When they entered Palestine as a religious minority, endogamy was seen as a means of preserving their distinctive religious beliefs.

The Indian caste system perhaps constitutes endogamy on the broadest scale. Indian society has traditionally been divided into thousands of castes and subcastes. They are based on such features as race, occupation, and religion. Persons are expected to marry within their caste and preferably within their subcaste, although males may marry members of lower castes if they cannot find suitable wives in their own group. This system has been defended as India's way of allowing diverse groups to coexist in peace while at the same time allowing each group to develop at its own pace.

Although rarely backed by law in late twentieth century North America, the pressure to remain endogamous still exists. Endogamy influences behavior in the United States insofar as persons are expected to limit themselves to dating and marrying others of the same race, ethnic background, religious affiliation, or social class. On the other hand, many states forbid marriage between first cousins, thus limiting endogamy within families.
—*Paul L. Redditt*

See also Cousins; Cross-cousins; Exogamy; Hinduism; Interfaith marriages; Jews; Monogamy; Muslims; Parallel cousins.

Engagement

Relevant issue: Marriage and dating
Significance: Whether by promise or contract, engagement is a custom whereby a man and a woman agree that they will marry at some future point in time

The custom of a couple getting engaged before marriage can be traced back to ancient history. Another name for this custom is betrothal. In societies in which premarital sex is tolerated or even encouraged, engagements or betrothals are more likely to have little or no importance. Generally, in societies in which a highly structured religious belief system is in place, the engagement is an important part of the entire marriage process. During biblical times it was customary for young Hebrew men and women to have their engagements arranged by either their parents or their guardians. For the Hebrews, as with many other societies, engagements were taken very seriously, and if parties decided to break off their engagements, they were assessed a penalty. In Islamic and Eastern societies it has historically been the practice for parents or guardians to arrange engagements. In

Modern engagements are less formal than those of earlier generations, but they remain important transitional periods in the lives of couples. (James L. Shaffer)

these societies future marriage is looked upon as an alliance between the families involved. The concept of romantic love bringing together a man and a woman is a very Western and modern phenomenon.

In ancient Rome it fell upon the elders to make engagement contracts. Prospective marriage partners were considered a good match if they were of like social standing. The equality of family wealth and the compatibility of religion would also be considered. During the Roman Empire, laws were passed that legislated marital choices. It was against the law for Jews and Christians to marry each other. Prominent male Romans could not marry actresses or former slaves. Historically, it was not until after the Middle Ages that it became more common for individuals to have any say about whom they promised to marry. During the Middle Ages many important political alliances were either established or solidified by arranged marriages. Tracing canon law back to Justinian's Code (named after the Roman Emperor Justinian), the Roman Catholic Church declared a canonical betrothal to be a "contract of promise to marry in the future." Church ceremonies were held to sanctify engagements.

The custom of men buying their fiancés engagement rings goes back to ancient times. (James L. Shaffer)

While the system of rules pertaining to engagements has been complex in many societies, there probably is none more complex than the system in place for arranging marriages in some tribes of central Australia. It is common for a marriage to be arranged before one of the parties is even born. While many societies have thought it necessary to make engagements binding, the Kwoma tribe of New Guinea allows for engagements to be broken. Since the two families involved have exchanged gifts of equal value, neither family feels slighted if the couple does not remain together. In most cases, the couple involved only breaks off the engagement if they come to the conclusion that they dislike each other.

Organized religion in Western societies does not exert as much authority in the twentieth century as it did in previous centuries. In previous times, if one party broke off the betrothal that had been sanctified by the Roman Catholic Church, it was then possible for the injured party to take the case to a Church court. For the most part, this practice has been done away with, and breach-of-promise suits are handled in civil courts. In most technologically advanced societies, such as the United States, Canada, and many European countries, engagement and marriage arrangements are made by the couples involved. It is common for men to give women engagement rings. This custom dates back to ancient times and signifies men's serious intent to marry the women involved.

While engagements are primarily a less formal step in the process that leads to marriage than existed in earlier generations in Western societies, it has remained a serious transitional period for couples. It is usually during the engagement period that prospective marriage partners reveal to each other their most intimate hopes and desires. They also become familiar with one another's families. The engagement period can help couples learn how compatible they are and how successful their future marriages could be. The length of engagements can be short or extremely long. Most authorities have stated that the ideal length is no more than six months. There are numerous books on marriage and courtship etiquette that outline the established steps for couples to follow. With the rise of the feminist movement, women have gained a more equal voice in the engagement process. While twentieth century Western societies allow for a wide range of acceptable courtship patterns, in many Islamic and Eastern societies the process has remained rigid.

—Jeffry Jensen

See also Arranged marriages; Bundling; Cohabitation; Couples; Courting rituals; Dating; Mail-order brides; Marriage; Marriage counseling; Matchmaking; Weddings.

Entertainment

RELEVANT ISSUES: Art and the media; Children and child development; Parenting and family relationships

SIGNIFICANCE: The definition and character of family entertainment have changed rapidly as the entertainment industry has increasingly shaped humankind's social mores and structure

Family entertainment can be described primarily as television and cinema products designed to provide a common entertainment experience for both children and parents. Therefore, it has traditionally represented the most conservative and wholesome values of society in an attempt to reassure parents that such entertainment will be a positive force in their children's lives. Although family entertainment is typically thought of as mirroring society's most traditional mores, there is growing evidence that it may be setting the agenda for the modern family and actually moving societal attitudes and values toward a more liberal bent.

Historical Perspective. Most early cinema, radio, and television programs targeted the family. The less refined marketing climate of the early to mid-twentieth century forced entertainment media to appeal to a broad audience. Variety shows, which offered a potpourri of music, skits, comedy, and drama, were a staple of the early entertainment industry.

Since the 1950's family entertainment has evolved into one of several lucrative niche markets, along with adult, action, young adult, teen, and youth markets. This specialized approach means that while programming appeals to a much narrower audience, its captures a larger market share of viewers.

Family entertainment targets the largest cross-section of viewers, but throughout the 1970's and

A traditional form of "wholesome" family entertainment is the hayride. (Mary LaSalle)

1980's it captured a comparatively small share of the market because of its perceived low level of entertainment value. Early situation comedies that depicted benign family and child issues, including such shows as *Father Knows Best, Ozzie and Harriet,* and *The Andy Griffith Show,* were designed for viewing in much the same way families had listened to radio—in the living room together. As media marketing became more sophisticated and audiences fragmented, traditional family television shows and cinema gave way to more biting humor and dramatic story lines focusing on interpersonal conflicts, sex, and other controversial issues. The traditional family became a dead-end market.

During the mid-1980's the media began to realize that the liberal baby boomers of the 1960's and 1970's were fast becoming the conservative parents of the 1980's and beyond. In response to this demographic shift, family entertainment reemerged as a distinct and lucrative niche market.

Family Cinema. Family cinema—films with G or PG ratings—is a multibillion-dollar industry. More than half of all top-twenty grossing films between 1994 and 1996 targeted family audiences. The industry leader, with a strong resurgence in popularity, was Walt Disney Studios, which earned more than $1.2 billion at the box office in 1996 with rereleases of its animated classics; new animated films such as *Toy Story, The Little Mermaid, Beauty and the Beast, The Lion King,* and *Pocahontas;* and several action films.

Disney's classics appeal to adults from a nostalgic perspective. Such films allow parents to feel confident that they are providing their children with wholesome entertainment that communicates traditional core values. Parents can also find a satisfying entertainment experience in films that allow them to revisit their childhood. Disney's more recent animated offerings rely on the studio's reputation for family entertainment but, in many cases, add mature themes and increased sexuality to the characters to appeal to adults as well as children. The antagonist in *The Hunchback of Notre Dame,* for example, clearly wrestles with lust for the alluring lead female character. In addition, unlike earlier Disney offerings, female characters

In the face of constantly developing thrill rides, the merry-go-round has remained a popular family draw and a favorite among young children. (James L. Shaffer)

in these films are stronger, more self-reliant, and less in need of rescuing. Males, on the other hand, are depicted as more human and less heroic.

Although Disney clearly leads the industry in family entertainment, the market extends beyond animated films. To appeal to a broad audience, blockbusters such as *Sleepless in Seattle*, *Mrs. Doubtfire*, and *Forest Gump* meld romantic themes and adult conflicts with children's concerns. Such offerings have redefined the family entertainment market by depicting nontraditional values such as unmarried cohabitation, premarital sex, homo-

sexuality, and adult language as acceptable behaviors. In addition, although not overtly marketed to the family audience, children and adolescents are key profit centers for many action films featuring graphic violence and sex.

Television. Despite the resurgence of family-oriented cinema, prime time television has, with few exceptions, failed to recognize the family as a specific, viable market. Exceptions include a handful of Christian-oriented dramas, as well as a few family sitcoms usually pitting acerbic-witted children against simple-minded parents.

Since the early 1950's television has become the single most popular form of family entertainment. (James L. Shaffer)

For the most part, television family entertainment remains synonymous with children's programming. This may be related to changes in viewing habits. Households with multiple television sets allow television programmers to target highly specific audiences. A mother can watch a situation comedy while a father views an action-oriented police drama. At the same time, children may watch *Leave It to Beaver* reruns in another room. The rationale is that parents can feel comfortable viewing adult-oriented entertainment knowing that their children are watching the same value-filled programming on which they were raised.

The reality, however, is that children—especially adolescents—frequently cross the boundaries to adult entertainment. Many shows focus on this tacit market. Programs such as *The Simpsons, Married . . . with Children,* and *In Living Color* combined adult themes with juvenile humor to capture a broad cross-section of age groups. A 1988 poll conducted by Louis Harris and Associates found that during the prime afternoon and evening hours—typical family viewing times—the three largest networks broadcast a total of 65,000 sexual references per year. In addition, shows targeting or depicting young teenagers also regularly feature adult themes. Programs such as *Roseanne, Doogie Howser, M.D.,* and *Blossom,* for example, often dealt with teen sex, frequently depicting it in a comical, positive, or value-neutral fashion.

Social Ramifications. The changing face of family entertainment may allow individual programming decisions to yield ever-larger revenues, but it has also impacted the social structure of the family. Even the most value-filled programming can produce a negative effect on the family. As early as 1951 researcher Elaine Maccoby suggested that when families view television together, interaction ceases except for occasional exchanges during commercials. Other studies indicate that when communication between family members is reduced or nonexistent, individuals pick up roles vicariously from television, acquiring social skills that are generalized to fit other life situations. As family interaction decreases, television's lessons become increasingly more powerful and significant.

Researcher Lewis Mumford speculated that, even more than real-life experiences, television shapes human judgment of what is "real" and "important." Media expert Jacques Ellul agrees, claiming that television destroys individual personalities and relationships, isolating and insulating viewers by creating a one-sided, illusory relationship between viewers and actors.

Children spend between 25 and 50 percent more time in front of the television than they do in a classroom. Media researcher George Gerbner indicates that exposure to violence and other explicit material on television directly affects children's behavior and may help account for increases in violent and sex-related crimes.

Media experts Neil Postman and Marie Winn contend that television weakens family structure and authority by eliminating vital barriers that filter out information not appropriate for children. "Through the miracle of symbols and electricity our own children know everything anyone else knows—the good with the bad. Nothing is mysterious, nothing awesome, nothing is held back from public view," said Postman. "It means . . . that in having access to the previously hidden fruit of adult information, they are expelled from the garden of childhood."

Many researchers blame the media, in part, for disturbing social trends such as the marked decline of Scholastic Aptitude Test scores and a threefold rise in teen suicides. They point out that cinema and television shows glamorize risky behavior and portray sex as inconsequential. The result, they say, is a significant increase in promiscuity, unwed mothers, and juvenile crime.

Although family entertainment may be less harmful than those offerings specifically targeting adults, it appears that rather than holding the line on traditional values, products in this market may only be marching a few steps behind other niche markets. The result may be that even products billed as "family entertainment" assist in the erosion of the traditional family structure.

—*Cheryl Pawlowski*

BIBLIOGRAPHY

Medved, Michael. *Hollywood vs. America.* New York: HarperCollins, 1992.

Postman, Neil. *The Disappearance of Childhood.* New York: Delacorte Press, 1982.

_____. *Technopoly: The Surrender of Culture to Technology.* New York: Alfred A. Knopf, 1992.

Spanier, Graham B., ed. *Journal of Family Issues* 4 (June, 1983).

Winn, Marie. *The Plug-In Drug.* New York: Penguin Books, 1985.

See also Advertising; Children's literature; Children's magazines; Community programs for children; Computer recreation; Cultural influences; Family economics; Family unity; Film depictions of families; Film ratings; Myths and storytelling; News media and families; Recreation; Television depictions of families; Television rating systems; Youth sports.

Equalitarian families

RELEVANT ISSUES: Economics and work; Parenting and family relationships
SIGNIFICANCE: Equalitarian families are those in which labor and power are shared evenly rather than unevenly on the basis of sex

A modern form of the married-couple or cohabiting-couple family, equalitarian families are defined empirically by the sharing of economic and domestic tasks (low or no sexual division of labor) and the sharing of decision making (balanced conjugal power). The equalitarian family is one in which adult partners share in the work and in family decision making. Members of equalitarian families are less likely to become impoverished because of unemployment or divorce.

Originally, ideology was used to define the equalitarian family. Attitudes of family members, usually spouses, were used to measure equalitarian ideas toward work and power. Attitudes do not necessarily correspond to behavior, but equalitarian couples hold more liberal attitudes toward gender status and work.

The equalitarian form of the married-couple family is contrasted with the patriarchal (male ruled) or matriarchal (female ruled) family. Patriarchal or male-dominated families are sometimes referred to as traditional families, but this is a normative rather than a statistical concept. In real life, there is tremendous variation in the situations of married-couple and cohabiting-couple families in terms of who makes the decisions and who does the work. Examples of families in the United States who tend to be most equalitarian include those in which the incomes of wives and husbands are similar, families of African American descent, families with one or no children living in the home, and

lesbian families. Within married-couple families, the best predictor of an equalitarian marriage is similar control over important resources such as income.
—*Elizabeth Maret*

See also African Americans; Baby-boom generation; Domestic partners; Dual-earner families; Gender inequality; Marriage; Men's roles; Women's roles.

Equality of children

RELEVANT ISSUES: Children and child development; Parenting and family relationships
SIGNIFICANCE: Equality in parenting is a challenge and skill based on children's individual temperament and the environment provided for them to grow in competence and self-esteem

Since the demise of primogeniture (the exclusive right of inheritance of the eldest son), treating all children in families equally has become one of the ethics of child rearing. Some countries are more conscious of the parenting ethic than others. Canada and the United States are particularly involved in family equity and child antibias issues. However, even the most idyllic family is not the picture of peace and tranquillity. Families are developmental, just as children in the family are developmental. They have to learn to work at equality while preserving individual differences and developmental appropriateness.

Different Children Are Treated Differently. What is right or appropriate for one child is not necessarily right for another. Children differ in age and temperament. Moreover, one child may be older, more aggressive, or shyer than another or in the midst of unusual circumstances. "Fair" does not necessarily mean the same thing for everyone. The equality strategy can be carried to ridiculous extremes. For example, to avoid showing favoritism, some parents may have their children's hair cut at the same time, even if only one child needs it. The other children may not want a haircut and may be unhappy with this idea of equality. Likewise, some parents may think it appropriate for their younger children to stay up late with their older children. In these examples, the idea of equality focuses on comparison rather than on needs. One set of rules or behaviors does not suffice for the entire family.

Even when trying to treat children equally, parents usually treat them differently because of their basic differences. Most parents create a mini-environment for each child that corresponds to individual needs. Siblings can experience such different environments in the same home that they may sometimes feel as if they do not live under the same roof. Because it is customary to treat siblings differently, it is of utmost importance that parents understand how and why they respond to each child as they do and what the consequences of their responses are.

Appreciating Temperament and Uniqueness. Healthy families have the ability to recognize and appreciate each family member. Children's differences are valued as bringing richness and diversity to the family structure. Children's temperament and biological personality characteristics determine how they respond to the environment and what ideas dominate their thoughts, opinions, and interests. Society often fosters conformity by valuing similarity of interests, attitudes, and behaviors rather than the uniqueness and individuality that make up each child's temperament. Alexander Thomas and Stella Chess, two renowned researchers in the area of temperament, define individuality as the interaction of nature and nurture, the style of behavior in response to environment and personality development that results from biological individuality and its interaction with the environment.

Each child brings a different personal style to the family. It can be a difficult challenge for any family to accommodate the different styles in the whole of family life. Children need to be parented according to their individual temperaments, and although parents want to be fair to all their children, they cannot treat them the same. To do so would not represent effective or confident parenting. Temperamental differences are influenced by people and events, while basic individual differences persist throughout the life span.

Environmental Factors. Some environmental factors that can have an influence on the temperament of children are gender, birth order, experiences, communication with family members, discipline in the family, peer relationships, and school or day care environment. Temperament is usually identifiable early in infancy, although it changes somewhat with children's development. Tempera-ment is biologically hereditary and is also influenced by environmental factors. It is relatively stable over time. The nine main dimensions of temperament include activity level, rhythmicity, approach or withdrawal, adaptability, sensory threshold, quality of mood, intensity of reactions, distractibility, and persistence and attention span.

Using these nine dimensions of temperament, children are categorized as "easy," "difficult," and "slow to warm up." Rather than looking for causes of behavior in parenting styles, parents can adapt parenting to children's temperament. "Goodness of fit" is the link between temperament and parenting. It is the match between children's characteristics and environmental expectations. For example, very active children reared by very quiet and studious parents who do not enjoy activity or understand how anyone could might be said to "fit poorly" in terms of this personality trait.

Parents' response to children's temperament characteristics can influence children's self-esteem and how children feel about parents, siblings, and the home. Parents who are frustrated by their children's behavior are usually tense and dissatisfied with the parent-child relationship and feel as if they have failed at parenting. Parents who observe their children and match their expectations to their children's capabilities will be the most successful types of parents. Because children have little control over their temperaments, parents must establish an environment to match their children's needs. Equality is thus not a matter of "equal goods" but a matter of meeting needs.

Reasons for Differential Parenting. Although families may differ from one another, there are strong patterns that promote differential parenting responses due to birth order (the order in which children are born) and gender. Some personality characteristics are affected by birth order. Only children tend to be responsible and achievement-oriented. They act mature early on and relate well to adults. They need opportunities to learn to play and cooperate with other children. Oldest children are similar to only children. They always try to do the right thing. Sometimes they are overly sensitive, bossy, or perfectionistic. Middle children are happy, friendly, and fun-loving. They can also be rebellious and stubborn. Such children are happy-go-lucky and the most relaxed of all. They can usually find humor in any situation. Youngest children enjoy being waited on and can get their siblings to serve them. Youngest children can be manipulative and convincing, even when they are not telling the truth. Birth order, or children's perception of their place in the family, may have a direct effect on children's behavior and parenting needs.

Gender stereotyping is subtle socialization in families that can deliver impressionable messages to children. Differences in dress, emotional expectations, tidiness, and risk taking can indicate differences in parental expectations between male and female children. Equality is particularly important when it comes to encouraging the growth and development of both sexes in a manner that does not stereotype possibilities and roles for girls and boys. Children usually perceive one another as equals in status and power. This can be observed in playtime activities or in friendships, as children give and receive directives without hesitation. Adults need only observe their children's interactions and follow their patterns of gender equality.

Democratic Family Meetings. Family meetings, at which issues of common concern can be discussed, are one way to foster equality, problem solving, and mutual respect. In family meetings, all persons may be invited to attend and leave as they wish. Decisions are made by consensus, and all members agree to abide by whatever compromises families decide upon. No family members can be allowed to use such meetings to manipulate, control, or embarrass other family members.

An equitable family is one in which parenting is fair, consistent, and individually suited to each child. It is a safe place to grow, in which all members are respected for who they are and in which all characteristics of temperament are valued and fostered in an equitable manner. It is a place in which children can make choices and learn diversity in lifestyles and thinking as they work and play together in mutual support and respect for one another. —*Patricia A. Ainsa*

BIBLIOGRAPHY

Bredecamp, S. *Developmentally Appropriate Practice in Early Childhood Programs Serving Children from Birth Through Age Eight.* Expanded ed. Washington, D.C.: National Association for the Education of Young Children, 1996.

Damon, William. *The Moral Child.* New York: Free Press, 1988.

Galinsky, Ellen, and Judy David. *The Preschool Years: Family Strategies That Work from Parents and Experts.* Toronto, Canada: Random House, 1988.

King, Edith, Marilyn Chipman, and Marta Cruz-Janzen. *Educating Young Children in a Diverse Society.* Boston: Allyn & Bacon, 1994.

Texas Association of School Boards. *Practical Parenting Education.* Austin, Tex.: Author, 1991.

Thomas, Alexander, and Stella Chess. *Temperament and Development.* New York: Bruner/Mazel, 1977.

See also Birth order; Disciplining children; Favoritism; Gender inequality; Primogeniture.

Erikson, Erik H.

BORN: June 15, 1902, near Frankfurt, Germany
DIED: May 12, 1994, Harwich, Mass.
AREA OF ACHIEVEMENT: Children and child development
SIGNIFICANCE: Erikson modernized and extended Freudian theory, postulating eight stages of psychosocial development; he was particularly well known for his description of the identity crisis experienced by adolescents

In 1927, Erikson made the fateful decision to accept a job teaching in a progressive school in Vienna. The school had been created by an American student of Sigmund Freud. In Vienna, Erikson was invited to receive psychoanalysis training with Anna Freud, who was particularly interested in the analysis of children. Upon completion of his training, he was made a full member of the Vienna Psychoanalytic Society. During this time, Erikson met and married Joan Serson, his life-long partner and editor. They eventually had three children. Because of the political events unfolding in Europe, Erikson and his wife left Vienna for the United States in 1933. Shortly before leaving he took the name "Erikson." (He had originally been named Homburger after his Jewish stepfather.) Emphasizing the importance of childhood experiences on later life, Freud had once observed that "the child is father of the man." Erikson seemed to pay homage to this view in renaming himself "son of Erik."

Despite his lack of formal academic credentials, Erikson secured academic posts at several presti-

Erik Erikson in 1970. (AP/Wide World Photos)

gious universities during the course of his long career, including Harvard, Yale, and the University of California, Berkeley, and he worked in a variety of cultural settings. He is best known for his eight stages of psychosocial development: trust vs. mistrust (infancy); autonomy vs. shame/doubt (toddler); initiative vs. guilt (preschool); industry vs. inferiority (elementary); identity vs. role confusion (adolescence); intimacy vs. isolation (young adulthood); generativity vs. stagnation (middle adulthood); integrity vs. despair (late adulthood). At each stage the individual faces a "developmental crisis" that may be resolved either positively or negatively. As an example, the preschooler who is continually reprimanded for "getting into things" and "making a mess" may develop a sense of guilt (as opposed to a sense of initiative) because of failing to live up to parental expectations. While Freud considered the first three of these stages as most critical, Erikson felt that each stage was important and attached special importance to the development of identity during adolescence. During the "identity crisis" of adolescence, adolescents struggle to decide who they are and what careers they plan to pursue. Erikson used the term "moratorium" to describe the period during which this struggle takes place and firm decisions have not yet been reached. Elaborating on this stage, James Marcia (1987) proposed four potential identity statuses: identity diffusion, identity foreclosure, moratorium, and identity achievement.

Erikson authored several influential books, including *Childhood and Society* (1950), *Young Man Luther* (1958), *Identity, Youth, and Crisis* (1968), and *Gandhi's Truth* (1969), and his theories remain central to many child development textbooks.

—Russell N. Carney

See also Freudian psychology; Love; Puberty and adolescence.

Eugenics

RELEVANT ISSUES: Health and medicine; Law; Race and ethnicity

SIGNIFICANCE: In the early part of the twentieth century, the eugenics movement became one of the largest legislative attempts to control reproduction—the most basic and private of family affairs

The eugenics movement was a historical attempt to "improve" the population through the use of legislatively controlled reproductive practices. Legislative implementation was multifaceted and included segregation and sterilization laws at the state level and laws restricting immigration at the federal. Furthermore, eugenics served as a foundation of the Nazi's "final solution," which led to the genocide of six million European Jews and millions of other "undesirables." In the aftermath of the Nazi era, eugenics fell into strong disrepute and was considered a pseudo-science by researchers in the field of genetics. However, with modern advancements in the field of genetic research, many eugenic ideals are again resurfacing.

Historical and Intellectual Foundations. The primary goal of eugenics is to increase the birth rates of desired groups while decreasing the birth rates of undesired groups. The eugenic philosophy was extremely popular throughout Western Europe and the United States during the early part of the twentieth century. While the implementation of eugenic principles has been repudiated, it is important to understand the social and intellectual climate in which these principles originated.

Three intellectual ideas popular in the late nineteenth and early twentieth centuries converged, leading to the advancement of eugenic principles. The most powerful of these was social Darwinism. Evolutionist Charles Darwin's monumental *On the Origin of Species,* published in 1859, influenced the thinking of the time. As is often the case with such profound works, the principles developed by Darwin to account for the variation of animal life were adapted to other fields of study. Social Darwinism attempted to explain social relations among races and economic classes as a function of evolutionary processes. There was a long history in European thinking that the nobility and the upper social classes had attained their position in society through birthright. Intellectual elitists of the nineteenth century took Darwin's notion of the "survival of the fittest" to be proof that the upper classes were of better "stock" than the lower classes. It was only natural for these upper classes to have a superior position in society.

The second intellectual idea that contributed to the development of the eugenics movement was the biological concept of race. The concept of race became analogous to the concept of species. As a result, the particular behavioral stereotypes held by the European-American elite about other races were held to be immutable. Furthermore, many feared that racial interbreeding would lead to contaminated germ plasm, thus degrading the "higher" races.

Finally, the earlier works of Gregor Mendel on selective breeding practices in horticulture were rediscovered around 1900 and served as the foundation of population genetics. Population genetics is the set of mathematical principles which can be used to predict the frequency of traits in the offspring of a species on the basis of the frequency of those traits in the parent population. Thus, it was believed that a more desirable race could be created by controlling the reproductive rates of desired and undesired peoples.

These three ideas converged in the thinking of Charles Darwin's cousin Sir Francis Galton. Galton formally established the eugenics movement in London in 1904 with an inauguration address to the Sociological Society. In this address, Galton concluded that since a person's character was of an inherited nature, and therefore immutable, and that since it was transferable through the germ plasm, it was imperative for the health of the superior races that their own members be preserved and the progeny of the inferior races and classes be limited, if not eradicated.

Three Avenues of Applied Eugenics. There were three primary avenues for the implementation of eugenic ideals: positive eugenics, negative eugenics, and preventive eugenics. Galton and his followers believed that comprehensive national policies utilizing all three of the above approaches were necessary to maintain the superior achievements of the Western European race (which included North Americans of Western European descent).

Positive eugenics is the encouragement of parenthood by "worthy" parents. This component was

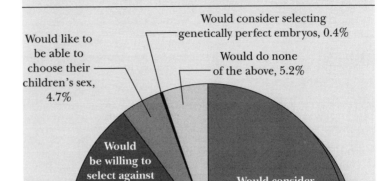

Parent's Opinions on Genetic "Tinkering"

Would consider selecting genetically perfect embryos, 0.4%

Would like to be able to choose their children's sex, 4.7%

Would do none of the above, 5.2%

Would be willing to select against or correct congenital defects, 17.8%

Would consider genetic makeup of prospective spouses, 39.4%

Would undergo prenatal testing for fetuses' suspected genetic defects, 32.5%

Source: Moms Online (1998)

Note: In early 1998 Moms Online conducted an informal survey among visitors to its website, asking them how far they would go in genetically manipulating their unborn children. This chart summarizes their responses.

to be achieved primarily through public education. Eugenic programs were implemented in schools catering to the upper social classes on the role of eugenics in the health of the nation and the upper classes's responsibility to pursue this aim. High school and college courses on how to maintain successful intimate and familial relations were implemented in order to encourage marriage among the social elite. In these educational and propaganda courses, the basic fundamentals of eugenics were explained, and young women were strongly encouraged to marry quickly and have many children. A rather negative portrayal was made of women who chose to pursue a career, not marry, or have few or no children. In their text *Applied Eugenics* (1933), Paul Popenoe and Roswell Johnson claimed that it is the confusion women have about pursuing their own interests and rights as citizens that has led to the degradation of marriages among socially worthy parents. Furthermore, they believed that young women must be educated about the costly errors of the women's rights movement.

Negative eugenics, conversely, is the discouragement of parenthood by the unworthy. The unworthy were defined to be the "lesser races" (anyone not of Western European descent) and groups commonly referred to as the feebleminded, imbeciles, prostitutes, paupers, and social and political deviants. The goals of negative eugenics were to be accomplished through programs of selective segregation, selective sterilization, and selective birth control.

Selective segregation was implemented almost universally across the United States, Canada, and England. Hundreds of thousands of the "mentally diseased," illiterates, and criminals were required by state laws to be institutionalized, denied contact with their families, and prevented from reproducing. These institutions ranged from large hospitals to less expensive labor camps. Many eugenicists believed that because the feebleminded were particularly adept at hard labor, the use of labor camps was doubly effective for society, for they gave "social degenerates" a way to contribute to society.

In addition to institutional segregation, nearly all states implemented antimiscegenation laws preventing individuals from different races from intermarrying and having children. The fallacious use of studies on racial intelligence led to the ranking of races according to genetic intellectual endowments. Basing themselves on Mendelian inheritance principles, eugenicists argued that if superior and inferior races were to mix, the progeny would be of the lower quality. These same studies on racial intelligence provided the foundation for the Immigration Restriction Act of 1924. Through this act thousands of Eastern European Jews and Slavs were denied immigration to the United States based entirely on the belief that they were of an intellectually deficient race and would degrade the Western European-derived elite of the United States.

In many cases it was felt that segregation alone was insufficient to prevent the spread of defective offspring. Thus, sterilization was considered a more appropriate course of action. Between 1900 and 1933, approximately 16,000 people were sterilized. Typically, more men were sterilized than women, because the procedure was more difficult in women. The one exception to this trend was in California, where the number of men and women sterilized was nearly equal. California's sterilization law was the most actively implemented and was thus taken as a model for the effective use of sterilization for eugenic purposes. By 1933 at least 8,500 people had been sterilized in California institutions and hospitals.

Because it was viewed as a model program, there was considerable research on the effects of sterilization in California. This research proclaimed sterilization to be a very effective eugenic method. Reportedly, nearly all branches of human services were happy with the procedure. These studies also suggested that the majority of individuals undergoing sterilization were happy with the results. In those cases in which participants were dissatisfied, researchers suggested that these persons were unhappy because of some mental deficiency. The California studies also claimed to provide evidence that the operation was in no way painful and that the vast majority of persons who underwent the operation preferred to be sterilized. While the validity of these studies were strongly questioned in later decades, they were taken to suggest that the sterilization laws were favored by both the public and the institutionalized themselves. The moral argument was made that sterilized persons were much better off after undergoing sterilization. It was argued that parole could be granted to many sterilized prisoners who would otherwise remain in institutions, that girls of suspect racial background could be allowed to marry, and that families that would otherwise have to be separated could remain intact if one of their members was sterilized.

In the early 1900's the lower social classes tended to produce offspring at a higher rate than that of the higher classes. As such, the leaders of the eugenics movement determined that research into effective contraceptive techniques and the dissemination of knowledge about contraceptives to lower social classes was necessary. This approach was less physically intrusive and Machiavellian in scope than segregation and sterilization laws. Nevertheless, it was among the more strongly contested aspects of the eugenics movement. Because of its opposition to the use of contraceptives, the Roman Catholic Church, whose membership largely belonged to targeted groups, protested against this aspect of the eugenics movement.

The third approach promoted by eugenicists was preventive eugenics. Preventive eugenics held that it was necessary to protect parenthood from racial poisoning. Racial poisons were defined as substances that were detrimental to the normal functioning of the germ plasm, most notably alcohol. As early as 1920 the negative effects of alcohol on both pregnancies and parenting practices had been observed. Alcoholics were subjected to institutionalization and perhaps sterilization. Furthermore, the findings on the effects of alcohol were used to support the prohibition movement of the 1920's.

Nazi Implementation and Western Recanting. The downfall of the eugenics movement came fol-

lowing World War II. The notion that race was a biological concept, in combination with applied eugenic principles, led to the Nazi's "final solution." The "Jewish problem," as it was referred to in early twentieth century Germany, had historically been approached from a reformist perspective. It was argued that if the Jews could be converted to Christianity and integrated into German society, they would not be such an evil threatening presence. However, the principles of eugenics led to a different conclusion. If race was biologically based and thus immutable, then the Jews could not be reformed. The Nazis railed that the "Jewish threat" emanated from Jews inside and outside Germany and that it was necessary to eradicate them.

Prior to World War II the Nazi application of eugenics was mostly applauded by Western Europe and the United States. In fact, the intro-

James Watson and Francis Crick, who shared the 1962 Nobel Prize for Medicine for their discovery of DNA. (Archive Photos)

ductory paragraphs of the Virginia eugenics laws and the German policies on Jews are quite similar. It was only after the war that eugenics was vilified by the Western scientific community as a whole and viewed as a product of fascist and racist ideologies.

Eugenics in the Last Half of the Twentieth Century. The discovery of the structure of DNA (deoxyribonucleic acid) by James Watson and Francis Crick in 1953 led to an explosion of genetic research and a resurgence of eugenic thinking. Although geneticists are careful to distance themselves from the earlier field of eugenics, the underlying ideology of eugenics can still be found. This ranges from quite explicit eugenic expositions, such as those professed in Charles Murray and Richard J. Herrnstein's controversial book *The Bell Curve* (1994), to more subtle implications of genetic technology.

There are several differences between the eugenics of the early twentieth century and genetic research since 1960. First, research in a number of disciplines has demonstrated that the assertions of social Darwinism, race as a biological concept, and the application of population genetics to individual cases are entirely erroneous. The method of genetic manipulation has also become more refined. The need to control reproductive practices through such means as sterilization has become unnecessary, because the actual structure of DNA itself can be manipulated. Finally, there is more discussion and dissension than there was previously within the scientific community in the late twentieth century as to the breadth of genetic research and the ethics of genetic technology.

As opposed to race perfection, genetic research at this more sophisticated level hopes to offer more choice to parents about family planning. For example, based on genetic testing, couples can be informed about the probabilities that their children will have genetic defects. This level of testing can also allow parents and physicians to take preventive steps to reduce the risks of genetic disorders. Ethical issues, such as whether parents should abort pregnancies based on the probability that they will give birth to children with genetic defects and whether parents with specific genetic makeups should be paid incentives not to have children that may be born with genetic defects, are very much in dispute. —*Ty Partridge*

BIBLIOGRAPHY

Goldhagen, Daniel Jonah. *Hitler's Willing Executioners: Ordinary Germans and the Holocaust.* New York: Alfred A. Knopf, 1996. Shows how the idea of race as a biological concept influenced eugenic practices, ultimately leading to the deaths of millions of people at the hands of what Goldhagen claims was a willing populace.

Gould, Stephen Jay. *The Mismeasure of Man.* New York: W. W. Norton, 1981. Cogently outlines the fundamental flaws in the basic eugenic idea that intelligence can be quantified, measured, and interpreted as biologically determined.

Hasain, Marouf. *The Rhetoric of Eugenics in Anglo-American Thought.* Athens: University of Georgia Press, 1996. Provides keen insights into the cultural ideologies that continue to support eugenic thinking in America, as well as the dissenting views of the minority groups most affected by the eugenics movement.

Kevles, Daniel. *In the Name of Eugenics.* Cambridge, Mass.: Harvard University Press, 1995. Complete overview of the historical context in which eugenics developed and a discussion of modern manifestations of eugenic logic.

Lewontin, Richard. *Biology as Ideology: The Doctrine of DNA.* New York: HarperCollins. 1992. Foremost text on the ideological assumptions supporting the eugenics movement as well as modern behavior genetics that presents a clear criticism of the eugenics movement and of the power ascribed to genes in the popular press.

McGee, Glenn. *The Perfect Baby: A Pragmatic Approach to Genetics.* New York: Rowman & Littlefield, 1997. Argues that much of the criticism of human genetic research is the result of unwarranted social fears and offers a positive view of the use of genetic engineering techniques to enhance human life.

Steen, Grant. *DNA and Destiny.* New York: Plenum Press, 1996. Shows how old-line eugenic approaches have been revitalized in modern research and transformed into the genetic bases of such behaviors as schizophrenia and sexual orientation.

See also Antimiscegenation laws; Birth control; Birth defects; Child prodigies; Childlessness; Euthanasia; Heredity; Infanticide; Sterilization.

Euthanasia

RELEVANT ISSUES: Aging; Health and medicine; Law

SIGNIFICANCE: The euthanasia controversy provides the opportunity for families to explore their own ideas and values that bear upon end-of-life decisions

A burning question in late twentieth century North America has been whether physicians should be permitted to end the lives of their patients upon request. This controversy engaged public attention in the 1990's when Jack Kevorkian, a retired physician, started to assist in the deaths of terminally ill people. The issue of euthanasia goes far beyond the activities of one physician and beyond the questions that have been addressed in courtrooms and legislatures. Every family has its own values to consult and its own decisions to make when the life of one of its members is nearing completion.

Euthanasia in Historical Perspective. The word "euthanasia" could be translated from the Greek as happy (*eu-*) death (*thanasia*). At first, this term referred to dying peacefully, without pain and suffering. This original meaning soon became overlaid with the idea of achieving a peaceful death by purposely bringing a life to an end rather than waiting for the dying process to take its course. Controversy developed when the question was posed as to whether it was ethical to prevent suffering by taking the lives of sufferers. This issue was divisive as long ago as the fifth century B.C.E. Some Greek physicians responded to the suffering of their terminally ill patients by providing "deadly medicine." Others strongly opposed this practice. From this controversy arose one of the most famous sections of the Hippocratic oath:

> I will give no deadly medicine to anyone if asked, nor suggest any such counsel; and in like manner I will not give to a woman an abortive remedy. With purity and with holiness I will pass my life and practice my Art.

Many modern physicians are not required to take the Hippocratic oath, nor is the oath included in the legal code. Some physicians see the Hippocratic oath as the articulation of fundamental ideals that they are committed to uphold, while others regard it as an inadequate guide to the realities of life and death in the modern world.

Euthanasia has never entirely been an issue for physicians. People have frequently encountered situations in which persons have died in agony. Soldiers have killed gravely wounded comrades or enemy soldiers on the battlefield with a swift sword thrust to prevent prolonged suffering. Dying persons have asked—even begged—to be killed, an act that has often been described as "mercy killing."

The idea of euthanasia took on a much darker meaning in Nazi Germany from 1933 to 1945. Many physicians complied with directives to kill helpless and dependent persons in hospitals and other institutions. The term "euthanasia" was applied to such acts, although the victims were neither terminally ill nor suffering. Physician compliance in killing their patients under the guise of "euthanasia" led to profound distrust of the term "euthanasia" and its advocates.

The modern controversy over euthanasia and assisted death is far removed from the Nazis' crimes against humanity. Nevertheless, some people are concerned that permitting even a limited form of assisted death will lead to widespread abuses. This is known as "the slippery slope" argument. Advocates of euthanasia believe that enlightened attitudes and suitable legal precautions will ensure that euthanasia remains within its agreed-upon bounds.

Active and Passive Euthanasia. A distinction is often made between active and passive euthanasia. Active euthanasia involves taking an action that directly ends a life. Administering a lethal drug is an example of active euthanasia. Passive euthanasia is the withdrawal of devices and procedures that support life. Removing patients from ventilators and disconnecting intravenous feeding tubes are examples of passive euthanasia. Another type of response to terminally ill people has been described at times as passive euthanasia—the decision not to start life-prolongation measures in the first place. Deciding not to place a person with massive brain damage on a life-support system is an example of this approach. Some people argue that whereas active euthanasia should be regarded as homicide, because in such cases persons directly terminate the lives of others, passive euthanasia is acceptable. Others argue that the distinction between active and passive euthanasia is irrelevant, because the outcome is the same in both instances.

There is a growing consensus that it is acceptable to forgo measures that prolong the dying process if they do not improve the quality of dying persons' lives. The living will, introduced in 1968, was an early expression of the belief that persons have the right to decide against medical interventions. Federal legislation later affirmed the principle of informed consent in the Patients' Self-Determination Act, which has been in effect since December 1, 1991. There are procedures that enable people to document their end-of-life preferences and appoint persons to safeguard this right should they become unable to speak for themselves. There is increasing public acceptance of

the right to demand the withdrawal of life-support measures when family and physicians agree that this is the proper course of action. When such situations have been brought before the justice system, mixed rulings have resulted, thereby creating a climate of uncertainty. Persons considering the decision to withdraw life-support measures often consult health law specialists. Much attention has been devoted to the development of standards and procedures to guide withdrawal-of-treatment decisions.

Arguments for Euthanasia. Most arguments in favor of euthanasia draw upon what is known generally as the "principle of autonomy" and judicially as the "liberty interest." The main assertion by proponents of euthanasia is that people have the right to make choices about what matters most to

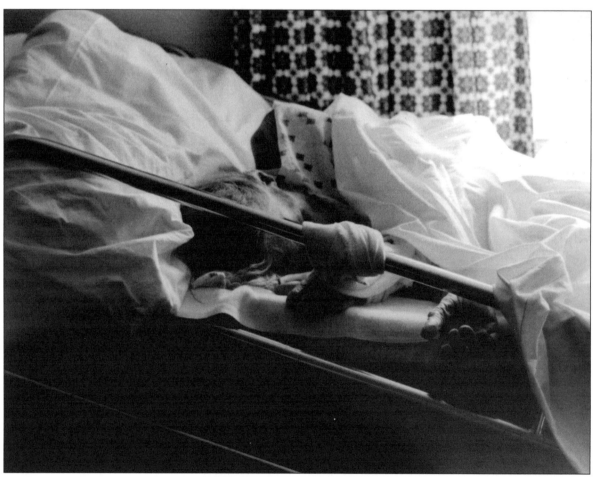

A major argument in favor of euthanasia is that terminally ill persons should not have to endure pain and despair from which there is no likely hope of escape. (AP/Wide World Photos)

them. It is argued that this right is protected by the due process clause of the Fourteenth Amendment to the United States Constitution. According to this view, the government has no compelling right to override the decisions of individuals to terminate their own lives. To abridge individuals' right to ask for merciful death is tantamount to abridging citizens' fundamental rights.

The other major argument in favor of euthanasia focuses on the suffering experienced by terminally ill people. People should not have to live and die in pain and despair; a more humane choice should be made available. Reports of the inadequate management of pain and other symptoms have been cited in support of this argument. It has been asserted that many physicians essentially abandon their dying patients and are either unskilled or unmotivated to provide effective relief.

Some proponents of euthanasia have limited their position to terminally ill and mentally competent adults who have the ability to make informed decisions. Other proponents broaden the scope of their arguments to include those with long-term illnesses who are not dying and to those who are not in a position to make their own informed choices. It is argued that the acceptance of physician-assisted, voluntary euthanasia in the Netherlands has demonstrated the value of this approach.

Arguments Against Euthanasia. Arguments against euthanasia emphasize placing limits on individual autonomy and liberty. According to such arguments, it is impermissible for people to inflict harm on others in the service of their own needs and desires. The state has both the right and the responsibility to prohibit actions that endanger and undermine society. Legalizing euthanasia for terminally ill people would encourage a form of homicide that could easily get out of control and also taint physicians as agents of death instead of life. The experience in the Netherlands with physician-assisted death is interpreted as a disaster rather than a success.

Opponents of euthanasia also assert that there are less extreme and more effective ways of comforting terminally ill people than terminating their lives. They note that hospice (palliative care) programs have had marked success throughout Canada and the United States. Pain can be alleviated. With loving care and competent assistance

terminally ill people can continue to find positive meaning in life. New programs have been developed to help physicians become more adept at providing comfort care in hospitals as well as through hospice programs. Comfort care has been recognized as an official treatment option in the U.S. medical system. Although many terminally ill persons experience moments when they wish "it were all over," most still find value in life, especially in their closest personal relationships.

Particular attention has been paid to the role of depression in the wish for euthanasia. Some of Kevorkian's patients and many others who have voiced the desire that their lives be terminated have suffered from depression. Depression can often be treated successfully. When depression is lifted, people no longer feel the need to end their lives through an act of desperation.

Intense Conflict in North America. The question of physician-assisted death has generated intense conflict in Canada and the United States. Whereas the medical associations of both countries have issued statements in opposition to the legalization of euthanasia, individual physicians have increasingly advocated it. Kevorkian has been tried on four occasions, but he has never been convicted for assisting death. The U.S. Supreme Court ruled on June 26, 1997, that states have the right to enact laws prohibiting assisted death. However, because this decision did not expressly prohibit states from enacting laws that legalize assisted death, the situation remained unsettled. Several local measures that legalize physician assisted death for mentally competent terminally ill adults have been subjected to review. By the late 1990's physician-assisted death was not clearly legal in any jurisdiction in Canada or the United States. Nevertheless, physicians have been permitted to prescribe medications in sufficient strength to relieve pain, even if doing so shortens patients' lives.

Families interested in preparing themselves for end-of-life discussions can find valuable material through hospice and palliative care services and through death education courses available at many colleges.   —*Robert Kastenbaum*

BIBLIOGRAPHY
Byock, I. *Dying Well.* New York: Riverhead Books, 1997.

Cox, D. W. *Hemlock's Cup.* Buffalo, N.Y.: Prometheus Books, 1993.

Kevorkian, Jack. *Prescription: Medicide.* Buffalo, N.Y.: Prometheus Books, 1991.

King, M. P. *Making Sense of Advance Directives.* Rev. ed. Washington, D.C.: George Washington University Press, 1996.

Lifton, Ralph J. *The Nazi Doctors.* New York: Basic Books, 1986.

Marker, R. *Deadly Compassion.* New York: William Morrow, 1993.

Quill, T. E. *Death and Dignity.* New York: Free Press, 1993.

See also Abortion; Death; Eugenics; Family crises; Family life cycle; Grief counseling; Health problems; Infanticide; Life expectancy; Living wills.

Exogamy

RELEVANT ISSUES: Marriage and dating; Parenting and family relationships

SIGNIFICANCE: Custom and law often require that marriage be exogamous, or the union of persons from different family groups

The term "exogamy" (from the Greek meaning "outside marriage") conventionally refers to the social requirement that spouses marry outside their culturally defined family group. Almost universally, this means that there is a taboo against incest, or engaging in sexual intercourse with members of one's biological family.

Explanations for the universality of the incest prohibition vary among anthropologists. Role theory posits that social order would be undermined if close kin were allowed to intermarry, as they could claim special rights over others in their extended family. Alliance theory hypothesizes that incest limits extended families' ability to compete economically and politically with other extended families, which can expand their influence through marriage.

Hebrew rules, as laid down in the book of Leviticus, prohibited marriage within the family, notably between a man and his son's wife, brother's wife, stepmother, father's brother's wife, wife's mother, or wife's sister. If a husband died, however, a brother could marry his widow. Although aunts and nephews could not marry, uncles could marry nieces, and cousins could also intermarry.

Legal prohibitions differ in defining the limits of exogamy. In Canada, England, and some U.S. states marriage is prohibited between aunts and nephews as well as uncles and nieces, but it is allowed between first cousins. Other U.S. states and some Roman Catholic countries also ban marriage between first cousins.

In sociology, exogamy has come to mean marriage across different ethnic, religious, and racial groups. Until the Supreme Court's ruling in *Loving v. Virginia* (1967), many U.S. states prohibited persons of different races from obtaining a marriage certificate.   —*Michael Haas*

See also Antimiscegenation laws; Clans; Cousins; Cross-cousins; Endogamy; Incest; Interfaith marriages; Interracial families; Marriage laws; Moiety; Nuclear family; Parallel cousins; Sexuality and sexual taboos.

Extended families

RELEVANT ISSUES: Kinship and genealogy; Parenting and family relationships; Sociology

SIGNIFICANCE: A minor form of family organization in American society, the extended family provides a network of material and emotional support to nuclear households

An extended family is a large family group composed of parents, their children, and other relatives whose residence, economic cooperation, authority, and emotional ties are formally organized by strict rules establishing the rights and obligations of each family member. The relatives other than members of the nuclear family may be grandparents, grandchildren, aunts, uncles, nephews, nieces, siblings, cousins, in-laws, and, in polygamous systems, other spouses and their children. The composition of an extended family varies with the organization of kinship; whether descent is bilateral, patrilineal, or matrilineal, whether marriage is monogamous, polygynous, or polyandrous, whether residence is patrilocal, matrilocal, or neolocal determines what an extended family is and how it lives.

In a patrilineal polygynous system such as the traditional family among members of the Church of Jesus Christ of Latter-day Saints (Mormons), unmarried children would live with their father,

Three generations of a California family in the late 1940's. (Arkent Archive)

mother, siblings, other wives of their father and the children of their father and his other wives— in other words, literally their half brothers and half sisters. Also, families may be extended vertically or horizontally. Stem families are composed of three generations living together. In this type of family, found in Japan and Ireland, unmarried children live with their parents and one set of grandparents. Joint families are composed of sets of brothers or sisters living together with their spouses and children. In this type of family, found in India, unmarried children live with their parents, uncles, aunts, and cousins.

The extended family is a form of family organization typically defined in relation to the nuclear family. An extended family is more than the collection of several nuclear families. It is composed of the living relatives who are part of a family descent group, meaning consanguinal kin who are descendants of a common ancestor, their spouses, and children. In this regard, the extended family overlaps with the consanguinal family. Also, extended families are more than the sum of their individual parts. Such families are entities in and of themselves, corporate groups whose interests and existence supersede those of its members. In this regard, the extended family overlaps with lineage and the clan.

Myth of the Extended Family. Anthropologists have found that in earlier times the extended fam-

In closely knit extended families uncles and aunts may play important roles in children's lives. (Hazel Hankin)

ily was the prevailing form of family organization. The extended family was particularly preferred in societies relying on agriculture for their livelihood. It would be erroneous, however, to believe that the extended family is the original and universal form of family organization. Anthropologists propose that nuclear family households, the standard in Western societies, were also typical of foraging societies, the least complex form of human organization found among such peoples as the Australian Aborigines and the southern African !Kung San. Anthropologists suggest that the need for mobility and the unpredictability of the food supply made it difficult for hunter-gatherers to maintain extended family households. There is evidence that extended family households came to prevail in societies where mothers and fathers were required to be absent from the home and thus could not fulfill their parental and domestic obligations. For example, in horticultural societies where women were expected to cultivate gardens and gather food, it was difficult for mothers to care for their children and perform expected household tasks at the same time. Similarly, when fathers were called away from the home to trade, fish, or engage in warfare, they could not provide the resources and protection required from males. In such cases, the presence of relatives in the household ensured the continuity of family life; elders watched over young children, sisters organized domestic duties, uncles or grandfathers fulfilled the economic and religious obligations of absent fathers.

Extended Family in American History. Historical and sociological research has dispelled the myth of the traditional American household as an extended family living happily on a self-sufficient farm. This stereotype portrayed the early American family as several generations living together with fathers working the family land, mothers tending to domestic chores, and obedient children under the watchful eye of grandmothers or a grandfathers. Historians have shown that this ideal family was not the dominant pattern in seventeenth century Europe and America. The most typical form of family was the nuclear family; houses were small, few grandparents lived with their grandchildren, and children left their parents' home once they married. This situation can be explained by demographic and economic fac-

tors. In colonial America, life expectancy was short; individuals could expect to live approximately forty-five years compared with eighty years in the 1990's. This is not to say that people did not live long; rather, the proportion of old people in the population and the likelihood that they lived with their grandchildren were much lower than they are in the late twentieth century.

Contrary to the popular belief that people married young in traditional societies, early Americans tended to marry in their mid- to late twenties. Marriage was more based on social and economic considerations than on romantic love. By marrying, men committed themselves to providing their wives and children with food, clothing, shelter, and protection. They could not marry if they lacked the economic means to fulfill this agreement, such as farms, shops, or professions. Moreover, the household was an economic enterprise in which goods and services consumed by the family were mostly produced and exchanged within the kin group. A couple could barely afford to accommodate nonproductive kin such as elders or collaterals.

If extended families have never been the norm in American society, the question arises as to the origin of this idealistic image. While debunking the myth of the original extended family, historians and sociologists have uncovered aspects of colonial and nineteenth century American family organization. For example, although not extended in structure, the traditional American household was extended in terms of living arrangements; in 1790 average family size varied between 5 and 7 persons. In addition to a married couple and their children, households frequently included nonrelated individuals such as servants, lodgers, boarders, apprentices, and slaves. They resided with families because they fulfilled a beneficial economic function: They paid rent, performed domestic chores, and contributed to the production of goods and services.

Historically, the extension of the American family beyond the normal nuclear family is linked to its adaptation to economic changes. In the nineteenth century, industrialization and urbanization resulted in a small but significant growth of extended families. The highest level of extended-family households in American history, 20 percent of all families, was recorded between 1850 and

1885. Working-class families in cities adopted this form of family arrangement out of dire necessity. The practice of "doubling up" in apartments allowed several generations or related nuclear families to cut the costs of lodging and pool all meager resources in order to avoid homelessness and indigence. All family members, including grandparents, children as young as three, and disabled adults, were expected to perform some labor. The dependence on kin and kinship networks was especially important in times of economic crisis; during the Great Depression of the 1930's, the number of extended families increased, so that one-sixth of urban households could be qualified as extended.

The Extended Family in American Society. The extended family is a form of family organization reportedly found among several racial, ethnic, and social groups in U.S. society in the late twentieth century. However, classifying the family structure among these groups as "extended" requires that the definition of the extended family be expanded beyond the concept used by historians and anthropologists to include relatives and sometimes nonrelated individuals who live in close proximity to and have frequent contact with one another. The existence of extended family networks is due to the maintenance of cultural traditions and adaptation to economic factors.

Extended families among Native Americans can be described as networks of several households of relatives and nonkin who engage in mutual aid, participate in ceremonial events, and perpetuate ancestral customs under the spiritual guidance of elders. Tribal tradition explains in part the importance of the extended family among Native Americans and Canadians; according to a 1986 report by the American Indian Law Center, in most tribes parents are not expected to shoulder all child-rearing responsibilities and can rely on the assistance of grandparents and other relatives living with them or nearby. It is erroneous, however, to speak of a typical Native American family because of the number of tribes (more than three hundred) and the diversity of family systems. The fact that approximately half of Native American men and women marry exogamously and live outside tribal lands clearly jeopardizes the maintenance of traditional ways. However, an ongoing revival movement has resulted in greater emphasis on the role of core native values—such as interdependence and harmony with nature—in social and family life.

Many African Americans spend some time of their lives living in extended families. Historian Steven Ruggles has suggested that 17.2 percent of African American households were extended in 1980, the majority of them composed of several generations living together. He estimated that 42 percent of elderly African Americans resided with relatives other than their spouses. The U.S. Census Bureau reported that 6.2 percent of African American children lived with relatives other than their parents in 1993.

When compared to other racial and ethnic groups, African Americans have been and still are more likely than whites and Hispanics to live in extended households: 1.4 percent of white children, 2.9 percent of Hispanic children, and 24 percent of white elderly persons live in such households. Contrary to popular beliefs, the extended family is neither part of the tradition or the modern preferred form of family organization of African Americans. Despite the fact that it was a feature of West African family systems, historians have shown that slaves and post-Civil War African Americans mostly lived in nuclear families. The single-parent family, composed of a single mother and her children in more than 90 percent of cases, emerged as the prevailing form of household in the African American community in the 1980's.

Economic and social factors such as poverty, unemployment, low educational attainment, low marriage rates, and high incidence of divorce explain why most African Americans do not live in nuclear families. In a poignant account of everyday family life in a poor urban black neighborhood, Carol Stack described how a network of relatives and nonkin individuals called "fictive kin" cooperate intensely; transportation and groceries are shared, tips on job and housing opportunities are passed on, assistance is provided in dealing with the welfare bureaucracy, constant adult supervision of young children is arranged. The extended family serves as a material and emotional surrogate for absent fathers, overworked mothers, unemployed adults, and poor elderly persons.

Cultural and economic factors contribute to making the extended family a significant, although not dominant, feature of immigrant families. The traditional value of familism and the religiously-based institution of the *compadrazgo*, or godparent, among Americans of Hispanic heritage encourage strong bonds of affection and cooperation between family members. Similarly, the emphasis on group needs and conformity and deference toward parents and elders among Asian Americans explain in part the emphasis on extended family obligations. There are significant differences within and between these groups, and acculturation leads to a weakening of extended family ties.

Nevertheless, the extended family represents for all minority groups a valuable resource which allows individuals to cope with an often hostile environment and maintain a well-balanced family life.

Social Issues and Public Policies. Because of the prevailing emphasis on the nuclear family and the changes it has experienced, the extended family is rarely addressed in social debate and in public policy measures. In fact, the extended family is mostly portrayed as a relic of the past or an unenviable adjunct of poverty and minority status. Such

Rites such as baptism typically bring members of extended families together. (James L. Shaffer)

a view is detrimental to groups and individuals accustomed or obliged to rely on their extended family networks. The official requirement by the U.S. Census Bureau that relatives share a common residence to be considered a family excludes those who live nearby regardless of their contribution to the material and emotional well-being of households. Inversely, according to the Internal Revenue Code, only relatives who live in taxpayers' homes qualify as dependents for whom a tax exemption can be claimed. Moreover, nonnuclear family members face restrictions from immigration and housing authorities.

Nevertheless, persons in the United States continue to care for their extended families. Research has shown that the elderly maintain frequent and close relations with their married children and grandchildren and that relatives are a vital source of assistance in the wake of family tragedies or natural disasters. Genealogical research, family reunions, and Internet postings also testify to the importance of extended family ties. The attention public policy has given to the extended family is narrow in focus, limited in scope, and uncoordinated. The Family and Medical Leave Act of 1993 includes distant relatives in its dispositions. From Massachusetts to British Columbia, legislative measures on foster care or adoption of children specifically refer to the rights of extended family members. —*Jacques M. Henry*

BIBLIOGRAPHY

Cochran, Montcrieff, et al. *Extending Families: The Social Networks of Parents and Children*. Cambridge, England: Cambridge University Press, 1990. Study of the parent-children networks detailing the influence of culture, race, class, and time on human development.

Coontz, Stephanie. *The Way We Never Were: American Families and the Nostalgia Trip*. New York: Basic Books, 1992. Provides an insightful look at the myths about American family life and concepts of the family.

Kephart, William, and William Zellner. *Extraordinary Groups: An Examination of Unconventional Lifestyles*. 5th ed. New York: St. Martin's Press, 1994. Presents eight different cultural groups and lifestyles found in the United States.

McAdoo, Harriet Pipes, ed. *Family Ethnicity: Strengths in Diversity*. Newbury Park, Calif.: Sage Publications, 1993. Collection of essays on the various forms of organization and lifestyles in American ethnic families.

Ruggles, Steven. *Prolonged Connections: The Rise of the Extended Family in Nineteenth Century England and America*. Madison: University of Wisconsin, 1987. Detailed study of the impact of economic and demographic factors on family structure during the rise of industrialization.

Skolnick, Arlene, and Jerome Skolnick, eds. *Family in Transition*. 9th ed. New York: Longman, 1997. Up-to-date collection of essays that presents modern trends in American family life in a historical perspective and examines concerns about gender issues, parenting, work, divorce, and family diversity.

Stack, Carol. *All Our Kin: Strategies for Survival in a Black Community*. New York: Harper & Row, 1974. Moving account of the everyday life of disadvantaged African American families in urban America.

Taylor, Ronald, ed. *Minority Families in the United States: A Multicultural Perspective*. Englewood Cliffs, N.J.: Prentice Hall, 1994. Presents Mexican, Puerto Rican, Chinese, Japanese, Native American, and other minority group families in the United States.

See also African Americans; Chinese Americans; Clans; Compadrazgo; Consanguinal families; Familism; Family: concept and history; Family unity; Godparents; Institutional families; Latinos; Lineage; Matrilineal descent; Native Americans; Nuclear family; Patrilineal descent.

Familism

RELEVANT ISSUES: Parenting and family relationships; Sociology

SIGNIFICANCE: Beliefs about the importance of the family influence both the behavior and the opinions of people about such issues as divorce, child rearing, family relationships, and the proper role of government in supporting families

Familism may be defined as a set of beliefs, values, and behaviors that give more importance to families than to individuals. Persons or groups who adhere to familism typically place family at the center of their social lives. From a familistic perspective, individuals are seen as owing numerous responsibilities and obligations to their immediate families and kin. Parents can exercise a great deal of power over children, often even after the children are fully grown. Parents may influence their children's choices of marriage partners or even select mates for their children.

Familist Beliefs. Children in such families generally remain at home until they marry and establish their own families. Even after grown children leave their parents' homes, they are still thought of as having heavy obligations to their parents, whom they often provide with money or other forms of material support. Parents, in turn, continue to help children throughout their lives, taking in unemployed grown children or acting as unpaid baby-sitters for their grandchildren.

Those who adhere to familistic principles generally disapprove of divorce or marital separation and tend to believe that individuals should sacrifice their own personal quests for happiness or self-fulfillment for the sake of their families. They see commitment to other family members as more important than personal achievements or accomplishments. They generally emphasize qualities such as obedience and respect for elders, rather than qualities such as self-assertion and ambition.

Decline of Familism in American Life. Individualism has long been a key American value. However, familism has also played an important role in

American social life throughout the nation's history. Until the late nineteenth century, most Americans lived and worked on family farms. Family tended to be the center of both their economic and social lives. Children and parents had to work together to plant and harvest crops, tend livestock, cook, and sew clothing. When grown children married, they often settled near the homes of their parents. They continued to have contacts with their parents, and kin networks were often concentrated within small geographical areas. Because there was no government Social Security system before 1935, parents relied on children for support as they grew old.

Even during the early period of American history, the frontier drew many individuals away from their families, causing them to leave their family ties and obligations behind. Familism began a more rapid decline, however, only with the rapid industrialization of the North American economy in the late nineteenth and early twentieth centuries. Economic activities steadily shifted away from family farms and shops toward offices and factories. As fewer people worked out of their homes, growing numbers of people uprooted themselves from their family homes and went to the cities to obtain jobs.

During the twentieth century women entered the labor force in increasing numbers. By the end of the century the majority of American women with children were employed full-time outside their homes. As grown children ceased to be able to work at home, they were increasingly expected to leave home after finishing their educations and establish their own lives. With the establishment of social security and other retirement programs, older people no longer had to look to their offspring for support. Simultaneously, an increasingly prosperous economy allowed people to think more about their own personal happiness and self-fulfillment, rather than self-sacrifice for the sake of the family. This growing emphasis on individualism, rather than familism, contributed to a rapid increase in the divorce rate and an expansion of the numbers of people living outside family households.

Ethnic Familism. Although the general trend in American society has been a movement away from familism, familistic values and attitudes have continued to be found in many sectors of the American population. Familism is particularly important among ethnic groups. Among Mexican Americans,

The core of familism is the belief that families are more important than their individual members. (James L. Shaffer)

Familism is especially important to members of ethnic communities. (Library of Congress)

for example, familistic views and practices are often strong. Family members are expected to help one another in times of economic hardship, and they often take care of one another's children. Unmarried children with incomes are expected to contribute to the incomes of parents by making gifts or regular payments. Parents place children at the centers of their lives, and grown children are expected to repay parental attentions by showing respect for parents throughout their lives.

Vietnamese Americans, one of the newest American ethnic groups, offer another example of familism as an ethnic cultural value. Family members are expected to place the family before their own needs. Older siblings with limited English-language skills often work long hours at their jobs in order to enable younger brothers or sisters—who are more fluent in English—to concentrate on their schooling. Grown children who obtain good jobs are expected to donate at least part of their incomes to their families.

As Vietnamese American children—as well as those of other new immigrant communities—adopt more of the values of the mainstream American culture, they often desert their ethnic familist traditions. This can lead to intergenerational conflict between familistic members of the older generation and individualistic members of the younger generation.

The "New Familism." The 1980's and 1990's saw a backlash against increasing individualism in American culture and calls for a new familism.

Some policymakers and social critics argued that the shift from responsibility to personal satisfaction as a basis for family life was undermining the family as a basic institution. They maintained that people who married for the sake of happiness and love would leave their marriages as soon as the emotional rewards ceased. While this phenomenon might have desirable consequences, such as escape from unfulfilling or abusive unions, it also threatened to weaken the capacities of families to perform basic social tasks. For example, some critics of the decline of American familism pointed out that most of the growth in poverty in general, and of the growth of child poverty in particular, after the 1970's resulted from an increase in single-parent, female-headed households. Child welfare expert David Popenoe pointed out that children growing up in single-parent families are two to three times more likely to suffer emotional and behavioral problems than children growing up in two-parent households. Popenoe claimed that the progressive weakening of the family should be a central issue for everyone concerned with the future of American society.

Popenoe argued that many people in the 1990's were beginning to recognize the importance of strengthening family life and coined the term "new familism" to describe this trend. It began, he maintained, with conservative movements such as the Christian family values organization Focus on the Family. However, he claimed that liberals also should attempt to revive two key characteristics of the traditional family: First, the sense of family obligations should be restored. Second, parents should strive to put the needs of their children ahead of their own. —*Carl L. Bankston III*

BIBLIOGRAPHY

Blankenhorn, David. *Fatherless in America: Confronting Our Most Urgent Social Problem*. New York: Basic Books, 1995.

Brown, Robin, ed. *Children in Crisis*. New York: H. W. Wilson, 1994.

Goldscheider, Frances K., and Calvin Goldscheider. *Leaving Home Before Marriage: Ethnicity, Familism, and Generational Relationships*. Madison: University of Wisconsin Press, 1993.

Melville, Margarita B., ed. *Mexicanas at Work in the United States*. Houston, Tex.: University of Houston Press.

Popenoe, David. *Life Without Father*. New York: Simon & Schuster, 1996.

Whitehead, Barbara Dafoe. *The Divorce Culture*. New York: Alfred A. Knopf, 1997.

Zhou, Min, and Carl L. Bankston III. *Growing Up American: How Vietnamese Children Adapt to American Society*. New York: Russell Sage Foundation, 1998.

See also Child rearing; Children born out of wedlock; Couples; Divorce; Extended families; Family unity; Family values; Fatherlessness; Generational relationships; Marriage; Nuclear family; Single-parent families; Vietnamese Americans.

Family advice columns

RELEVANT ISSUES: Children and child development; Divorce; Marriage and dating; Parenting and family relationships

SIGNIFICANCE: Useful advice on coping with problems such as dating, marriage, raising children, and divorce is available in a variety of columns in newspapers, magazines, and online services

More than one thousand different advice columns are available from North American syndicates offering publishers a wide choice of content and style. These columns discuss home repairs, household problems, gardening, cooking, beauty, and fashion. Family advice columns started with the *New York Journal*'s "Beatrice Fairfax" in 1900. Inviting readers to submit questions on a wide range of family problems, these advice columns provide interesting indications of the mores of the times.

Mother Confessor to Millions. In 1896, at the age of thirty-three, Elizabeth M. Gilmer started writing to overcome her personal depression and earn money to care for her sick husband. At the end of her career some fifty years later, she was a millionaire whose daily columns were read by more than 60 million people. She began the practice of publishing letters from readers along with her advice-to-the-lovelorn responses. On a typical day she received 100,000 letters. The format was so successful that it was followed throughout the twentieth century.

Gilmer introduced frankness in depicting women, who until then had been mentioned in the paper only at the time of their birth, marriage, and death. People turned to her writings for views on dating, marriage, careers, problem solving, and morals. They wrote to her about extravagant wives, interfering mothers-in-law, cruel husbands, how to propose marriage, or how to wriggle out of affairs. Gilmer provided advice to those in need in areas that concern everyone: how to attract a mate, how to make do on a limited budget, how to improve the quality of life, and how to escape the despair of depression, alcoholism, or unemployment.

Her decisive responses generally advocated that people take control of their lives and face their problems. A typical letter was written by an indignant woman who was tired of her husband's infidelity and wanted advice on the merits of a pistol versus poison. Another was from a seaman expressing concern over whether various girlfriends around the world were faithful to him. One woman wrote that her husband kept telling her to go to hell and asking if she could take the children with her. An engineer, writing that he had been forced at gunpoint to marry a pregnant girl whom he did not know, wanted to know what to do about it.

To couples contemplating marriage, Gilmer suggested that they sit together for three or four hours to see if they enjoyed talking of matters other than love. She composed an oft-quoted list of ten rules for happiness that suggested that people make the best of their lot, not cherish enmities and grudges, and not seek trouble. She often suggested that her readers not worry about what they did not know and instead focus on what they did. The ninth and tenth rules were to do things for persons less fortunate and to keep busy.

From Etiquette to Ann and Abby. The longest-running advice column was started by Emily Post in 1930. Born Emily Price in 1873, she became the world's authority on standards of dress, manners, and speech. Her book *Etiquette*, first published in 1922, was kept up to date with subsequent editions, and her column appeared in 150 newspapers. Post believed that etiquette is a realistic code of conduct that makes relations with others as pleasant as possible. Her keys to compatible relationships were consideration and unselfishness.

Another leading columnist on etiquette was Amy Vanderbilt. However, she did not to tell people how to behave but how the "best people" behaved. Her column appeared in such magazines as *McCall's, Better Homes and Gardens, and Ladies' Home Journal.* While her advice was prim and formal, she believed in keeping up with what was actually happening in society. Offering advice that would have shocked early advice columnists such as Beatrice Fairfax and Dorothy Dix, Vanderbilt wrote that it was all right for a couple in love to live together.

Esther Pauline Friedman and Pauline Esther Friedman, twin sisters who got married in a double ceremony in 1939 to Jules Lederer and Morton

Abigail Van Buren (Courtesy Abigail Van Buren)

Phillips, became known to the world as Ann Landers and Abigail Van Buren ("Dear Abby"). They started writing in the 1950's, adding humor and abrasive wit to advice columns while removing much of the reluctance to talk openly about sensitive modern issues. Ann Landers wrote that her most difficult column was the one announcing her own divorce in 1975. The sisters also started the practice of consulting experts—lawyers, doctors, dentists, and clergy—on readers' more complex problems. Drug use, sexual dysfunction, and venereal disease were among the problems they addressed that had been ignored by earlier columnists.

Health Columns. A popular form of family advice is written by doctors. The first syndicated medical column, "Personal Health Service," was started by William Brady in 1914. After Brady's death in 1972, his column was replaced by "For Women Only" by Lindsay Curtis, a specialist in obstetrics and gynecology. Curtis's column recognized that the majority of readers of such columns were women. He wrote on such topics as natural childbirth, smoking, and alcohol and drug addiction.

The authors of health columns are often older, conservative, well-educated practitioners making the equivalent of house calls through the media. Style and subject preferences vary, however, and subject matter has become more explicit within the restraints of publishing in family newspapers and magazines. They also often offer pamphlets on such topics as acne, arthritis, diet, stomach trouble, skin problems, life changes, coronary disease, sleep disorders, and medical research.

In 1972 Jean Mayer, who earned a Ph.D. in physiological chemistry at Yale University, started "Food for Thought," a column on nutrition that provided information on family diet. He argued that typical high school students enter middle age upon graduation because they have high-fat, low-nutrient diets and follow fad diets making confusing claims. Mayer said that hamburgers and french fries are not bad for active teenagers if they also eat other foods.

Other doctors have provided advice on psychological health in columns on child development, parent problems, and the generation gap. Melvyn Berke, for example, started a column called "After Divorce" for the Los Angeles Times Syndicate in 1977. Joyce Brothers, a psychologist widely known from television soap operas, quiz shows, and talk shows, replaced Beatrice Fairfax and was promoted as a new type of advice columnist—one with professional qualifications.

Family Advice in the Information Age. The problems that attract readers' interest have changed little since family-advice columnists first made their appearance. What has changed is the explicitness of the problems, the training of the columnists, and the widespread availability of the advice. Frank discussions about sex and such social issues as homosexuality, premarital sex, acquired immunodeficiency syndrome (AIDS), and birth control have become common. Marriage therapists discuss "Can This Marriage Be Saved?" in the *Ladies' Home Journal,* one of the outlets for Dorothy Dix's column. In 1997 the Disney Company launched an Internet home page offering a variety of professional advisers on family life with such topics as "How to raise an unspoiled child" and "Convincing a preteen not to smoke."

—*Roger D. Haney*

BIBLIOGRAPHY

Gilmer, E. M. *Dorothy Dix, Her Book: Everyday Help for Everyday People.* 2d ed. New York: Funk and Wagnalls, 1937.

Kane, Harnett T., with Ella Bentley Arthur. *Dear Dorothy Dix: The Story of a Compassionate Woman.* New York: Doubleday, 1952.

Landers, Ann. *Ann Landers Says . . . Truth Is a Stranger.* Englewood Cliffs, N.J.: Prentice-Hall, 1982.

————. *Ann Landers Talks to Teenagers About Sex.* New York: Fawcett, 1981.

Van Buren, Abigail. *Dear Teen-Ager.* New York: Bernard Geis, 1959.

Weiner, Richard. *Syndicated Columnists.* 3d ed. New York: Richard Weiner, 1979.

See also Child rearing; Couples; Disciplining children; Divorce; Emotional expression; Family counseling; Health problems; Mental health; Parenting; Support groups.

Family albums and records

RELEVANT ISSUES: Kinship and genealogy; Parenting and family relationships; Religious beliefs and practices

SIGNIFICANCE: From photo albums to oral histories, family records provide a sense of history, linking the children of today to earlier generations

From "Baby's First Picture" to golden anniversary portraits, capturing a visual record of important milestones has long been a tradition in family life. Before the nineteenth century, art was the only means of preserving such moments, and family portraits were a luxury reserved for royalty and the upper classes. Traditional types of portraits included betrothal, marriage, and family groupings. Sitting for an artist was a long and tedious process, and only the well-to-do could remain idle long enough to be captured on canvas. These images were often idealized, as an unflattering likeness could cost the artist his commission.

Paintings and Photo Albums. This changed with the 1839 invention of the daguerreotype, an early method of capturing images on copper plates lightly coated with sensitized silver and developed using mercury fumes. This new medium offered a relatively inexpensive alternative to painted portraits, and many families took the opportunity to preserve their images for posterity. The cheaper ferrotype, or "tintype," as it was more commonly known, used iron plates and made photographs even more accessible. The lengthy exposure time limited its usefulness to portraiture, and early entrepreneurs made their livings traveling from town to town photographing families dressed in their Sunday best.

In 1888 George Eastman introduced roll film and the simple Kodak box with the slogan "You push the button, we do the rest." Families now had the means to take photographs themselves. While portraiture did not completely vanish, amateur photographers could easily move out of the studio and capture the family at work and play. These early photographs offer historians an invaluable glimpse of the past, showing turn-of-the-century parties, picnics, and other social occasions, which until then had not been visually documented. By the end of the nineteenth century, most households owned a family album, which included cabinet portraits, cartes-de-visite (framed photographs mounted on cards), and tintypes.

With improvements in cameras and film throughout the twentieth century, film remained the cheapest and best way to preserve family memories. Most households still have photo albums, now filled with everything from gap-toothed grins at birthday parties to multigenerational assemblies in front of the Grand Canyon. The milestones remain—weddings, graduations, anniversaries, and annual school pictures share space with family reunions, holidays, and birthdays.

Advances in digital and computer technology have provided prospective archivists with a variety of ways to maintain photographic records. High-resolution digital cameras record and store images that can be read by a computer and transferred to diskette or CD-ROM. Using personal computers and scanners (devices that record images for computer editing and display), enthusiasts can duplicate and restore existing photographs, even creating family portraits from individual pictures of ancestors who have never met. Pictures duplicated in this manner can be viewed and stored in a variety of ways, including on videotape, CD-ROM, and, of course, in the traditional photo album.

Home Movies. With the introduction of user-friendly 8-millimeter movie cameras in the mid-1930's, moving pictures became part of some family albums. Proud parents captured birthday parties, graduations, and vacations on 8-millimeter and later Super 8 film (developed in 1965). The outlay was considerable: Early home movies required that persons have a camera, projector, and screen, and only families with the time, money, and inclination attempted to document their lives in this manner.

The "camcorder," a portable device that combined a video camera and videocassette recorder, changed everything. The benefits were obvious; instead of using film, the camcorder records images on videotape, which are then viewed through a videocassette recorder. As the technology improved, many opted to transfer their old home movies to videotape. The transfer process also allows family archivists to edit their films to include still photographs and slides and even add music or narration. By the late 1990's, camcorders were nearly as common as cameras, giving rise to the criticism that some parents were so busy recording their children's lives that they only saw the important moments through a two-inch viewfinder.

Family photo albums help link past and present generations. (James L. Shaffer)

Genealogy. Genealogy is the record of the descent of a person or family. Whereas some persons can trace their ancestry back only a few generations, others can trace their ancestry back to the days of the Mayflower and beyond. What was once an isolated hobby has blossomed into a big business, as more and more people began to search for their ancestors. Some observers attribute this increased interest in family history to Alex Haley's 1976 book and subsequent television miniseries, *Roots,* which dramatized the author's search for his own ancestors. Most North Americans have ancestors who emigrated from other countries, and genealogical research can bridge the gap for those who may have lost touch with their ethnic heritage.

Genealogical records are tracked in two manners. The first begins with a common ancestor and shows all of his or her descendants. The second works backward from the current generation. Using special computer software, professional and amateur genealogists can create multigenerational family trees and search Internet databases for census and other archival information.

Detailed genealogical records have benefits beyond their historical value, especially if each family members' medical histories are included in the tree. Doctors can use this information to watch for early warning signs of inherited diseases such as hemophilia, sickle-cell anemia, and certain cancers. Information from the horizontal line (brothers, sisters, aunts, uncles, and cousins) is as important as information from the vertical line (parents, grandparents, and great-grandparents).

Videotaping has become a modern alternative to the traditional photo album; however, magnetic media, such as audio- and videotape, lack the long-term durability of printed photographs and are not likely to be permanent. (James L. Shaffer)

Being aware of the risk can lead to the prevention, early detection, and treatment of some diseases.

Oral Histories. For centuries oral histories were the only family records. They required no technology, only an apt storyteller and an audience. Complete histories passed down from generation to generation, imbued with a rich sense of tradition and ancestry. The oral tradition continued well into the twentieth century, when the rise in literacy rates allowed family archivists to put their stories down on paper. Since then, photographs and the written word have all but supplanted oral histories. Fortunately, in many families there is still one person who assumes the role of historian and is eager to pass the legacy on to younger generations. Both storytellers and listeners derive benefits from oral history: Storytellers gain a sense of their own historical importance while listeners acquire the gift of learning about their origins.

Types of Family Records. Despite the widespread use of personal computers, for most persons paper is still the medium of choice. Family bibles provide persons with historical links to earlier generations, in many cases the only links they have, as many government records were destroyed during the Revolutionary and Civil Wars. For the families of slaves and the transient poor, scribbled notes in the family bible were often the only records that existed of their families. Birth certificates, report cards, newspaper clippings, and marriage licenses are also part of family life. Scrapbooks are sometimes used to preserve letters, postcards, ticket stubs, and other fragile mementos. Letters to loved ones from overseas, love missives pledging eternal troth, even newsy Christmas cards can give future generations a glimpse of who came before.

Family records are not limited to traditional means, and there are a wide variety of ways to keep the past alive. Heirloom plants are those transplanted from the family farm or a loved ones' garden. Marking children's height on a doorjamb is another family tradition. Family cookbooks are also handed down from generation to generation. Some families opt for time capsules, to be opened on a child's distant birthday. These can contain toys, tapes of favorite music, recorded messages, anything that might bridge the gap between the years.
— *P. S. Ramsey*

BIBLIOGRAPHY

Arnold, Jackie Smith. *Kinship: It's All Relative.* Baltimore: Genealogical Publishing Co., 1990.

Davis, Cullom, Kathryn Back, and Kay MacLean. *Oral History: From Tape to Type.* Chicago: American Library Association, 1977.

Fletcher, William. *Recording Your Family History.* Berkeley, Calif.: Ten Speed Press, 1989.

Haley, Alex. *Roots.* New York: Doubleday, 1976.

Jones, Vincent L., Arlene H. Eakle, and Milfred H. Christensen. *Family History for Fun and Profit.* Salt Lake City, Utah: Publishers Press, 1978.

Pladsen, Carol, and Denis Clifford. *Family Records: How to Preserve Personal, Financial and Legal History.* Berkeley, Calif.: Nolo Press, 1987.

See also Ancestor worship; Coats of arms; Family gatherings and reunions; Family History Library; Family trees; Holidays; Kinship systems; Lineage; Myths and storytelling.

Family and Medical Leave Act (FMLA)

DATE: Proposed in Congress as Public Law 103-3 and enacted on February 5, 1993

RELEVANT ISSUES: Economics and work; Health and medicine; Law

SIGNIFICANCE: With increasing numbers of working women, single-parent families, and workers caring for elderly parents who are living longer, federal laws have tried to make the workplace more family friendly

After years of controversial congressional debate, the Family and Medical Leave Act (FMLA) was passed and signed by President Bill Clinton in February of 1993. This act protects employees who previously had risked losing their jobs by taking time off for a sick child or relative or a newborn infant. The law provides up to twelve weeks of unpaid leave each year for the birth or adoption of a child or the illness of a family member or oneself. The leave days need not be consecutive, but may be intermittent. Workers are allowed to return to the same or an equivalent position with no loss of benefits. Employers may require that employees use paid vacation or sick leave first.

Balancing work and family responsibilities is a problem for both women and men in the work-

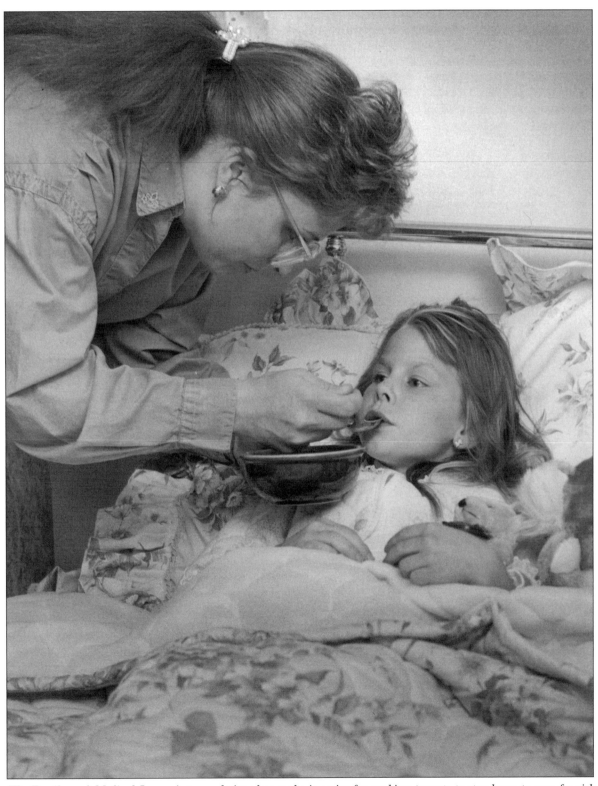

The Family and Medical Leave Act was designed to make it easier for working parents to stay home to care for sick family members. (James L. Shaffer)

States with Family Leave Laws in 1994

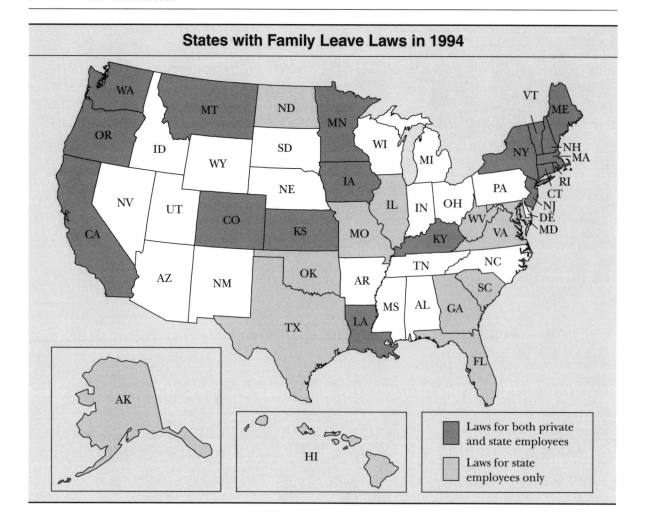

Legend:
- Laws for both private and state employees
- Laws for state employees only

force. The act covers about 40 percent of employees, exempting small firms. Only 2 to 4 percent of workers eligible to take a leave have done so. Some may not be able to afford unpaid leave. Policies in Canada and many other countries (including Austria, France, Japan, and Sweden) are more generous, some offering longer and partially or fully paid leaves.
—*Betsy B. Holli*

See also Dual-earner families; Family-friendly programs; Health of children; Health problems; Maternity leave; Pregnancy Discrimination Act; Sandwich generation; Single-parent families; Work.

Family businesses

RELEVANT ISSUES: Economics and work; Parenting and family relationships

SIGNIFICANCE: Family businesses represent the oldest form of business enterprise in the world and have continued strongly to effect the economy in the late twentieth century United States

From ancient pottery makers of Mesopotamia to the family farm of nineteenth century America, a natural form of business organization consisted of using the varied talents of family members to achieve efficiency. Indeed, the very concept of "home economics" implies that all families had to operate—at times—like businesses in their allocation of scarce resources and utilization of labor. The rise of the modern corporation in the mid-1800's reduced the overall influence of family firms on the economies of nations but did not eliminate family businesses or reduce their popularity.

Background. Prior to the mid-nineteenth century, most business organizations, especially in the United States, were family firms. These included farms, plantations, small shops, and factories and covered areas of endeavor as varied as banking, mining, textile manufacturing, bookselling, and rice planting. On family farms or plantations, husbands generally oversaw "outdoor" activities, such as planting, harvesting, and mining. In the case of artisans or merchants, husbands managed the shop floor or store office. On farms, wives managed purchases for personnel, and on larger plantations they managed the "inside" work related to the plantation houses and slave quarters, such as clothing and feeding the people in residence as well as their own family members. In cities, wives helped clean stores, keep books, take orders, and—in cases of illness or death of their husbands—they actually managed the businesses. Children were viewed as a source of unpaid labor, with the understanding that they were learning a trade as well as earning their keep. In some cases, parents sent male children to other merchants or artisans as apprentices to "learn the business," as was the case with the American banker J. P. Morgan. The division of labor allowed the family to retain as profits all the money they would have had to spend paying laborers and training employees.

Decline of the Family Business. Several factors contributed to the decline of family firms as the

A traditional "mom and pop" grocery store. (AP/Wide World Photos)

most prominent form of business enterprise. Farming families found that their land could support only one or two heirs; eventually children could not be retained indefinitely as laborers when there was no prospect that they would take over family farms. Also, city dwellers were increasingly subjected to a new ethos demanding public education of children, thus removing children as stable components of the labor force for parent-owned businesses.

More important, however, the rise of industrialization introduced two other factors that greatly reduced the appeal of family firms. Large-scale enterprises such as railroads, with their high capital demands, brought about a separation of owner-ship from management of businesses. This dramatically reduced the ability of families to control large-scale enterprises, as evidenced by the fact that virtually the only "family" that managed to retain substantial control of a large railroad was the Vanderbilts, and even they lost control after a generation. Industrialization also introduced the factory system, with its emphasis on mass production and wage labor. The appeal of the factory, with its promise of steady pay, often drew farm boys who had watched their parents struggle through unpredictable weather, disastrous crop failures, and heavy debts. Large-scale enterprise did not eliminate family firms, but by the 1920's it had seriously weakened their impact on the econ-

Restaurants are among the most common types of family businesses. (James L. Shaffer)

omy. The dynamic rise of General Motors, eclipsing family-dominated Ford, characterized that era.

Revival of Small Business and the Family Firm. After World War II, small firms offered a welcome alternative to factory work, despite the fact that the economy continued to be dominated by "big businesses," which—with a few exceptions such as the Gettys and the Fords—were seldom run by a single family. Small businesses also had a more relaxed pace that offered an alternative to the pressures felt by the "Organization Man," who rarely saw his family. Suburbanization added to the demand for millions of new dry cleaners, appliance stores, drug stores, and grocery stores, many of them owned and operated by families. Both husbands and wives managed their operations, kept the books, and handled "the front," with children filling in after school, on weekends, and during vacations. In contrast to the past, however, most small business owners did not expect their children to "grow up to run the business," but instead used some of their income to send them to college in the hope they might attain higher-paying and more prestigious jobs. The revival of "mom and pop" stores coincided with an intensive lobbying effort in Washington and the creation of the Small Business Administration (SBA) in 1953, which provided special tax incentives and easy credit for individuals starting or operating small businesses.

More important to the revival of small businesses than the SBA, however, was the appearance of a new form of business expansion: franchising. Made popular by McDonald's Restaurants, franchises have allowed families to purchase businesses with built-in advertising, a national reputation, and professional managerial support. Franchises reduced the risk of initial investments, while providing much of the independence associated with family business ownership. Auto dealerships, long a favorite of families operating franchises, were joined by Baskin-Robbins ice cream, Howard Johnson motels, drug stores, and, later, pizza delivery services and health clubs.

Family-owned large firms had not disappeared entirely. Frank Gerber and his son turned a small canning company from the 1920's into a booming baby-food manufacturer in the 1950's; A. P. Giannini and his family dominated the powerful Bank of America from the 1920's to the 1960's; and Sam

Walton and his family ran the gigantic Wal-Mart in the 1980's and 1990's. Families found, however, that maintaining family control over large business corporations was extremely difficult. Walt Disney's family finally had to relinquish control of the Disney company when they were unable to generate a hit film. The Gettys lost control of Getty Oil, which was taken over in a controversial merger by Pennzoil in the early 1980's. Even the Gianninis could not retain management control over the Bank of America in the 1980's.

Such difficulties in keeping family control of businesses illustrate the individual nature of wealth creation. A 1978 study of male multimillionaires revealed that only one-third of them had inherited a significant portion of their money, and of those whose net worth exceeded $2 million, almost three-quarters had no inherited assets at all. Additionally, a study of 1,100 millionaires found that 80 percent of American millionaires were first-generation rich, and more than half of all millionaires never received any inheritance at all. In contrast, with the exception of John F. Kennedy, Jr.'s foray into publishing, not one of the inheritors of Joseph P. Kennedy's fortune has gone into business.

Immigrants and Family Businesses. For generations, immigrants have comprised an important segment of family businesses, from Italian restaurants to Chinese landscapers. Beginning in the 1960's and 1970's, new waves of Cuban, Vietnamese, Lebanese, and Mexican immigrants came to the United States. More than 200,000 Cubans arrived in Florida in the first two years after Fidel Castro came to power, creating 25,000 new businesses in Dade County alone. Michael Zabian, a Lebanese refugee who settled in Lee, Massachusetts, developed a family-run business that eventually encompassed a grocery store and a department store.

The key to these immigrants' success—and that of previous generations of European immigrants—is their commitment to hard work through harnessing the efforts of their extended families. Lebanese businesses, for example, stay open between 16 and 18 hours a day. A study of Korean family businesses in Atlanta found that they worked an average of 60 hours a week. The work habits of Jamaican immigrant families were so pronounced that they were spoofed in many of

A more restricted form of family business is the home business, such as this woman's Christmas decoration business. (AP/Wide World Photos)

the skits performed on the cutting-edge variety series *In Living Color*. Unfortunately, most statistics concerning wealth accumulation in the United States have not accounted for the labor or on-the-job experience gains of family members, thus dramatically underestimating the value and influence of family-owned companies. Ironically, legislation designed to limit part-time work and require minimum wages has reinvigorated family businesses paying no detectable wages at all, for families' children have become the only labor that many low-profit operations can afford.

Regulations and the Revival of the Family Small Business. As immigrants have quickly learned, many of the regulations enacted between 1960 and 1990 have enhanced the desirability of owning small businesses predominantly operated by family members. Small dry cleaners, independent restaurants, or tanning salons cannot hire many employees at the increasing minimum wage rates and stay competitive. People hoping to develop and sell new products and needing employees to operate telephones and offices cannot afford the rising taxes required by the government. Very few small businesses can begin to comply with the blizzard of regulations related to employee health and protection, sexual harassment, disabilities acts, and dozens of other expensive laws and regulations. As a result, small firms have increasingly turned to family members to help operate their businesses. There is no way of determining how many of the 14 million sole proprietorships in the United States in 1995 were family firms, but evidence suggests that the number was large and growing, as witnessed by the fact that "microbusinesses" (firms with fewer than five employees) constituted the most rapidly growing category of all enterprises.

The arrival of widespread computer technology and the Internet, with its commercial operations on the World Wide Web, have accelerated the expansion of microbusinesses and broadened the appeal of the family firm. A family of four, with a capable teenager who is computer competent, can operate a thriving Web-based business from the home, thus avoiding government regulations that apply to hired employees. This is seen in the fact that most corporations have less than $100,000 in total assets. Yet while the U.S. economy has continued to grow, the sales of the top corporations has

fallen steadily as a share of gross national product (GNP), buoyed only by the spectacular rise of a few companies such as Microsoft.

One of the most rapidly rising new areas of family business—again, dominated by immigrants—are nail salons. By 1996 nail salons constituted a $6 billion industry (equal to that of the video-game market dominated by Japanese corporations such as Nintendo), a figure that industry analysts suggest underestimates the level of activity. Family-owned salons have appeared in "upscale" malls, and in Los Angeles County alone the number of nail technicians rose from 9,700 to 15,200 in five years, with more than 80 percent being Vietnamese-born. In the 1980's virtually no economist predicted the growth of such family businesses, and the Bureau of Labor Statistics did not even track the listing for manicurists as late as 1979.

A significant problem facing small business family firms, which has implications for the entire family, is that nearly half of the 800,000 new firms launched annually fail. The central fact of entrepreneurial life is that of risk, and every family enterprise confronts the competition of the market each day. Unlike arrangements whereby family members might be employed by different companies and are thus somewhat protected against layoffs or business failures, family business failures can imperil the structure of the family itself. Yet, virtually all of the founders of successful family businesses have failed at least once. Automobile manufacturer Henry Ford, banker A. P. Giannini, and retailer Sam Walton all either declared bankruptcy or were kicked out of companies they created.

In general, most small firms have small annual incomes hovering around $16,000, as compared to General Motors' annual sales of $126 billion. Nevertheless, many family-owned small businesses remain small deliberately, with adults choosing to work fewer hours or to be less aggressive at expanding their enterprises in order to focus on nonbusiness family relationships. The number of individual family businesses that become large, however, represents an ever-increasing share of all business activity, because the overall pool of small businesses and family firms continues to swell.

Expansion of the Internet can further accelerate the advantages already enjoyed by home-based, family-run operations. In 1997, the Internet service provider America Online recorded more than 16 million "log ons" in a single day, most of which the government has little control over. Businesses can take and ship orders, determine customer satisfaction, and maintain all records without expanding their employee base outside the family. The economic cost of regulation and taxation facing large firms with many employees, combined with the computer/Internet revolution, can accelerate the increasing number of family businesses and their influence on the market. Mandatory retirement ages and the desperate need for reliable employees by small businesses means that retirees will increasingly be approached by family members for part-time employment. Finally, family farms—the essence of the family business in previous eras—still exist and even thrive in modern society. —*Larry Schweikart*

BIBLIOGRAPHY

Bruchey, Stuart. *Small Business in American Life.* New York. Columbia University Press, 1980. Essay collection that features an excellent overview by the author and contains a number of specialized, highly useful essays on small business growth and operations.

Fucini, Joseph J., and Suzy Fucini. *Entrepreneurs: The Men and Women Behind Famous Brand Names and How They Made It.* Boston: G. K. Hall, 1985. Well-researched book that provides snapshots of dozens of successful entrepreneurs, including family businesses such as Gerber and Mary Kay Cosmetics.

Gilder, George. *Recapturing the Spirit of Enterprise.* San Francisco, Calif.: C. S. Press, 1992. An updated version of his *The Spirit of Enterprise* (1984), this work approaches entrepreneurship with attention to analysis of macroeconomic data and to numerous case studies.

Min, Pyong Gap. *Ethnic Business Enterprise: Korean Small Business in Atlanta.* New York: Center for Migration Studies, 1988. Excellent source dealing with the situation of Korean small businesses.

Neff, Alixa. "Lebanese Immigration into the United States: 1880 to the Present." In *The Lebanese in the World: A Century of Emigration*, edited by Albert Hourani and Nadim Shehadi. London: Taurus, 1992. Details the history of Lebanese immigration to the United States.

Schweikart, Larry. "Business and the Economy." In *American Decades: The 1950's*, edited by Richard Layman. Detroit: Gale Publications, 1994. Includes material dating to World War II dealing with such business developments as franchises, the revival of the family firm, and the dominance of large corporations.

Sowell, Thomas. *Race and Culture: A World View.* New York: Basic Books, 1994. Synthesizes a great array of data on immigrants to various nations, emphasizing their contributions to the economies in their new homes.

See also Corporate families; Family economics; Institutional families; Wealth; Work.

Family caregiving

RELEVANT ISSUES: Aging; Health and medicine; Parenting and family relationships

SIGNIFICANCE: The provision or management of extraordinary assistance to family members has many forms and costs and is performed primarily by wives and adult daughters

In the late twentieth century, the convergence of several life-span and life-course factors ushered in a remarkable decrease in fertility rates, greater public concern for healthy lifestyles, and a concomitant increase in the numbers of North Americans fulfilling their life-span potential. As a direct outcome of these factors, by the late 1990's the fastest-growing segment of the population comprised those aged eighty-five and older. The favorable physical and demographic conditions of aging, however, have to be considered in the context of what has been called the "compression of morbidity": Many illnesses have not been eradicated; rather, their onset and debilitating effects have been delayed. Periods of significantly ill health are thus compressed and may increase in proportion with advanced age.

These factors together suggest that at least part of shared family life may be spent with family members in ill health who require assistance in performing daily routines, such as bathing, walking, laundry, and meal preparation. These forms of assistance are central in the conceptualization of caregiving.

Who Cares? Although less than 10 percent of older Americans reside in long-term care settings,

The growing lifespans of Americans have increased the demands on adults to care for their parents. (James L. Shaffer)

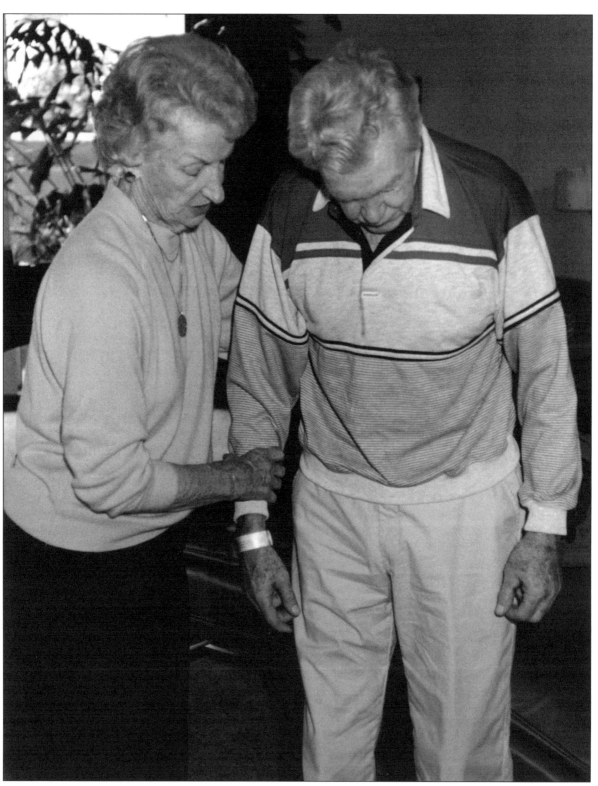

The burden of caring for an elderly Alzheimer's victim is magnified by the fact that the victim may neither recognize nor thank the person providing the care. (Ben Klaffke)

old age increases the likelihood of institutionalization. It has been estimated that almost one-third of North Americans eighty-five years old and older spend at least some time in an institution. It is important to note, however, that institutionalization does not end family caregiving careers. Caregivers report frequent and lengthy visits to their institutionalized family members and continue to provide care in the form of bathing, writing correspondence, or managing finances.

The vast majority of dependent elders receive care in informal or community settings. Essentially, these communities are families; community care is, in practice, elder care by family members. Moreover, there is typically a primary caregiver—one whose time is significantly devoted to the care of an older family member. More than one in seven adults in the United States provide care for a relative or friend. These caregivers include spouses (approximately 35 percent), adult children (approximately 45 percent), siblings, other relatives, and friends. Most of these spouses are wives, partially because women outlive men and tend to marry men older than themselves. The adult children are typically daughters or daughters-in-law; roughly 80 percent of adult-child caregivers are women, and almost 20 percent of all middle-aged women are caregivers. Family care, and therefore community care, is typically care by women.

This is not to say that men do not care. There appear, however, to be differences between how women and men give care. Women have been described as care providers, delivering services directly to care recipients and being somewhat more involved than men; men have been described as care managers, arranging for care to be provided and overseeing its provision. Men may also perform such time-limited tasks as laundry and preparing meals.

Masked in the discussion of gender, however, is the analysis of generation. That is, wives and husbands may provide different patterns of care from that provided by daughters and sons. This issue remains relatively unexplored, although differing levels and types of intimacy and expectations (including filial responsibility) characterize these family relationships. Moreover, because spouses are older than their children, they may themselves be dealing with ability losses. Elaine Brody has written about "women in the middle," referring to those caregiving daughters in their middle years, in the middle generation (potentially caring for both parents and children), and in the middle of multiple demands upon their time (including family and employment). It is important to recognize these gender and generational differences; the support needed by daughters and wives differs from that needed by husbands and sons.

Costs of Caregiving. The goal of support programs is typically to ease the burden experienced by caregivers. The difficulties, stresses, and strains reported by caregivers—usually in terms of anxiety, exhaustion, and isolation—have been the focus of much research. One central burden on caregivers is the amount and type of care provided. It has been found that care provision creates greater burdens than care management. Furthermore, those caregivers who are more involved in the direct provision of care report greater burden; thus, spouses are more burdened than children, and children are more burdened than other relatives. Similarly, those caregivers who share their residences with care recipients are more burdened than those with independent residences. Spending great amounts of time providing care means that other activities either suffer or are sacrificed. The tasks may also be burdensome—such as personal hygiene assistance, which violates people's personal boundaries. Interestingly, caregivers also report that interacting with professionals is stressful.

A second factor associated with increased burden is the condition of the care recipient. A major component is the level, cause, and permanence of the functional disability of the older person in need of care. A poignant example might be caring for someone with Alzheimer's disease who no longer recognizes the caregivers.

A third factor concerns the situation of the caregivers themselves. These include age and gender. Older caregivers report greater exhaustion and more concern for the future of the care recipients. Women report greater burden than men—perhaps because of the amount of work they do or because of their greater ease in expressing burden. "Women in the middle" appear to have an especially burdensome load.

Solo caregivers and reluctant caregivers report greater burden. Employment status also plays a role. Many women report leaving the paid labor force or cutting back work hours in order to provide care for their aging parents. This may become a prelude to poverty in the caregivers' later years as a consequence of reduced pension contributions and reduced earnings. It should also be noted, however, that home employment may serve as a helpful respite from the burden of caregiving.

Further Thoughts. Despite the extreme conditions and hardships experienced by those on the front lines, caregiving involves more than burden. What little research exists suggests that caregiving can also be associated with an increased sense of mastery or competence; caregivers may also derive satisfaction from their experience in enabling desirable outcomes, such as the delay or avoidance of institutionalization, or the opportunity to express their love, duty, and commitment.

A neglected area of caregiving involves older parents who care for adult children. A relevant example concerns older parents as caregivers of mentally ill adult children. The rapid deinstitutionalization of mental patients has resulted in the discharge of an estimated 65 percent of such persons from hospitals. Most of them return to their parents, and a slightly smaller proportion return to their spouses. Expressions of burden are reported by these caregivers and are often exacerbated by parents' anticipatory grief and mourning for their child's lost future. In caring for children with acquired immunodeficiency syndrome (AIDS), parents, and especially mothers, take on unanticipated caregiving responsibilities in later life, responsibilities also assumed by large numbers of domestic partners and intimate friends.

—*Brian de Vries*

BIBLIOGRAPHY

Aneshensel, C. S., et al. *Profiles in Caregiving: The Unexpected Career.* New York: Academic Press, 1995.

Brody, E. M. *Women in the Middle.* New York: Springer, 1990.

Finch, J., and D. Groves. *A Labour of Love: Women, Work, and Caring.* London: Routledge & Kegan Paul, 1983.

Jarvik, L., and G. Small. *Parentcare: A Compassionate, Commonsense Guide for Children and Their Aging Parents.* New York: Bantam Books, 1988.

Marks, N. "Caregiving Across the Lifespan: National Prevalence and Predictors." *Family Relations* 45 (1996).

Walker, A. J., C. C. Pratt, and L. Eddy. "Informal Caregiving to Aging Family Members: A Critical Review." *Family Relations* 44 (1995).

See also Acquired immunodeficiency syndrome (AIDS); Aging and elderly care; Alzheimer's disease; Child care; Elder abuse; Filial responsibility; Foster homes; Generational relationships; Health problems; Men's roles; Parenting; Sandwich generation; Substitute caregivers; Volunteerism; Women's roles.

Family: concept and history

RELEVANT ISSUES: Children and child development; Divorce; Kinship and genealogy; Law; Marriage and dating; Parenting and family relationships; Religious beliefs and practices; Sociology

SIGNIFICANCE: The role of the family, which has changed throughout history and which impinges on kinship, marriage, and divorce, has been to organize religious, economic, political, and social behavior

Family values had become a hot political issue at the end of the twentieth century. This buzzword seems to move people to want to create a society in which family values are paramount. The trouble is that few people can agree on what family values mean. Consequently, the family-values movement has involved a good deal of harking back to some notion of the good old days, when the family consisted of a mother, father, and children. The father went off to work and the mother stayed home and raised the children. This notion of the nuclear family is largely unreal.

The reality seems to be that the very definition of family has constantly fluctuated throughout history. From kinship through clan through extended family through nuclear family, family types and ties have changed. Perhaps the only constant in the concept of family is the emotional support the family has provided to its members and the human need for some kind of identity with kinship.

Prehistory. Because humans stand upright, have small pelvic openings, and undergo a short gestation period, the need for prolonged maternal care for children is important. These factors, combining with the increasing complexity of social inter-

Amid changing definitions of family, one constant has been the emotional support that families provide for their members. (James L. Shaffer)

Throughout human history parents have played a central role in educating and training children. (James L. Shaffer)

action, led to the evolution of the human brain and the development of the family unit. As survival demanded adopting a broad-based diet with a food-sharing social group, the combination of families increased the complexity and unpredictability of daily life. Kinship, therefore, has played a fundamental role in organizing religious, economic, and political behavior.

The earliest Paleolithic persons, *Homo erectus*, who lived approximately 600,000 years ago, organized themselves into small bands for protection and food gathering. The basic social unit in this hunter-gatherer society was the family. Because of women's roles as gatherers and bearers and raisers of children, a gradual division of labor along gender lines arose, which may date from this time. Neolithic society, which existed approximately 10,000 years ago, became settled. The family remained the basic unit with, perhaps, the extended family taking on a more prominent role. This would have provided the labor for agricultural tasks. Women may have even enjoyed a higher status than men owing to their importance as planters and gatherers during the agricultural revolution. Mythology suggests that the subjugation of women did not occur until the introduction of the animal-drawn plow about 5,000 years ago.

All known societies have recognized marriage and condemned incest. The forms of marriage have differed. Monogamy, marriage in which a spouse has only one mate, is widely practiced in the modern Christian world. However, polygamy, or marriage in which a spouse has more than one mate at the same time, was sanctioned by the Bible and is still practiced in the Muslim world. Polyandry, marriage in which women have more than one husband is rare, and group marriage, in which two or more men marry two or more women is the rarest of family types.

History. The Code of Hammurabi in Mesopotamia (c. 2100 B.C.E.) provided one of the earliest legal codes in the Western world. It spelled out the rights of husbands and wives and of parents and children. Men could practice polygamy, have mistresses, and sell their wives and children into slavery. Men could also divorce at will. Women could divorce only by demonstrating cruelty or neglect. They could, however, own property and enter into contracts. Fathers had absolute control over their

children until the latter married. Marriages were arranged by parents and sealed by contract. Fathers could not disinherit sons unless they had twice committed major offenses. The code greatly influenced Hebrew legal principles embodied in the Bible.

The generally tightly-knit patriarchal family continued through Greek and Roman times into the Byzantine Empire, which existed from approximately the fourth century C.E. to the thirteenth century. The social role of women was defined within the confines of the nuclear family, which was the heart of the social structure. Women did make some gains. An eighth century law treated women and men as equals with respect to property and gave widows with children total control over their property. By the late eleventh century the nuclear family had broadened into the extended family, because a kinship network offered political control. Under this arrangement, women became more active in court and aristocratic circles.

In East Asia, Confucianism as a governing philosophy had taken control by the fifth century B.C.E. Because of the patriarchal nature of this system, fathers had control over all members of their families, but they were expected to set a good example. Confucianism taught "right-relations" for virtuous behavior: father-son, husband-wife, older brother-younger brother relations. Sons were more important than daughters and women were subservient to men.

Meanwhile, dark-skinned peoples spread across sub-Saharan Africa. They shared a common heritage in which family and kinship were primary. Extended families grouped into tribes with chieftains picked by family elders. Showing great diversity in inheritance patterns, some tribes recognized the primacy of the female line while others recognized the primacy of the male line.

By the sixteenth century Europeans began to move away from the extended family, which remained common in Asia and Africa. In place of the extended family the conjugal or nuclear family began to take hold in Europe. In both Europe and Asia monogamy prevailed, whereas in the Muslim world, Africa, and among some South American Indian tribes polygyny was the rule. Although family structures varied throughout the world, all societies valued children for a variety of reasons, including for the labor they performed and the social security they offered.

Arranged marriages were common among European aristocrats and Asian families until the sixteenth century. Both supported the concept of the domination of the husband-father as a ruler figure over the family. Both also supported the desirability of sons over daughters. Thus, Europeans sometimes forced "surplus" daughters into becoming nuns, while the Chinese just threw them away. The Asian family, however, took on a very different role from that of the Europeans. The Asian family was hierarchical and extended. It was not uncommon for three generations to live under one roof together, with the grandfather as the dominant figure. Responsibility and loyalty were owed to the group. Individuals succeeded only as members of families, castes, clans, or guilds.

The European model, on the other hand, moved away from kinship dominance to an emphasis on individuality and individual responsibility. Protestantism stressed the nuclear family and marital affection. Meanwhile, Protestant Europe planted the seed for the ultimate weakening of the family unit by establishing the principle of divorce. As the nation-state developed, responsibility for social control shifted from kinship to the state. This decline in the role of kinship reinforced the nuclear family and a diminishing sense of kin responsibility for individual acts. The Napoleonic Code (1804) confirmed the flow of authority downward from the state through the patriarchal family. It further confirmed the status of the husband-father. Women could own property only with husbands' written consent. At fathers' command, children could be imprisoned for up to six months, and until they reached the age of thirty they had to gain their fathers' consent in order to marry.

The Family and the Industrial Revolution. Modernity led to secularization and authority based on rational-legal principles. It also gave rise to capitalism. The Industrial Revolution of the early nineteenth century dramatically altered the family structure along class lines. Because the textile mills favored the employment of women and children and women could also find domestic employment, the previously dominant and responsible husband-father was left relatively underemployed. Women and children were, moreover, cruelly exploited by their employers. The family broke down. Single-parent households, high rates of illegitimacy, child delinquency, prostitution, and theft became much in evidence.

In contrast, bourgeois and working-class families tended to become more child-centered. The home with the dutiful and comfortable "Ma" that was always there to satisfy both children and husbands became the ideal. Women were stereotyped into the role of docile subordinates, who existed only to support family breadwinners and take care of the children. As the middle class expanded in both Europe and North America, legal power became concentrated in the hands of husbands and fathers. Property rights passed through fathers, and whereas husbands could divorce their wives on the grounds of adultery, wives could not divorce their husbands. Boys went to school to receive a classical education or to learn a profession, while girls stayed home to learn domestic work and religion.

Well into the twentieth century women's main occupations were in domestic service, the textile trades, and garment making. Moreover, the female workforce was largely single. By 1911 only 9.6 percent of married women were employed. Even as the world wars of the twentieth century changed the composition of the workforce by allowing women to take traditionally male jobs, the notion of the domestically-tied married woman and the man-as-sole-breadwinner lasted well past mid-century.

The Concept of Family. The ancient Greek philosopher Plato, arguing that the family was too weak to be trusted with the socialization of children, believed that children should become wards of the state. The nineteenth century French philosopher Auguste Comte worried that the French Revolution had weakened social ties and broken down monogamy. Late twentieth century American politicians played on the notion that the modern welfare state is responsible for breaking down "family values." The status of the family as a social institution has long been debated and is always in flux.

The family is a universal social institution. The form and function of the family, however, differs widely in a cross-cultural context. In the Navajo family, for example, husbands and wives live under separate roofs—wives live with their mothers, sisters, and their children, while husbands live in communal men's houses. The Masai of East Africa consider it impolite for a wife to refuse "sexual hospitality" to a husband's good friend. In Samoa, children are members of an extended family and roam from house to house at will. The most commonly practiced form of marriage in the world is monogamy. This does not, however, mean that men and women are necessarily limited to one lifetime spouse. Because more than half of American marriages end in divorce and most divorced people remarry, Americans, for example, practice "serial monogamy."

Despite massive pressures for change, family ties have been shown to remain strong. (James L. Shaffer)

Traditionally, the four functions of the family have been the regulation of sexual activity, reproduction, socialization of children, and the economic function of providing food, shelter, protection, and health care to its members. Industrial and postindustrial societies have altered these functions. The connection between sex and reproduction has been broken by such medical advances as the birth control pill. Consequently, sex before and outside marriage is widely practiced. To some extent, because of the complexity and unpredictability of modern society and its volatile job market, modern schools have taken over the socialization role. Finally, some governments have assumed a large economic role through such programs as socialized medicine and social security. The one family constant has been emotional support for its members.

The Changing Family. The American pollster George Gallup, Jr., has suggested that four pressures on the family were responsible for a late twentieth century change in the traditional family unit. Because this unit has been responsible for transmitting stable cultural and moral values from generation to generation, new cultural and moral values are altering manners and mores into the twenty-first century.

Gallup cited the increasing incidence of alternative lifestyles. Gay men and lesbians have begun to gain the right to marry and adopt children. Many heterosexual single adults have begun single-parent households by adopting children. Some women have chosen to bear children out of wedlock or through artificial insemination. Polls have indicated that young people consider living together without the benefit of marriage an acceptable long-term alternative. Additionally, many married couples choose to remain childless. Gallup also recognized a changed sexual morality. Premarital and extramarital sex are commonplace. With acceptance comes a desire for more promiscuity within society and a denial of the importance of the family unit.

The family unit may likewise feel pressure from changing economic circumstances. The employment of women in large numbers outside the home has become the rule rather than the exception. Families feel the need for extra income in order to afford child rearing itself. Child rearing has thus suffered as a result of economic changes in society. Finally, Gallup has suggested that the pressure of grassroots feminist philosophy has contributed to change in the traditional family. Women have shunned the subservient domestic role, demanding equal opportunity with men, and have entered the workforce in ever-increasing numbers in order to assert their rights.

Despite these pressures, evidence indicates that family ties remain strong. The extended family, which sociologists define as three or more blood generations living in close proximity or under the same roof, was bemoaned as a lost ideal during the 1950's and 1960's. In truth, it had been changing throughout the twentieth century. The modified extended family is now a more accurate model. This is a network of relatives who live in separate residences, often miles apart, but maintain close family ties.

Myth of the Nuclear Family. A convenient myth has been that of the ideal nuclear family, consisting of a husband and wife and their dependent children living in a home of their own. In this myth husbands are breadwinners and wives household servants. The media helped to foster this myth with its popular TV sitcoms of the 1950's, such as *Ozzie and Harriet* and *Leave It to Beaver*. While it is true that the rates of divorce and out-of-wedlock births in the 1950's were half of what they became in the 1990's, the picture painted of American family life in the 1950's was an aberration. The nuclear family of the 1950's represented a break from a long-term pattern of social change. Since 1900 the gender gap in education had been narrowing and the divorce rate rising. The image of the "happy housewife" masked women's boredom and lack of fulfillment, presaging the social angst of the 1960's. Moreover, postwar affluence hid "socially invisible" poverty. Some forty to fifty million people, 25 percent of all Americans, lived in poverty. Half of two-parent African American families lived in poverty and 40 percent of mothers in these families worked outside the home.

By the 1990's several identifiable trends in the changing American family emerged. Among the most important of these were the increasing age at which people first married, the proportion of young adults remaining single, divorced adults, adults living alone, unmarried couples, single-parent families, working wives and mothers, and

A postmodern trend among American families has been the declining strength of links among the generations. (James L. Shaffer)

dual-career families. Concurrently, couples were bearing fewer children.

U.S. Census Bureau figures show the change in American households. From 1970 to 1995 the proportion of adults who never married rose from 18.9 to 26.8 percent for males and 13.7 to 19.4 for females. From 1970 to 1993 the birthrate per 1,000 women decreased from 87.9 to 67.6. From 1970 to 1996 the proportion of out-of-wedlock births nearly tripled. From 1965 to 1994 the divorce rate rose from 2.5 to 4.6 per 1,000 people. From 1970 to 1996 the number of Americans over fifteen who lived alone more than doubled. By 1996, 63.5 percent of women with children under six years of age and 76.2 percent of women with children between six and seventeen years of age were in the labor force. The trend of these figures has remained constant throughout the industrialized world. For example, in Canada between 1961 and 1991, households with a married couple and children decreased from 51 to 30 percent, households with married couples without children increased from 27 to 33 percent, single-parent households increased from 4 to 6 percent, and single-person households increased from 9 to 23 percent.

By 1992, 27 percent of American children lived in one-parent families. Estimates suggested that 50 percent of all children and 80 percent of African American children would live in a single-parent environment before they reached eighteen. The vast majority of single parents are mothers. Between 1960 and 1992 births to unmarried mothers increased fivefold. The absolute number of out-of-wedlock births is highest for white mothers, but the percentage is higher for minorities.

Ratios for out-of-wedlock births are about the same for all Western countries. The United States, however, has the highest rate of teenage pregnancy, even though teenagers in Canada and Europe have the same rates of sexual activity. Poverty and low educational attainment seem to be key factors in the high rate of teenage pregnancy in the United States.

The United States also has the highest divorce rate of any industrial nation. About half of U.S. marriages end in divorce. The divorce rate is influenced by several factors: the age at which couples first marry (couples who marry in their teens are twice as likely to get divorced as those who marry in their twenties); socioeconomic status (the lower the family income, the higher the divorce rate); race (depending on socioeconomic status); religion (Protestants are more likely to divorce than Roman Catholics); and children (more and speedier divorces among the childless).

Nevertheless, because of shifting cultural moods, the rate of divorce seems to be leveling off and may even decline into the twenty-first century. Living and having children outside formal marriage has lost some of its stigma. Alternative lifestyles are more accepted. Moreover, the acquired immunodeficiency syndrome (AIDS) epidemic may influence stronger monogamous ties.

The increasing incidence of single-parent families through out-of-wedlock births and divorce has produced a new extended family. Owing to stagnating wages, the high cost of urban housing, and the need for child care, multigenerational households have been on the rise. Three-quarters of single parents live with their parents or other relatives. Nevertheless, the notion of the nuclear family holds a powerful attraction for Americans. Polls indicate that most Americans rate a good marriage and family life as important to them. Studies further indicate that married persons are generally healthier and happier both physically and mentally than nonmarried persons.

Family, Race, and Ethnicity. Race and ethnic variations in the United States affect family structure and function. For the African American family the legacy of slavery, racism, and economic disadvantage has had profound effects. The divorce rate is high. Women are more likely than men to head African American households. Families tend to be young and poor. Half of African American children are born to single mothers, and four out five will live in a female-headed household at some time in their lives. This is due partly to economic factors and partly to the fact that women outnumber men at every age past childhood. Fortunately, African Americans have strong extended family ties. They are far more likely than whites to live in classical three-generation extended families. Families tend to pool resources and develop strong bonds of kinship and friendship as a buffer against discrimination.

Likewise, Hispanics hold to the extended family. Many see *la familia* as the center of their lives. They also tend to be young and poor. They maintain close bonds of kinship and live near their extended kin. Asian American families, on the other hand, while true to the notion of the extended family, tend to be strictly patriarchal. Interfamily discipline is strict. Children must defer to their parents' wishes. They tend to have a higher socioeconomic status than other minorities. Among Asian American families, marriage rates are higher and divorce rates lower than the average.

The Family and Poverty in Postmodern Times. In the first half of the twentieth century poverty was seen as a pervasive condition involving the working class. By mid-century, poverty was seen as a minority problem. At century's end, poverty has been seen as part of the breakdown of the family and the emergence of an urban underclass. In the United States and Canada, for example, families headed by divorced or separated women have low incomes, low levels of home ownership, low savings, and low participation in pension plans. Several trends have influenced this "new poverty." Greater social mobility and individual freedom have abetted female freedom. An extended liberal state has increased individual autonomy and encouraged alternate ways of living and working. The gendered family structure and gender division of labor has created a "feminization of poverty."

Thus, the postmodern trend is toward weaker links among generations, a declining commitment to marriage, and a lack of meaning for women in domestic life. This loosening social structure has contributed to the greater influence of commercialism and to a more material culture. The rise of materialism has heightened the stigma of poverty.

Whatever the form and function of the family, poverty plays a key role in determining its stability. Conversely, family stability plays a key role in determining poverty. A direct correlation exists between family income level and divorce. Only 19.1 percent of American children with families whose income level is below $5,000 per year live with both parents, while 91.4 percent of children whose family income is above $40,000 live with both parents. James Q. Wilson, Professor Emeritus of political science at UCLA, summed up the problem in a 1997 speech: "You need only do three things to avoid poverty in this country—finish high school, marry before having a child, and produce the child after the age of twenty. Only 8 percent of families who do this are poor; 79 percent of those who fail to do this are poor." Clearly, then, this "new poverty" will call into question income redistribution schemes well into the twenty-first century.

It seems to be a matter of perspective whether one is optimistic or pessimistic about the consequences of the changing family. If one sees the family as an instrument for providing emotional support and companionship to its members, there may be reason for optimism. If, however, one sees the family as primarily an instrument for child rearing, there may be reason for pessimism. The only certain thing is that the family will continue to adapt itself to changing historical circumstances. *—Brian G. Tobin*

BIBLIOGRAPHY

Cheal, David. *New Poverty: Families in Postmodern Society.* Westport, Conn.: Greenwood Press, 1996. Scholarly work that employs statistical analysis to compare the relationship between families and poverty in the United States and Canada.

Fagan, Brian. *The Journey from Eden: The Peopling of Our World.* London: Thames and Hudson, 1990. Work examining the history and genesis of the family in different parts of the world.

Gallup, George, Jr. *Forecast 2000.* New York: William Morrow, 1985. Well-known pollster looks at trends regarding families, marriage, divorce, and childbearing as society faces the twenty-first century.

Gelles, Richard J., and Ann Levine. *Sociology: An Introduction.* New York: McGraw-Hill, 1995. Updated survey of key definitions and sociological pressures affecting individuals and families.

Greaves, Richard L., Philip V. Cannistraro, Robert Zaller, and Murphey Rhoads. *Civilizations of the World: The Human Adventure.* 2d ed. New York: Harper-Collins, 1993. Comprehensive overview of the history of civilizations throughout the world.

Harris, John, ed. *The Family: A Social History of the Twentieth Century.* Oxford, England: Oxford University Press, 1991. Readable and illustrated look at how modernity has affected families throughout the world.

Lauer, Robert H. *Social Problems and the Quality of Life.* 7th ed. New York: McGraw-Hill, 1998. Work that explores the interrelationship of problems affecting the lives of families.

Rosman, Abraham, and Paula G. Rubel. *The Tapestry of Culture: An Introduction to Cultural Anthropology.* New York: McGraw-Hill, 1992. Work that surveys the role of families in a broad cultural context.

See also Divorce; Extended families; Family unity; Family values; Fatherhood; Gender inequality; Literature and families; Marriage; Marxist critique of the family; Men's roles; Monogamy; Motherhood; Nuclear family; Single-parent families; Women's roles.

Family counseling

RELEVANT ISSUES: Children and child development; Marriage and dating; Parenting and family relationships

SIGNIFICANCE: Counseling helps hurting families
facing a variety of problems find solutions by
learning to work together and communicate
more effectively

Helping families in emotional and behavioral distress find the courage, love, strength, and wisdom
to heal themselves when they are hurt by life is the
job of family counselors. When successful, family
members feel more successful as a team and better
about themselves as individuals. They are better
able to talk with other family members about their
wants and needs. Counseling can enable family
members to manage stress and anger constructively and can help families and family members
experience less depression, anxiety, and physical
symptoms.

Counseling Techniques. Using a variety of approaches, interventions, and techniques, counselors can help families strengthen themselves and
develop stronger and more satisfying relationships. Counselors offer families and family members support in times of turmoil. They work with
individuals and groups within families. Counseling
can help all types of families—those with children,
stepfamilies, extended families, dual-career families, single-parent households, and even adults
with their own parents.

Family counselors focus on the problems that
cause dysfunctional behavior within families. They
are more interested in the present than the past.
Counselors concentrate on patterns of communication—how family members express their wants,
needs, anger, and other emotions.

Solving Problems. Practitioners contend that all
counseling is family counseling, because working
with individuals to change behavior cannot help
but affect the feelings, attitudes, and behavior of
others with whom they live, especially children.
Family counseling differs from individual counseling in that counselors must be involved in families'
communication patterns, relationships, and power
blocs. Family counseling is the process of solving
problems for the good of the whole family and in
the best interests of individual family members.

Perhaps most important, family counselors believe
that individuals' behavior must be understood in
the context of the whole family and may even be a
sign that the family is hurting or being hurt.

Family counseling involves changing behavior
and communication patterns to preserve and to
strengthen families. Such counseling can be
highly effective when family members have difficulty getting along with one another, or are depressed, anxious, hurting, or scared. Counseling
can be helpful when parents argue too much or
when family members hit, touch, or talk to one
another in ways that cause anger or emotional or
physical pain. It is useful when families' own efforts to solve their problems and to communicate
do not work or when problems worsen or become
chronic.

The keys to successful family counseling and
behavioral change are the right counselors and
the willingness of family members to do what is
best for their families and their members. It is
about finding workable solutions to problems, not
about placing blame. Counseling sessions are supposed to be safe places to find better ways of interacting and talking. Family members must feel
comfortable enough with counselors to express
themselves and work to cope with or change their
situations. Confidences must be kept and decisions respected.

Types of Counselors. Counseling is conducted
by a variety of professionals, including clergy, social workers, and other individuals not licensed as
psychologists or psychiatrists. For example, pastors
who provide family counseling services may address spiritual questions and use spiritual tools
such as Scripture and prayers. They are, however,
not licensed to provide medical or psychological
counseling or therapy. Pastoral counselors acknowledge that physical or environmental influences may cause some problems and that physicians or psychiatrists might better serve families'
needs. Clinical psychologists also provide counseling services, although their expertise is geared
more toward the management of major mental
illness. In settings such as community mental-
health centers and hospitals, helping professionals
all essentially do the same things.

Professionals approach family counseling from
a variety of theoretical standpoints, including psychoanalytic, humanistic, and behavioral perspec-

tives. Whatever their orientation, most counselors acknowledge that people have the capacity to change and to learn alternative behaviors and problem-solving skills. They recognize the critical roles early childhood experiences and home environment play in personality development. They

respect the need to make their clients feel accepted, respected, and understood. Empathy is a key helping skill.

Families are referred to counselors for many reasons, but they seek out counselors especially when their family well-being is at risk. Abuse, alco-

The job of family counselors is to help families regain the emotional strength and close ties lost during times of crisis. (James L. Shaffer)

Religious leaders often serve as informal family counselors. (James L. Shaffer)

holism, divorce, death, and serious illnesses, such as acquired immunodeficiency syndrome (AIDS) and cancer, are problems that may impel families to seek professional help. Families may struggle with one or more problems. Physicians, teachers, family members, or significant others may recommend counseling. Sometimes, counseling may even be required by foster-care agencies and juvenile court judges seeking to decide whether to terminate parental custody of children. Counseling then becomes part of a plan to preserve or reunite families, especially when children are placed in foster care because of alleged abuse or neglect. Treatment may involve one counselor or a team of professionals and other community resources, such as drug rehabilitation and anger management programs.

The Counseling Process. Counseling is a process that uses various skills, strategies, and techniques to promote positive changes in behavior. Five stages make up the counseling process: counselors' establishment of a working relationship with families, analysis of problems and their causes, an explanation of the problems, development of a formula for change, and termination of counseling. Counselors must create a caring and therapeutic environment that enables families or family members to mature in self-understanding and self-acceptance. Counselors help families to understand their strengths and weaknesses and develop a more realistic self-evaluation. They help families establish stronger and healthier social relationships, develop independence, and take on the responsibility to make sound choices. Counselors may ask clients to explore different ways of expressing themselves and their anger.

Before the counseling process begins, counselors must learn about the families they are treating, about individual family members, and about family relationships and dynamics. This understanding is gained through interviews, questionnaires, testing, informal techniques such as drawing and storytelling, and observations by family members, teachers, social workers, the police, and counselors themselves. Counselors sometimes use a diagnostic tool called a genogram, which is a map of all the members of a family over several generations, including their power structures, alliances, conflicts, and connections. Counselors use the information gleaned from these techniques to develop a hypothesis about what is causing the problem and preventing its solution by the family. Effective counseling requires that counselors win the trust of families and their members, especially during this information-gathering process.

Treatment of Family Problems. The next step is the development of a treatment plan and strategy. Counselors, in concert with families and various professionals, set goals to resolve problems and restore family well-being. Most counselors focus on facilitating behavioral change and developing healthy family and individual relationships. Strategies might include the use of support and addiction recovery groups, confidence-building exercises, social skills development, therapy, and referrals to physicians and other appropriate professionals. The strategies are designed to leverage the strengths of families and their members to aid in the recovery process. Counselors view family members as partners in the process. The coopera-

Psychiatrists who treat children may have to use different methods of evaluating the patient's emotional and mental problems, such as asking the child to create drawings that illustrate feelings and states of mind.

tion of family members is important but not always guaranteed. Lack of cooperation and even resistance to counseling, especially when there is a threat that children may be removed from the family, can be a problem. Trust plays a critical role in making the counseling process work. Counseling sessions can become emotionally charged.

Treatment is successful when the original problems have mostly disappeared or have greatly abated. Counseling is effective when family members have learned how to solve their own problems and express their wants and needs without the help of counselors. In addition, family members must have begun to practice what they have learned in counseling. If problems recur or new ones develop, families may reenter therapy. Counseling can teach families how to get help when they need it.   —*Fred Buchstein*

BIBLIOGRAPHY

Annunziata, Jane, and Phyllis Jacobson-Kram. *Solving Your Problems Together: Family Therapy for the Whole Family.* Washington, D.C.: American Psychological Association, 1994.

Carlson, J., and J. Lewis. *Family Counseling: Strategies and Issues.* Denver: Love Publishing, 1991.

Cutler, Jeffrey A., and Robert W. Brown. *Introduction to Therapeutic Counseling.* 3d ed. Pacific Grove, Calif.: Brooks/Cole Publishing Company, 1996.

Hewlett, Sylvia A. *When the Bough Breaks: The Cost of Neglecting Our Children.* New York: Basic Books, 1991.

Kagan, Richard. *Turmoil to Turning Points: Building Hope for Children in Crisis Placements.* New York: W. W. Norton & Company, 1996.

Orton, Geraldine Leitl. *Strategies for Counseling with Children and Their Parents.* Pacific Grove, Calif.: Brooks/Cole Publishing Company, 1996.

Thompson, Charles L., and Linda B. Rudolph. *Counseling Children.* 4th ed. Pacific Grove, Calif.:Brooks/Cole Publishing Company, 1996.

See also Behavior disorders; Divorce mediation; Dysfunctional families; Family advice columns; Family crises; Family therapy; Grief counseling; Marriage counseling; Mental health; Parenting; Parents Anonymous (PA); Recovery programs; Social workers.

Family courts

RELEVANT ISSUES: Divorce; Law; Parenting and family relationships
SIGNIFICANCE: There has been a growing trend in the United States to resolve legal issues relating to family matters in special courts

The governments of most U.S. states have recognized a need for judicial expertise in the resolution of purely family law issues and have delegated these matters to specialized courts. States have often created separate court systems for family law matters, giving these courts various names, such as family courts, domestic relations courts, or juvenile courts. Other jurisdictions have created special sub-branches of their general court systems to hear family law matters. Still other jurisdictions have parceled various family law issues among a bewildering variety of courts.

Unified Family Courts. The types of issues addressing the attention of family law courts vary among jurisdictions, but they typically include such matters as divorce, child and spousal support, child custody, paternity determinations, juvenile delinquency, child neglect, adoption, and domestic violence. It is not unusual, however, for one state to have several different types of courts with the power to resolve particular issues of importance to families.

Various family law matters may be delegated to different courts in ways that family members may not find easy to predict. For example, jurisdiction in adoption proceedings may be conferred upon the courts having jurisdiction in probate matters in some states, while it is conferred upon juvenile courts or family courts in others, or upon courts of general jurisdiction or equity courts in still others. In some states, different kinds of courts have power to deal with a single issue. In many jurisdictions, family members may find themselves tossed from one court to another in their quest to penetrate the thicket of laws and procedures affecting their lives. Different courts, for instance, may deal with problems involving juvenile delinquency and those involving child custody, or problems involving domestic violence and divorce.

Some advocates have suggested that states should create—where they have not already done so—unified family courts which would have the

Most U.S. states have created systems of family courts to deal with purely family issues. (James L. Shaffer)

power to address the myriad issues involving families. Such proposals are winning growing national support. This kind of consolidation, its advocates claim, would ease the confusion of seeking solutions for family law problems in a tangle of different courts. Moreover, it would give the unified family courts power to craft more comprehensive solutions to family law matters, which have traditionally been carved into smaller pieces and committed to separate courts with no ability to act in concert. Unified family court systems would combine all the elements of traditional family and juvenile courts under one roof to render comprehensive services to those appearing before them.

Family Court Personnel. Family courts generally employ a much wider range of personnel than

other U.S. courts. The U.S. system of justice has generally relied upon parties involved in legal disputes to gather evidence and present it to courts of law. Under this scheme, court personnel serve mainly to schedule, document, and assist in the conduct of judicial proceedings. Family courts, though, differ in important respects from this general pattern.

For example, family courts take a far more active role in the investigation of matters relating to the family and in attempts to link family members with needed social services. The investigative role of family courts is most pronounced in dealings with children. Their interests are not always the same as those of their parents, so they may not be adequately represented by the attorneys repre-

The types of courts that deal with problems of juvenile delinquency vary among the states. (James L. Shaffer)

senting their parents. Consequently, family courts frequently have third parties act as liaisons (guardians *ad litem*) between the court and the families to ensure that the interests of children are being protected.

Courts appoint guardians *ad litem* (guardians for the suit) to serve a variety of functions. Persons who act as guardians *ad litem* are often expected to gather information about the parents and the children and report back to the court recommending which parent should have custody of the children. Sometimes, a guardian *ad litem* is simply a lawyer appointed to represent the legal interests of the children. At other times, guardians *ad litem* are expected to mediate discussions between divorcing parents on child custody and support. In whatever capacity they serve, guardians *ad litem* are frequently lawyers. Courts also sometimes appoint liaisons, often social workers, to gather facts about the family relevant to issues such as child custody.

The Courts and Other Agencies. In addition to personnel who advocate the interests of children or investigate family circumstances, family courts also often work closely with—or supervise directly—a variety of social service personnel. These personnel respond to the wide range of problems that may afflict a family. A family, for example, may need assistance with obtaining welfare benefits or housing or counseling regarding alcohol abuse. Other family contexts may suggest a need for psychological services of some sort. Family courts are frequently in the best position to recognize these needs; they either use their own personnel to assist families or refer families to social service agencies that work in cooperation with the family court to meet these needs.

During the 1980's and 1990's, family courts increasingly attempted to organize or support education programs. These have proliferated most in the area of providing information to divorcing parents about the postdivorce needs of their children.

Continuing Supervision of Family Law Issues. Most American courts do not retain ongoing supervisory roles over matters after they have been presented in trial and judgments have been rendered. Family courts differ from other courts, however, in the degree to which they continue to supervise family issues for extended periods of time. For example, while a divorce may end a marriage, it seldom resolves all problems associated with who is to have custody of the children, under what circumstances, and with what support. Moreover, changes in family circumstances—particularly changing income levels—seldom make it practical for courts to determine such issues once and for all in single proceedings. Consequently, it is not uncommon for family courts to exercise supervision of particular matters over an extended period, during which family members—or former

family members—appear before them on multiple occasions as their individual circumstances change.

Alternatives to Family Courts. Family courts have not been immune to the overcrowded dockets and underfunded budgets that plagued virtually all U.S. courts in the last decades of the twentieth century. Many states have attempted to ease the burden on family courts by exploring alternative methods of resolving family disputes. The most popular among these alternatives is mediation. By the late 1990's somewhat more than half of the jurisdictions in the United States allowed family law courts to force interested parties (such as divorcing spouses) to mediate their disputes.

The mediators to which parties are assigned generally receive specialized training designed to assist them in their efforts to help family members agree on matters such as child custody, child support, and property division. The aim of mediation is both to relieve some of the burden on family courts and to provide a more congenial atmosphere for the resolution of family problems than can be attained in formal court proceedings. To encourage the success of mediation programs, many family courts provide, or insist upon, completion of pre-mediation education programs by family members so that they will be prepared in advance to participate in the mediation process.

—Timothy L. Hall

BIBLIOGRAPHY
Belli, Melvin M., and Mel Krantzler. *Divorcing.* New York: St. Martin's Press, 1988.
Boumil, Marcia Mobilia, and Joel Friedman. *Deadbeat Dads: A National Child Support Scandal.* Westport, Conn.: Praeger, 1996.
Clark, Homer H., Jr. *The Law of Domestic Relations in the United States.* 2 vols. St. Paul, Minn.: West Publishing, 1987.
Harwood, Norma. *A Woman's Legal Guide to Separation and Divorce in All Fifty States.* New York: Charles Scribner's Sons, 1985.
Sack, Steven Mitchell. *The Complete Legal Guide to Marriage, Divorce, Custody and Living Together.* New York: McGraw-Hill, 1987.
Sheindlin, Judy, with Josh Getlin. *Don't Pee on My Leg and Tell Me It's Raining: America's Toughest Family Court Judge Speaks Out.* New York: HarperCollins, 1996.

See also Adoption processes; Child custody; Child support; Divorce; Divorce mediation; Family law; Juvenile courts; Marriage laws; Uniform Child Custody Jurisdiction Act (UCCJA); Uniform Marital Property Act (UMPA); Uniform Marriage and Divorce Act (UMDA).

Family crises

RELEVANT ISSUES: Children and child development; Parenting and family relationships

SIGNIFICANCE: Family crises are developmental or catastrophic events that demand change and coping in the family system and from which families may emerge stronger or may not emerge intact

The Chinese orthographic character for "crisis" reveals a deep understanding of the nature of crises. This character is a combination of two simpler characters: one meaning danger, the other meaning opportunity. A crisis carries the danger of deterioration, because old ways no longer work. If the change demanded by a crisis is resisted, the danger exists that families or persons will be destroyed by it. However, crises also involve opportunities for growth and strengthening.

Normative and Nonnormative Crises. All families experience stress and crisis. Such stress and crises may range from the pressures of adjusting to predictable developmental challenges within the family life cycle to the shock of a natural disaster.

Normative, or developmental, crises are those changes or transitions that are expected or pre-

In times of family crisis, many people turn to public services maintained by volunteers. (James L. Shaffer)

dictable, which most or even all families experience over the life cycle and which require that family members and the family system adjust and adapt. Such adjustment and adaptation may be as intense as when sudden extraordinary events occur. Normative crises occur because family members and the family system develop psychologically and physically over time. Stress and potential crisis is part of this development process.

Family development theory has established that there are predictable stages over the course of the family life cycle and that within each stage there are developmental tasks for each individual member and for the family as a collective group. It is during the movement from one stage to the next that families are most vulnerable to developmental stress. For example, most married couples plan to have children, yet research shows that nearly all couples struggle greatly in adjusting to this normative event and the transition to this stage of family life.

Nonnormative crises are not predictable, expected, or experienced by most families at anticipated times. They are sometimes referred to as situational, catastrophic, and even "act-of-God" crises. They may include, for example, natural disasters, unexpected loss of employment, the birth of a handicapped child, or out-of-wedlock births.

Objective Characteristics of Stressor Events. Both normative and nonnormative events vary. Objective characteristics, or the nature of events and transitions, refer to the extent of the demands and hardships associated with events. Some events require more extensive adaptations on the part of families than do others. If the source of events is internal rather than external, they are often more difficult for families to address directly, and generally there is less sympathy and support from friends and community. For example, family members and communities rally around and assist the victims of a home fire or flood, but it is more difficult when problems arise within families themselves, such as in cases of spousal abuse or alcoholism. Another way to examine the nature of events objectively is to consider their duration. Events of temporary duration are less difficult to cope with than events of permanent duration, but both types of events are easier to handle than events whose duration is uncertain, as is the case with missing children or undiagnosed illnesses.

The total number of events, both normative and nonnormative, with which families must contend at any given time is referred to as "pile-up of stressor events." Most families deal with more than one event at a time. Stressor events overlap each other. Normative events overlap and may be complicated by nonnormative events. The consequences of this pile-up of events are a magnification of the demands and adaptations required of families at particular moments.

Family Crisis-Meeting Resources. Each family is unique, with its own composition of strengths and resources. Some resources may be well matched to aid families in the event of certain types of crisis situations; other resources may be less helpful. Although there is no magic list of resources that protects families from the stress of crisis events, many resources are recognized as being helpful. Economic resources can often provide a cushion for families in times of stress. Conversely, families in lower socioeconomic groupings are restricted not only in their income but also in their health, energy, space, and strategies for coping with crises.

Families' social supports are often regarded as critical to meeting the demands of stress and crisis. Social supports may come from extended family and kinship members, close interpersonal friendships, neighborhoods, churches, professionals (for example, mental health counselors), and mutual self-help support groups (for example, Mothers Against Drunk Driving, Parents Without Partners, and Alcoholics Anonymous).

The stressfulness of particular events depends on the balance between families' deficits and resources at the time such events occur. In addition to social supports, families also benefit from particular patterns of interaction. For example, families who ordinarily exhibit balanced levels of closeness (or family cohesion) respond better in difficult times of stress than do families who are either disengaged from each other or smotheringly close. Likewise, families who have balanced levels of flexibility (family adaptability) cope better than rigid inflexible family types or chaotic families that do not possess stable routines and role patterns.

Coping. Coping is the process of using the resources that families have at their disposal. Families that cope well experience much less stress than families that cope poorly. Families that are unable

Families are less likely to find outside support if the source of their trouble is internal to the family. (James L. Shaffer)

to cope find that they move from a state of stress to a state of crisis. In crisis situations, the family system becomes immobilized, and families can no longer perform their basic functions. Coping includes the cognitive and behavioral problem-solving strategies used to respond to stressor events. Coping thus reflects efforts undertaken by families to decrease or avoid stressors, manage hardships, activate and develop resources, and change family processes in response to the demands of stressor events.

In a most basic way, strategies for coping involve problem resolution, emotion management, or both. The purposes of coping strategies are to minimize families' perception of stress, decrease or eliminate the hardships associated with stressor events, influence the environment and change circumstances leading to stressor events, recruit various kinds of social supports, and protect families from negative physical or psychological consequences resulting from the pile-up of demands.

Cognitive coping efforts reflect how families perceive particular events. They reflect families' subjective definition of stressors, accompanying hardships, and their effects. They reflect families' values and previous experiences in dealing with change and meeting crises. To identify stress as a crisis leads to crisis. Families may ultimately destroy themselves by broad, catastrophic interpretations of events. Conversely, effective cognitive coping efforts include clarifying the hardships families face so that they become more manageable, deemphasizing the emotional components of crises, trying to maintain the functional properties of the family system, and continuing to support members' social and emotional development.

Behavioral coping strategies refer to what families actually do to manage stress. The most effective coping efforts are those that produce adaptations that reduce stress while supporting the growth and well-being of all family members. The unique stressor events families must manage interact with the coping resources they and their members possess to produce unique coping strategies. While some coping strategies may not seem optimal, they may represent the best efforts of families to deal with demands, given the available resources they have at their disposal. The effectiveness of these coping strategies is determined by the extent to which families are able to continue executing their basic tasks. As long as families are able to fulfill their basic tasks, they may be under stress but not in a crisis situation.

When the coping process breaks down, so too does the ability of families to manage their basic tasks. In such situations, family members feel alienated and isolated from one another, anxious, and perhaps depressed. Family members' roles and responsibilities become confused. The family breaks into factions, which interferes with their ability to manage conflict and support their members. Family members are then no longer assured of receiving needed physical, social, emotional, and psychological benefits, and the survival of the family may be in question. *—Gregory E. Kennedy*

BIBLIOGRAPHY

Boss, Pauline. *Family Stress Management.* Newbury Park, Calif.: Sage Publications, 1988.

Burr, W. R., and S. R. Klein. *Reexamining Family Stress.* Thousand Oaks, Calif.: Sage Publications, 1994.

Hobfoll, S. E., and C. D. Spielberger. "Family Stress: Integrating Theory and Measurement." *Journal of Family Psychology* 6 (1992).

McCubbin, H. L., E. A. Thompson, A. I. Thompson, and J. E. Fromer, eds. *Sense of Coherence and Resiliency: Stress, Coping, and Health.* Madison: University of Wisconsin Press, 1994.

Ross, C. E., J. Mirowsky, and K. Goldsteen. "The Impact of the Family on Health: The Decade in Review." In *Contemporary Families: Looking Forward, Looking Back,* edited by A. Boom. Minneapolis: National Council on Family Relations, 1991.

See also Death; Dysfunctional families; Family counseling; Family life cycle; Homeless families; Midlife crises; Mothers Against Drunk Driving (MADD); Parents Without Partners (PWP); Recovery programs; Shelters; Suicide; Support groups.

Family demographics

RELEVANT ISSUES: Demographics; Race and ethnicity; Sociology

SIGNIFICANCE: Since demography is the study of the characteristics of human populations, family demographics indicate families' major characteristics and how these characteristics differ over time and among various groups in a population

Demographers study how many people there are in a given population and attempt to describe the population in terms of variables such as age, race, gender, income, education, and religion. The size of a population is determined by birth rates, death rates, and migration rates. The family, therefore, is a central demographic issue, since every birth occurs in some type of family or creates a family. Families, like individuals, have their own demographic traits. On average, parents may be comparatively young or comparatively old, families can encompass greater or fewer children and adults, live at different income levels, and differ in terms of religious and racial background. All of these demographic traits tend to change over the course of time.

Numbers and Types of Families. The governments of the United States and Canada use the concept of the "household" to describe the living arrangements of their inhabitants. A household includes all people living together in common quarters. A family household is defined as people related by blood or marriage who live together in common quarters. In the U.S. census only couples who have entered into formal marriages are counted as "married," since most of the states do not recognize common-law marriage. Canada recognizes as married couples those who have lived together for a certain period of time.

According to the March, 1997, estimates of the U.S. Census Bureau, there were 101,018,000 households in the United States. Of these, 70,241,000, or 70 percent, were family households. Another 25 percent consisted of people living alone and 5 percent were other types of nonfamily households, such as institutions or roommate arrangements. Slightly more than 76 percent of the families in the United States in 1997 were married-couple families. Of these, an estimated 25,083,000

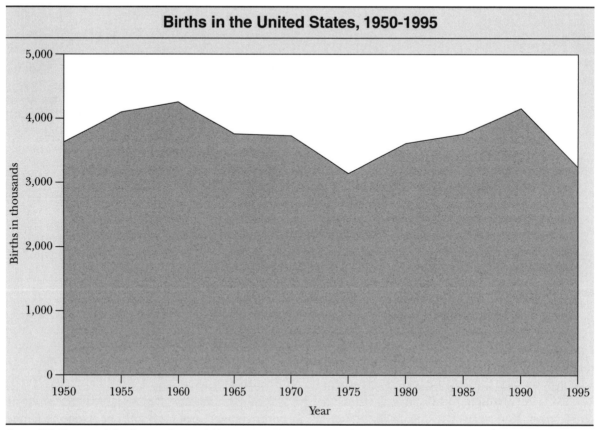

Source: U.S. Bureau of the Census, *Statistical Abstract of the United States: 1997.* Washington, D.C.: GPO, 1997.

had children in the home and 28,521,000 had no children in the home. Thus, 47 percent of married-couple families had children living at home. Many married-couple families without children were composed of older persons whose grown children had their own households. Slightly less than 18 percent of U.S. households were headed by single women and about 5 percent were households headed by single men.

The 1996 Canadian census shows similar patterns, with an estimated 39,190,000 family households. Slightly under 86 percent of Canadian families were identified as married-couple families. This percentage is greater than that of the United States, because the 4,600,000 couples living together in Canada who were not formally married were counted as common-law couples. If common-law couples are ignored, about 74 percent of Canadian families were married-couple families, a figure almost identical to that of the United States. Canadian families were slightly more likely than U.S. families to have children at home: 51 percent of Canadian married-couple families had children. Canadians were apparently also slightly less likely than persons in the United States to live in single-parent families: 12 percent of single-parent families were single-mother households and 3 percent were single-father households.

In all of North America, therefore, most people live in families, and married-couple families are the most common type. However, despite the continued importance of married-couple families in American society, recent decades have seen some changes in the types of families and family characteristics.

Growth of Alternative Family Types. Families that do not fit the dominant married-couple form are often referred to as alternative family types. Many varieties of alternative families became more common during the second half of the twentieth century.

A steady increase in single-parent families, particularly single-parent families headed by women, was one of the most notable trends in family demographics from the 1960's through the 1990's. In 1960 just under 10 percent of family households in the United States were headed by single women and just under 3 percent were headed by single men. Ten years later, in 1970, about 11 percent of U.S. families were headed by single

women and about 2 percent by single men. By 1975, 13 percent of U.S. families were headed by single women and just under 3 percent by single men. In the 1980 census the proportion of families headed by single women had climbed to 15 percent and the proportion of families headed by single men remained constant at 3 percent. Estimates from 1985 indicate that families headed by single women had risen to 16 percent and families headed by single men had risen to between 3 and 4 percent. By 1990 families headed by single women made up between 16 and 17 percent of families in the United States and families headed by single men made up more than 4 percent. Seven years later, families headed by single women and men had increased to 18 and 5 percent, respectively.

The increase in single-parent families in Canada was not as dramatic as in the United States, but it was detectable. In the 1986 Canadian census 10 percent of family households were headed by single women and 2 percent by single men. According to Canada's 1991 census 11 percent of families were headed by single women while about 2 percent continued to be headed by single men. In 1996 the proportion of families headed by single women jumped to just over 12 percent while the proportion of families headed by single men rose to about 3 percent.

There are two demographic sources of single-parent families: divorces and children born to never-married mothers. Divorces in North America appear to have become more common through the 1960's and 1970's, increasing from 2.2 divorces for every 1,000 people in the population in 1960 to 3.5 for every 1,000 people in 1970 and 4.8 in 1975. The divorce rate peaked in 1980, with 5.2 divorces for every 1,000 persons. Throughout the 1980's and into the 1990's, the divorce rate remained constant at about 4.7 to 4.8 divorces for every 1,000 people. About one-half of couples aged twenty-five to thirty-four years married in 1980 were expected to divorce at some point during the course of their marriages.

Thus, divorce was one factor contributing to the increase in single-parent families from 1960 to 1980. After 1980, however, most of the increase in single-parent families was due to childbearing by mothers who had never been married. In the United States only about 5 percent of all children

One of the most pronounced demographic trends of the late twentieth century was a rise in the numbers of households headed by single mothers. (James L. Shaffer)

Marriages and Divorces in the United States, 1950-1995

Source: U.S. Bureau of the Census, *Statistical Abstract of the United States: 1997.* Washington, D.C.: GPO, 1997.

were born to unmarried mothers in 1960. By 1980 slightly under 20 percent of children were born to unmarried mothers. Ten years later, this increased to about 30 percent of all births in the United States. Canada showed a similar trend, with out-of-wedlock births increasing from just more than 4 percent in 1960 to 17 percent in 1986, with a continued rise through the 1990's. North America shared this demographic trend with most other economically developed countries.

Another alternative family type that became more common in America in the late twentieth century was cohabitation. Cohabitation may be defined as a relationship between members of the opposite sex who behave as if they are married. Canada defined most cohabiting couples as common-law families of husbands and wives, and these increased from 7 percent of Canadian families in 1986 to 12 percent in 1996. In the United States, where most states do not recognize

common-law marriage, the number of cohabiting couples increased from about a half million in 1960 to nearly three million in 1990. Thus, by the 1990's about 3 percent of the U.S. population aged fifteen and older cohabited with members of the opposite sex without being legally married.

Ethnic and Racial Variations in Family Types. Although alternative family types, especially single-parent families, have become much more common among almost all groups in North America, there were significant variations among ethnic and racial groups. The rate of single-parent, female-headed families increased most among African Americans. This becomes clear when one looks at the living arrangements of children under eighteen years of age. In 1960, 22 percent of African American children lived in single-parent households, with 20 percent of all African American children in mother-only families. By 1995 the proportion of African American children in single-parent households had increased to more than 56 percent, with 52 percent in mother-only families. The mother-only family, therefore, was the dominant family form among African Americans by the middle of the 1990's.

Among white, non-Hispanic children in the United States, only 7 percent of children under eighteen years of age lived in single-parent homes in 1960, with 6 percent in mother-only families. Thirty-five years later, 21 percent of white children lived in one-parent households, with 18 percent in mother-only families. The 1960 figures for Hispanic children are not available, but 22 percent of Hispanic children lived in one-parent households in 1970. Twenty-five years later, this had grown to 33 percent, with 28 percent in mother-only families.

Aging and Shrinking of American Families. American families became older and smaller during the course of the late twentieth century. These two trends are related. The American population expanded rapidly in the period following World War II. However, Americans born during the baby boom (1946 to 1964) tended to have fewer children than their parents, so that the population grew older as the baby boomers aged. According to 1997 estimates of the U.S. Census Bureau, the average U.S. family with minor children contained only 1.86 children. Moreover, a majority of U.S. families (52 percent) contained no children. Average U.S. family size dropped from 3.58 in 1970 to 3.27 in 1980 to 3.16 in 1990. Although Canadian families have generally been somewhat larger than U.S. families, family size in Canada has followed trends similar to those in the United States. Average family size in Canada dropped from approximately 3.90 in 1966 to 3.70 in 1971 to 3.50 in 1976. Canadian family sizes continued to shrink throughout the 1980's and into the 1990's.

American families have aged and shrunk because of the tendency of Americans to marry older and have children later than was previously the case. In 1960 only 28 percent of U.S. women between the ages of twenty and twenty-four had never married. Thirty years later, 63 percent of U.S. women in this age group had not married. The median age at first marriage in the United States changed from 20.3 for women and 22.8 for men in 1960 to 24.5 for women and 26.9 for men in 1995.

Even after marrying, many couples delayed having children. The 1980's and 1990's saw dramatic increases in childbearing among women in their thirties and forties. As parents grew older, women had fewer years to have children, intensifying the trend toward smaller families. Increasing levels of education, especially for women, and the increasing participation of women in the workforce were the primary causes of delayed marriage and childbearing.

The aging and shrinking of families raised questions about society's ability in the twenty-first century to provide for the support of aging baby boomers during their retirement years. As more baby boomers reach age sixty-five and older, there will be comparatively fewer young workers in the workforce. This demographic trend also means that industries such as health care and funeral services will become increasingly important parts of the North American economy.

Family Economic Situations. The income available to families is a major measure of family well-being. During the economic expansion of the 1980's, family incomes appeared to increase. However, this was largely because dual-earner families became increasingly common. In 1960 only 37 percent of all adult women, married or unmarried, were in the labor force. By 1990, 61 percent of mothers with children under eighteen years of age were in the workforce. Earnings of women became critical to family incomes. Among whites, median family income was $37,840 in families in which only fathers worked, $30,657 in families in which only mothers worked, and $50,064 in families in which both parents worked. Among African Americans, the median family income was $28,827 in families in which only fathers worked, $24,471 in families in which only mothers worked, and $43,273 in families in which both parents worked. Although the gap between the incomes of men and women narrowed steadily, this was largely a result of the fact that men's incomes remained stagnant or decreased. Throughout the 1980's and into the 1990's inequality between families' incomes increased, with high-income families holding more wealth and receiving more income and low-income families holding less wealth and receiving less income. Families living below the official poverty level in the United States increased from 6.8 percent of white families and 26.9 per-

In 1997 households headed by single fathers numbered less than a third of those headed by single mothers in both the United States and Canada. (James L. Shaffer)

cent of black families in 1974 to 9.4 percent of white families and 31.3 percent of black families in 1993.

The growth of single-parent families was a significant part of the increase in income inequality among families. Families with only one earner had lower incomes than families with two. Also, children usually lived with their mothers, and the incomes of women were lower than those of men. In the United States in 1993, 5.7 percent of white married-couple families lived below the poverty level and 12.3 percent of African American married-couple families lived below the poverty level. By contrast, 29.2 percent of white families headed by single women and 49.8 percent of African American families headed by single women had incomes below the poverty level. Throughout the 1980's and 1990's more than one out of every five children in the United States lived in poverty, the majority of whom lived in single-parent families. Families headed by divorced mothers and out-of-wedlock mothers showed high poverty rates, but long-term poverty was much more common among out-of-wedlock mothers.

—*Carl L. Bankston III*

BIBLIOGRAPHY

Dunn, William N. *The Baby Bust: A Generation Comes of Age.* Ithaca, N.Y.: American Demographics Books, 1993. Examines the consequences of low birth rate among baby boomers.

Fast, Timothy. *The Women's Atlas of the United States.* New York: Facts on File, 1995. A compilation of statistics on American women.

Owram, Douglas. *Born at the Right Time: A History of the Baby Boom Generation.* Toronto: University of Toronto Press, 1996. Follows major changes in American society from the birth of the baby-boom generation through the 1990's.

Roberts, Sam. *Who We Are: A Portrait of America Based on the Latest U.S. Census.* New York: Times Books, 1993. Provides a readable description of major demographic characteristics of the United States, based on the 1990 U.S. Census.

Russell, Cheryl. *The Master Trend: How the Baby Boom Generation Is Remaking America.* New York: Plenum Press, 1993. Discusses consequences of the large cohort of children born in the years after World War II.

See also Baby boomers; Birth control; Dual-earner families; Family life cycle; Family size; Fatherlessness; Household; Life expectancy; Marriage squeeze; Only children; Retirement; Sandwich generation; Second shift; Single life; Single-parent families; Vanier Institute of the Family (VIF); Zero Population Growth movement.

Family economics

RELEVANT ISSUES: Demographics; Economics and work

SIGNIFICANCE: Careful planning and budgeting of limited money resources allow for financial independence, which improves the quality of family life and the relationships among family members

Problems relating to money frequently cause family fights. This may represent a positive trend toward more open discussions of family finances. By contrast, families' main breadwinners historically made most of the financial decisions, with little input from other family members. Cooperation and open communication among all family members have positive effects on the budget process, reducing the stress caused by limited finances. If family members feel their needs are being considered, they may be willing to make sacrifices for the common good.

Family Budgets. Family budgets represent the planned distribution of family income to satisfy needs and wants. They may contain spending and saving requirements, as well as debt reduction plans. Budgets are plans of families' prioritized goals. Important advantages of budgeting include a clear recognition of how families spend their money, capping undirected spending activities, and saving for future goals. Approximately 60 percent of the American population keep budgets. The most frequently cited reasons for starting to budget are the birth of a child and a move to a new home. Other reasons include major medical expenses, divorce, retirement, and financial difficulties. Approximately 10 percent of consumers routinely overextend their budgets.

Household budgets include two major categories: income and expenses. Expenses are deducted from income. Income, called disposable personal income, is the money remaining from paychecks after taxes and other deductions. Expenses can be divided into two types: fixed and variable. Fixed expenses do not vary monthly and can be anticipated with accuracy. For example, housing and automobile payments are constant from month to month. Some fixed expenses are paid annually, such as insurance, and should be proportionally deducted each month to ensure that enough money is set aside to make payments when they are due. Variable expenses, which include the purchase of standard and luxury items, are less precise, but they can also be closely estimated. For example, food expenses are necessities that may vary from week to week. Entertainment expenses are considered luxury items that may also vary weekly.

Calculating Budgets. Family budgets can be prepared with a minimum of accounting knowledge. To develop a budget, the fixed and variable expenses are itemized and added together, resulting

The growing complexities of household finances and planning for retirement have caused increasing numbers of couples to rely on professional financial advisors. (James L. Shaffer)

in a total expense calculation. Total dollar expenses should be compared with the income figure. Ideally, the income figure should exceed the expense figure. If all expenses are carefully estimated, however, the total expense figure may nearly equal the total income figure. If expenses exceed income, the family should reconsider luxury expenditures, such as entertainment or dining out. These expenditures may need to be lowered so that basic needs can be accommodated.

Living within a budget may initially seem like a difficult task, but there are ways for families to reduce budgeted items without feeling that enormous sacrifices are necessary. Family members can simplify the budgeting process by following a few simple tips. First, parents should leave credit cards and checkbooks at home to reduce impulse buying. Second, families should include a "savings" section as part of their budget. Third, families can save money by not paying bills early, but rather as they come due. Fourth, extra or unexpected income, such as bonuses and tax refunds, should be earmarked for planned purchases rather than spent impulsively. Finally, families should not try to account for every penny. They should budget enough extra money to cover minimal expenses. Whereas the concept of "penny-pinching" typically has a negative connotation, saving money is appealing and allows families to stretch their income dollars. Purchasing products in bulk or economy sizes, using coupons, and choosing generic brands and private labels enables families to spend less on necessities and more on luxury items.

During the 1990's the Dacyczyns, a California family of eight, was highly publicized for taking penny-pinching to a frugal extreme. In 1996 the Dacyczyns kept their household expenditures to $17,580, or less than half of the typical expenditure of $39,537 for a family of six. They were so confident of their efforts to reduce expenses that they began publishing a monthly newsletter called the *Tightwad Gazette*. Because the newsletter infringed on family time, the Dacyczyns opted to cease publication, continuing to share tightwad tips in published books that went by the same name as their newsletter. Most families have neither the time nor the interest to pinch pennies like the Dacyczyns. Family awareness of unique budget options, however, allows for more edu-

cated decisions and, consequently, more successful budgets.

Family Income. Average household income in the United States has been increasing, while average household income in Canada has remained fairly stable. The U.S. Census Bureau reported in 1997 that average annual household income was $44,938 in 1995. From 1990 to 1995, average family income in the United States rose an average of 2.44 percent each year. *Statistics Canada* reported in 1997 that the 1995 average annual household income was $55,247. Although average income in Canada appears higher than in the United States, the difference reflects the different values of the countries' currencies.

Families must decide which members will be the primary income earners. Although males historically have been the primary wage earners among married couples, the proportion of male primary wage earners has declined. From 1980 to 1993 the number of U.S. families in which husbands were the sole wage earners decreased by 28.7. The number of families in which females were the sole wage earners increased by 34.7 percent during the same period. Among families maintained by single women or men, household income levels increased from 1980 to 1993.

Families must choose whether they want to have one or more than one wage earner by weighing the potential sacrifices and gains. Their decision will be correct if they are financially independent and their earnings cover their basic family needs. Families often decide to rely on sole wage earners so that mothers can stay home and care for the children. Wives may have been employed prior to childbearing, leading to a loss of income when they decide to leave the workforce. Creative budgeting thus becomes more critical, and families may have to sacrifice some luxury items in order to stay within the limitations of their budgets.

Consumer Debt. Although family incomes have increased, family debts have increased at a faster rate. The ratio of consumer debt to disposable per person income in the United States was 18 percent in 1993, 19.7 percent in 1994, and 21.3 percent in 1995. Budgets are often created in response to families' financial debts, which often arise from overspending and credit card charges. Families are constantly bombarded with advertising and marketing messages telling them to "buy now, pay

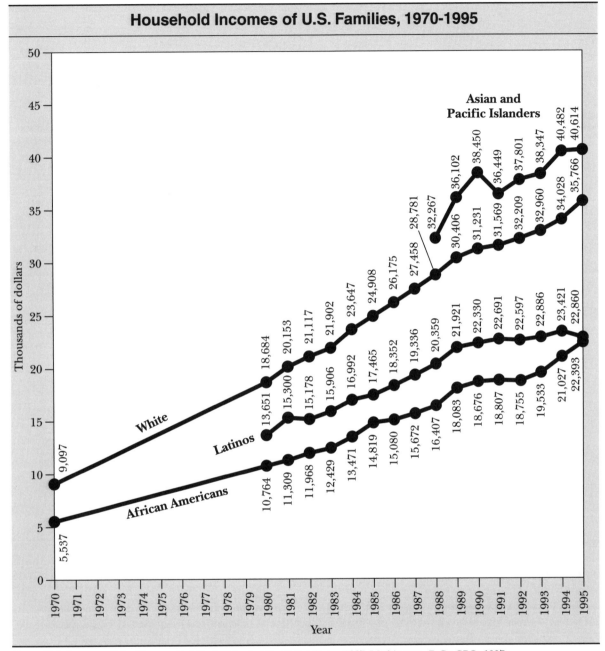

Household Incomes of U.S. Families, 1970-1995

Source: U.S. Bureau of the Census, *Statistical Abstract of the United States: 1997.* Washington, D.C.: GPO, 1997.

later." The ease of gaining credit and the desire to "keep up with the Joneses" create debts that are often overwhelming.

Credit reports are available to companies issuing credit to consumers. A "credit rating" is a financial biography of persons' credit purchases and payment history. Credit information is pro-

vided by company subscribers to credit bureau services. The most likely subscribers are bank creditors who supply charge cards, major department store creditors, and travel and entertainment creditors. Because only subscribers to bureaus' services supply information, credit reports may not be a complete history of consumers'

Median Household Incomes in the United States in 1995

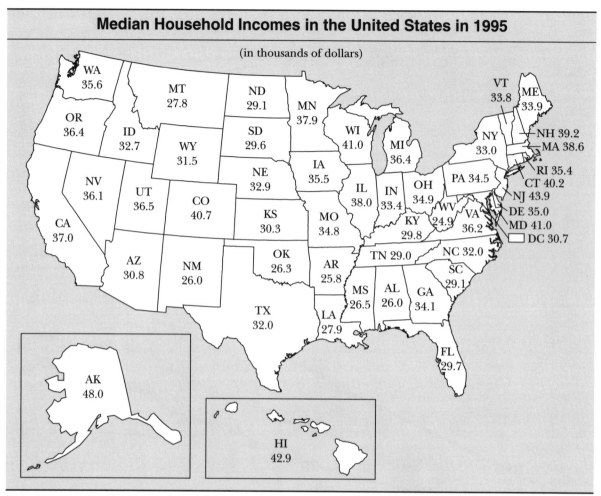

(in thousands of dollars)

WA 35.6
MT 27.8
ND 29.1
MN 37.9
VT 33.8
ME 33.9
OR 36.4
ID 32.7
SD 29.6
WI 41.0
NY 33.0
NH 39.2
MA 38.6
WY 31.5
NE 32.9
MI 36.4
PA 34.5
RI 35.4
CT 40.2
NV 36.1
UT 36.5
CO 40.7
IA 35.5
IL 38.0
IN 33.4
OH 34.9
NJ 43.9
CA 37.0
KS 30.3
MO 34.8
WV 24.9
VA 36.2
DE 35.0
MD 41.0
KY 29.8
DC 30.7
AZ 30.8
NM 26.0
OK 26.3
AR 25.8
TN 29.0
NC 32.0
SC 29.1
TX 32.0
LA 27.9
MS 26.5
AL 26.0
GA 34.1
FL 29.7
AK 48.0
HI 42.9

Source: U.S. Bureau of the Census, *Statistical Abstract of the United States: 1997.* Washington, D.C.: GPO, 1997.

spending and repayment patterns. They may provide a distorted picture of persons' finances. If household incomes are inadequate to cover monthly bills, families may want to pay at least the minimum monthly payments on credit cards. These are most likely to affect credit ratings. Credit experts recommend keeping credit purchases to less than 20 percent of family incomes so that families have enough money to pay housing costs and finance other necessities.

Credit histories are important for future credit purchases. They provide creditors with information about consumers' potential for timely repayment. Both women and men should have individual credit reports. Although husbands and wives often pool their incomes, it is recommended that each have a separate credit history. A credit his-

tory will develop if both spouses maintain separate checking accounts, even if they maintain a joint account. They should own credit cards in their own names. Occasionally, they should examine their own credit reports. An estimated 48 percent of credit reports are distorted by inaccurate reporting, of which consumers may not be aware. *Consumer Reports Money Book* recommends that women continue to keep credit in their own (maiden) names after they marry in order to maintain their financial identities. They should apply for credit using their own first names rather than those of their husbands. By maintaining separate credit histories, husbands and wives can prevent some financial problems from arising in the future if divorces or loss of jobs should afflict their families.

Families who do incur debts and have difficulty repaying them have options to assist them in managing their financial resources. Their first course of action should be to notify creditors and inform them of the financial difficulties. Families may want to entrust creditor notification to credit counselors or attorneys. It is important that families not ignore their credit problems, which serves to aggravate the situation, create emotional stress for family members, and possibly increase penalties and interest. Creditors who believe families are sincere may be willing to reduce monthly payments or stop levying additional finance charges or penalties.

Families may want to resolve their difficulties themselves. It is recommended that they visit their bank, share their problems with bank officers, and permit these experts to assist them in developing a payment plan. *Consumer Reports Money Book* cautions families against debt consolidation loans, because unsecured loans, such as charge card purchases, may be converted to secured loans that require collateral. Interest rates on consolidation loans may also be higher than previous rates. Bankruptcy is an option, but it may not alleviate all the problems. Some debts, such as alimony, child support, and income taxes, are not usually dischargeable. The purpose of bankruptcy is to give debt-ridden families a fresh start.

Achieving Financial Independence. Family budgets are short-term solutions to achieving financial independence. Financial planning is a continuous process, which should begin early in life and last a lifetime. By making savings a regular component of their monthly budgets, families can work toward a financially secure future. For most families, it is more realistic to develop ways to reduce expenses than to increase incomes. Families may be willing to reduce expenses so that one parent can remain or become a homemaker. Families may also reduce expenses so that primary earners can leave corporate employment, either voluntarily or involuntarily.

The 1990's have been credited as a decade of corporate downsizing, during which many former corporate employees have begun their own companies. Entrepreneurship, defined as owning one's own business, is prevalent among individuals between the ages of twenty-five and thirty-five, possibly the result of layoffs from corporate downsiz-ing and young persons' willingness to take risks. Former corporate employees may be tired of inflexible hours, long commutes, lack of variability in job responsibilities, inadequate salaries, and time spent away from their families. In spite of negative publicity, corporate downsizing has achieved some positive outcomes. Having gained experience working for corporations, former employees have often begun their own companies with ideas that fill market niches or voids left untapped by their previous employers or competitors.

Layoffs due to corporate downsizing have forced wage earners to look for other income options and replace complacency with aggressiveness. Terminated employees may seriously consider entrepreneurial options. Although the risks of entrepreneurship are high, personal satisfaction may be emotionally fulfilling. Relationships among family members may improve if they have been part of the decision-making process and are supportive of wage earners' endeavors. Families may have to make sacrifices during early entrepreneurial stages. Spouses may have to go to work. Teenage children may have to find employment to help pay some expenses. All family members should contribute to performing household chores and should concentrate on the positive aspects of their changing life roles and standards. The same financial common sense that applies to maintaining a household should be applied to owning one's own business. Expenses and income must be closely monitored. The first two years after a new business start-up are critical to success and family income.

Families should carefully budget their financial resources. Stress on family relationships can be reduced if money concerns do not affect communications among family members. By living within their income limits, families can make productive economic decisions that ensure a stable future. Financial independence can be achieved through strong work ethics, business plans, careful budgeting, and families' mutual love and support.

—*Celia Stall-Meadows*

BIBLIOGRAPHY

"Average Annual Income for Selected Family Types and Unattached Individuals." *Statistics Canada* (1996-1997). Compilation of statistics on Canadian society detailing aspects of family incomes. Also available on the Internet at http://www. statcan.ca, these statistical tables provide basic demographic data about Canadians.

Bamford, Janet, Jeff Blyskal, Emily Card, and Aileen Jacobson. *The Consumer Reports Money Book.* Yonkers, N.Y.: Consumer Reports Books, 1992. Comprehensive guide to personal, financial decision making that includes information on consumer loans and on how to deal with loan problems as they arise.

Dacyczyn, Amy. *Tightwad Gazette II.* New York: Villard, 1995. Book by the author of the *Tightwad Gazette* newsletter, published by the Dacyczyn family, presenting tips on how families can employ substantial money-saving techniques that take penny-pinching measures to frugal extremes.

Famighetti, Robert, ed. *The World Almanac and Book of Facts, 1997.* Mahwah, N.J.: K-III Reference Corporation, 1996. General almanac detailing statistics and facts on many subjects, such as comparative family incomes and inflation levels.

Johnson, Otto, ed. *The 1997 Information Please Almanac.* Boston: Houghton Mifflin, 1996. Atlas and yearbook containing sections on business, economy, and nations' statistics including statistics on wage and price levels, types of occupations, and poverty levels.

Miller, Roger L., and Alan Stafford. *Economic Issues for Consumers.* Belmont, Calif.: Wadsworth, 1997. General resource for family economics including facts about incomes, budgeting, and credit issues.

Porter, Sylvia. *Sylvia Porter's New Money Book for the 80's.* New York: Avon, 1980. Covers the spectrum of consumer finance including spending, insurance, borrowing, and investing.

U.S. Bureau of the Census. "Labor Force, Employment, and Earning." *Statistical Abstract of the United States: 1995.* 115th ed. Washington, D.C.: Author, 1995. Statistics pertaining to aspects of working life and incomes in the United States. Also available on the Internet at http://www. census.gov, this site provides statistical tables detailing demographic data about Americans.

See also Advertising; Allowances; Corporate families; DINKs; Displaced homemakers; Dual-earner families; Family businesses; Intergenerational income transfer; Single-parent families; Tax laws; Wealth; Welfare; Work.

Family-friendly programs

RELEVANT ISSUES: Economics and work; Law; Parenting and family relationships

SIGNIFICANCE: Family-friendly programs offered by organizations to their employees have the potential to help workers balance the important responsibilities of work and family

In 1996, families consisting of a working husband, homemaker wife, and two or more children accounted for less than 7 percent of U.S. households, yet most workplaces and benefit plans were set up with that type of household in mind, reflecting workforce demographics of the past. In 1950, 15 percent of women with young children were in the workforce. By 1970, that proportion had grown to 30 percent, and in 1990 to 60 percent. It is projected that by the year 2000, 75 percent of all families will be run by dual-earner couples and single parents.

As women entered the workforce, workplace arrangements based on old workforce demographics began to be problematic. Companies had difficulty retaining women, and women had difficulty balancing work and family roles. In addition, the 1990's saw an increasingly vocal call for recognition of gay and lesbian and other types of families that are often not acknowledged as families.

The Need for Family-Friendly Programs. Prior to the Industrial Revolution, work and family were not separate spheres of life. Work tasks were gendered, but the tasks were not divided so clearly into "work" and "family" spheres. An extended family and kinship group was often an economic unit, and men and women both performed tasks that would lead to direct economic gain and tasks that would not. It was only with the Industrial Revolution that sex roles began to separate into "private" or "family" roles (for women) and "public" or "work" roles (for men).

Since the 1950's, women increasingly have joined men in holding paid labor roles, but most of the home-based work is still done solely or primarily by women, many of whom come home from a paid job to a "second shift" of household

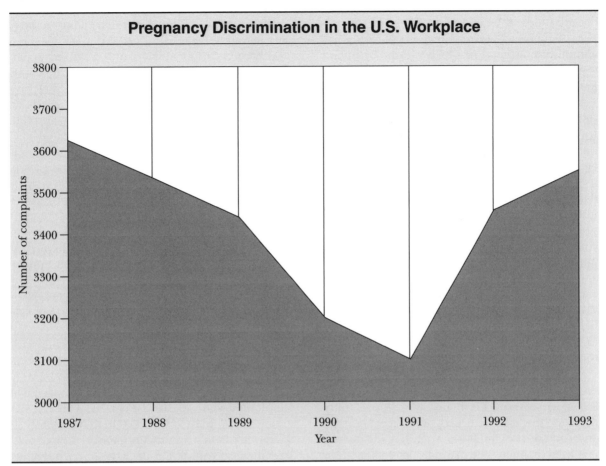

Pregnancy Discrimination in the U.S. Workplace

Source: Equal Employment Opportunity Commission

chores and child care. In addition, most of the emotional tasks of nurturing children and supporting a marriage or relationship are taken on by and expected of women.

Many women do not want to be full-time homemakers, and of those who do, many cannot afford to. At the same time, men do not seem to be choosing the homemaking role. Partially because of these issues, many women left typical corporate positions in the late 1980's and 1990's for other types of work arrangements such as entrepreneurship. The majority of small business start-ups in the 1990's were by women.

In the late 1980's, some companies started to focus on being "family friendly," ostensibly as a way to retain women and encourage or enable women and men to participate in both work and family. "Family friendliness" is a term used to indicate the degree to which a company is responsive to the family-related needs of employees. The primary way in which a company is judged in the popular business press as "family friendly" is by its family-friendly programs. Publications such as *Business Week* and *Working Mother* have published lists of family-friendly employers.

Types of Programs. Although family-friendly programs vary widely, there are two primary types of programs. Some, such as on-site child care, directly address family concerns. Others, such as flexible working hours, include everyone in an organization but are viewed as family-friendly because they facilitate meeting family responsibilities. In some cases, employees must show family responsibilities to be allowed to use the benefits. Programs that are available only to those with families (as defined by the organization) include primarily family leaves and dependent care support.

Many family-friendly programs are viewed by

organizations as employee benefits and thus are part of compensation and benefits planning and administration, most of which is done by human resource managers. In some cases, a specific work-family manager position exists.

Family leaves include paid and unpaid maternity leave, paternity leave, parental leave, and leaves for illness and deaths in the family. Companies vary widely in offering these leaves, and many employers do not. In the United States, paid maternity leaves may be covered by companies' standard disability leave. The Pregnancy Discrimination Act of 1978 requires employers to treat pregnancy as they would any other disability; thus, companies that provide paid leave for disability must provide paid maternity leave. The Family and Medical Leave Act (FMLA) of 1993 requires employers with more than fifty employees to provide twelve weeks of unpaid leave with medical benefits after the birth or adoption of a child, or to care for a seriously ill child, spouse, or parent, for some employees.

Despite this legislation, the United States offers significantly less unpaid leave than most Western European countries, Canada, and Japan. Canadian workers' situations vary because of different government policies, but overall, Canadians have the legal right to paid parental leaves and have longer unpaid leaves available. In the United States, paid family leave remains very rare, in sharp contrast with Western Europe and Japan.

Dependent care support programs vary widely. The most common is reimbursement accounts that allow employees to pay for qualified child-care expenses with pretax dollars. A less common benefit is child-care referral services. One 1990 study showed that 29 percent of responding employers offered this low-cost benefit. This study also showed that 12 percent of responding companies offered child-care subsidy, 11 percent elder-care referral services, 8 percent near- or on-site child care, 3 percent some form of sick-child care, and 3 percent elder-care subsidy. Firms with strong family-friendly programs are more likely to respond to such surveys, so these numbers may be overestimates.

In the United States, there is no government supported child-care policy, unlike in Canada, much of Western Europe, and Japan. Other programs include written family policies, family-related education for supervisors and workers, and adoption benefits.

A broad type of family-friendly program, generally available to all employees, concerns flexibility about when and where work gets done. Such programs include compressed workweeks in which the typical five days at eight hours apiece are compressed, usually to four ten-hour days, and flextime (also known as flexitime), in which there is often a core time when all employees must work, but the remaining hours of the workday can be worked when the employee desires as long as the workplace is open.

Options for those who choose to work less than full-time include job sharing (in which two people share one job) and part-time work. Both options frequently come with reduced benefits and lower pay rates. Other flexibility programs include telecommuting and work-at-home options. Some programs include time off to participate in certain activities, such as volunteer work and children's school performances and conferences.

Issues of Providing Programs. Family-friendly programs can act to reduce stress on individual employees who are also caregivers. This has the potential to positively affect both relationships within the family and family members' emotional and physical health. On the surface, then, family-friendly programs seem beneficial to employees at low cost to employers, but many problems exist.

First, the definition of "family" in most of these programs is narrow. For example, the FMLA essentially defines family as children, spouse, and parents, but many individuals live in less traditional arrangements. Second, relatively few workers in the United States are eligible for any of these work-family benefits. Even the FMLA is available to only 60 percent of the U.S. workforce and is of questionable value to many who cannot afford to take unpaid leave.

In addition, for those to whom the most benefits are available, the effect is often more a work support than a family support. In other words, the programs often act to free workers from their family responsibilities instead of helping them balance the responsibilities (for example, sick child care). This results, in part, from two longstanding societal assumptions. First, a "good employee" is assumed to be aggressive, able to work at any time to help out in a crisis, and able to spend many hours of overtime at work. This assumption does not fit women or men who choose to be involved with their families and results in negative consequences (or stigma) for workers not matching this profile.

Second, caregiving, whether paid or unpaid, is seriously undervalued. Taking care of children and elderly, disabled, and ill individuals is one of the lowest paying occupational sectors. Often, such caregiving is a "free" service, provided mostly by women. As single-parent and dual-earner families grow in their proportion in the workforce, more families will find that they no longer have access to this "free" service because the workplace demands all the hours formerly devoted to caregiving.

Even workers at "family-friendly" firms face stresses related to caregiving unless they can afford to work part-time. As the work day lengthens, parents spend less time with children, and quality child care is hard to find and/or unaffordable.

The reality of family life in the United States has changed, but the basic structures and assumptions of the workplace have not. Family-friendly programs can help, but in many cases they are not enough. Continuing changes in the workforce are likely to result in changes in the workplace to accommodate their needs.   —*Teresa J. Rothausen*

BIBLIOGRAPHY

Dunn, Dana. *Workplace/Women's Place.* Los Angeles: Roxbury, 1997.

Gilbert, Lucia Albino. "Workplace Family Policies." Chapter 6 in *Two Careers/One Family.* Newbury Park, Calif.: Sage Publications, 1993.

Neal, Margaret B., Nancy J. Chapman, Berit Ingersoll-Dayton, and Arthur C. Emlen. *Balancing Work and Caregiving for Children, Adults, and Elders.* Newbury Park, Calif.: Sage Publications, 1993.

Noe, Raymond A., John R. Hollenbeck, Barry Gerhart, and Patrick M. Wright. *Human Resource Management: Gaining a Competitive Advantage.* 2d ed. Chicago: Irwin, 1997.

See also Alternative family types; Child care; Dual-earner families; Family and Medical Leave Act (FMLA); Family Protection Act; Gender inequality; Maternity leave; Mommy track; Second shift; Single-parent families; Women's roles; Work.

Family gatherings and reunions

RELEVANT ISSUES: Kinship and genealogy; Parenting and family relationships

SIGNIFICANCE: In the face of mobility, which places stress on American families by robbing them of support from extended-family members, gatherings and reunions can help strengthen family ties

There is tremendous variety in family gatherings and reunions. They vary from two grown siblings spontaneously deciding to meet for coffee to annual family picnics or holiday celebrations to elaborate weekend reunions of many extended-family members who may have traveled hundreds or thousands of miles to attend. Family gatherings and celebrations have no doubt existed as long as there have been families, but written reports of family reunions in the U.S. and Canada seem to have begun in the mid-1800's. In 1968 Congress passed legislation proclaiming the second Sunday in August as Family Reunion Day. In 1970 *Better Homes and Gardens* carried an article titled "Family Reunion: Help Stamp out the Generation Gap," and in 1979 author Alex Haley made an appeal for holding family reunions following the final segment of the very popular television miniseries *Roots, the Next Generation.* Thus, by the 1970's family reunions were an important part of popular culture in America. However, formally arranged, large family reunions, often at resorts, seem to be a relatively recent phenomenon that grew in popularity in the 1990's.

Family Gatherings. The informal gatherings of immediate family members, who probably live near each other, are often designed to celebrate birthdays, anniversaries, or holidays. These gatherings tend to last for a few hours, include a meal or refreshments, and take place at the home of a parent or grandparent. The organization of these events is often determined by ongoing family or cultural traditions that dictate who hosts what events, who brings what kinds of food, and what is done during the gathering. Thus, little formal planning for these gatherings may be necessary, but there may well be extensive preparations by designated individuals. These gatherings serve to maintain family contact and, hopefully, encourage support among family members. Some may view

A midwestern family reunion held in 1900. (Wendy Sacket)

participation in such gatherings as a matter of obligation, especially if they occur among in-laws. Family gatherings may even be dreaded by some participants because they bring back memories of or reenact earlier sibling rivalries, parental favoritism or control, and in-law disapproval. Family gatherings force persons to confront issues that some members may prefer to avoid.

A variant of small, relatively frequent gatherings of immediate family members is the annual extended-family picnic or holiday party. These gatherings have been especially common among rural families in the United States and Canada. Journalistic accounts of such reunions began to appear in the mid-1800's. In this type of reunion, cousins, aunts, uncles, and other extended family members meet, usually for a potluck meal and various activities such as a ball game. Specific activities, types of food, inclusiveness and size of the group, and the location and frequency of such gatherings no doubt vary depending on the specific family and their cultural and ethnic traditions; however, little systematic information exists from which to make meaningful generalizations about group differences. Weddings and funerals are also occasions for gatherings of extended family members and can serve some of the same functions.

Changes in American Society. The United States has always been a nation of immigrants who have usually left behind family members in their coun-

Birthdays may be the most common occasions on which members of extended families gather. (James L. Shaffer)

tries of origin. In addition, mobility due to job transfers and interstate marriages has tended to scatter extended families. This pattern has made it less convenient for families to get together sponta-neously or for brief gatherings. Thus, extended family members are less likely than in the past to know each other. For some this is no problem; they may even prefer the lack of obligations to

Wedding anniversaries are most likely to bring families together when they celebrate landmark occasions, such as a fiftieth anniversary. (Hazel Hankin)

family and the relative anonymity of suburban or city life. However, others feel a need for the connectedness and sense of history that knowing relatives and roots can provide. Many people want to have a better sense of personal heritage and to leave for future generations a sense of who they were. This has led to increased interest in genealogy and family histories. Most cities and many towns have genealogical societies whose members are interested in exploring their family histories and finding living relatives and ancestors. One of the products of family reunions is often some sort of family history, perhaps in the form of booklets, photo albums, or videos. A survey by *Reunions Magazine* found that many families want their children to become more aware of their heritage and see reunions as a way to achieve this goal. These trends have led to an increase in formal family reunions and in resources to help plan and conduct them.

Formal Family Reunions. Large and often carefully planned events, formal family reunions have become big business and quite popular in recent years. Each year about 200,000 American families hold reunions. The *Reunions Magazine* survey found that more than fifty people, on average, attend formal reunions, and one-third have more than one hundred participants. Close to half of such reunions last three or more days. One and two-day events each account for about 25 percent of formal family reunions. June, July, and August are the primary months to hold reunions, encompassing 85 percent of these family gatherings.

Although many family reunions are held at the homes of family members, more than half take place at hotels, motels, campgrounds, and resorts. Resorts attract many longer reunions due to the variety of activities they offer for persons of all ages, and this seems to have become more common. For example, the Young Men's Christian Association (YMCA) of the Rockies in Estes Park, Colorado, has doubled its reunion business in the 1990's, hosting about seven hundred family reunions per year at its two centers. Some of these reunions are for all persons of a certain ethnic group who want to attend, even if they are not related. For example Welsh and Cornish Americans have recently held such gatherings.

Ethnic Groups and Reunions. Family reunions are a pervasive aspect of American life. They oc-

Days Celebrating Family Togetherness

A variety of annual events celebrate family gatherings. Clio, Michigan, for example, stages Visit Your Relatives Day every May. The Wellness Permission League encourages Americans to celebrate Family History Day on Flag Day in June. Participants are encouraged to share family traditions and stories with each other.

cur in all regions of the country and among families of all ethnic and social groups. Most journalistic reports of family reunions are about specific European-American families, but there is reason to believe that family reunions are also popular among minority families.

For example, each year one million African Americans travel hundreds of miles to participate in family reunions. One estimate is that 45 percent of African Americans' travel expenses are related to family reunions. These facts indicate that for African Americans reunions hold a special place that is unlikely to be matched by other ethnic groups. Although family was at the center of African tradition, slavery disrupted the roles of the family, because legal marriages and parental control of children was forbidden. However, after emancipation the extended family became crucial for African Americans' psychological and financial support and morale, and family reunions have been a means of keeping extended families strong. As for most American ethnic groups, the African American extended family has been scattered geographically, so that many African American family reunions alternate between the North and South to connect those who have moved from one region to the other. Although little has been written about family reunions among other American minority groups, it seems likely that reunions play a role in facilitating their family cohesion.

—*George A. Morgan and Hildegarde S. Morgan*

BIBLIOGRAPHY

Ayoub, Millicent. "The Family Reunion." *Ethnology* 5 (1966).

Beasley, Donna. *The Family Reunion Planner.* New York: Macmillan, 1997.

Brown, Barbara, and Tom Ninkovich. *Family Reunion Handbook.* San Francisco: Reunion Research, 1996.

McGoldrick, Monica. *You Can Go Home Again: Reconnecting with Your Family.* New York: W. W. Norton, 1995.

Mergenhagen, Paula. "The Reunion." *American Demographics* 52 (April, 1996).

Swenson, Geta. *Festivals of Sharing: Family Reunions in America.* New York: AMS Press, 1989.

Wagner, Edith, ed. *Reunions Workbook and Catalog.* Milwaukee: Reunions Magazine, 1998.

See also Family albums and records; Funerals; Genealogy; Holidays; Weddings.

Family History Library

DATE: Founded in 1894

RELEVANT ISSUES: Kinship and genealogy; Religious beliefs and practices

SIGNIFICANCE: The Family History Library allows visitors, regardless of religious affiliation, to search, free of charge, genealogical records containing more than 2 billion names

The Family History Library of the Church of Jesus Christ of Latter-day Saints, located in Salt Lake City, Utah, is the world's largest repository of genealogical information. The five-story library houses more than 258,000 books, two million rolls of microfilm, and 523,000 microfiche containing billions of names of deceased persons. The books include city directories, compiled genealogies, and state, local, and community histories. The microfilm and microfiche contain copies of birth, marriage, property, parish, death, and other vital records. These collections focus on North America and Europe, but the library also has numerous oral histories from Africa, Asia, Australia, and the Pacific islands. These centrally located collections draw professional and lay researchers from all over the world.

As of 1997, the Family History Library had more than 2,800 branches in sixty-four countries. Patrons at these branches have access to the main library's computer database and borrow approximately 80,000 rolls of microfilm from Salt Lake City each month.

The Family History Library employs librarians and skilled genealogical consultants. Hundreds of volunteers are also available to answer questions for the 2,600 daily visitors. First-time patrons at the main library may attend an orientation lecture describing the resources and introducing them to the computer system.

Technology has tremendously facilitated family history research. In 1938 the library began microfilming records in foreign countries. Library staff members have worked closely with numerous countries, libraries, archives, and religious organizations to preserve historical records and lists of names.

The library's computer programs and databases expedite genealogical research. One computer program, FamilySearch, allows patrons to search the International Genealogical Index (IGI). The IGI contains more than 243 million names and increases by seven million names a year. A second program named Ancestral File contains more than nine million names. Another program, Family Registry, has an alphabetical list of more than 360,000 surnames. This program connects individuals working on the same family lines, helping researchers coordinate their efforts and share results. There is no fee to register with this program or to search its contents. Family Registry is updated periodically, and additional genealogical information or family histories are always welcomed. All these programs are available on CD-ROM at the Family History Library's branches located throughout the world.

The Family History Library is owned by the Church of Jesus Christ of Latter-day Saints. The library began with the formation of the Genealogical Society of Utah in 1894. Fifty years later, it became the Genealogical Society for the Church of Jesus Christ of Latter-day Saints. In 1987 it was again renamed, this time as the Family History Department. It is this department that operates the Family History Library.

For more than a century, church leaders have encouraged their members to search for their ancestors. Latter-day Saints believe in the eternal significance of the family. After death, they hope to be reunited with both immediate and extended family members. The Family History Library supports and facilitates this objective.

—*Heather M. Seferovich*

See also Family albums and records; Family trees; Genealogy; Lineage; Mormons.

Family law

RELEVANT ISSUES: Divorce; Law; Parenting and family relationships

SIGNIFICANCE: Family law pertains to the laws and legal procedures and issues involving the lives of families

The law regulates many features of family life, from the inception of family relationships through marriage or adoption to the termination of these relationships through legal procedures such as annulment, divorce, or even death. Lawyers play a central role in assisting clients in family law matters. They do so partially because the laws and procedures pertaining to the family are often complicated, and those who must navigate these laws and procedures do well to obtain expert pilots. Lawyers also play a crucial role in the legal affairs of family life, since family members sometimes find themselves at odds with one another and seek legal assistance in protecting their respective rights.

Marriage. Although the laws of most jurisdictions have a good deal to say about who can be married, most couples seeking marriage do not encounter these laws in a direct way and most have no need for the services of lawyers. Normally, couples seeking to be married must obtain a marriage license and demonstrate that they are of legal age to be married. Furthermore, many states require couples to have blood tests for venereal diseases. Finally, in most cases couples must participate in a formal marriage ceremony—whether religious or civil—to cement their marriage commitment. Although the various legal requirements relating to marriage are sometimes numerous, they are typically administered by state officials who administer these requirements and see that marriage applicants satisfy them. Thus, couples may generally marry without having to consult a lawyer. They simply follow time-worn traditions and the instructions provided to them by government personnel at offices that issue marriage licenses.

Lawyers do occasionally play a role in the formation of the marriage relationship, particularly when couples wishing to marry want to enter into prenuptial agreements. According to such agreements, soon-to-be-married couples determine spouses' rights and obligations in the event that they divorce or one partner dies. In many cases, wealthy marriage partners attempt to use prenuptial agreements to avoid losing property if their marriage ends in divorce. Like other contract negotiations, the negotiation and drafting of prenuptial agreements frequently involves the services of one or more attorneys, although this is not legally required. Lawyers for wealthy persons, for example, may draft prenuptial agreements favorable to such persons' interests, whereupon wealthy partners may insist that anticipated spouses sign the agreement. The mere fact that anticipated spouses sign such agreements without legal counsel of their own does not generally suffice to render them unenforceable. However, courts sometimes rescue weaker partners from prenuptial agreements that are grossly unfair to them, especially in cases in which weaker partners have had no legal counsel. Accordingly, prenuptial agreements are more likely to survive later court challenges if both couples have obtained independent advice from lawyers regarding the terms of such agreements.

Adoption. Would-be parents seeking to adopt children have a variety of avenues open to them, for which they are at least partially required to seek lawyers' guidance. Individuals or couples seeking to adopt children can contact government agencies that handle adoptions or charitable institutions that assist in placing children with adopted parents or seek to make private arrangements with mothers who wish to give up their children for adoption. However, because adoptions in all cases must ultimately be officially approved by a court, those seeking to adopt must generally turn to attorneys to obtain necessary adoption orders.

Attorneys should be able to give some indication to those seeking to adopt children as to whether or not they meet the eligibility requirements of the states in which they reside and whether or not they are likely to be successful in adopting children. Furthermore, particular attorneys specialize either in assisting clients in their encounters with adoption agencies or in arranging private adoptions. Lawyers specializing in private adoptions are especially useful in arranging the appropriate consent from natural parents. Finally, lawyers are able to advise clients as to how they can best prove to the satisfaction of the court that they will make suitable parents.

A family court judge meets with newly adoptive parents. (James L. Shaffer)

Divorce and Separation. Both the law and lawyers make their most pronounced appearance in family life during divorces and their attendant legal proceedings. Couples contemplating a divorce often separate from one another prior to divorcing. Separation periods may serve as a trial run at divorce or, for those with moral or religious scruples against divorce, they may be an attempt to escape marital turmoil without actually severing the legal bond of marriage. Although one or more lawyers will almost certainly be involved in the event of actual divorces, lawyers may also provide valuable assistance for those seeking legal separations. Legal separations not only result in separate living arrangements, but they are also an attempt by couples to obtain specific agreements concerning matters such as support and child visitation rights. Such formal separations require either the preparation of separation agreements, the issuance of court orders, or both, and they generally involve the services of attorneys to draft separation agreements and to obtain separation decrees from a court.

More commonly, attorneys assist couples seeking to terminate the marriage relationship through a divorce. Some divorces are generally amicable, with spouses having mutually agreed upon matters such as property division, child custody, and child support. In these cases, one or more lawyers may assist couples in formalizing their agreements through a court-ordered decree of divorce incorporating these agreements. In contested cases, however, marriage partners will typically retain attorneys to represent their individual interests, both by negotiating on their behalf and, if necessary, appearing in contested court proceedings. If their attorneys cannot negotiate an agreement on the contested matters—such as property division—they will ask a court to decide the matters. In this situation, the parties—generally through their lawyers—will present evidence and arguments supporting their respective wishes, and the court will resolve the issues. These kinds of court proceedings are relatively rare, however. As many as 95 percent of divorces resolve themselves short of contested court proceedings. Lawyers in such cases remain valuable assistants to their clients in negotiating acceptable arrangements.

Child Custody and Child Support. When spouses with minor children cease living together or terminate their marriage through divorce, they must provide living arrangements and support for their children. Unlike some other issues relating to separation and divorce, issues of child custody and support involve the interests of more than simply the married partners. Therefore, their agreements as to these issues are not necessarily decisive. In most jurisdictions, family law courts are required to consider the best interests of the children of marriages, even if this requires living, visitation, or support arrangements different from those to which the parents have mutually agreed. In cases in which parents can reach no agreement

and a court must decide questions of child custody and support, the judicial decision again is supposed to reflect the best interests of the children rather than the mere preferences of the parents.

Many states recognize the diverging interests of parents and children in divorce proceedings and take pains to see that the children have independent representation in these divorce proceedings. Courts in such states appoint an independent representative for minor children, called a guardian *ad litem*, who represents neither fathers nor mothers but only the interests of the children. In these cases, the guardian *ad litem* makes an independent recommendation to a court concerning the custody and support arrangements that will be best for the children of a marriage. Often the guardian *ad litem* is an attorney.

Because child support issues are of vital concern to state and federal governments, these matters are increasingly regulated and not left simply to the adversarial skills of divorce lawyers. Federal law now requires that states implement guidelines for family law courts to use in determining the appropriate child support in particular cases. Unfortunately, the existence of a court order mandating child support is not an automatic guarantee that the support will be paid. Surveys have suggested that as little as 50 percent of child support obligations are paid in full, 25 percent paid in part, and 25 percent not at all.

Parents with custody of children to whom a support obligation is due, called custodial parents, have a number of options when confronting former spouses who fail to make child-support payments. One possible recourse is to hire an attorney to demand payment from recalcitrant spouses and to pursue available legal remedies should payment not be forthcoming. These remedies may include filing a motion to hold nonpaying spouses in contempt of court for failure to pay, garnishment of wages or other funds, or attachment of property. Custodial parents with insufficient financial resources to hire a private attorney may consider seeking assistance from a legal-aid clinic. In addition, the attorney general's office of many states prosecutes parents who fail to make court-ordered support payments.

Wills and Estates. Most family members wish to provide for their families in the event that they die. Even if they do not, the laws of various states generally attempt to see that spouses, children, and other relatives receive the assets of deceased persons without a will. These laws, sometimes referred to as laws of "intestate succession," generally distribute assets to the persons most closely related to the deceased. Nevertheless, these intestate succession laws do not always provide for the precise distribution that the deceased may have intended. It is wise to have attorneys prepare a will that designates specifically how persons' assets are to be distributed upon their death. An attorney who specializes in this area may also be able to structure an estate plan in such a way as to minimize the costs of probating an estate and minimize the taxes paid on the estate.

Attorneys' Ethical Requirements. Lawyers play an important role in many family law matters as advisors, negotiators, trial advocates, and drafters of important legal documents, such as separation agreements or wills. In this work, lawyers are subject to a variety of ethical requirements, some of which apply particularly to common family law issues. For example, lawyers generally may not represent clients with competing interests or conflicting interests. In many jurisdictions, this general conflict of interest requirement means that a single lawyer cannot represent both spouses in obtaining a divorce. In contested divorces, of course, each spouse will generally hire a lawyer to represent his or her interests. In more amicable divorces, however, a couple simply needs an attorney to help them finalize their divorce, according to terms to which they mutually agree, by obtaining the appropriate judicial decree. Even in these "friendly" divorces, however, many jurisdictions forbid a single attorney from acting as the representative of both spouses. In practice, to avoid incurring the expense of hiring two attorneys, spouses in these circumstances commonly agree that only one of them will hire a lawyer to obtain a divorce upon the terms to which they have agreed.

Lawyers' ethical rules collide with family law matters in another important way. The law generally prohibits attorneys from arranging to receive contingency fees in divorce or child-custody matters. Contingency fees are those in which lawyers' recovery fees from clients depend wholly or partially upon lawyers' success in obtaining a particular result and are widely used in some kinds of legal matters. For example, a lawyer may represent someone who has been injured because of another's negligent action and stipulate that the fee will be 30 or 40 percent of the settlement money from the opposing party or the opposing party's insurance company. In divorce and child-custody cases, however, lawyers are generally precluded from accepting such contingency fees. Instead, they generally charge clients hourly fees. For clients able to afford an hourly rate, this limitation on contingency fees may impose no hardship. However, for divorcing spouses without financial assets, the inability to offer a lawyer a contingency fee arrangement or to pay a hefty hourly charge might severely limit their ability to obtain a good lawyer. At least in some jurisdictions family law courts seek to counter this problem by allowing divorcing spouses without substantial assets to petition the court to have opposing spouses pay the legal fees.

—*Timothy L. Hall*

BIBLIOGRAPHY

Belli, Melvin M. and Mel Krantzler. *Divorcing.* New York: St. Martin's Press, 1988. Book by a noted trial attorney and an expert in divorce psychology that emphasizes both the legal and psychological aspects of divorce.

Boumil, Marcia Mobilia, and Joel Friedman. *Deadbeat Dads: A National Child Support Scandal.* Westport, Connecticut: Praeger, 1996. Both a description of the social forces that have produced a crisis in child support and an attempt to explain the realistic possibilities of obtaining support from absent parents.

Clark, Homer H., Jr. *The Law of Domestic Relations in the United States.* 2 vols. St. Paul, Minn.: West Publishing, 1987. In-depth survey of legal issues relating to the family.

Harwood, Norma. *A Woman's Legal Guide to Separation and Divorce in All Fifty States.* New York: Charles Scribner's Sons, 1985. Book by a female attorney for women, which surveys a variety of legal and financial issues relating to divorce and separation and the different ways that various states treat these issues.

Sack, Steven Mitchell. *The Complete Legal Guide to Marriage, Divorce, Custody and Living Together.* New York: McGraw-Hill, 1987. Practical guide to family law issues, including sample legal documents and information about hiring and paying lawyers.

See also Adoption processes; Alimony; Child custody; Child support; Common-law marriage; Divorce; Family courts; Guardianship; Living wills; Marriage laws; Prenuptial agreements; Tax laws; Uniform Marriage and Divorce Act (UMDA).

Family life cycle

RELEVANT ISSUES: Demographics; Parenting and family relationships

SIGNIFICANCE: Families go through predictable stages as parenting roles change in response to children's maturation, although demographic changes have decreased the utility of a life cycle model

Family systems theory views the family as a network of reciprocal and interdependent relationships. Because of aging and consequent changes in the developmental stage of each family member, every family shows its own "life cycle," with changes in the various relationships among members.

The Presence of Children. The earliest and most influential description of the family life cycle was developed by Evelyn Duvall in the 1950's. According to this description, stages in the family life cycle are determined by the presence and ages of children. Prior to the birth of a first child, a married couple is in its "honeymoon phase." Different issues present themselves to parents of infants and of preschool- and school-aged children, adolescents, young adults in the "launching" stage, and adult children who have left home for marriage or employment. Although other family life cycle theories have been developed, a focus on the changing concerns of parents is common.

The oldest child has a particularly influential effect on the parents' and family's developmental status. The youngest child has a marked impact in signaling transitions involving launching into adulthood. The exit of the youngest child from the parental household indicates the end of the active parenting stage.

Infancy and adolescence are often peak stress times in family life. Newborns bring changes in personal responsibility. Infants require personal attention and time, and they are emotionally demanding. Adolescents are beginning their own transition to adulthood, triggering their own assertions of independence and a growing awareness in

parents of their own mortality and aging. The launching period frequently extends these concerns more than expected by either parents or children. Although school-aged children in this account might seem the easiest to care for, each age poses its own dilemmas. The need to coordinate schedules and respond to institutional demands can create family stress.

After Children Leave. After children leave home, parents often renew or reemphasize other relationships in the extended family system. Relationships among adult siblings may be renewed or strengthened. Parents may find that the time and emotional energy freed by children leaving home is taken up by the need to care for a different generation, their aging parents. Because of changing demographics and longer life spans, middle-aged couples can find themselves caring for both aging parents and adolescent or young adult children, a phenomenon placing them in what has been called the "sandwich generation."

When their own parents become ill and die, middle-aged adults confront their own mortality as well as a shifting sense of self associated with being the oldest generation in the family line. Continuing transitions in family status include becoming a grandparent and later a great-grandparent. There is a greater sense of voluntariness to these relationships, and research shows much greater variability in how people behave in these roles. The grandparent role can vary from having child custody to tremendous geographic and emotional distance. Active grandparents can define their role as one of providing fun, or one of providing wisdom.

Misconceptions About Family Development. An overemphasis on parenting as the dominant family role left common misperceptions unchallenged. Social scientists in the 1970's were concerned with the empty nest syndrome, an adjustment problem they linked to depression in middle-aged women who lost their mothering role when children left home. Subsequent research found that only about one-fourth of women experience this problem, and that it is usually mild and transient. It is a greater concern immediately prior to the departure of the first and last child than after the "nest" is actually empty. Moreover, men are just as likely to experience a problem as are women.

When adult children leave home, parenting responsibilities continue. Viewing the nest as empty obscures ongoing emotional and financial support from aging parents to adult children. Many elderly people give high satisfaction ratings to their relationships with adult children. Just as grandparenting roles show marked variability, so do parent-child relationships in aging parents.

Effects of Demographic Change. Traditional family life cycle theories assume a marriage that produces children who grow up within the context of that marriage. This assumption always excluded a significant portion of the population, and demographic trends in the United States and Canada (and throughout the industrial world) greatly increased the size of that excluded portion during the last half of the twentieth century.

Marriage at later ages and decisions not to marry, as well as rising divorce rates, contributed to an increased number of single-adult households. In the United States, between 1960 and 1993, the average age of first marriage changed from 22.8 to 26.5 years for men, and from 20.3 to 24.5 years for women. Corresponding Canadian data showed a shift from 25.0 to 28.8 years for men and 22.5 to 26.7 years for women. Some 25 percent of households in the United States in 1993 contained only one person, compared with 17 percent in 1970. Trends toward delayed childbearing and voluntary childlessness also were evident.

At the other end of child rearing, data reveal complications in the concepts of launching and the empty nest. Single adults continued to reside with their parents until later ages than was previously the case. In the United States in 1994, 60 percent of men and 46 percent of women aged eighteen to twenty-four were living with a parent, compared with 52 and 35 percent respectively in 1960. The same trend was apparent in Canada, with about two thirds of adults aged twenty to

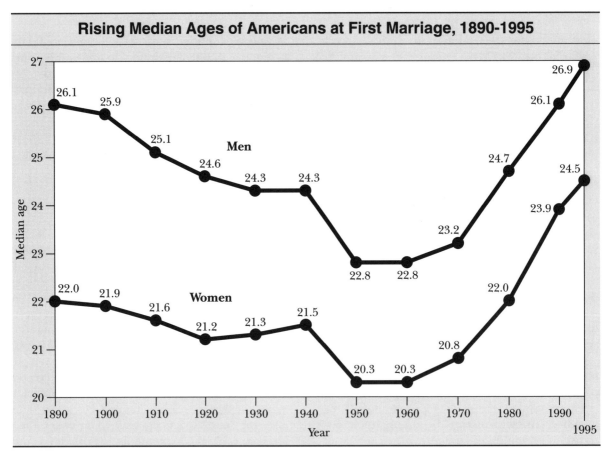

Source: Bureau of the Census (1992)

twenty-four living with a parent in 1993. Moreover, many adults living with a parent had left but returned, often for economic reasons or because of divorce.

Effects of Divorce and Aging. Divorce was a fact of family life when Duvall developed her model in the 1950's. Between 1965 and 1995, however, the divorce rate in the United States doubled to a peak of nearly 50 percent of all marriages. A similar trend in Canada brought the divorce rate as high as 40 percent. More than 70 percent of divorcing adults in both the United States and Canada in the 1990's were likely to remarry. Thus, remarriages, as a proportion of all marriages, increased from 31 to 46 percent in the United States between 1970 and 1988. Canadian data showed a growth in the percentages of remarriages from 13 percent in the 1950's to 33 percent of all marriages in the early 1990's.

Owing both to the divorce rate and an increase in out-of-wedlock childbirth during the late twentieth century, there was an increase in the number of single-parent households. Between 1960 and 1993, the percentage of U.S. children under the age of eighteen living in a single-parent household grew from 9 percent to more than 25 percent. A similar increase in Canada resulted in 14 percent of minor children living in single-parent households in the 1990's.

Finally, increases in the life span and in the economic independence of the elderly contributed to a growing percentage of households consisting of elderly couples and single elderly adults. Between 1960 and 1995, the proportion of the population over the age of sixty-five increased by 40 percent in the United States, with similar data for Canada. Family life cycle models are weakest in considering these families.

With the changing character of the family, the predictability of a family life cycle was partially lost. Divorce by parents or by young adult children overwhelms the "normal" crises associated with each life stage. Single-parent and remarried households confront issues of work sharing, discipline, and schooling in a more complex manner. In a combined household with children from two prior marriages, one set of children may be in the launching stage while the other is entering school. Additionally, a new couple may decide to become parents together.

Demographic change alerted social scientists to the increasing limitations of family life cycle models, but various exceptions to the aforementioned standard life cycle (and others such as involuntary childlessness and early widowhood) have always existed. Many families follow the outline, at least for several years, and for these families, a family life cycle model remains useful. Even for families outside the traditional nuclear family model, many of the parenting issues described are pertinent to the development of complex family systems. Experts on the family continue to use family life cycle models, although with an awareness of their limitations.   —*Nancy E. Macdonald*

BIBLIOGRAPHY
Carter, Elizabeth A., and Monica McGoldrick. *The Family Life Cycle: A Framework for Family Therapy.* New York: Gardner, 1980.
Duvall, Evelyn. *Marriage and Family Development.* 5th ed. Philadelphia: J. B. Lippincott, 1977.
Gladding, Samuel T. *Family Therapy: History, Theory and Practice.* Englewood Cliffs, N.J.: Prentice Hall, 1995.
Lamanna, Mary Ann, and Agnes Riedman. *Marriages and Families: Making Choices in a Diverse Society.* Belmont, Calif.: Wadsworth, 1997.
Sloane, Philip D., Lisa M. Slatt, and Peter Curtis, eds. *Essentials of Family Medicine.* Baltimore: Williams & Wilkins, 1993.

See also Blended families; Empty nest syndrome; Family demographics; Family life education; Midlife crises; Nuclear family; Parental divorce; Remarriage; Sandwich generation; Sheehy, Gail; Single-parent families; Stepfamilies.

Family life education

RELEVANT ISSUES: Education; Marriage and dating; Parenting and family relationships

SIGNIFICANCE: Because being a good spouse, parent, or other family member does not come naturally, all persons need family life education throughout their lifetimes

According to one commonly accepted definition, put forth by Richard Kerckhoff, family life education includes facts, attitudes, and skills related to dating, marriage, and parenthood. It includes family relationships; the roles of individual family

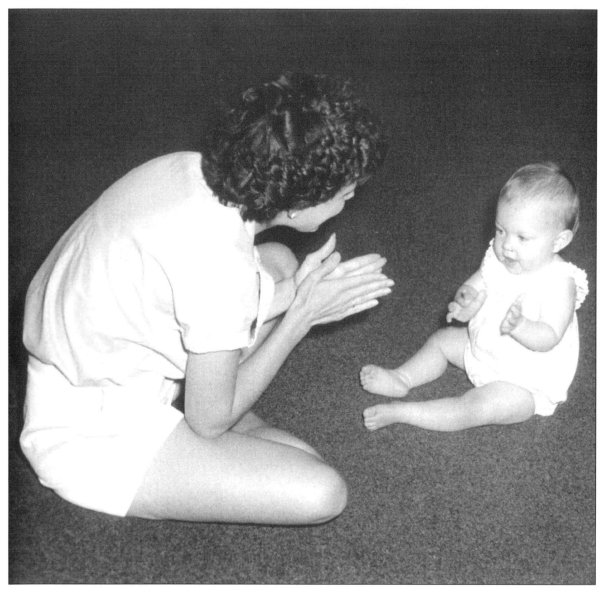

Family life education begins in infancy. (James L. Shaffer)

members; the role of the family in society; the development of feelings and attitudes toward and within the family; dating, courtship, marriage, and family behaviors and responsibilities; love and its place before and during marriage; pregnancy, prenatal care, and childbirth; the child's place in the family; family consumption and economics; family communication and problem resolution; and education about expression of sexuality.

The Lifelong Educational Process. Family life education is a lifelong process. During infancy, a baby needs to learn how to adapt to the demands of the outside world. During the preschool years, a child begins to be socialized, to develop a conscience, and to learn interpersonal skills. During middle childhood, a child becomes socialized by the peer group and learns to understand and accept the facts of his or her own sex.

Three significant events for adolescents between the ages of ten and twenty affect their present and future family life. First, their pubescent changes will require that they adjust to their changing physical and sexual bodies. Second, they must emancipate themselves from parental control as they move toward young adulthood. Third, they begin relating to the other sex in a way they have not done previously, as they begin dating, engaging in mate selection, and participating in interpersonal sexual activities.

During young adulthood, many people marry and begin to have children. They must learn the roles of being a husband or wife, as well as the role of being a parent. During the middle adult period, they continue their spousal and parental roles, and increasingly they find that they are a part of the "sandwich generation," forced to adjust and adapt to care for both children and aging parents. In later adulthood, they often find that they must accept being a widow or widower, as well as relating to their adult children and grandchildren in an acceptable manner.

Formal Education. The first college courses in preparation for marriage were offered at Boston University in the early 1920's, and then a few years

A child's socialization begins in the preschool years. (Cindy Beres)

later at the University of North Carolina. These are considered to be the first formal family life education courses.

In recent years, it has been recognized that education for family living must take place when children are in elementary school and must continue well after graduation from high school or college. In elementary school, the emphasis is more likely to be on the improvement of family attitudes, social skills training, and gender-role development. In junior and senior high school, in addition to classes geared toward preparation for marriage and parenthood, adolescents learn about family living in their home economics, social studies, biology, and health classes. All these formal classes, as well as the socialization that occurs from being part of a school group, help adolescents adjust to being independent, self-sustaining individuals and prepare them for the demands and responsibilities of marriage and parenthood that they might later face.

Education Within the Family. Although family life education is thought of as formal training for marital and family living delivered through the schools, the family into which one is born is perhaps a more powerful teacher of family life concepts. The family teaches the child about love, affection, security, trust, and how to relate to other people. By having to accommodate to the demands of parents and siblings of both sexes, children learn how to relate to authority figures and to peers.

The family also plays an important role in the development of personal attitudes. Through their family experience, children develop attitudes about such topics as sexuality, the meaning of money, sharing, and caring about other people. The family also provides a child with his or her first living habits. The habits learned in the family concerning such things as expressing feelings, eating, and personal hygiene often remain with a person throughout his or her life.

Sexuality Education. Traditionally, a major part of family life education has been education in human sexuality. In its broadest sense, sexuality education is much more than teaching about reproduction. Sexuality refers to human relationships and interrelationships between the sexes. It involves an examination of the roles of men and women in society, how they relate and react to and

supplement each other, the responsibilities of each, and the responsible use of sexual expression as a creative and re-creative behavior.

Like the more inclusive family life education, education for healthy sexuality begins when a newborn is cuddled in the parents' arms. This affectionate gesture is the first and often one of the most significant events in a child's learning about love and being close to another person. During the preschool years, children learn about their bodies, as well as the answer to the question, "Where did I come from?" During elementary school, their sex education consists primarily of learning gender role behaviors and responsibilities.

Because of the many changes that occur during adolescence, teenagers must learn about their bodies and about responsible sexual behavior. They also must learn appropriate role behaviors in dating, marriage, and familial situations. Education for human sexuality in its broadest context is close to family life education. Sexuality education is concerned not only with physical relationships but also with emotional and interpersonal relationships. It develops in adolescents an understanding of feelings, sexual urges, and sexual responsibility in the context of a society that discourages people from engaging in sexual activity until they have made career choices, become self-supporting, and are able to support children.

Parent Education. Some people assume that by growing up in a family and having parenting models, people automatically learn how to be good parents themselves. Such is not the case. Although modeling is powerful as an educational tool, it does not always teach all the lessons to be learned. In addition, many children grow up in less than ideal family situations with no proper role models.

Parent education is a complete field of study, and many colleges and universities train individuals to become parent educators. Parent education helps parents and prospective parents fulfill their responsibilities, as well as helping children develop into mature and responsible citizens. Classes teach awareness of child development principles to enable parents to understand and correctly interpret the growth and behavior of their children. Learners become competent in dealing effectively with the day-to-day child rearing situations that confront them and become aware of expert advice and opinions on how to rear children.

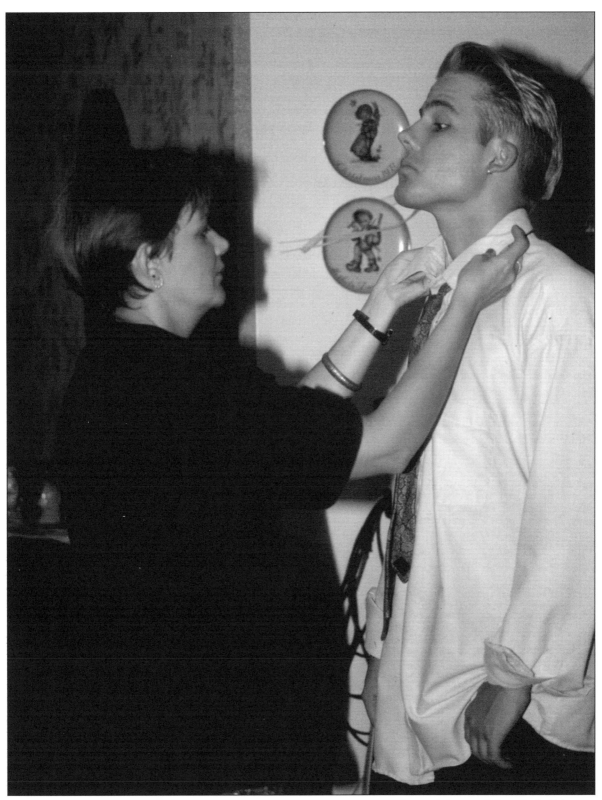

During adolescence teenagers learn about such matters as appropriate dating behavior. (Mary LaSalle)

Transitions to New Families. The transition from married couple status to parenthood is often stressful and painful. Becoming parents requires a rapid reorganization of a couple's lives into a three-person or triangular group system. They find that living as a trio is more complicated than living as a pair. Most couples are not prepared for the changes that parenthood forces on them. They also find that their parental roles frequently are in conflict with their other role commitments; as a result, they find that parenthood puts them in a temporary crisis. The goals of parent education are to prepare them for how their lives will change, to explain to them how their lives have changed and what to do about it, and to provide them with some problem-solving resources.

Goals over the Life Course. The true worth of family life education can be measured in terms of desirable attitudes and action behaviors. There are no concrete and definitive tools to adequately measure behavior that takes place long after a person has left the original family. Behavior patterns develop over a period of time and may be judged completely only over the entire course of a lifetime.

Knowledge is an essential first step in appropriate behavior, and it is fairly easy to measure concepts and facts through testing. Family life education, however, is a three-step process. People must have knowledge before they can make intelligent decisions. Understanding their emotions, attitudes, and values regarding themselves and others is a crucial second component, and behaving in a mature, rational, and responsible manner also is necessary for successful adaptation to family life. Family life education attempts to help people achieve all three goals throughout their lives.

—Sander M. Latts

BIBLIOGRAPHY

Calderone, Mary, and James Ramey. *Talking to Your Child About Sex.* New York: Ballantine, 1982.

Dinkmeyer, Donald, Sr., Gary McKay, and Donald Dinkmeyer, Jr. *Parent's Handbook.* Circle Pines, Minn.: American Guidance Service, 1997.

Dreikurs, Rudolph. *Children: The Challenge.* Des Moines, Iowa: Meredith, 1964.

Gordon, Thomas. *Parent Effectiveness Training.* New York: Peter Wyden, 1970.

Kerckhoff, Richard. "Family Life Education in America." In *Handbook of Marriage and the Family,* edited by Harold Christensen. Chicago: Rand McNally, 1964.

Lamanna, Mary A., and Agnes Riedmann. *Marriages and Families.* Belmont, Calif.: Wadsworth, 1997.

See also Cultural influences; Disciplining children; Emotional expression; Family life cycle; Love; Marriage; Moral education; Myths and storytelling; Sandwich generation; Sex education; Systematic Training for Effective Parenting (STEP).

Family Protection Act

DATE: Proposed on September 1, 1979
RELEVANT ISSUES: Law; Parenting and family relationships
SIGNIFICANCE: Introduced in the U.S. Senate in 1979, this act was a major platform statement for what was then the emerging New Right in American politics

The Family Protection Act of 1979 was a long, detailed statement of the social policies of the new conservative movement. The primary sponsor of the act was Senator Paul Laxalt, a Republican from Nevada, but it was more broadly supported by organizations of the New Right. There was little expectation that the act would be passed quickly, either in whole or in part. Instead, it was intended to serve both as an organizing tool and as a basis for challenging what was seen as the liberal underpinnings of existing social policy.

The legislation was intended to reshape social policies—in education, taxes, senior and child care, welfare, labor law, legal services, and judicial procedures—in order to strengthen the traditional family. The act's provisions were intended to affect women more directly than men, both positively and negatively. It included thirty-five major provisions. For example, among the provisions with direct implications for families were incentives for employers to establish child-care facilities, the elimination of the so-called marriage tax, a prohibition on legal services spending for both divorce and abortion cases, and an affirmation of states' rights in the area of spousal abuse. While the Family Protection Act was presented in legislative form, its primary purpose was to shape political debate and mobilize public opinion against what its supporters considered to be the antifamily liberal bent of government programs.

—David Carleton

See also Abortion; Aid to Families with Dependent Children (AFDC); Child care; Divorce; Domestic violence; Family-friendly programs; Marriage laws; Welfare.

Family size

RELEVANT ISSUES: Demographics; Sociology

SIGNIFICANCE: Appearing to be related to the educational and economic success of children, family size varies among ethnic groups, cultures, and social classes, and affects relations within families

One of the problems with discussing family size is that the word "family" can mean different things. Alternative family forms, for example, may include households of several unrelated adults or same-sex couples. Some people may consider cousins, aunts, and uncles to be part of a family, while others would define a family as consisting only of parents and children. For the sake of clarity, however, one can use the definition of family employed by the governments of Canada, the United States, and many other countries: a group of people related by kinship, marriage, or adoption, all of whom live in the same household.

Cultural Influences on Family Size. Cultural attitudes toward marriage and family can influence family size. In ancient Rome, for example, a male-dominated culture caused men to undervalue women and to limit family size in order to limit family obligations. Abortions and infanticide, the practice of leaving newborn infants exposed to the elements to die, helped to keep families small. These practices also tended to keep the female population small, since women sometimes died from abortions and female babies were more likely than male babies to be abandoned. The size of the average Roman family is difficult to determine, but many scholars estimate that dual-parent families had an average of about three children. This was small for pre-industrial families, because the lack of modern health care and sanitation led to a high child mortality rate. In France in the mid- to late 1700's, for example, the average family had four to five children.

Cultural attitudes may be one source of the variation in family size among modern ethnic groups. The 1990 U.S. Census showed that the average family size among white, non-Hispanic Americans was only 3.00 people per family. African Americans had slightly larger families, with 3.45 people. Among Hispanics, Mexican Americans had the largest families, with an average of 4.11 people per family. This probably reflects the emphasis Mexican American culture places on the family and the central influence of Roman Catholicism, a faith that discourages contraception. Among Asian Americans, the Hmong, a refugee group from Southeast Asia, have the largest families. Having large families is part of the cultural tradition the Hmong have brought with them from their homeland.

Ethnic differences in family size can affect the ethnic composition of nations. Groups with larger families grow faster than groups with smaller families. In part because of the greater numbers of children in Hispanic and Asian families, the Hispanic and Asian populations in the United States grew more rapidly in the late twentieth century than the non-Hispanic white and African American populations.

Cultural expectations within any group regarding family size may change over the course of time. In North America during the 1930's and early 1940's, parents generally expressed a preference for two- and three-child families. During World War II, three-and four-child families became the most widely desired size. By the late 1960's the two- and three-child family had once again become the ideal, and by the 1990's people in the U.S. and Canada most often identified the two-child family as optimal.

One factor influencing these changing cultural expectations by the late 1960's was a growing perception of global overpopulation. In the 1970's groups such as Zero Population Growth began advocating one- or two-child families as a way of stopping the increase in population size. This change in attitude was accompanied by technological changes that made it easier to limit family size: Most of the effective means of birth control, including oral contraceptives and intrauterine devices (IUDs), were developed after 1960. Planned Parenthood, an organization founded in 1921 as Planned Parenthood of America and later re-

Among Latinos, Mexican Americans have the largest average family size. (James L. Shaffer)

named Planned Parenthood-World Population, played an important part in educating parents or potential parents about birth control methods and in helping them plan the number and timing of births.

Economic Influences on Family Size. Economic development also affects family size. People who live in cities and work for wages tend to have smaller families than people who live in rural areas and earn their livings on family farms. On family farms, each family member is a potential worker, so children can contribute to the economic well-being of their families. Furthermore, farm children can consume food produced by the family itself. In the cities and suburbs, however, parents must usually support families by working at jobs outside the home. As the economy becomes more based on manufacturing, services, and management, and less on agriculture, jobs require greater formal education and children become more expensive to educate. They also become more expensive to feed and house.

The education and full-time employment of women, also characteristics of economic development, contribute to smaller family size. The more educated women are, the longer they tend to wait before having children. In addition, when both parents work outside the home, it becomes difficult for them to care for large numbers of children.

In examining average family size over the course of U.S. history, it is possible to illustrate the effects of economic development. According to the ten-year U.S. Census, the size of the average family in the United States in 1850, when 60 percent of American men were farmers, was 5.60 people. Throughout the nineteenth and early twentieth centuries, a time of rapid industrialization and urbanization, average family size declined steadily from 5.00 in 1880 to 4.70 in 1900 to 4.30 in 1920. The first year in which the U.S. Census showed a majority of the American population living in or around cities instead of in rural areas was 1920. Accordingly, during the 1920's family size decreased markedly, so that by 1930 the average U.S. family consisted of 3.40 people.

Although the United States became an increasingly urban society, the baby boom following World War II kept family size at about 3.60 to 3.70 people. During the 1970's and 1980's, however, families with two parents employed full-time became the norm. In 1970 only 29 percent of the mothers of preschoolers were in the labor force. By 1988 this number had climbed to 53 percent and during the 1990's to more than 60 percent. Partly because of these changes, the average size of families in the United States dropped from 3.58 in 1970 to 3.27 in 1980 to 3.16 in 1990.

Although Canadian families have generally been somewhat larger than U.S. families, family size in Canada has followed a similar pattern. Average family size in Canada dropped from approximately 3.90 in 1966 to 3.70 in 1971 to 3.50 in 1976. The size of families in Canada continued to shrink throughout the 1980's and 1990's.

Family size is related to economic inequalities; it also helps to perpetuate economic inequalities. Families with less well-educated parents who work in lower-status occupations tend to have more children. Because children from large families tend not to be academically as successful as children from small families, family size appears to be one way in which economic advantages and disadvantages are passed from generation to generation.

Family Size and Achievement. Studies of the effects of family size have found that children from large families tend to complete fewer years of schooling than children from small families. In a study conducted in the 1970's and 1980's, sociologist Judith Blake found that male only children completed, on average, almost thirteen and a half years of school, or high school plus some college. Female only children averaged about twelve and three-quarters years of school, or slightly more than a high school education. Male children with three siblings averaged about twelve and a half years of school and female children with three siblings about twelve years. On average, both male and female children with five or more siblings did not complete high school.

Family size also seems to have some relationship to how children score on intelligence tests. Children from smaller families tend to get higher scores on tests for verbal ability, or the ability to use language, than children from larger families. For both male and female children, researchers have found that the larger the family of origin, the lower the children's intelligence quotient (IQ) scores. This relationship appears to be stronger for women than for men. Furthermore, the negative relationship between IQ scores and the number of children per family seems to have become more pronounced among children of the post-"baby-boom" generation—that is, among those born in the 1970's and later. Only children may be an exception to the general rule that children from smaller families display higher IQs. Some studies have indicated that only children tend to perform slightly poorer on intelligence tests than children from two-child families. These studies have been inconclusive, but it is possible that children benefit from being able to interact with at least one brother or sister.

Family Size and Adulthood. Family size continues to affect children after they leave school and enter adulthood. While taking into consideration that lower-income persons tend to have larger families, researchers have found that persons from larger families tend to be relegated to lower-status jobs and receive lower wages. This appears to be primarily the consequence of school achievement: Since education is the main route to upward mobility in a modern society, large families often limit their children's life chances by hindering their school performance and reducing the years of schooling they complete. There is some evidence that persons who grow up in large families frequently develop poorer self-images than those who grow up in small families, thus possibly affecting their achievement throughout life.

The most likely explanation for the apparent disadvantages of large family size is the importance of the time and attention parents pay to each child. The fewer children in a family, the more time, attention, and psychological support parents can give to each child. This explanation is bolstered by some of the exceptions to the correlation between family size and achievement. Researchers who have studied Vietnamese American children, for example, have found that these children may actually show higher levels of school performance when they come from large families. Within Vietnamese American families, brothers and sisters often perform schoolwork together, and older siblings frequently help their parents by tutoring younger siblings. Therefore, brothers and sisters become sources of time, attention, and support for each other. This suggests that large families may actually be able to help the development and achievement of their children if they are highly cooperative.

Findings on religion and family size may also

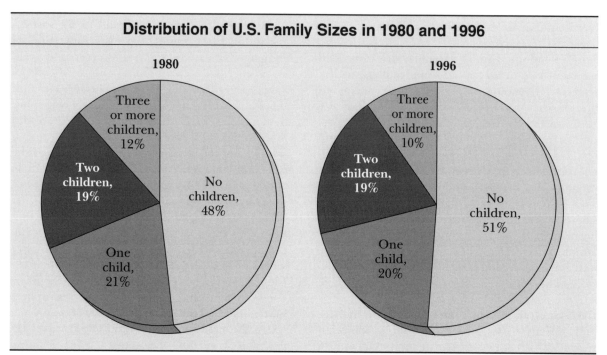

Distribution of U.S. Family Sizes in 1980 and 1996

1980

Three or more children, 12%
Two children, 19%
No children, 48%
One child, 21%

1996

Three or more children, 10%
Two children, 19%
No children, 51%
One child, 20%

Source: U.S. Bureau of the Census, *Statistical Abstract of the United States: 1997.* Washington, D.C.: GPO, 1997.

support the view that the relations within families helps determine the effects of family size. Roman Catholics tend to have somewhat larger families than adherents to many other faiths. Roman Catholic children who come from large families, however, appear to do somewhat better in school than non-Roman Catholic children who come from large families. It appears, then, that Roman Catholicism provides social supports that supplement the efforts of parents, thereby lessening the negative effects of large families.

Similarly, members of the Church of Jesus Christ of Latter-day Saints, commonly known as Mormons, tend to have large families and also show high levels of educational achievement and economic success. This may be because the Mormon church stresses close family interaction and mutual assistance. In addition, individual families receive help from other church members and extended family kinship networks, so that the burden of child care does not fall exclusively on mothers and fathers.

Family Size and Family Relations. There is some evidence that brothers and sisters in large families tend to be emotionally closer to one another in later life than siblings who grow up in small families. Those in large families, however, also experience more sibling conflict as children. Both parents and children in larger families tend to be more family-centered because the family tends to play a more important part in the lives of families with many children than in the lives of those with only one or two children.

Fathers in families with many children are generally more involved in family life than fathers in families with few children. Fathers in large families also tend to be more authoritarian, however; they are more likely to demand obedience from their children and to employ strict, inflexible discipline. This may reflect in part the comparatively low social standing of many large families, since authoritarianism is often found to be a characteristic of lower-income fathers. However, paternal authoritarianism may also be a matter of practicality, since households with many children may require more control than households with one to three children.

Researchers have found that the relations between parents in larger families tend to be poorer than those between parents in smaller families.

Mothers and fathers with many children are at greater risk of hypertension and a variety of other physical ailments. Poor marital relations and health troubles may be attributed to the strain of caring for several children of different ages, who place a variety of demands on parents.

—*Carl L. Bankston III*

BIBLIOGRAPHY

Blake, Judith. *Family Size and Achievement.* Berkeley, Calif.: University of California Press, 1989. Authoritative work containing complex statistics and readable chapter summaries on how family size affects life chances.

Caplan, Nathan, Marcella H. Choy, and James K. Whitmore. *Children of the Boat People.* Ann Arbor, Mich.: University of Michigan Press, 1991. Straightforward study of Vietnamese American children and their families that discusses why large families do not seem to handicap Vietnamese students.

Gerson, Kathleen. *Hard Choices: How Women Decide About Work, Career, and Motherhood.* Berkeley, Calif.: University of California Press, 1985. Discusses the factors that influence women's decisions on family size and on how to balance between work and family.

Polit, Denise F., and Berman, Judith. *Just the Right Size: A Guide to Family Size Planning.* New York: Praeger, 1984. Offers advice on family planning and describes issues, such as income and life goals, that parents should consider when planning their families.

Rossman, Isadore. *Two Children by Choice: The Why and How of the Two-Child Family.* New York: Parents Magazine Press, 1970. Presents the argument for small families for the sake of population control and gives advice on birth control.

Wasserman, Pamela. *Planning the Ideal Family: The Small Family Option.* Washington, D.C.: Zero Population Growth, 1990. Describes the benefits of small families for individuals and society and argues for small families as a way of limiting population growth.

See also Birth control; Birth order; Dual-earner families; Family demographics; Fertility and infertility; Multiple births; Only children; Planned Parenthood Federation of America (PPFA); Siblings; Zero Population Growth movement.

Family Support Act

DATE: Enacted on October 13, 1988

RELEVANT ISSUES: Economics and work; Law

SIGNIFICANCE: Passed with broad bipartisan support and signed into law by President Ronald Reagan, the Family Support Act of 1988 was a major effort to change the focus of Aid to Families with Dependent Children (AFDC) from an income maintenance program, sustaining families at a basic level, to a transitional program helping to build independent, self-sustaining families

Based largely on proposals drafted by Senator Daniel Patrick Moynihan of New York, the Family Support Act introduced four major changes. First, it strengthened the enforcement and collection of child-support payments from absent parents. Second, it required states to create Job Opportunities and Basic Skills Training (JOBS) programs and to enroll at least 20 percent of AFDC recipients by 1995. Third, health and child-care benefits were extended while recipients were in a JOBS program and for up to a year after entering the workforce. Fourth, states were allowed to require minors who were parents on AFDC to live with their own parents or under the supervision of other adults. Each provision was intended to help move welfare families toward financial self-sufficiency.

By the early 1990's, however, the Family Support Act was generally viewed as ineffectual, because large numbers of AFDC recipients were being exempted from its provisions, and it was difficult to find employment for people in the midst of a national recession. Only eight years after its passage, therefore, more far-reaching welfare reform was enacted in the Personal Responsibility and Work Opportunity Reconciliation Act of 1996.

—*David Carleton*

See also Aid to Families with Dependent Children (AFDC); Child support; Child Support Enforcement Amendments; Personal Responsibility and Work Opportunity Reconciliation Act.

Family therapy

RELEVANT ISSUES: Health and medicine; Parenting and family relationships

SIGNIFICANCE: Family therapy is an increasingly popular and promising treatment method for many problems facing individuals, couples, and families

The profession of family therapy, which is often referred to as "marriage and family therapy," originated in the United States in the 1950's. According to Carlfred Broderick and Sandra Schrader in volume two of the *Handbook of Family Therapy*, family therapy is one of several social movements concerned with family life that originated in North America during the late eighteenth century and the first half of the nineteenth century. Other movements dealt with social work, sex education and reform, child guidance, marriage counseling, and social psychiatry.

History of Family Therapy. Although the family therapy movement began in the United States, Broderick and Schrader note that clinicians in England and other parts of the world were also beginning to experiment with treating more than one family member at a time. The dominant mode of therapy at that time was individual therapy. If persons had problems, they were identified as patients and seen by therapists. Clinicians were reluctant to see more than one person in therapy, because they were concerned that doing so would interfere with the therapeutic relationship between therapists and patients.

One frustration of early family therapists, many of whom were psychiatrists, was that they would treat patients—for example, young schizophrenic adults—and then send them home from the hospital. Within a few months these patients would suffer a relapse and return to therapy. Incidents such as this led early pioneers in the field of family therapy to hypothesize that dysfunctional family interactions caused mental illnesses such as schizophrenia. Given this assumption, the whole family was seen as the cause of the problem and it was thought necessary to treat the whole family in order to cure individuals' problems. Thus, early family therapists began experimenting with hospitalizing whole families or at least seeing them together in therapy sessions.

Initially, the pioneers of family therapy worked independently at several sites across the country. Commonly identified as the founders of family therapy in the United States were John Bell,

Nathan Ackerman, Christian Midelfort, Theodore Lidz, Lyman Wynne, Murray Bowen, Carl Whitaker, Gregory Bateson, Jay Haley, John Weakland, Don Jackson, Virginia Satir, Ivan Boszormenyi-Nagy, Gerald Zuk, and James Framo. By 1961 many of the original family therapists corresponded with one another, met together, and began working on a book and a professional journal (*Family Process*). During the 1960's the family-therapy movement began to slowly gain in popularity and win more adherents. The number of family therapists steadily increased over time. According to figures of the American Association for Marriage and Family Therapy (AAMFT), the number of family therapists, estimated to be 1,800 in 1966, grew to 7,000 in 1979 and to more than 46,000 by 1997. Family therapy is recognized by the National Institute of Mental Health (NIMH) as one of the five core mental health disciplines alongside psychiatry, psychology, social work, and counseling. In 1997, forty of the fifty U.S. states licensed or certified family therapists. None of the Canadian provinces licensed family therapists in 1997, although efforts to attain licensure were in progress.

Defining Family Therapy. Family therapy has been described as a profession; an orientation to human problems; a method of treatment; and a field of study with a knowledge base about families, their problems, and how to solve them. Many practitioners of family therapy refer to themselves as family therapists, have received a graduate or postgraduate degree training in family therapy, are members of the AAMFT, and subscribe to professional journals focusing on family therapy. For such practitioners, family therapy fits the first description: It is a profession.

The second description of family therapy is that it is a systemic orientation to human problems utilized by those who are open to viewing mental illness and problems in living from a systemic perspective. One of the key features of family therapy is its use of systems theory to understand and explain problems in living. A system is a holistic set of interacting elements that cannot be understood simply by examining each individual part. When a family is viewed as a system, this implies that family dynamics and relationships cannot be understood by studying each individual family member; the dynamics of the group as a whole must be studied. Family therapists have employed systems theory to understand individuals, couples, families, agencies, and other social organizations.

The third definition of family therapy is that it is simply one modality or method of psychotherapy. Depending on the problems clients exhibit and clinicians' expertise and training, clinicians may perform various individual, group, couple, or family therapies to address clients' problems. Therapists with a variety of professional identities—for example, psychologists, social workers, psychiatrists—might all indicate that they practice family therapy without identifying themselves as family therapists. Thus, from this perspective, family therapy is simply another tool that clinicians may choose in meeting clients' needs. This view of family therapy also implies that training programs in a variety of disciplines can provide training in family therapy along with other therapy modalities.

The fourth way to describe family therapy is to view it as a field of study with an accessible collection of theories, research, and publications about families and the practice of family therapy. Clinical training programs, researchers, and theorists both inside and outside the field of family therapy can utilize this information for research and applied purposes. Similar bodies of knowledge exist within other fields, such as psychology, developmental psychopathology, psychiatry, and social work. Researchers and clinicians in the field of therapy have been encouraged to be more open to and accepting of the knowledge from these other fields, while family therapists have also urged those in other fields to be more accepting of family therapy theories and research.

These four descriptions of family therapy capture the different ways that family therapy is viewed by those both within and outside the field. There is no consensus as to which, if any, of the four descriptions are the "correct" way to define and view family therapy.

Practice of Family Therapy. Family therapists work with all types of clients, including individuals, couples, families, and groups. In fact, surveys of family therapists routinely find that they see more individuals in their practices than they do couples and families. However, what makes family therapists unique has more to do with how they think about their work than how many people they see in the treatment room. Family therapists focus on the relationships between people as the means to understanding the problems clients are experiencing.

Accordingly, when prospective clients call to inquire about beginning therapy, family therapists usually request that all members of the family attend, even if the problem only appears to involve one member of the family. Because family therapists operate this way, clients sometime resist participating in family therapy. When individuals experience a problem, they, and often members of their family, believe that the problem is an individual one. However, many family therapists believe that even if dysfunctional relationships within the family do not "cause" the problems experienced by one or more members of the family, all family members are likely to be affected by them. Hence, at least initially, family therapists believe there is benefit in working with all members of the family. During the course of treatment, family therapists may meet individually with different members of the family or with different family subsystems (the parents one week, the children the next), in addition to meeting with the family as a whole. While a primary concern for therapists and clients alike is solving the problems that brought clients to therapy in the first place, many family therapists also hope that the overall quality of family relationships and satisfaction will improve as a result of participating in family therapy.

Different Family Therapy Approaches. As research on the causes of mental illness discovered that many illnesses have genetic or biological components, family therapists moved away from the early assumption that families *cause* mental illness. Instead, they came to adopt a more holistic view, acknowledging that individual or biological factors can cause problems while choosing to focus on the relational consequences of individual disorders and seeking to understand how family processes can effect the course of the problem or disorder. For example, researchers have identified what they call "expressed emotion" to refer to family patterns that involve emotional overinvolvement, intrusiveness, criticism, and a generally hostile emotional climate. In the course of studying families with members diagnosed as schizophrenic, researchers discovered that while the amount of expressed emotion does not cause mental illness, it can affect relapse rates and the course of the illness. Hence, family therapy with

schizophrenia takes the form of what is called "psychoeducation." Patients receive the standard treatment for the disorder (usually involving medication and some form of individual and group therapy), while family members are educated about the nature and course of the disorder and family therapy. This combination has been found to be more effective in reducing relapse rates than standard treatment alone.

Family therapy is practiced in a wide variety of settings, which commonly include private practices, community mental health centers, inpatient facilities, social service agencies, schools, universities, health maintenance organizations, and employee assistance programs.

There are several schools or theoretical approaches to family therapy. Eight schools or models of family therapy are commonly recognized: psychodynamic, behavioral, experiential, structural, strategic, feminist, solution-focused, and narrative. These schools tend to share some of the same ideas that view the family as a system. However, they differ in terms of how therapists view problems, solutions, and the means to bring about solutions. In reality, few therapists are purists, utilizing a single therapy model. Most are eclectic, borrowing concepts and methods from whatever therapy model best helps their clients.

Family Therapy Research. There is a growing body of outcome research evaluating the efficacy of family therapy for a host of individual, couple, and family problems. In 1995 William Pinsof and Lyman Wynne in a special issue of the *Journal of Marital and Family Therapy* summarized much of the existing data about the effectiveness of family therapy. The data supporting family therapy's efficacy is encouraging, but much more systematic research must be conducted before any definitive claims can be made. Hence, claims about the effectiveness of family therapy must be accepted tentatively.

Pinsof and Wynne offered six conclusions based on their research. First, family therapy does produces positive results. Family therapy (which includes marital therapy) is more effective than no psychotherapy for adult schizophrenia, outpatient depressed women in distressed marriages, marital distress and conflict, adult alcoholism and drug abuse, adult hypertension, elderly dementia, adult obesity, cardiovascular risk factors in adults, adolescent conduct disorder, anorexia in young adolescent girls, adolescent drug use, child-conduct disorders, aggression and noncompliance in children with attention-deficit hyperactivity disorder, childhood autism, chronic physical illnesses in children, child obesity, and cardiovascular risk factors in children.

Second, family therapy is not harmful. Research has not indicated a pattern of clients in family therapy who are in worse condition than those who received no psychotherapy.

Third, family therapy is more effective than the standard or individual treatment approaches for several disorders, problems, and patients, including adult schizophrenia, depressed outpatient women in distressed marriages, marital distress, adult alcoholism and drug abuse, adolescent conduct disorders, adolescent drug abuse, anorexia nervosa in young adolescent females, childhood autism, and various chronic physical illnesses in adults and children.

Fourth, although a variety of schools or models of family therapy exist, the available data do not demonstrate the superiority of any particular family therapy approach over another.

Fifth, a trend noted in a few studies is that family therapy is more cost effective than standard inpatient and residential treatment for schizophrenia, severe adolescent conduct disorders, and delinquency. Preliminary data also indicate that family therapy may be more cost effective than other treatments for adult alcoholism and adult and adolescent drug abuse.

Sixth, while family therapy is a helpful component in many effective treatments, it is not sufficient in itself to treat many severe problems and disorders. Many of the treatment packages that include family therapy also include additional components, such as medication, individual and group therapy, and education about the nature of the disorder.

While evidence about the efficacy of family therapy is promising and continues to accumulate, much more systematic, controlled research is necessary before it can be definitively established that it works, why it works, and for what problems it works best. Nevertheless, the practice of family therapy is growing in acceptance and popularity and is widely practiced in both the United States and Canada.
                                        —*Mark B. White*

BIBLIOGRAPHY

Gurman, Alan S., and David P. Kniskern, eds. *Handbook of Family Therapy.* Vol II. New York: Brunner/Mazel, 1991. Comprehensive overview of the history of family therapy, the main approaches, and some of the pressing issues in the field.

Napier, Augustus Y., and Carl A. Whitaker. *The Family Crucible.* New York: Harper & Row, 1978. Classic discussion, written for the general public from the perspective of therapists, of one family's experience in experiential family therapy.

Nichols, Michael P. *The Power of the Family.* New York: Simon & Schuster, 1988. Written in the form of a novel, this book combines dramatized vignettes from family therapy sessions with a fictional family and includes discussion of their family process and dynamics.

Nichols, Michael P., and Richard C. Schwartz. *Family Therapy: Concepts and Methods.* 3d ed. Boston: Allyn & Bacon, 1994. Popular introductory text that presents an overview of the primary family therapy theories and intervention methods.

Pinsof, William M., and Lyman C. Wynne, guest eds. *Journal of Marital and Family Therapy* 21 (1995). Special issue on the effectiveness of marital and family therapy that contains ten articles summarizing the research literature about the effectiveness of family therapy for a variety of disorders and problems.

Roy, Ranjan, and Harvy Frankel. *How Good Is Family Therapy? A Reassessment.* Toronto: University of Toronto Press, 1995. Critique and overview of research documenting the effectiveness of family therapy, spelling out what is known and still unknown and providing directions for future research.

See also American Association for Marriage and Family Therapists (AAMFT); Attention-deficit hyperactivity disorder (ADHD); Behavior disorders; Bradshaw, John; Disabilities; Divorce mediation; Dysfunctional families; Eating disorders; Family counseling; Gray, John; Parents Anonymous (PA); Recovery programs; Social workers.

Family trees

RELEVANT ISSUES: Kinship and genealogy; Parenting and family relationships

SIGNIFICANCE: A family tree graphically displays genealogical relationships between family members across generations as well as between members of a single generation

A family tree is perhaps the most common way of displaying genealogical information about an extended family. Usually the family tree is presented in the form of a many-branched tree or bush indicating the ancestry or descent of individuals, with relationships marked by thin lines like branches.

Although the English term itself is fairly recent—dating only from the 1860's—the concept itself is far older. Genealogies and family trees have long played important roles in social and political history. In all societies that place an emphasis on inheritance, people have had to be able to document and trace their family histories and display them in the form of family trees. One of the most famous family trees is found in the first seventeen verses of the Gospel according to Matthew, in which the writer traces the ancestry of Jesus Christ. He begins with Abraham, the first patriarch of the Hebrews, moves on through David, the first king of a united Israel, and ends with Joseph, son of Jacob and father of Jesus. In this list of ancestors and descendants, the writer does something that all modern creators of family trees do: He establishes a sense of the development of the family through time, and he relates the subject of the genealogy to famous historical figures and events.

Family trees have always been important in modern America among certain religions and denominations, such as the Jews and the followers of the Church of Jesus Christ of Latter-day Saints (Mormons). Genealogy received a great surge in popularity in the late 1970's after the television adaptation of Alex Haley's novel *Roots* aired. The dramatization of Haley's book brought a new sense of the importance of family history to young Americans, who felt alienated from their past after the political and social upheavals of the 1960's. Genealogies became very popular, especially among previously neglected ethnicities and minority groups, such as African Americans, Latinos, Asian Americans, and those whose ancestors came from Eastern Europe. Resources such as the Family History Library in Salt Lake City, Utah, expanded their archives to satisfy the demand for information on thousands of immigrants.

For individuals, family trees are a valuable way of connecting with extended families across time as well as across space. Knowing one's own ancestry can make the past relevant in ways histories or chronologies cannot. Being able to name one's ancestors can give a sense of familiarity or of belonging to families, helping them to stay together.

—Kenneth R. Shepherd

See also Ancestor worship; Family albums and records; Family History Library; Generational relationships; Haley, Alex; Lineage.

Family unity

RELEVANT ISSUES: Children and child development; Parenting and family relationships
SIGNIFICANCE: Since the family is the basic unit of society, developing and maintaining family unity is essential to the foundation of a strong nation and society as a whole

The ancient Chinese, Egyptians, Greeks, Hebrews, Romans, and Hindus of India were all family-oriented peoples. All these cultures had strong patriarchal families and built family unity and traditions by participating together in games, public entertainment, hunting, fishing, and work projects. Chinese and Roman households were large and closely knit and included not only the nuclear family, but maintained strong ties with the extended family.

For pioneer families in the United States, family unity was both a necessity and a natural result of their way of life. Pioneer families lived, worked, and played together. They cleared the land, planted, cultivated, and harvested crops together. Family members relied heavily on one another for companionship, education, religious instruction, recreation, safety, and survival.

In recent decades, a very mobile society has led many persons to change jobs and homes several times during their lives. As a result, people have learned to depend less on the family. In addition, television and outside activities frequently demand persons' time and attention, and family unity has broken down as family members have become isolated from one another. The isolation of family members has also occurred frequently in the wake of divorces or after the deaths of parents.

Playing games together is a family tradition with ancient roots. (James L. Shaffer)

As children grow older, the nature of the games they play with their parents tends to change. (James L. Shaffer)

Since the 1950's television has helped to bring families physically closer together, but at the cost of reducing communication. (AP/Wide World Photos)

The key factor in the maintenance of family unity is that family members take time to talk and listen to one another. Keeping communication lines open builds self-esteem, respect, and mutual love, providing a wholesome atmosphere in which problems can be discussed and solved. Development of family unity helps family members learn the skills of cooperating and working with others, tolerating fads and individual habits, and contributing positively to society as a whole. Whether it be the traditional nuclear family or other family patterns, family unity is essential for the effective functioning and longevity of the family unit.

Since time is at a premium, many families hold periodic family councils to discuss matters of common family interest, to agree upon things to be done, and to plan activities, work projects, and service projects that will build family traditions and unify the family. Many of these topics can also be discussed at regular family meals. Families can meet together once a week for an hour or two of activities, during which they can discuss family problems, values and religious principles, personal problems, and their family needs. Such meetings can be held in an atmosphere of open communication tempered with kindness and love,

One of the most intimate forms of family unity is the family outing. (James L. Shaffer)

during which family members can learn that changes occurring outside the home do not affect fundamental family relationships.

—*Alvin K. Benson*

See also Extended families; Family: concept and history; Family values; Love.

Family values

RELEVANT ISSUES: Children and child development; Education; Marriage and dating; Parenting and family relationships; Religious beliefs and practices; Sociology

SIGNIFICANCE: Growing numbers of working women, the increase in the numbers of women engaged in political life, U.S. Supreme Court

rulings on civil rights and religion, the rise of the Christian Right, and feminism have all contributed to the use of the term "family values"

The idea of "family values" has its roots in the religious beliefs of colonial North America. The concept of a Judeo-Christian god and of his interest in the founding of the nation is reflected in the wording of the Declaration of Independence and the U.S. Constitution. These documents reflected Protestantism and fundamentalism, which were reinforced by the industrial capitalism of the nineteenth century. The waves of immigrants during this period were predominantly Protestants and Roman Catholics from Western European countries. These events led to a rising white middle class, whose interest in mirroring European social culture coincided with the U.S. government's interests. From this beginning emerged the late twentieth century concept of "family values."

The Industrial Revolution brought with it a growing middle class able to educate its children. Boys were reared to be businessmen and professionals, while girls were reared to provide a home suitable to a husband's new status. While the leisure and education of the middle class provided men with more time to engage in social and civic pursuits, some women grew restive at their con-

fined sphere. Rising materialism also threatened to dilute, if not extinguish, the higher moral values that were prized by the society. The solution to this was the establishment of what Linda Kerber has termed "republican motherhood." Based on the concept of women's place in civil society—the home—and a fundamentalist interpretation of the Bible on women's proper place, republican motherhood taught women that they could best serve their families, their country, and their own salvation by providing a moral atmosphere for

The 1948 film I Remember Mama, *which examines an immigrant Norwegian family in San Francisco, is a nostalgic classic about family values.* (Museum of Modern Art, Film Stills Archive)

husbands and children in the home. Emphasis was placed on the concept that a strong society must rest on the foundation of strong homes and families.

The Christian Right. Corwin E. Smidt and James M. Penning trace the roots of the Christian Right movement in the United States to reformed revivalism at the beginning of the twentieth century, with its ability to mobilize politically. As social protest became popular in the 1960's, including a revival of the feminist movement, and especially when the U.S. Congress passed a resolution proposing the Equal Rights Amendment (ERA) in 1972 and sent this proposed amendment to the states for ratification, the Christian Right created organizations with strong moral overtones such as the Moral Majority and the Christian Voice. Such organizations spoke of "putting God back in the government" and urged "pro-family" antiabortion policies, school prayer, reinforcement of parental rights, and religious equality as a counterweight to secular views in the classroom. With the defeat of the ERA, the Christian Right movement became uncoordinated but was rescued after religious broadcaster Pat Robertson's unsuccessful 1988 presidential campaign. Managed by Ralph Reed through the umbrella Christian Coalition, it developed into a nationally coordinated coalition of political pressure groups and campaign finance committees at the federal level and throughout the states.

The goal of this campaign was to elect to state and federal office conservative Republicans who would support a "family values" platform, opposing government policies that allow or encourage nontraditional family structures such as gay-lesbian parenting arrangements or same-sex marriages. They sought to overturn *Roe v. Wade*, the 1973 Supreme Court decision that granted women the right to abortion on demand within the first three months of pregnancy, and expressed support for a constitutional amendment prohibiting abortion. They supported a return to teaching basic Christian values in the schools and a constitutional amendment allowing prayer in public schools.

Political conservatives essentially coopted the term "family values" for themselves, charging that Democrats, feminists, and nontraditionalists support antifamily values. Political conservatives play on a deep and continuing cultural ambivalence about whether women with young children should stay at home or work and oppose programs that encourage a family structure other than that consisting of traditional breadwinning fathers and at-home nurturing mothers.

Attempts to Broaden the Term. The feminist movement of the 1960's and 1970's concentrated on broadening women's personal, political, and economic options and in so doing downplayed the traditional role of women in the family. The

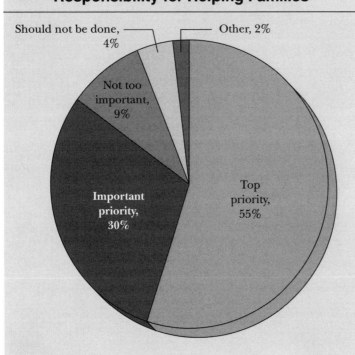

U.S. Public Opinion on Government Responsibility for Helping Families

Should not be done, 4%
Other, 2%
Not too important, 9%
Important priority, 30%
Top priority, 55%

Source: The Pew Research Center

Note: In early 1998 the PEW Research Center conducted a nationwide survey in which 1,200 adults were asked how high a priority dealing with the problems of families should be for the federal government in the coming year. This chart summarizes responses.

Many conservative Americans lament court rulings that have outlawed religious training in the public schools, such as this Bible class conducted in a Misssissippi school in 1964. (Library of Congress)

leaders of feminist organizations, who were accused of being antifamily, classist, and racist, emphasized in the 1980's and 1990's the importance of women's right to choose, including the right to choose a traditional role. Leaders of these organizations attempted to counteract the perception that feminists are antifamily while insisting that the term "family values" must be seen as inclusive of all types of family configurations and of more than simply traditionalist values. They argued that traditionalist values perpetuate the po-

litical and economic inequality of women.

Feminists, liberals, and Democrats point to statistics showing that only about 7 percent of households fit the traditional concept of the family: a breadwinning father, an at-home mother, and at least one child under the age of eighteen. Nearly half of all families comprise adult male and adult female wage earners, with or without children. The next most common family types are single-parent families and unmarried, cohabiting couples, followed by individuals who live alone. Gay

Modern notions of "family values" trace their roots to religious beliefs held in the colonial era. (James L. Shaffer)

and lesbian couples, some with children, are increasingly visible and vocal. In his 1997 State of the Union address Democratic president Bill Clinton used the term "family values" repeatedly in an attempt to weaken the Republican Party's ownership of the term.

Different Interpretations. Different interpretations of the concept of "family values" illustrate the prevailing differences in viewpoints. A 1998 Democratic proposal to increase federal support for day care included tax credits for families who place their children in day care, tax breaks for businesses offering child care, larger subsidies for low-income parents, and investment in programs to improve day-care quality. Republicans countered with a proposal that would expand tax credits to families in which child care is provided by stay-at-home mothers.

Differing views of family values have also come to light as gay men and lesbians have demanded that single homosexuals or same-sex couples have the right to adopt children, that same-sex marriages be legally recognized, and that laws be enacted granting same-sex companions health care benefits. The education of children has also sparked arguments around family values. While Christian Rightists insist that sex education should be confined to teaching abstinence, their opponents argue that sex education should include information on sexually transmitted diseases and the issuing of condoms.

There have been contentious debates about the degree of control that parents should have over what their children see and hear on television, in movies, and on tapes and CDs, and the extent to which the media should be regulated by government or at least required to provide ratings. However, these debates do not often seem to be based on liberal versus conservative or religious beliefs. In 1996 Congress mandated as part of a sweeping Telecommunications Act that parents be provided with timely information about the nature of upcoming television programs and be provided with a means to block shows they do not want their children to see. The act granted manufacturers a two-year hiatus in which to develop V-chips, which would allow parents to block programs, and stipulated that all televisions with thirteen-inch screens or larger would eventually have to contain this blocking device. —*Erika E. Pilver*

BIBLIOGRAPHY

Diamond, Sara. *Roads to Dominion: Right Wing Movements and Political Power in the United States.* New York: The Guilford Press, 1995.

Kerber, Linda K. *Women of the Republic: Intellect and Ideology in Revolutionary America.* New York: W. W. Norton & Co., 1980.

Kerber, Linda K., and Jane DeHart-Mathews, eds. *Women's America: Refocusing the Past.* New York: Oxford University Press, 1987.

Shanley, Mary Lyndon, and Carole Pateman, eds. *Feminist Interpretations and Political Theory.* University Park: Pennsylvania State University Press, 1991.

Smidt, Corwin E., and James M. Penning, eds. *Sojourners in the Wilderness: The Christian Right in Comparative Perspective.* New York: Rowan and Littlefield, 1997.

Tuana, Nancy. *Woman and the History of Philosophy.* New York: Paragon, 1992.

See also Alternative family types; Cult of True Womanhood; Cultural influences; Family: concept and history; Family unity; Focus on the Family; Gay and lesbian families; Gender inequality; Moral education; Motherhood; Nuclear family; Sex education; Single-parent families; Women's roles.

Family Violence Prevention and Services Act

DATE: Enacted on October 9, 1984

RELEVANT ISSUES: Health and medicine; Sociology; Violence

SIGNIFICANCE: The act was the first comprehensive federal measure to address the problem of domestic violence

The Family Violence Prevention and Services Act of 1984, Title III of the Child Abuse Amendments of 1984, provided $65 million to states to fund shelters for abused women and for research into domestic violence. It authorized, among other things, state demonstration grants to provide shelter and related services. It also established a National Clearinghouse on Family Violence.

The programs established by the act were intended to emphasize support for effective community-based projects operated by non-profit organizations, particularly those whose primary purpose is to operate shelters for victims of family violence and their dependents and those which provide counseling, treatment for alcohol and drug abuse, and self-help services to victims and abusers. The federal government distributed funds under the Act according to states' population size, although each state was guaranteed a minimum of $50,000. Sixty percent of this money had to be spent on immediate shelter and related assistance to victims of family violence. In 1994 the act was amended to include provisions making interstate domestic violence a crime. In general, the new provisions make it a crime to cross a state line and commit domestic violence or to cause spouses or intimate partners to cross a state line and then commit domestic violence against them. *—Timothy L. Hall*

See also Child abuse; Cruelty as grounds for divorce; Domestic violence; Marital rape; Shelters; Violence Against Women Act.

Father-daughter relationships

RELEVANT ISSUES: Children and child development; Parenting and family relationships
SIGNIFICANCE: While fathers help to shape their daughters' feelings about themselves as females and about the role that men are expected to play in their lives, men's attitudes can help daughters develop their capacities to the fullest or keep them relegated to traditional female roles

A major determinant of the nature of father-daughter relationships is the feelings that fathers, as men, have about the opposite sex. Some fathers subscribe to patriarchal views that see females as inferior to males; they react to their wives and daughters accordingly. These men believe that their wives and daughters should be subservient to their needs and that there should be a strict sexual division of labor inside and outside the home. They may have little to do with the child-rearing process, and their expectation levels for their daughters are relatively low.

Traditional Psychoanalytic Theories. Austrian psychoanalyst Sigmund Freud offered a theory of father-daughter relationships that has continued to have a strong hold on psychological thinking. According to Freud, when girls and boys become aware of the anatomical differences between

them, girls assume that the absence of a penis means that they are deformed, causing them to develop "penis envy." In Freud's theory, girls try to compensate for the lack of a penis through attachment to their fathers, hoping thereby to possess their penis. This sexualized desire for the father has been called the Electra complex, a corollary of the Oedipus complex, in which boys develop sexual cravings for their mothers.

A constellation of personality traits accompanies the Electra complex. Girls supposedly develop feelings of inferiority because of their anatomical lack of a penis, narcissism (to compensate for their feelings of inferiority), masochism (the wish for intercourse to obtain the penis), and contempt for mothers, who also lack a penis. While many modern theorists, including women, subscribe to modified versions of the Electra complex, some interpret whatever envy girls experience as the envy of the prerogatives that males enjoy rather than envy of the male organ itself.

Research on Father-Daughter Relationships. Relatively little research has been conducted on father-daughter interactions. Available data show that fathers relate very differently to daughters than to sons. To begin with, most fathers-to-be want to have sons rather than daughters, especially if they only intend to have one child. They feel that only sons can carry on their name and tradition. As a reflection of fathers' greater involvement with sons than with daughters, research also indicates that fathers concentrate more on their sons, offer them more support, and encourage them to help in fathers' pursuits, be it learning auto mechanics or baseball. Fathers may not only fail to encourage their daughters to achieve mastery in "masculine" areas, but they may also actively discourage them from doing so. Interestingly, those daughters who do receive active encouragement from their fathers tend not to have male siblings. In a study of top female executives, Margaret Hennig and Ann Jardim found that all twenty-five subjects had no brothers.

Sexualization of the Father-Daughter Relationship. The aspect of the traditional female role that fathers expect their daughters to fulfill is being physically attractive and feminine. Research indicates that fathers are more tender with infant girls than with boys and have more eye contact with them. Girls cuddle more with their fathers than

The nature of father-daughter relationships derives from attitudes that the fathers themselves may have about male and female sex roles. (Dick Hemingway)

A key to raising daughters to be independent is for fathers to avoid gender-biased behavior. (R. Kent Rasmussen)

boys, sit on their laps, and mold their bodies to them. Culture expects girls to have a romantic attachment to their fathers. Unlike the term "mama's boy," the term "daddy's girl" carries positive connotations. The father-daughter romance has its counterpart in other relationships in which young women may become involved with men "old enough to be their fathers," be it college professors, doctors, or bosses.

Unfortunately, it is not uncommon for the father-daughter relationship to become sexualized. As Miriam and Otto Ehrenberg point out in their book *The Intimate Circle: The Sexual Dynamics of Family Life*, the chemistry that makes the father-daughter relationship special from the beginning also makes it problematical as daughters mature. According to the Ehrenbergs, when fathers become aroused by their daughters' sexuality, they may react in destructive ways. Some become aloof in order to defend themselves against their feelings of sexual attraction; some turn against their daughters, becoming critical of their growing womanliness in order to curb their own distress; some engage in "pseudoincest" by being sexually seductive; and some, in extreme cases, cross the line and engage in actual incest. Although it is difficult to estimate the actual number of instances of father-daughter incest, it has become increasingly clear that it occurs all too often. Cases have been reported of fathers sexually molesting daughters under one year of age. The incidence increases with daughters' increasing sexual maturity. Studies indicate that father-daughter incest is most apt to occur in households in which fathers are the dominant figure and sexually repressive in other ways as well. Such fathers are prone to put the onus on their daughters when incest occurs, blaming it on their daughters' seductiveness. As

the most important member of their families, these fathers also tend to feel a sense of entitlement in having their needs met by the females in the household, whether by their wives or daughters.

Obviously, incest has devastating consequences for daughters, but even pseudoincest is harmful, because it makes daughters feel guilty about their sexuality and perpetuates the double standard ac-

Relatively little research has focused on father-daughter relationships, but it is clear that fathers relate to daughters very differently than they do to sons. (James L. Shaffer)

cording to which women who do not suppress their sexuality have nobody but themselves to blame if they are sexually assaulted or raped.

Absent Fathers. An increasing number of fathers are not a part of the family unit. In the African American community, for example, almost half of all families have a female head of household. The impact of absent fathers on daughters is not necessarily negative. On the positive side, girls who grow up in father-absent homes may grow up with aspirations that are less gender stereotyped, following the lead of their mothers. On the negative side, they may grow to believe that men are not dependable or caring, and they may place few demands on the men they encounter in their later lives, having learned to expect very little.

Future Prospects. Several feminists have pointed out that the way to raise daughters who are more independent is to eliminate gender biases in the division of labor within households. If fathers play a more active role as actual caretakers they may learn to appreciate their daughters more as people and less as sex objects. They also can set the stage for breaking down rigid gender roles and open up new possibilities for their daughters.

—Miriam Ehrenberg

BIBLIOGRAPHY

Appelton, William. *Fathers and Daughters.* Garden City, N.Y.: Doubleday, 1981.

Boose, Lynda E., and Betty S. Flowers, eds. *Daughters and Fathers.* Baltimore: The Johns Hopkins University Press, 1989.

Chodorow, Nancy. *The Reproduction of Mothering.* Berkeley: University of California Press, 1978.

Ehrenberg, Miriam, and Otto Ehrenberg. *The Intimate Circle: The Sexual Dynamics of Family Life.* New York: Simon & Schuster, 1988.

Herman, Judith L. *Father-Daughter Incest.* Cambridge, Mass.: Harvard University Press, 1981.

Lamb, Michael E., ed. *The Role of the Father in Child Development.* 2d ed. New York: John Wiley and Sons, 1981.

See also Abandonment of the family; Electra and Oedipus complexes; Equality of children; Father-son relationships; Fatherhood; Freudian psychology; Gender inequality; Incest; Mother-daughter relationships.

Father figures

RELEVANT ISSUES: Children and child development; Parenting and family relationships

SIGNIFICANCE: Father figures are adult males who personify some of the characteristics of fathers, exercising some degree of paternal oversight, warmth, care, companionship, protection, or material support toward others and toward whom emotional attachment and filial appreciation are focused

The term "father figure" conveys the same meaning as the 1930's term "father image" or the British terms "father-substitute" and "father surrogate." Although the origin of the term "father figure" is not precisely traceable, it has its conceptual roots in antiquity. In more than thirty references, the Old Testament mandates the protection of and provision for the fatherless. In the first epistle to the Corinthians, Saint Paul asserts that he had become their "father in Christ," which by the 1300's also became known as a "spiritual father." The term "father figure" may colloquially extend to anyone with fatherly characteristics or functions, such as role models, mentors, coaches, or teachers. Father figures may be connected to families through formal support organizations, such as Big Brothers, but most often the father-figure relationship is established informally through extended family relationships (uncles, grandfathers, or mother's boyfriends), through stepfathers, or through the community (coaches, mentors, teachers, male godparents).

Because of the high incidence of single-parent, female-headed households resulting from divorce and out-of-wedlock births, the need for father figures received increased attention in the late twentieth century. Psychologically, constructive father figures are thought to make positive contributions to children's self-concepts; sex-role modeling; and spiritual, cognitive, and career development. While these benefits of father figures can be realized in intact families in which fathers are uninvolved or inept, it is in father-absent families that father-figure relationships are most commonly recognized.

—Rob Palkovitz

See also Extended families; Fatherhood; Fatherlessness; Godparents; Men's roles.

Father-figure relationships are most often established informally through extended-family ties. (CLEO Freelance Photography)

Father-son relationships

RELEVANT ISSUES: Children and child development; Parenting and family relationships

SIGNIFICANCE: Fathers play an important role in the social, emotional, cognitive, and sex-role development of their sons

Four aspects of family life in North America put the father-son relationship into proper perspective. Mothers have traditionally provided most of the day-to-day care of infants and children and have also tended to spend more time with their children than fathers. Thus, the primary parent-child relationship for most boys is with their mothers. As a result, the contribution of fathers to child development was often overlooked in the past. However, researchers have begun to focus on the unique contributions of fathers to the well-being of their children.

Fathers who have warm, supportive, and accessible relationships with their sons are an ideal but not necessarily the rule. (James L. Shaffer)

Boys tend to model their own behavior on that of their fathers. (Hazel Hankin)

There is great variability in the quality and nature of father-son relationships in the United States and Canada. Some fathers abandon their children, while others are distant or abusive. Some fathers are in and out of their boys' lives, while others are warm, supportive, and available. In addition, the nature of a particular father-son relationship also depends on the individual characteristics of fathers and their sons.

There are class, racial, and ethnic differences in the father-son relationship. For example, some research suggests that middle-class African Americans may be more involved in the lives of their children than middle-class white American fathers. Also, the father-son relationship does not exist in a vacuum. It affects, and is affected by, other relationships in the family. To illustrate this, there is research suggesting that the quality of men's fathering is significantly influenced by the quality of their marital relationships, with better marital quality associated with more constructive parenting. Furthermore, the nature of the father-son relationship also depends on the composition of the family. Boys who have only sisters tend to receive more attention from their fathers than do boys with other brothers. Sons whose parents have divorced tend to have less contact with their fathers than do boys from intact families.

Theories of the Father-Son Relationship. At least three theories seek to explain how fathers influence their sons. The first, Freudian psychology, focuses on the mother-father-son triangle. Freud proposed that boys during their preschool years go through several stages (the Oedipus complex) in which they are attracted to their mothers, feel like rivals and competitors of their fathers, fear their fathers, and then seek to identify with and be like their fathers. Boys whose fathers are nurturing and involved pass through these stages more successfully than boys whose fathers are either distant and unavailable or harsh and punitive. Negotiating this process is thought to be necessary for healthy adult functioning.

The second theory, social learning theory, suggests that sons observe and imitate their fathers. Accordingly, sons of fathers who are alcoholics, who abuse their wives or children, or who engage in antisocial behavior are viewed as more likely to repeat these same behaviors. On the other hand, fathers who are involved in their sons' lives, who

are loving but firm, and who have successful marriages are more likely to have sons who repeat these patterns.

The third theory, biological-genetic models, posits that fathers influence sons through the genetic inheritance they provide them. Using twin studies (comparing twins who were raised together and those who were raised apart), researchers have sought to separate out the effects of the environment from genetic influences. When such heritable traits are identified (such as intelligence, sociability, activity level, alcoholism, schizophrenia), biological-genetic models suggest that if a parent exhibits the trait, the child is more likely to exhibit the trait as well.

These three theories have been proposed as frameworks for understanding how the father-son relationship influences sons. A growing body of research, from two different perspectives, has focused on fathers and their impact on their sons.

Father-Absence vs. Father-Presence Research. One line of research that has considered the impact of fathers has studied sons who have had very little contact with their fathers. This "father absence" research postulates that if boys who do not have a relationship with their fathers are different from those who do, the importance of fathers can be inferred. Such research has raised concerns about boys raised in father-absent homes, suggesting, in general, that males who do not have fathers in the home tend to have problems with sex-role and gender identification, school performance, psychosocial development and adjustment, and aggression control. However, it is difficult to separate out the important factors that contribute to these challenges on the part of sons. It remains to be determined whether the lack of a father, the lack of a father's income, or the increased stress on the single-parent mother explains the poorer outcomes for these boys or, given that many single-parent families are created by divorce, whether factors associated with divorce, such as chronic marital conflict, explain these poorer outcomes. Furthermore, since not all boys without fathers develop in an unhealthy manner and not all boys with fathers develop normally, there must be other factors to consider. Fortunately, there is another line of research, which explores a father's presence and involvement, not just his absence. This research has documented several contributions of

As boys move into adolescence they tend to spend less time with their fathers than they do with their mothers. (Ben Klaffke)

fathers to the social, emotional, and cognitive development of their children, including investigations of father-son relationships at different developmental periods.

Father-Son Relationship over the Life Cycle. Fathers have been shown to be as competent as mothers at caring for infants, although in most families mothers continue to provide the majority of routine care. Mothers are also usually the primary attachment figures—the persons to whom infants can turn when they are distressed and in need of contact and comfort. However, fathers also serve as attachment figures for their infants, although their primary role with infants and toddlers has been that of playmates. Fathers are known for their rough-and-tumble, stimulating style of play, which may differentiate them from mothers.

Soon after their children are born, many fathers tend to interact more with infant sons than with infant daughters. This differential treatment of sons and daughters often continues throughout infancy and the toddler stages. It has been suggested that the last half of the infancy period (from eighteen months to three years of age), is the critical time when parents shape the gender identity of their children. Although contradictory findings exist in the literature, there is some research suggesting that fathers reinforce their sons for behaving in sex-stereotypical ways during interactions and play at this stage of life.

As their infants become preschoolers, fathers remain secondary to mothers in terms of the amount of time they spend caring for their children. Nevertheless, positive father involvement is associated with favorable cognitive, social-emotional, and moral outcomes at this stage of development and as sons reach school age. Specifically, the available research indicates that the cognitive development of boys whose fathers are highly involved is enhanced and that these boys do better in school than those whose fathers are less involved. Furthermore, boys' ability to be empathic, their social skills, and their degree of peer acceptance are associated with a healthy father-son relationship. Additionally, boys' sense of responsibility, a healthy self-concept and gender identity, and their ability to exercise self-control and avoid delinquent acts are all predicted by constructive father involvement.

During adolescence, as peers become more important and adolescents are engaged in more activities, fathers and sons tend to spend less time with one another. On average, adolescent sons spend less time with their fathers than they do with their mothers, although they report spending more of their free time with their fathers than with their mothers. In general, sons report greater intimacy and more frequent communication with their mothers but less conflict with their fathers. Thus, for male adolescents, fathers play the roles of recreation partner, disciplinarian, and consultant for solving problems and discussing future educational and career goals. Hence, while fathers are generally less involved and close to their adolescent sons than are mothers, they continue to have an impact on their sons, particularly in specific areas in which they are more involved (such as discipline) or in which they tend to be role models (such as attitudes toward alcohol, since drinking is commonly viewed more as male behavior in American culture).

Long-term Effects of the Father-Son Relationship. The consequences of a healthy father-son relationship persist over the life span. Links between the father-son relationship in childhood and adolescence and several behaviors or characteristics in adulthood have been found, including constructive fathering, positive personality characteristics, emotional stability, social competence, and occupational success. These are all general findings and they may not apply to any one father-son relationship, but they speak to what is possible. As role models and as sources of support and guidance for their sons, fathers can have a positive lasting impact.

—*Mark B. White*

BIBLIOGRAPHY

Biller, Henry. B. *Fathers and Families.* Westport, Conn.: Auburn House, 1993.

Hawkins, Alan J., and David C. Dollahite, eds. *Generative Fathering: Beyond Deficit Perspectives.* Thousand Oaks, Calif.: Sage Publications, 1997.

Lamb, Michael E. *The Role of the Father in Child Development.* 3d ed. New York: John Wiley & Sons, 1997.

Larson, Reed, and Maryse H. Richards. *Divergent Lives: The Emotional Lives of Mothers, Fathers, and Adolescents.* New York: Basic Books, 1994.

Shulman, Shmuel, and W. Andrew Collins, eds.

Father-Adolescent Relationships: Development and Context. San Francisco, Calif.: Jossey-Bass, 1994.

Snarey, John. *How Fathers Care for the Next Generation: A Four-Decade Study.* Cambridge, Mass.: Harvard University Press, 1993.

See also Attachment theory; Father-daughter relationships; Fatherhood; Fatherlessness; Freudian psychology; Mother-daughter relationships; Mother-son relationships.

Fatherhood

RELEVANT ISSUES: Children and child development; Parenting and family relationships

SIGNIFICANCE: The roles and functions fathers have played in family life have varied over time, but despite these variations it is clear that fathers' roles have predominantly centered on caring for the needs of their children

A survey of both historical and modern research on fatherhood gives a glimpse into the multifaceted roles fathers play in families. One limitation in understanding fathers' roles in the past is the lack of historical research on fatherhood. From what is known about fathers, their participation in family life may have changed more than that of all other family members combined. The roles and functions that fathers have played in family life have varied over time, but despite these variations, most fathers have focused their roles on caring for the needs of their children. The needs of children are consistent. Children's material needs are satisfied by fathers who provide them with food, shelter, and clothing. Children also have emotional, moral, and educational needs that fathers satisfy by providing them with love, learning, and interaction.

It is possible to understand how fathers' roles in families have changed through the years by examining their roles during the preindustrial, industrial, and the late industrial or postindustrial periods. The pre-industrial period is generally identified as the seventeenth and eighteenth centuries. The industrial age encompasses the nineteenth century and roughly the first half of the twentieth, and the late industrial or postindustrial era is typically identified as the social and economic life of advanced societies. Modern North America is a postindustrial society.

Fathers' Roles in the Preindustrial Period. In the preindustrial era husbands and wives shared emotional and work roles in and out of the home. Not only did men participate in the household production of the family, but they also shared in the emotional nurturing and care of their children. Although family chores were segregated along sex-based lines, men and women still shared collective tasks. For example, at times mothers and daughters worked in the fields while husbands sometimes spun and wove cloth after they had finished their chores; male apprentices helped with household tasks; and mothers educated the children when they were young while fathers generally educated them when they were older. Men and women worked in the fields together and ensured family survival not only to meet their material needs but also to allow time for fathers to be with their children. This time together not only helped children to develop work skills for later employment but also allowed fathers to spend time with their children and to teach them.

Some research suggests that fathers may have taken a greater responsibility for parenting than their wives in the preindustrial period. Fathers took major responsibility for the moral and religious education of their children, for their literacy, and for their courtship and marriages. Fathers were also role models, as it was thought that fathers provided the best examples of moral character and behavior. Many roles and beliefs relating to fathers' parenting responsibilities in this period may be attributed to stereotyped gender beliefs. Yet, this does not diminish the fact that fathers played an active role in almost every aspect of their children's lives.

Fathers in the preindustrial period were thought to be active in many parenting roles. They were thought to play predominant roles as psychologists, companions, and caregivers. As psychologists, fathers were thought to be more sensitive than mothers in perceiving the psychological needs of their children. Because of the abilities attributed to fathers at that time, fathers were also likely to counsel their children on personal matters. Besides sensitivity to the psychological needs of their children, they also exhibited sensitivity and nurturance in their role as caregivers. As parents and moral overseers according to the common law of the time, fathers retained custody of

The popular 1989 film Parenthood *starred Steve Martin (right) as a man struggling to be the best father he could be for his son Jasen Fisher.* (Museum of Modern Art, Film Stills Archive)

their children in the event that they separated from their wives. Despite the preferred status of fathers in this period, their responsibilities would soon be almost totally transferred to mothers.

Fathers' Roles During the Industrial Age. During the Industrial Revolution parenting roles switched from fathers to mothers. Industrialization reshaped the structure of American families, as fathers left home to work in factories and other workplaces. As fathers entered the workplace and became salaried employees or wage laborers, their family roles were taken over almost completely by mothers.

As mothers inherited almost exclusive responsi-

bility for housework and child care, emphasis on family life and motherhood became paramount. Many new magazines were published to help mothers perform their primary function of caring for the household and the children. In contrast, books for fathers centered around the competitive nature of the workplace and included handbooks about how to conquer in the competitive work environment outside the home and how to become self-made men.

As fathers' home roles diminished, their abilities as parents came into question. During this period, women were depicted as unselfish, calm, and pure. Their moral purity elevated them far above men as parents. The superiority mothers attained in this period can be seen in the area of child custody. Child custody in the preindustrial era was generally given to fathers in the event of marital separations. In the industrial era of heightened domestic awareness, however, courts began to declare that mothers were the most proper parents to attain custody of their children. It is during the industrial age that expressions such as "the missing man," "the forgotten man," or "the "almost invisible father" came into vogue. Clergymen and others lamented that fathers played only limited roles in their families, echoing similar statements regarding women in the preindustrial period.

Because of the absence of fathers during the Industrial Revolution and the glorification of motherhood, expressions such as the "cult of motherhood" and the "cult of domesticity" entered the scene. As women's roles in the home became glorified, men's roles became limited. This gave rise to the idea of the "part-time parent" or "part-time father." The only roles that fathers continued to play in the family were as audiences, playmates, disciplinarians, and discussion leaders. However, of all these roles, fathers as providers took precedence.

As fathers focused on their primary responsibility of providing for their families, they came to be labeled as "incompetent" for their lack of active daily participation in the home, not because they were incapable of participating fully in home life. The myth of the "incompetent" father was so prevalent in society at this time that fathers were depicted as such in comics, theater, and later television. They were cast as a bumblers who were implicitly patronized by their wives and children. Research done in the 1950's and 1960's even claimed that fathers' participation in child rearing was inappropriate and of little importance.

Contrary to the myth of incompetency, fathers expressed great interest in and devotion to their children during the period of industrialization. They made many sacrifices working and providing for the material needs of their families and cherished the time they had with their children, typically on weekends. Contrary to the image of the part-time father, fathers were active in the physical, moral, and mental development of their children. Fathers typically influenced children's physi-

cal development by serving as their playmates, which also strengthened the emotional bonds between them. Fathers also influenced their children's moral and mental development by giving them advice and supporting their education with financial and emotional support.

Fathers' Roles During the Postindustrial Era. Modern fathers play a wide variety of roles and functions in families. These roles are in many respects a combination of the roles fathers fulfilled during the preindustrial and industrial eras. Although many fathers are still the primary providers of material necessities for their families, mothers have increasingly entered the workforce and shared the provider role with their husbands. As more women have increasingly begun to work outside the home, it has become necessary for husbands to share more of the housework and child care with their wives. Not only have structural factors in society, such as greater numbers of working women, influenced fathers to be more involved in the daily care of their children, but changing cultural and societal images of "good" fathers have also changed. This new style of fathering has been called "androgynous," "involved," or "highly participant" fatherhood. It emphasizes fathers who are present at the births of their children and who are involved in their daily care from infancy on. "New" fathers are also sensitive to their children's needs and are as involved with their daughters as they are with their sons. Obviously, this image is an ideal, but it nevertheless represents many modern fathers and their involvement with their children.

Despite the many roles that modern fathers play in their families, it is also true that some fathers

---

Father's Day

This annual holiday can be traced back to 1910, when the mayor of Spokane, Washington, proclaimed June 19 to be Father's Day, and it was supported by an additional proclamation by the state's governor. President Calvin Coolidge publicly supported Father's Day in 1924; however, it was not given the semiofficial national sanction until President Lyndon B. Johnson proclaimed the third Sunday of every June to be Father's Day in 1966.

It is through consistent involvement and interaction with their children that fathers learn about caring and nur-turing. (Dick Hemingway)

neglect or flee entirely from their family responsibilities. Some fathers who live with their children fail to involve themselves with them in any meaningful or consistent way. Other fathers fail to pay child support or visit their children when they do not have custody of them. When fathers fail to be involved with their children, not only does children's development suffer, but fathers' development suffers as well.

Fathers' Role in Child Development. Research has documented several ways in which fathers can influence their children's development. Affectionate fathers help their children to develop positive relationships. Children of affectionate fathers are more sure of themselves than children of unaffectionate fathers, and they feel that they have greater control over their lives when they have involved and accessible fathers. Such children also have higher cognitive abilities and fewer stereotypical gender beliefs about the roles that women and men should play in society than children with uninvolved and inaccessible fathers. When fathers play an active role in their children's intellectual, social, and physical development by helping them with their homework, taking them to museums, and playing games, children are more likely to have greater educational and occupational success when they become adults. Fathers who spend time with their children and are available to meet their children's needs also have better relationships with them. Children with involved fathers tend to have more self-control, self-esteem, and better social skills than children with uninvolved fathers.

Father Involvement and Development in Fathers. Research highlights how fathers' involvement with their children not only influences child development, but also father development. Fathers must actively participate in housework and child care to perpetuate and further develop their parenting skills. At the births of their children, many fathers demonstrate nurturing and sensitive

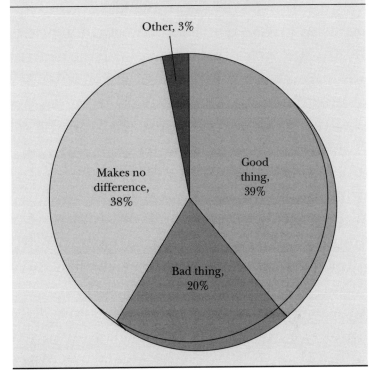

Women's Attitudes Toward Stay-at-Home Fathers

Other, 3%

Good thing, 39%

Makes no difference, 38%

Bad thing, 20%

Source: The Pew Research Center (1998)

Note: A cross-section of American women were asked if the trend of more fathers staying at home with their children was a good or a bad thing for society.

caretaking abilities by touching, kissing, talking to, and feeding their infants. It is through consistent involvement and interaction with their children that fathers learn to care for and nurture them. Fathers learn to care for their children much like they perform any other job; parenting skills are acquired through participation and practice. As mothers participate more heavily in the workforce outside the home, fathers acquire greater parenting skills. Since fathers often spend less time with their children than mothers, they feel less confident as parents over time and can become less sensitive to their children's needs. Nevertheless, fathers who do participate actively in the care of their children gain the skills and confidence needed for sensitive care. Fathers who fail to involve themselves with their children, particularly when they lack custody, suffer from isolation, loneliness, and depression later in life. It can be said that if they want the support and love of their children when they grow older, fathers must support and love their children while they are young.

Fathers' roles throughout history have varied and changed according to structural changes, such as those of the Industrial Revolution and the increasing involvement of women in the labor force. Fathers' roles have also been influenced by predominant cultural beliefs, including the presumed superiority of mothers during the industrial era and the changing culture of "new" fatherhood. Despite changes in fathering through time, it is clear that fathers' roles have primarily centered on caring for the needs of their children.

—*Shawn L. Christiansen*

BIBLIOGRAPHY

Demos, John. *Past, Present, and Personal: The Family and the Life Course in American History.* New York: Oxford University Press, 1986. Examines the changing American family and fatherhood from a historical perspective.

Hawkins, Alan J., and David C. Dollahite, eds. *Generative Fathering: Beyond Deficit Perspectives.* Newbury Park, Calif.: Sage Publications, 1997. Discusses several contexts and ways in which fathers care for their children, and offers ideas on how to support fathers' involvement with their children.

Lamb, Michael E., ed. *The Role of the Father in Child Development.* 3d ed. New York: John Wiley & Sons, 1997. Examines unique types of fathers such as gay fathers, young fathers, stepfathers, and fathers of children with special needs and reviews the literature on the effects of father involvement on child development.

Marsiglio, William, ed. *Fatherhood: Contemporary Theory, Research, and Social Policy.* Newbury Park, Calif.: Sage Publications, 1995. Examines diverse kinds of fathers such as inner-city fathers, stepfathers, and single fathers while considering research, theory, and policy and their influence on fatherhood.

Popenoe, David. *Life Without Father: Compelling New Evidence that Fatherhood and Marriage Are Indispensable for the Good of Children and Society.* New York: Free Press, 1996. Discusses some of the negative changes in the fatherhood role and the need to support father involvement and marriage.

Snarey, John. *How Fathers Care for the Next Generation: A Four-Decade Study.* Cambridge, Mass.: Harvard University Press, 1993. Studies the reciprocal nature of father involvement and how both children and fathers develop through this interaction.

See also Child care; Child support; Dual-earner families; Father-daughter relationships; Father figures; Father-son relationships; Fatherlessness; Men's roles; Parenting; Patriarchs; Unwed fathers.

Fatherlessness

RELEVANT ISSUES: Children and child development; Divorce; Parenting and family relationships

SIGNIFICANCE: The consequences of fatherlessness are a source of major concern in the United States and Canada for children and society as a whole

Fathers play an important role in the development, adjustment, and well-being of their children. The most common ideal includes fatherhood in a coparent setting, in which fathers and mothers share the tasks and responsibilities of raising their children. In reality, however, many children grow up in family structures that do not include fathers.

Rates of Fatherlessness. In 1990 about 36 percent of all children under age eighteen lived apart from their biological fathers. Approximately 25 percent of these children lived in single-parent homes, and about 3 percent of these children lived only with their fathers. In 1993 the ethnic distribution of children under age eighteen living in single-parent homes was 17 percent for white children, 30 percent for Hispanic children, and 58 percent for African American children.

This fatherless state of families has been caused mainly by the high divorce rate and the large number of out-of-wedlock births. In 1993 it was estimated that approximately one-half of all marriages in the United States would end in divorce, and more than half of such divorces would involve children. In addition, about 25 percent of all children were born to unmarried mothers. This figure was up from 5 percent in 1960. Six percent of births to unmarried teenagers were among whites, 10 percent were among Hispanics, and 21 percent were among African Americans. Unmarried teen mothers make up one of the highest risk groups of children, with 88 percent of them living in poverty. These conditions pose a definite and long-term threat to all children, especially to African American children. Data indicate that African American families have the highest rate of father absence in the nation.

In *Life Without Father*, David Popenoe indicates that the media and many social scientists in the 1970's discounted the negative effects of fatherlessness. By the 1990's the view of social scientists had shifted. This shift occurred because of new evidence that was directly linked to the negative effects of fatherlessness on families. In the 1980's many children from fatherless homes entered their teen years and provided the subjects for new research. It is during the teenage years that the most devastating effects of father absence can be seen.

Role of Fathers. Fathers have traditionally played the role of providers and protectors of their families. In 1990 about 60 percent of women with children under age six and 75 percent with children between the ages of six and seventeen were employed in the U.S. work force. This trend has enhanced the nurturing and caregiving roles of fathers as they have assumed more responsibilities for home and children. Fathers enhance the lives of children through material resources. They also strongly affect the development of their children's identities, characters, and competence. Children in fatherless homes have difficulty in each of these areas.

It is largely through identification with their fathers that sons learn how to be men. The traditional ideal of manhood in Western society includes achievement, male responsibility, independence, acceptable assertiveness, and the ability to relate to women. Making the shift from boyhood to responsible manhood is difficult, since sons must break away from mothers' nurturance and bond with their fathers. In addition, daughters must learn from their fathers certain aspects of achievement, heterosexual trust, intimacy, and an appreciation of their own femininity.

Impact of Fatherlessness. For the first time in the history of the United States, the majority of all poor families in 1986 were father-absent families. In 1990 children living in fatherless homes were six times more likely to live in poverty than children in father-present homes. By 1992 about 22 percent of all children under age eighteen and 25 percent under age six lived in poverty. The conditions for female-headed families were worse, with 35 percent of white, female-headed families and 57 percent of African American, female-headed families living in poverty. In dual-parent families only 6 percent of white families and 18 percent of African American families lived at the poverty level. In Canada about 14 percent of all children lived in poverty in 1991.

In 1993 only 43 percent of white mothers, 18 percent of Hispanic mothers, and 17 percent of African American mothers received any alimony or child support from absent fathers. Many young adults who reach the age of eighteen no longer receive financial support from their fathers, even though they need support for college or for becoming established in an occupation. For many young adults, this lack of economic support contributes to downward social mobility.

Problems of Youths in Fatherless Homes

Drawing on a variety of government and nongovernment sources, *Getting Men Involved: The Newsletter of the Bay Area Male Involvement Network* claimed in its Spring, 1997, issue that children growing up in fatherless homes accounted for:

- 63% of all youth suicides
- 90% of all homeless and runaway children
- 85% of all children exhibiting behavioral disorders
- 80% of all rapists motivated with displaced anger
- 71% of all high school dropouts
- 75% of all adolescent patients in chemical abuse centers
- 70% of all juveniles in state-operated institutions
- 85% of all youths sitting in prisons

Source: Fathermag.com website (1998)

More than half of the American children living in fatherless homes are African Americans. (AP/Wide World Photos)

Father absence is the single most powerful reason for child poverty. Children who grow up without fathers are far more likely to move down the socioeconomic ladder than children with fathers. Sons are especially affected, because they are the traditional beneficiaries of occupational guidance and role modeling. Although the negative impact of poverty on children has been well documented, it cannot be separated from the social and psychological outcomes of fatherlessness. In *Life Without Father* Popenoe estimated that no more than half of the social and behavioral outcomes of growing up without a father could be attributed to the economic status of children.

Studies have shown that children who live apart from their biological fathers suffer more emotional, behavioral, and intellectual problems than children who live with their biological fathers. They are more at risk of suicide, mental illness, juvenile delinquency, teenage pregnancy, alcohol and drug use, and dropping out of school. Children in fatherless homes are also more at risk of physical abuse by mothers and their boyfriends.

Impact on Boys. A major negative consequence of fatherlessness for boys is juvenile delinquency and violence. A disproportionate number of male youths from father-absent homes become involved in crime. Approximately 60 percent of rapists, 72 percent of adolescent murderers, and 70 percent of long-term prison inmates come from fatherless homes. In *A General Theory of Crime* Michael R. Gottfredson and Travis Hirschi conclude that in most studies which compared children from intact and broken homes, those living with two biological parents had lower crime rates. Fathers serve as role models to help their sons develop self-control and feelings of empathy toward others. These are traits that are absent in violent youths. The male role model is also important in controlling the behavior of teenage boys.

Impact on Girls. For girls, the negative effects of fatherlessness most often emerge during adolescence in precocious sexuality. Girls who grow up without fathers are at much greater risk of early sexual activity, adolescent childbearing, divorce, and early marriage than girls who grow up with fathers. Girls of both widowed and divorced mothers are less able to interact successfully with men than girls with married mothers.

Those who lose their fathers through death are more likely to be shy, whereas girls who lose their fathers through divorce are more likely to be overly responsive to men.

Of all first births to teenagers between the ages of fifteen and seventeen, 81 percent are born out of wedlock. Most of these children will grow up in fatherless homes. This situation presents a major concern for society, because the presence of fathers plays a key role in the development of female sexual behavior. In 1988 the teen birth rate per 1,000 teenagers was 54.8 in the United States and 23.1 in Canada. Approximately 56 percent of girls said they had become sexually active by age eighteen. Approximately 26 percent had become sexually active by age fifteen compared to 4.6 percent in 1970. Other risks of fatherlessness for girls include a higher risk of sexual abuse from mother's boyfriends or male strangers. It seems that the presence of fathers provides a protective role for young girls.

Conclusion. For boys, the most socially acute manifestation of fatherlessness is juvenile violence; for girls, it is out-of-wedlock births. The effects of fatherlessness can also be seen when young adults are unable to form lasting relationships of their own. Fatherless children grow up without role models for sons and male-relationship models for girls. They also lack positive models in the form of mother-father interactions. In *Daddy We Need You Now!* Herman A. Sanders states, "There is no father-substitute who can fill the place which is left empty by the child's father. The father's presence in the family is necessary if the child is to be afforded every opportunity to grow normally."

—*Davia M. Allen*

BIBLIOGRAPHY

Blankenhorn, David. *Fatherless America.* New York: Basic Books, 1995.

Center for the Study of Social Policy. *Kids Count Data Book.* Washington, D.C.: Author, 1993.

Gottfredson, Michael R., and Travis Hirschi. *General Theory of Crime.* Palo Alto, Calif: Stanford University Press, 1990.

Mackey, Wade C. *The American Father: Biocultural and Developmental Aspects.* New York: Plenum Press, 1996.

National Commission on Children. *Beyond Rhetoric: A New American Agenda for Children and Fami-*

lies. Washington, D.C.: U.S. Government Printing Office, 1991.

_____. *Just the Facts.* Washington, D.C.: U.S. Government Printing Office, 1993.

Popenoe, David. *Life Without Father.* New York: Free Press, 1996.

Sanders, Herman A. *Daddy, We Need You Now! A Primer on African-American Male Socialization.* Lanham, Md.: University Press of America, 1996.

See also Child support; Fatherhood; Juvenile delinquency; Parental divorce; Paternity suits; Poverty; Single-parent families; Teen mothers; Unwed fathers.

Favoritism

Relevant issues: Children and child development; Parenting and family relationships; Race and ethnicity; Religious beliefs and practices

Significance: Children are extremely sensitive to signs of real or perceived parental discrimination, and favoritism by parents or other family members can be potentially harmful

Parents often discover that they favor one child in the family over another in spite of their efforts to be impartial. Children become aware of real or perceived injustices in their own families at a very early age. All humans have the psychological mechanisms for detecting inequities in treatment. Siblings in particular engage in frequent comparisons between themselves and brothers and sisters. Some evidence suggests that siblings' personalities vary because they adopt different strategies of behavior in a universal quest to be in parental favor. Favoritism may arise from parents' religious or cultural backgrounds and is reinforced by exposure to nuclear family members such as grandparents.

The self-concepts that children form can be greatly affected by their birth order, their sex, how close in age they are to their siblings, the number of children in the family, and the involvement of nuclear family members. The family value system that has been handed down from earlier generations affects the relationships of all members of the family and sometimes leads to favoritism. In large families, favoritism between siblings may also occur and impact on the personalities of favored children and those who are not so favored. Early

attachment or bonding between parents and children may also influence whether or not parents show favoritism toward a child. If some children's personalities or temperaments are similar to parents' own, it may appear as if they are being favored, because there is more agreement between them and their parents than between their parents and their siblings.

Birth Order. In general, first-born and only children tend to reflect the values of their families and to be slightly more achievement oriented than children who are born later. Second- and third-born children seem to have greater social skills and are better able to function outside the confines of the family. Birth order may affect parental attitudes toward their children. Fathers who wish to have a son to carry on the family name or business or who believe that a son will share their interests and serve as a companion may be sorely disappointed by the arrival of a daughter and allow their disappointment to surface. Even if parents accept the birth of a child regardless of its gender, the later birth of other children who require attention may make the first-born child feel that the younger ones are being favored by the parents.

Younger siblings receive much of their learning from older siblings because parents cannot devote their exclusive attention to later-born children. Older siblings can deliberately encourage wrong behavior in younger siblings in order to keep their own status intact and to gain favor with one or both parents. Parents may show strong disapproval of children who vary from the family system of rules and expectations. The effects of this disapproval is seen as favoritism toward "good" children. Disputes over parental affection create rivalries, and any conflicts that arise may cause children to apply their competitive edge, such as physical size, to gain back parental favor. Parents should discourage this type of rivalry, pointing out positive traits to their children instead of overly praising the more compliant ones.

Gender, Cultural, and Religious Favoritism. Many of the world's religions believe that women are inferior to men in many ways. Families from various religious and ethnic backgrounds may show overt favor to children of a particular sex and relegate children of the other sex to a lower position in the family. In religions that favor males,

Even at an early age children are sensitive to real and imagined signs of parental favoritism. (James L. Shaffer)

female children may feel that they are incapable of performing certain activities, such as athletics, merely because they are female. Grandparents may promote favoritism based on their cultural values or religious beliefs and treat some of their grandchildren less affectionately or give them fewer monetary rewards than their other grandchildren. This practice certainly promotes rivalries between children, and parents should take an active role in asking grandparents to equalize their treatment of their grandchildren as much as possible.

Attachment and Bonding. Three types of attachment behavior in infants have been identified. In avoidant attachment behavior, infants who are separated from their mothers are not particularly distressed by the separation and are easily comforted by strangers. Mothers who have such infants may find it difficult to become close to them, because they feel that the children reject them. Children displaying securely attached behavior play comfortably with toys and react positively to overtures from strangers. However, when their mothers are absent, they become distressed, and when their mothers return, they go immediately to them, initiate contact, and calm down after being taken into their arms. Mothers of such children favor them and may extend their favoritism to them as they mature. Children displaying resistant behavior are not as content as securely attached children when their mothers are present and resist contact and show anger when their mothers return after an absence. Even when their mothers are still in the room, such children remain visibly upset.

Children who smile and make eye contact tend to encourage and reinforce parental reactions. It is not the parents alone who set the initial pattern of interaction; children are not passive recipients of parental action but can actually provide stimuli to their parents. Parental reactions to the different types of attachment behavior help children to form healthy relationships, but when children are not securely attached to their parents, some subtle signs of rejection on the part of parents may occur. Naturally, children's interpretation of parent approval or rejection is critical throughout childhood. When a later sibling is born who attaches more securely to parents than an earlier sibling, the first child is acutely aware of the difference.

Sibling Rivalry. Siblings who are less than five years apart in age and of the same gender tend to be more competitive than those with five or more years between them. The frequency and intensity of competition between siblings can be discouraged or encouraged by parents. Parents should treat each of their children as unique individuals and support their individual interests and skills. The more parents compare their children, the more competitive they will become. Spending individual time with each child is critical to reducing sibling rivalry. Parents should respect the wishes of their children to have their own possessions. Children who are continually forced to share their possessions with younger siblings tend not to develop attitudes of generosity.

Parents who intervene in children's disputes beyond very early childhood find themselves in the permanent role of arbitrators, and if children sense that disputes are solved unfairly, sibling rivalry will intensify. Any unintended favoritism may be perceived as real, and children are quick to decide that parents love their siblings more than themselves based on "who wins" in disputes. By placing the responsibility of solving minor disputes on the children, parents can help them learn to deal with situations throughout life that require cooperation. Parents who make a concerted effort not to favor one child over another find that episodes of sibling rivalry decrease. Despite the best efforts of many parents, children may still perceive that other siblings are their parents' favorites. Evidence has shown that siblings' personalities may vary not just because of genetics but because they deliberately adopt behaviors to win parent's favor. If early efforts to win parental approval fails, they may deliberately adopt behaviors that gain them negative attention.

—*Stephanie G. Campbell*

BIBLIOGRAPHY

Bank, Stephen P., and Michael D. Kahn. *The Sibling Bond.* New York: Basic Books, 1982.

Daniels, Denise. "Favoritism in Families." *Journal of Personality and Social Psychology* 51 (1986).

Segal, Julius, and Herbert Yahraes. *A Child's Journey.* New York: McGraw-Hill, 1978.

Sulloway, Frank J. *Born to Rebel: Birth Order, Family Dynamics and Creative Lives.* New York: Pantheon Books, 1996.

See also Bonding and attachment; Competition during childhood; Cultural influences; Equality of children; Family values; Generational relationships; Siblings.

Feminist sociology

RELEVANT ISSUES: Economics and work; Parenting and family relationships; Sociology

SIGNIFICANCE: Feminist sociologists are critical of past research on family life that ignored gender-based domination in families and the strict adherence of family members to traditional male and female social roles

Humans have always lived in groups and are tied to one another by binds of obligation (economic, political, and social) and affection. The discipline of sociology is oriented toward scientifically studying how small groups (such as families) and large groups (such as bureaucracies or entire societies) are organized, as well as how this organization affects individuals on a daily basis. Sociologists are interested in the outside forces that affect people and on how people give meaning to and internalize their particular, historically situated, experiences.

For feminist women and men, gender is a central organizing feature of social life. Feminists have identified bias and distortions in sociological research and theory. For example, much more attention has been paid to organizations where men are most prominent, such as government and religious hierarchies, than to family life. Ignoring private life leads to biases in concepts, as when the word "work" is used to refer exclusively to paid employment, neglecting the economic value of housework and child care, tasks performed primarily by women.

Feminists also are critical of patriarchal (male) domination, and they challenge the idea that learned masculine traits inherently are more important than feminine traits. Because the full human potentials of both men and women are limited by strict adherence to traditional, usually unequal, masculine and feminine roles, feminists argue that gender-based equality is a positive goal. A basic assumption is that gender is a learned trait that has varied historically; because gender is socially constructed, gender roles can be changed.

Prior to the 1970's, sociological research typically ignored the significance of gender and issues relevant to women's lives. Since then, researchers have made contributions to sociology by asking new questions and by studying issues of particular importance to women and children. Topics of special concern with respect to family life include domestic violence, gender role socialization, inequality in parenting and household work, the economic dependence of women in families, critiques of traditional conceptions of what constitutes a family, and women's reproductive rights and responsibilities. Feminist scholarship also recognizes the multiple realities of women's lives by taking into account the ways in which race and ethnicity, social class, sexuality, and other variables are intertwined in the construction of human experience. Much feminist research is inclusively multicultural.

Housework and the Domestic Division of Labor. With the onset of industrial capitalism, the family economy became based outside the home in the form of paid labor. Although variation by class, race, and ethnicity occurred, women no longer played as crucial a role in producing basic necessities or supervising the family's farm or business. Instead, they were relegated to the care and nurturance of children and the maintenance of the household. This unpaid work, largely private and invisible, went unmeasured in the industrial economy. Moreover, men's monopoly over the public sphere soon translated into power and authority at home.

Although child care and housework are crucial to family life, they continue to be undervalued. Despite significant shifts in attitudes about gender roles and an increase in the number of women who work in the paid labor force, these undervalued types of work continue to be predominantly female. Research consistently has shown that women spend approximately fifty hours weekly on housework, whereas men contribute a maximum of about eleven hours. The unequal household responsibilities do not diminish as women enter the workforce, and working women end up laboring twice as long at what has been termed the "double day."

Economic Dependence. Even though the proportion of dual-earner families increased from one-half to two-thirds between 1960 and 1995 in

One outgrowth of the feminist movement has been a slowly growing tendency among men to value and share in the child-rearing responsibilities traditionally relegated to women. (James L. Shaffer)

the United States, women's average earnings remained lower than men's. Although less economically dependent than in the past, women continue to contribute lower earnings to families than their male partners or spouses. This disparity has been attributed by many researchers to segregation of men and women into different sectors of the labor market, with women in lower-paid positions, as well as to lower pay for women when they hold the same jobs as men.

Women's economic well-being affects institutional processes such as political power, access to education, and control in the home. As long as sex segregation in paid employment persists, keeping women from advancing and earning what men earn, the distribution of power in families will remain skewed.

The cycle of dependency and inequality between the sexes is fostered when family obligations such as child care and housework either keep women out of the paid labor force or restrict their opportunities once they enter it. Thus, disadvantages in the marketplace are reinforced by asymmetrical responsibilities at home.

For female-headed families, the burden of juggling home and employment is even greater than for married women. Research has shown that social support systems, such as high-quality, affordable public child care, coupled with the availability of jobs that pay women living wages, can help shift the burden of responsibility from individual family members to the broader community. In the United States, however, no lasting commitment to do so has been made.

Domestic Violence. Estimates of the extent of family violence vary widely, but most show that between 10 and 30 percent of American households are arenas of interpersonal violence. Research has demonstrated that although some domestic violence is directed against husbands and parents, children and wives are the most frequent victims.

Although children are taught to avoid potentially violent strangers, children are far more likely to experience violence in their homes. For children of all ages, the home is often the most dangerous place they go. Between 1.5 and 2 million children are abused by their parents, and almost 2,000 children are killed annually in the United States.

Force or the threat of force is common between spouses in America. One type of violence involves the need for husbands to exert control over wives. This type of violence has been termed "patriarchal terrorism" because it involves the tradition of male superiority that dictates that the husband should always be in charge. Because Western culture and laws have for centuries approved of the use of violence against wives to "keep them in line," domestic battering continues to be a difficult public issue to combat.

Domestic violence is found in all social classes and has many causes. The roles of socialization (the process by which people internalize the expectations of their society) and culture (the sets of ideological beliefs) are central. Males are still socialized in ways that reward them for being aggressive and tough, and females are still taught to be passive and vulnerable. Male folklore and pornography also reinforce the view that females enjoy aggressive treatment by men, that men are superior to women, and that intimidation and violence are ways to solve disputes. Research also has demonstrated that without the economic means to do so, battered women are reluctant to leave even the most horrendous of domestic situations.

Alternatives to Traditional Families. Feminist sociologists examine families that have different organizational structures and exhibit variations in gender roles. One such variation occurs when a husband takes on the tasks traditionally assigned to a wife. One study found that men who choose this role, or men who are forced into it by disability or a job layoff, gain insight into the problems female homemakers face. They may become more appreciative of their family and form more egalitarian attitudes in their marriages.

Family structures are complex, constantly in flux, and highly sensitive to outside influences such as the economy, politics, legal changes, and social and cultural trends. The institution of the traditional nuclear family—consisting of a married heterosexual couple, a breadwinning male spouse and a homemaking female spouse, along with their children—is idealized in popular culture but accounts for less than 20 percent of modern families. Other family forms include those headed by women, two wage earners, or pairs of lesbian women or gay men; interracial couples; and blended families that include children from previous marriages. In addition, between 1970 and 1995 the numbers of childless couples increased, as did the numbers of unrelated people who cohabited outside wedlock.

For feminist sociologists, gender is a centrally organizing process that sets opportunities and boundaries in women's and men's daily realities. In practice, feminist sociologists typically are oriented toward facilitating social change that brings about economic and physical freedom and security for women, children, and all people who suffer the burden of subordination.

—Eleanor A. LaPointe

BIBLIOGRAPHY

Freeman, Jo, ed. *Women: A Feminist Perspective.* Mountain View, Calif.: Mayfield, 1995.

Gerstel, Naomi, and Harriet Engel Gross, eds. *Families and Work.* Philadelphia: Temple University Press, 1987.

Hess, Beth B., and Myra M. Feree, eds. *Analyzing Gender: A Handbook of Social Science Research.* Newbury Park, Calif.: Sage Publications, 1987.

Hochschild, Arlie. *The Second Shift: Working Parents and the Revolution at Home.* New York: Viking, 1989.

Jaggar, Alison M., and Paula S. Rothenberg, eds. *Feminist Frameworks: Alternative Theoretical Accounts of the Relations Between Women and Men.* New York: McGraw-Hill, 1993.

See also Alternative family types; Child rearing; Domestic violence; Equalitarian families; Family economics; Gay and lesbian families; Gender inequality; Hochschild, Arlie Russell; Patriarchs; Women's roles.

Feminization of poverty

RELEVANT ISSUES: Divorce; Economics and work; Sociology

SIGNIFICANCE: Feminization of poverty leads to a significant increase in the number of children in poverty who will likely become unproductive and impoverished adults, creating a vicious circle of poverty and undermining family life and societal well-being

"Feminization of poverty" refers to the relatively high incidence of poverty among female-headed families compared to married-couple and male-headed families. Female-headed families are those in which a single mother is the main breadwinner and often the only adult responsible for dependent children in the family. The picture of the poor family has dramatically changed since the 1960's. Typical poor families in the late twentieth century included not only elderly rural couples in the South and large families headed by housewives and their minimum-wage husbands, but also increasing numbers of single mothers juggling housework and paid employment. In the mid-1960's female-headed families comprised 26 percent of the poor in the United States. By the mid-1990's, 55 percent of all poor families in the United States were female-headed.

Poverty has become feminized for several reasons. First, there has been a change in the structure of the family as a result of the general rise in the number of female-headed families. Between the mid-1960's and the mid-1990's the number of families headed by single mothers doubled. This increase has been attributed to the increase in the divorce rate, women's growing socioeconomic independence, and the growing number of unmarried teenage parents with their own households. There has also been a decline in the poverty rate of married-couple families. This decline has been attributed primarily to the major increase in the labor force participation and earning capacity of married women. The expanded Social Security system has greatly reduced poverty for the elderly. During this same period, real income increased, lifting a great number of working couples above the poverty line. The federal government and American-based employers have been criticized for their failure to generate innovative and continuous opportunities for groups most vulnerable to poverty—particularly young, nonwhite, and less-educated women—so that they can achieve the highest potential earnings. As the feminization of poverty persists, all efforts to maximize family well-being, reduce crime and substance abuse, increase and improve education, and achieve social justice are severely hampered.

Finding solutions to the problem of feminized poverty has stirred considerable public policy debate. Federal and state governments can adopt programs to encourage women to work while providing them with education, training, job placements, and child care. The success of such reme-

There is a much greater incidence of poverty among mother-headed families than among father-headed or two-parent families. (Ben Klaffke)

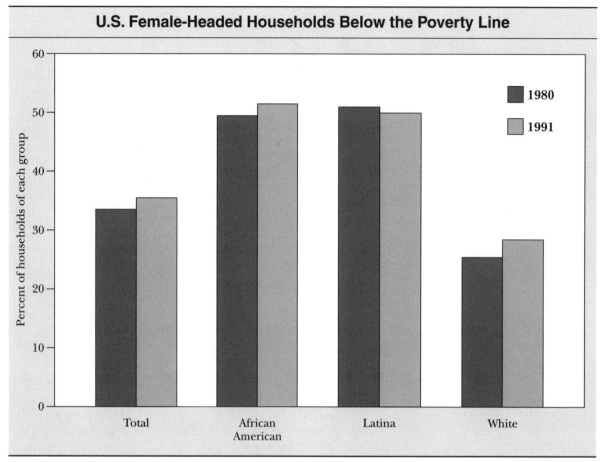

U.S. Female-Headed Households Below the Poverty Line

Source: Bureau of Labor Statistics of the Department of Labor

dies will be evident only if they enable poor women to rise above the poverty line by working in jobs that pay higher than minimum wages. The arguments concerning such programs have focused on their costs and who will pay for them. Government can also provide income supports and guarantees. As in the case of welfare, the policy debate surrounding such programs has focused on how expensive they are and how they may discourage work and foster dependency. The mid-1990's income-tax exemption program has been criticized for helping affluent families more than the poor, many of whom pay little or no income tax. —*M. J. Alhabeeb*

See also Alimony; Child support; Culture of poverty theory; Displaced homemakers; Gender inequality; Poverty; Single-parent families; Tax laws; Wealth; Welfare.

Fertility and infertility

RELEVANT ISSUES: Children and child development; Health and medicine; Parenting and family relationships

SIGNIFICANCE: Because many persons assume that they will parent a biological child at some point in their lives, issues of fertility and infertility profoundly affect family life

More than five million couples of childbearing age in the United States suffer from infertility. Infertility is defined as failure to achieve pregnancy after one year of unprotected intercourse. The percentage of people with this condition has not increased greatly since the 1960's, although the absolute number of sufferers has increased due to population growth. Forty percent of problems related to infertility are attributed to female factors,

40 percent to male factors, and 20 percent to both male and female factors and to unexplained causes. Contrary to popular belief, infertility generally is not the result of psychological problems stemming from sexual hang-ups or apprehensions. In most cases, infertility is a physical problem that commonly places tremendous stress on persons suffering from it. Most infertile individuals experience a loss of self-esteem and feel guilt, sadness, fear, and shame. Struggling with disbelief when they first become aware of their condition upon trying to conceive children, many individuals keep their infertility a secret. Because infertility is usually a shared condition affecting both partners, this secrecy seriously affects families.

Fortunately, more than half of these persons can be helped with modern infertility treatments. Like the symptoms, however, the treatment comes with a cost. Dealing with infertility, a process that can take years, requires a large commitment of time, energy, and resources that places physical, financial, and emotional strains on families and individuals.

Causes of Infertility. Despite years of scientific research, the exact reasons why infertility strikes certain individuals remain a mystery. Women's fallopian tubes, for example, may be blocked, causing infertility, but it might not be clear if the blockage has been caused by an undiagnosed infection or a pelvic disease or if it is a side effect of a ruptured appendix. It is known that women's fertility decreases with age. Most specialists agree that women may have problems conceiving after the age of thirty-five, with a dramatic decrease after the age of forty. These statistics even apply to women in remarkable physical shape, because the

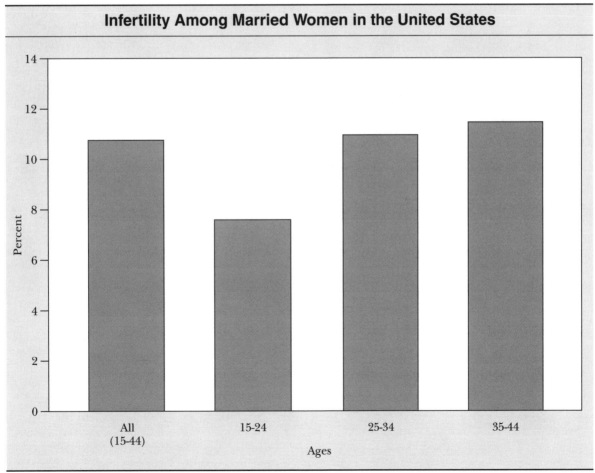

Infertility Among Married Women in the United States

Source: National Center for Health Statistics

Reasons for infertility among couples are evenly divided between male and female causes. (James L. Shaffer)

Common Causes of Female Infertility

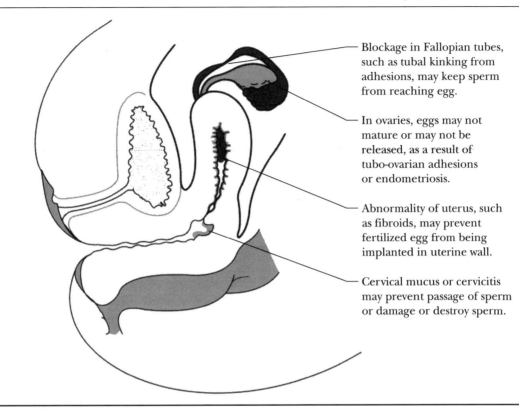

Blockage in Fallopian tubes, such as tubal kinking from adhesions, may keep sperm from reaching egg.

In ovaries, eggs may not mature or may not be released, as a result of tubo-ovarian adhesions or endometriosis.

Abnormality of uterus, such as fibroids, may prevent fertilized egg from being implanted in uterine wall.

Cervical mucus or cervicitis may prevent passage of sperm or damage or destroy sperm.

internal workings of the body are not related to physical conditioning, women's supply of eggs dwindles as they age, and their eggs are not as healthy as they once were. Male fertility does not seem to be similarly affected by age, since healthy males continually generate new sperm. Some studies published in the 1990's have shown, however, that infertility problems related to lower sperm count or sperm quality may be more common and serious as men get older than previously thought.

It is also known that certain conditions in females and males are associated with infertility. Endometriosis, a disease which usually strikes women in their thirties, occurs when the normal uterine lining implants itself outside the uterus, often on or within the ovaries or fallopian tubes. Although the relationship between infertility and endometriosis is as puzzling to physicians as the disease itself, it is known that between 30 and 40 percent of women who have endometriosis have infertility problems. It is also known that 20 per-

cent of infertile women are diagnosed with this problem. One example of a condition affecting male infertility is varicocele, a mass of varicose veins around the testicles that hinders sperm function, perhaps by increasing scrotal temperature and reducing sperm production. About 40 percent of all infertile men have detectable varicosity, although it may affect fertility in only half of these cases.

Sexually transmitted diseases, affecting both males and females, are probably among the most understood causes of infertility. In men, chlamydia and mycoplasma can cause duct obstruction, inhibiting the sperm's journey to the urethra. In women, gonorrhea, chlamydia, and syphilis often damage and block fallopian tubes. In both males and females, sexually transmitted diseases may work insidiously so that persons never seek treatment, leaving them infertile years before they try to conceive a child. Sexually transmitted diseases are not the only concern for those who are sexually active. Intrauterine devices used for contraception have been known to cause pelvic inflammatory disease, a condition that often leads to infertility.

Other serious causes of infertility that are not thoroughly understood are related to environmental factors. Some experts argue, in part based on studies conducted on animals, that fertility rates in both men and women may be affected by environmental pollutants, alcohol and drug abuse, exposure to X rays or workplace toxins, or even the modern stressful lifestyle.

Diagnosing Infertility. Besides seeking infertility treatments in cases in which women fail to achieve pregnancy within a one-year time period of unprotected intercourse, women might also seek these treatments for a variety of health problems and concerns including ovulation problems, the menopause, hirsutism, a history of genital infections, use of diethylstilbestrol (a synthetic compound used as a potent estrogen), irregular menses, unusual sexual development, and multiple miscarriages. In order to diagnose infertility problems, evaluation of males and females should occur simultaneously beginning with simple and risk-free tests.

Diagnostic treatment begins as both partners undergo a history and physical examination followed by laboratory studies to measure hormones during the menstrual cycle. Other simple tests include monitoring women's basal body temperature to determine when ovulation might occur, observing the quality and cellular characteristics of women's midcycle cervical mucus and sperm's reaction to it, taking a semen analysis to determine the number and quality of the sperm, and performing a scrotal/rectal ultrasound to look for varicoceles or duct obstruction in males. More invasive procedures include an endometrial biopsy, which examines the condition of the lining of the uterus; a hysterosalpingogram (HSG), which diagnoses tubal blockages; and a hysteroscopy, which allows physicians to view the inside of the uterus through a narrow telescope inserted through the cervical opening. For some infertility patients, minor surgical procedures performed under anesthesia are diagnostically necessary.

Techniques for Treating Infertility. Modern research has offered new treatments and options for infertile couples. Although the quality of treatment at different infertility clinics may vary, a protocol that each follows for treatment is relatively similar. Most patients are first diagnosed and treated for individual infertility problems in the hope that improved fertility will allow them to conceive naturally through intercourse. For women, this treatment might involve performing minor surgery to treat endometriosis or stimulating the ovaries with fertility drugs so that they produce more than one egg, thus increasing the chance of conception. For men, treatment might involve sperm washing to separate sperm from the seminal fluid, thus increasing the sperm's viability, or hormone therapy to increase sperm count. Only after treatments such as these fail do physicians turn to more advanced techniques.

With the advent of in vitro fertilization (IVF) and the birth of the first so called test-tube baby in 1978, infertility treatment reached a new plateau. This new treatment has helped approximately 50 percent of infertile couples who could not achieve pregnancy with natural-conception infertility treatments. In advanced assisted reproductive technology (ART) procedures, the eggs and sperm are taken from the body and immediately combined by a technician in a laboratory before being placed in the uterus as embryos three days after the fertilization has taken place. Other ART procedures stemming from IVF, including gamete intrafallopian transfer (GIFT), zygote intrafallopian transfer (ZIFT), and tubal embryo transfer (TET), offer some infertile couples even better chances for conception by returning gametes or embryos to the fallopian tubes instead of the uterus. Physicians have found that the tubal environment, which cannot be duplicated in the laboratory, fosters pregnancy.

Other advanced IVF procedures have also increased the chances for pregnancy. In assisted hatching, the outer shell of the egg is chemically or mechanically thinned prior to embryo transfer in order to improve the likelihood that the cells will burrow into the uterine wall. In intracytoplasmic sperm injection (ICSI), which was rarely practiced prior to 1994, the egg is held under the microscope and a single sperm is injected into its interior. Cryopreservation has also become possible with the advent of in vitro fertilization. In this procedure, embryos can be frozen in liquid nitrogen for years in order to initiate a future pregnancy without the need for repeated egg retrieval.

IVF is not without problems. This expensive and emotionally difficult procedure has only about a 20 percent success rate per attempt. Furthermore, besides the minor discomforts and pain associated with it, the long-term effects of infertility drugs on patients is not known. One of the biggest risks associated with all infertility treatments, and especially IVF, is multiple births. The multiple pregnancy rate from IVF results in twins in about one out of four, triplets in about one out of twenty, and quadruplets in about one out of fifty pregnancies. The multiple birth rate is determined by the quality of embryos transferred to the patient as well as the number of embryos transferred. Women in their late thirties and early forties whose embryos are not as viable as those of younger women are not at as much risk of having multiple births. While most women can tolerate a twin pregnancy, more than two fetuses threatens the health of mothers as well as that of babies; mothers suffer from high blood pressure and uterine bleeding while babies are prone to premature births and all attendant complications.

Because of the frequency of multiple births and their dangers, many physicians encourage patients to undergo what is called selective reduction if they are carrying more than two fetuses. In this procedure the development of one or more fetuses is terminated so that the remaining fetuses have a better chance of healthy delivery. Many individuals and groups question the morality of this procedure.

Infertility and the Third Party. In many cases, couples' infertility problems cannot be solved

Over-the-counter products such as pregnancy-testing kits are market responses to the concerns of couples about their fertility. (James L. Shaffer)

without help from donors. Sperm donation, which has existed for nearly a century in the United States, helps couples when the woman's reproductive system is normal and the man's semen contains little or no sperm. This process involves inseminating women by using a small plastic tube to implant donated sperm, either fresh or frozen, at the cervix. Egg donation is a newer and more complicated process which helps couples when the man's reproductive system is normal but the woman's ovaries do not function properly. Volunteer donors, who undergo a treatment similar to that administered to women undergoing in vitro fertilization, furnish multiple healthy eggs that are combined with the man's sperm in the laboratory before being placed as embryos into the infertile woman's uterus. In some cases, when both partners have fertility problems, a donated embryo can be used. The supply of donated embryos comes from former patients who have undergone IVF but no longer wish to use their cryopreserved embryos.

Surrogacy is yet another solution to couples' infertility. Surrogate mothers are women who agree to intentionally bear and sometimes conceive a child for others to parent. Couples often use surrogacy when women have infertility problems, whereby surrogates are artificially inseminated with the man's sperm. A second kind of surrogacy, called IVF surrogacy, involves combining infertile women's eggs and their partners' sperm in the laboratory before transferring them to surrogates. IVF surrogacy is used when an infertile woman's uterus has been removed or when serious medical conditions exist that make pregnancy dangerous for her. Although standard in vitro fertilization is a controversial infertility treatment, the procedures that involve the participation of third parties have generated even greater ethical, legal, financial, psychological, and emotional controversy.

Resolving Infertility. Although advanced infertility treatments allow many couples to give birth to biological children, not all infertility problems can be solved. Some couples who have conceived one child may experience secondary infertility and find that they must deal with the trauma of infertility even while parenting a biological child. Many infertile couples adopt in order to achieve their dream of having children, while many decide to live child-free, a decision that is often reached after couples have undergone some form of infertility treatment. —*Cassandra Kircher*

BIBLIOGRAPHY

Harkness, Carla. *The Infertility Book: A Comprehensive Medical and Emotional Guide.* Berkeley: Celestial Arts, 1992. Extensive and sensitive discussion of infertility with frequent excerpts from individuals who have dealt with the ramifications of being infertile.

Marrs, Richard, et al. *Doctor Richard Marrs' Fertility Book: America's Leading Fertility Expert Tells You Everything You Need to Know About Getting Pregnant.* New York: Delacorte Press, 1997. Written by one of the first practitioners of assisted reproductive technology, this book covers the medical, emotional, and financial aspects of infertility.

Perloe, Mark, and Linda Gail Christie. *Miracle Babies and Other Happy Endings for Couples with Fertility Problems.* New York: Rawson Associates, 1986. Thorough discussion of infertility, especially its causes.

Robin, Peggy. *How to Be a Successful Fertility Patient: Your Guide to Getting the Best Possible Medical Help to Have a Baby.* New York: William Morrow, 1993. Includes interviews with more than one hundred infertility patients, presenting the subject of infertility and fertility from the patients' point of view.

Rosenthal, M. Sara. *The Fertility Sourcebook.* Los Angeles: Lowell House, 1996. Provides information about infertility with a large section on infertility prevention.

Sher, Geoffrey, et al. *In Vitro Fertilization: The A.R.T. of Making Babies.* New York: Facts On File, 1995. Thorough discussion of in vitro fertilization, one of the treatments available to infertile couples.

Tan, S. L., et al. *Infertility: Your Questions Answered.* Secaucus, N.J.: Citadel Press, 1997. Presents a question-and-answer format that answers patients' most frequent questions about infertility.

See also Adoption issues; Birth control; Childbirth; Childlessness; Health problems; Life expectancy; Menopause; Multiple births; Pregnancy; Reproductive technologies; Sterilization; Test-tube babies; Twins; Zero Population Growth movement.